Jerry's Riot

The True Story of Montana's 1959 Prison Disturbance

Sky Blue Waters Press
2005

Jerry's Riot

The True Story of Montana's 1959 Prison Disturbance

Kevin S. Giles

*To Dad, who knew a guard's life,
and to Mom, who helped me remember.*

ABOUT THE AUTHOR

Kevin S. Giles is a native Montanan. Like many sons and daughters of prison guards, he finds some of his past at Old Montana Prison in Deer Lodge, his hometown. He is a journalism graduate of the University of Montana in Missoula, and has worked as a reporter and editor for several daily newspapers. He is preparing his first book, "Flight of the Dove: The Story of Jeannette Rankin," for a second edition. He can be contacted at jerrysriot@hotmail.com

Table of Contents

Prologue

I was a young teenage boy when I first saw the inside of Montana State Prison. It was a winter night in 1964, about the time the Beatles made their sensation on The Ed Sullivan Show, and I went to see the fights.

Going inside the prison to witness a boxing match was a coming of age for the son of a prison guard. My father, Murry Giles, was a lieutenant of custody. I had never seen him at work inside the walls.

Dad arranged my visit for a Friday night that he worked. I remember huddling at the main tower entrance with my classmate, Rocky Barton, and his dad, Harold, squinting through a tiny window. We watched a guard unlock a door at the far side. Dad entered. The gold badge on his cap glittered under the naked light bulbs.

Once the guard locked that door, he let us inside. That place under the tower was like a sandstone tomb. I looked at the keys and locks and felt a curious mix of fear and wonder at going into the prison. I thought Dad looked more official than I had known him. This impression stays with me more than forty years later.

With Dad in the lead, we left the tower and entered a white building where an old guard behind a barred door welcomed us with some blue language. (Around town, Dad often spoke rampant profanity in the company of prison guards that he carefully avoided at our house.) From the guard's bony hand several large keys dangled from a worn metal ring resembling a miniature hula-hoop.

On the other side of the building another guard waited inside a barred cage between the lobby and the prison yard. After the steel door clanged shut and the big key rattled in the lock, Rocky and I tried not to look at two convicts who watched us with simmering eyes from behind more bars. They wore patches on their shirtsleeves that allowed them into certain areas. In prison vernacular, I learned

xi

later, they were called "runners" because they ran errands for guards.

The turnkey opened the outside door. We once again walked in the frigid night air, but on the inside of the prison now. Our rubber boots crunched on the snow. Yellow light spilled from the high windows of the theater. That's where we would watch inmates box.

Silhouettes emerged from dark towers. Guards with rifles stood on the wall, watching us walk to the theater. Another guard inside the theater sent us up the west staircase to the balcony, where we sat alone. Somebody locked a door behind us. Below, Dad watched from near the boxing ring as convicts streamed into the wooden folding chairs.

Lieutenant Murry Giles

I never would have imagined this scene. They came in waves, dressed in khaki, hair glistening with oil, crude brown and black shoes, white socks. Some seemed much too old to be in prison. Most were white or Indian, a few black. Plenty of them looked tough, but maybe it was my innocence or the tattoos I could see from way up high and how they rolled up their sleeves to show them off. Some looked like friendly neighbors. Some were young enough to attend high school. I tried to guess the really bad ones among them.

I watched Dad. He was the only guard on the floor in that sea of hard men. He was an uncommon man with a common background. Before he came to the prison he sold groceries, then sold cars. In the years around my birth he worked construction, harnessed high above the river at Hungry Horse Dam near Glacier Park in northwestern Montana. In 1958 he came to Deer Lodge to be a prison guard, working six- and seven-day shifts. My mother, brother, sister and I stayed behind in Columbia Falls for nearly eight months until he earned enough money to rent us a house. During that time he lived in the guards' quarters at the prison.

Dad could shoot the breeze with anybody. He was that kind of man. In the theater that night, I watched him joke with convicts, but he wouldn't be intimidated. He just stepped right into the rows when he had to straighten someone out. I was beginning to understand why he was a successful keeper of men. Dad made a good prison guard because he talked the rough talk, and the inmates understood him.

Only a few years later, when I was a senior in high school, he had a heart attack downtown and nearly died after driving home and collapsing on the living room floor. He spent a few more years as manager of the prison canteen before retiring on disability.

When I better understood the full story of prison guards, it became apparent that Dad and others valued their survival most. To leave the "joint" once and for all brought the privilege of never having to look back. Only as Dad's life withered in his sixtieth year did he consent to revisit the old prison, abandoned nine years earlier for a newer one west of town, and sold to the City of Deer Lodge for a single dollar. That bright July day was a magnificent one. I remember the clip-clip-clip of sprinklers on the yard's grass. Wandering tourists thumbed their guide maps in what had become Old Montana Prison. Dad trudged behind his granddaughters, visibly troubled by his memories of this sad place. Only after the girls rained questions on him did he tell some of what he knew, and when he did, he seemed for a short while the confident lieutenant I remembered that night of the boxing match. Before we left the prison that afternoon, he consented to pause in front of Cell House 1 to have his picture taken with his granddaughters. That was his last visit.

Dad's memory of the 1959 riot tumbled out over the years. He had known the riot up close and personal. He was one of two guards working the second shift on April 16, 1959, who escaped being taken hostage. Like many men who had witnessed the riot, he sometimes had trouble talking about it. I captured many facts and anecdotes from our informal conversations, which at least provided me dozens of clues when I began researching the riot in 1995. A front-page picture from the *Seattle Post-Intelligencer* shows Dad crouched atop the wall outside Tower 7 in the dark. He's reaching to help rifle-bearing Highway Patrol officers climb onto the wall from ladders. That clipping made him proud. He kept it folded in an envelope in his closet.

Dad died of congestive heart failure on April 11, 1989, five days short of the riot's thirtieth anniversary. Several years later, as I researched records and interviewed the last remaining men who survived those thirty-six hours, I wished Dad were here to guide me.

On summer days when I walk beneath empty towers I think of that night, cold and raw and thick with a boy's fear of a dangerous and unfamiliar place. I hear my father calling out to rough men in the wild commotion of a boxing match. Dad is gone now and so is the theater. It's a shell now, set afire in the closing days of the old prison's life by an inmate arsonist.

Men die, but their memories should live. That's why I wrote this book. In the charm of a Montana evening, when the sun falls farther still, a pink glow falls on the red brick facade of Cell House 1. Inside it's gloomy and cold and there's a silence like death. The old prison hides secrets from its past. If you listen close, you can hear the men who made this story.

Kevin S. Giles

Cell House 1 just hours after the National Guard ended the riot. Bazooka rounds hit top windows of the cell house tower, left.

AP/Wide World Photos

"And I will give unto thee the keys of the kingdom of heaven: and whatsoever thou shalt bind on earth shall be bound in heaven: and whatsoever thou shalt loose of earth shalt be loosed in heaven."

Matthew 16:19

A ghost's whisper

A board falling flat to the floor is thunder to the heart. And so it
was that when prison guard Clyde Sollars heard a hard clap,
he stiffened in fear. For a few seconds he listened, breathless.

Sollars looked at his wristwatch, an anniversary gift from his
wife. The hands showed almost four o'clock. He reached into the
canvas bag he had carried into the prison from the main office
across the street. Inside the tiny mailroom that was nothing more
than a cubbyhole with shelves, wedged at the end of a short
hallway, he sorted the day's last letters. That noise, sharp and
urgent, echoed in his head. The convict carpenters working with
hammers and saws near the deputy warden's office must have
dropped a board. The day suddenly felt used and cold, like frost on a
flower. Feeling a chill that he couldn't understand, he worked faster.

An hour earlier, Sollars waited outside the prison's rock walls,
across the street, while his wife Helen censored the last letters. She
was the new matron in the Women's Unit, a small stockade behind
the main prison. They told her that if she worked with the mail
superintendent for a few weeks she would know the prison better.
Every morning she and another matron marched eleven of the
thirteen female prisoners from their quarters to their jobs in prison
offices outside the walls. Clyde felt lucky to see her during working
hours. He was one of two mail and transportation officers,
alternating with another guard on road trips to return parole
violators to Deer Lodge. The most recent assignment had been to
North Dakota. The other guard asked for it, hoping to visit relatives
along the way.

On this Thursday, April 16, 1959, Clyde Sollars might have been
driving hundreds of miles to the east, free as a bird on the perpetual

plains of eastern Montana. Instead he stacked mail into a bag, looked at his watch, and decided that before he ended his shift he would walk one more time into Montana State Prison.

"See you at home, Mom," he had said to his wife. That was what he called Helen sometimes. They had two daughters, grown and gone, and it felt good to speak to his wife as if the children were still at home.

He had come to the prison in 1957. Like many of the guards before him, who found their way to Deer Lodge from the sawmills and the mines and the timber crews, he arrived at the prison with dirt on his heels. After leaving the Army after World War II he went to work in the grain elevators in Charlo, Ronan, Polson, Pablo and Paradise, all towns in northwestern Montana. Sollars was an ordinary blue-collar worker, as unadorned as the other guards who filed in and out of those imposing sandstone and granite walls. He was about to find out how plain men take on new worth in a crisis.

He swung the canvas sack onto his shoulder and walked forty paces across Main Street and into the lengthening shadows of two mighty cell houses. The fortresses stood four stories high. Castle-like turrets clawed at the pale sky from each of the eight corners. One cell house had been built before the turn of the century, the other, during Teddy Roosevelt's presidency. They made an awe-inspiring sight to travelers who drove into town on Highway 10, a two-lane ribbon of asphalt, and stopped and pointed their Brownies to snap pictures. The forbidding prison, by some accounts one of the worst in the country, made for interesting vacation snapshots next to the more pastoral elements of Montana, like steaming geyser spray from Old Faithful in Yellowstone National Park.

Like most prison guards, Sollars saw little romance in the rugged architecture of the cell houses. He thought them ugly and wretched because he knew of the misery that they hid. He felt them staring at him with their troubled swollen eyes. The prison had eyes everywhere. The hundreds of prisoners watched and remembered all they saw, as did the guards if they knew what was good for them. The seven wall towers watched what was inside, and everything inside stared back. Eyes watched from everywhere. It was said that the prison's ears heard all, even a ghost's whisper.

Wind swept the scent of spring snow off the mountains that loomed like a painted backdrop behind the prison. The scent stung his nose but felt fresh and clean. Only when Sollars arrived at the looming stone entrance did he shiver. Instinctively he zipped his blue uniform jacket.

He tilted the bill on his police-style cap to shut out the sun, which already was fading behind the prison. Then he looked up. On the wall outside the tower, known as Tower 7 or the main gate, a guard stood with a loop of clothesline rope. He uncoiled it and let it drop twenty feet or so to Sollars, who unclipped from it a brass key that filled his hand. At the front of the tower, standing almost on Main Street where the cars rolled past, Sollars unlocked an ornate black grill door to enter the base of the two-story tower. Here, the easy innocence of small-town Deer Lodge dissolved into a dark cave of sandstone rock. A naked bulb cast dull yellow light that didn't penetrate the corners. The room was cold and drafty. Sollars felt a change in him as he always did when he went inside.

He locked the grill door behind him. This time, the rope dangled through a round opening in the ceiling. The guard who had stood on the wall a minute earlier was now inside the tower, up in the eagle's nest where he could see the guts of the prison through its broad windows. Sollars attached the key, tugged on the rope, and the guard above pulled it back. Seconds later the rope returned. A new key rattled inside the tin tube. Sollars used it to unlock a wooden door, as thick as his hand was wide, on the opposite side of the tower. He swung open the door, stepped into the prison yard, and locked it again. The other guard, standing outside on the wall again and facing the prison now, dropped the rope. Sollars surrendered the key.

He crossed a short courtyard to ten steps that led upward to another barred door. Behind it was Inside Administration, where guards brought their prisoner counts. Convicts came for medicine, or to get their teeth pulled in the dental office, or to shine the guards' black leather shoes. In the photo office, they took pictures of the "fish," the new men who arrived through the main gate and wrote descriptions of their scars and tattoos in case of escape. The visiting room was here, too. Inside Administration was the business district of this town of criminals.

The cell houses, like big brothers, pressed against the chalk-white Inside Administration on either side, dwarfing it. On the south end, to Sollars' left, was the 1896 version. This cell house had buckets for toilets. Despite all the technological inventions before its construction, it more resembled a Civil War-era fortress with its galleys of wood and its cell doors that had to be locked individually. It was made of dark brick, the color of dried blood. Its round turrets had roofs that came to a point, where in the early days big flags flew. To the north, the 1912 cell house was much the same in its rectangular construction, although its brick looked more orange by contrast and its square turrets flared at the top. Even forty-seven years after it was built, guards called this building the "new" cell house because it had plumbing and interlocking cell doors.

***

None of the guards would doubt that this was Floyd Powell's prison. The new warden from Wisconsin State Prison, a champion of reform, had proclaimed at his arrival eight months earlier that he would change this reputed hellhole into a model institution that would be the envy of every prison in America. Not everyone shared his enthusiasm. Some residents of Deer Lodge greeted his presence with skepticism, others with disdain. The town wasn't accustomed to a warden of such outward determination, and the prospect of an improved prison was a new idea. In Wisconsin he had a reputation as a bit of a daredevil because he was willing to go into prison cells to talk inmates out of knives or other weapons. From childhood he lived a hard life and was determined to overcome it. As a boy, and the oldest son, he took over the family farm when his father became disabled in a car accident. He also hired out as a laborer to bring extra money home. He was a driven, determined self-made man.

4

The new warden arrived in Deer Lodge to repair decades of decay and mismanagement at the only prison in Montana's vast landscape. It was an outpost of sorts, planted in a town of fewer than 4,000 residents in a tall empty county – Powell County, coincidentally – where Hereford cattle outnumbered people. The prison had stood at that spot along the Clark Fork River since Montana was a territory, when sluice miners crawled the snow-fed creeks and road agents fleeced them of their gold nuggets. It had been a familiar face to three generations of Deer Lodge folk who worked there. The old prison was a tolerated place, if not tolerable, a dark ripple in the stream of a good life. In a wide lonesome valley that felt like cupped hands beneath the heavens, the prison's purpose was a spoiling, a footprint of humanity's inevitable sorrowful deeds. Montanans liked their prison kept quiet, much like ignoring a sleeping dog for fear of its bite. With Floyd Powell's arrival, that was about to change. There, between folds of the Rocky Mountain Front that wore some of the best forests in Montana on its flowing cape, his agenda for reform took shape.

As summer waned, Powell charged ahead with uncommon energy, trying to change everything at once. He recruited Ted Rothe, his friend and ally, from Wisconsin State Prison. To make the prison safer, he hired more guards. To know the troublemakers, he started classifying prisoners by crimes and behavior. He even fired the "con bosses" who had supervised their peers in the industries and shops. Powell was a whirling dervish. In his quest to bring the prison into modern times, he was upsetting the balance of power inside of it.

Clyde Sollars felt a haunting at the prison. The prison felt dead and ugly. Knowing the men held inside was like ripping open a psychological veil. Behind it were the inmates' victims and their personal agonies. Civilization built prisons to hide what they didn't want to see. Sollars and all the other guards discovered that in the midst of convicted men they met hell, exposed and raw and full of pain. Guards coped with two evils: real dangers and apparitions. They sensed in Floyd Powell's vision a change in wind direction. It felt like a storm building on the mountain. To many Montanans, prison reform was worse than a futile gesture. It was a violation of faith.

If anything, a guard's life was a fertile field for conversation. On the outside, off shift, guards cracked their foaming Great Falls Selects and smoked their unfiltered Camels and ranted of how it was, how it *really* was, and lamented Powell's policies and the joint and the torment of their working lives.

***

At the top of the steps at the barred door into Inside Administration, Sollars pushed a button that sounded a buzzer. Officer James "Little" Jones, the second-shift turnkey, appeared at the door. He was as short as his nickname implied, but a muscled, wiry man, and his hair was thick and black. "Last trip for today?" he asked Sollars. He opened the door for Sollars to pass and then swung it shut. Metal crashed against metal. He turned the big key until the lock slid closed with a thunk. Jones made small talk before Sollars entered a little hallway to his right. He had been sorting the mail for fewer than ten minutes before he heard the noise that scared him.

Jones worked two grill doors that day. On the west side of the building, opposite from where Sollars had entered, two grill doors spaced twelve feet apart created a vestibule, where on most days one door would be locked before the other was opened. Those doors admitted convicts from the yard. Usually a second turnkey guard worked between the doors and had to work them with care to avoid being trapped with both sets of keys. Today Jones was working alone. On such days when the afternoon shift was short a man, the outside grill door was left open. Convicts who had business to do came up the steps from the yard on the west side of Inside Administration and walked right up to the second grill door in the vestibule. As a matter of policy, Jones would order them to step back before he unlocked the door.

Standing now inside his claustrophobic mailroom, Sollars was thinking again about the noise that bothered him. Like other guards he had become accustomed to listening beyond clanging doors and crude language for true and ominous signals of trouble. This noise had ricocheted around the jungle of concrete rooms like a clap of thunder. Had he heard a board falling flat to the floor, blasting the air away? Or had he heard something else? His suspicion grew.

For a few moments only silence came to his ears, and in prison, silence deafens. Here, a dictionary of sounds lay open in Clyde Sollars' mind, as it did for every guard, ready for quick reference. In this prison of a thousand eyes, danger usually came first to the ears. Sounds that fill the prison alarm new guards. As months pass those sounds become a pattern of routine. The prison at its safest was a numbing routine and a guard was soon to learn that he should listen close when the routine changes.

From somewhere in the maze of rooms came an urgency of shoes on tile. They weren't squeaks of new shoes but the warnings of a struggle. Sollars felt curious and then afraid. He crept into the lobby. Here in this gloomy room, where convicted men had tromped a trail in the linoleum, he saw no carpenters, nor did he see anyone else. Where was Jones, the turnkey guard? And why were both barred doors to the yard standing open?

That very second, as Sollars comprehended a guard's greatest fear, a squat and sweating convict rumbled into the lobby from Deputy Warden Ted Rothe's office. His big fist clutched a thin ugly knife, red with blood.

Sollars recognized him at once. He didn't know the man well, in fact couldn't recall a conversation with him, but in an instant Sollars sensed the man's frightful confidence.

***

Like a mad bull, Jerry Myles snorted through a flattened nose that listed to the left. Rivers of purple and red ran across his flushed face. His bully scowl, accentuated with heavy eyelids and full pouting lips, promised trouble. His high forehead, where only a tongue of wavy salt-and-pepper hair remained, shined with sweat. He tilted his head backward a bit, daring Sollars to defy him. Sollars had heard this man was nicknamed "Shorty" and could see why. Myles stood only a shade over five feet, and despite thick arms and a chest as round as a rain barrel, his feet were dainty like a woman's. His shoes seemed too petite for a man who propelled his stout body with such authority. He was a bull on tiny feet.

Although a common burglar, Myles had a reputation among the guards as a jocker, meaning he stalked young men for sex. They also called him "Little Hitler," alluding to his remorseless and domineering behavior in the cell house. He courted violations of the rules in an effort to draw attention to himself, and when he was caught, tried to make amends in pitiful ways.

At 125, his IQ was far higher than most of his fellow convicts. He wrote poetry, enjoyed the strategic challenges of chess, and had learned to play the violin. Had he not been a psychopath, he might have been a scholar. Little good had come from his intellect. Other than occasional regret over his troubled loveless life, he reserved most of his thinking for petty hates and distorted illusions.

Sollars thought he saw a flicker of compassion in the eyes of this mad bull before him. When Myles spoke, his voice came softer than Sollars had expected. "This is a riot and if you want to live, Cap, do what I say," Myles advised him.

At first Sollars didn't understand that Myles was even more dangerous than he appeared. Prison was his home. Now forty-four years old, he had spent most of the past twenty-five years at Alcatraz Island and five other federal and state prisons. Mutinies came to him as second nature. He thought he knew prison life better than anyone who had guarded him. Myles was determined to impress on his captors that because of his long history of confinement he deserved special privileges. It soon would become clear to everyone in Montana that he desired to run the prison.

Myles stepped toward Sollars. He guided the knife in front of his short bulk like he was trying to clear a path with it. Sollars didn't doubt that Myles would kill him. He raised his hands in surrender. Sollars had been to war and seen a few fights at the grain elevators but knew nothing about confronting armed convicts. Behind Myles came Lee Smart, the kid with eyes of ice. Sollars knew him as the teenage murderer. He was skinny and had a girl's countenance but everyone knew he was a psychopath and gave him room. Smart had a sassy defiant way about him. He walked around the prison with his trousers drooping.

Between Myles and Smart stood Sergeant Bill Cox. Blood soaked the shirtsleeve on his left arm from shoulder to wrist. He had a jaw of rock that made him look fierce but now his strength was gone and his face white and dazed. Cox worked in the captain's office between the lobby and Ted Rothe's office. As Sollars tried to understand what he was seeing, he wondered for an instant why the scene didn't include Deputy Warden Rothe. Then he looked closer at the boy.

Smart pointed a lever-action rifle at Sollars. He gripped the barrel not as a hunter would with a thumb on one side and fingers on the other for a clear view, but with his fingers wrapped all the way around. The ominous opening at the barrel's tip looked larger than life. Sollars smelled gunpowder. He saw Smart's other hand at the trigger, coaxing it. Sollars felt a violation of the basic order of life. He blinked hard behind his glasses. He wouldn't forget Lee Smart's blank cold face.

- 2 -

Rifles and two men at odds

In Floyd Powell's prison, the rules of engagement were clear. A guard who carried a rifle had to be willing to shoot it. He had to be willing to kill a man with it, or at least to disable him, because if he weren't, his bluff wouldn't intimidate the cons. The warden knew they had their shanks and stingers and other contraband weapons stashed in every secret nook and cranny, but that they coveted guns most of all. Every warden knew that. Some cons, and Powell had a few names in mind, would kill guards.

The psychopaths, the remorseless criminals who lived to dominate other men, worried Floyd Powell the most. Those cons would want the rifles. Those rifles were pivots of power. Held by guards, they meant authority. Held by cons, they meant revolt. Parading a gun inside a prison, not from the high tower walls or from inside a barred gun cage but from unprotected catwalks, was like dangling a lollipop to a pouting child. Powell knew he was breaking a cardinal rule of security by allowing the Winchesters. Outside those walls, such guns at least had recreational purposes. Inside a prison, a gun would kill.

As Floyd Powell stood in the inmate dining room on Thursday, April 16, 1959, he looked forward to a remarkable afternoon. Eight months earlier he had become the new warden in Deer Lodge. As he waited in the convict serving line for his lunch, surrounded by men wearing plain blue cotton shirts, their darker blue denim trousers conspicuously marked by white stripes sewn from belt to cuff, the new warden fretted about the rifles on the catwalks. Each of the two cell houses had one of the Winchesters. Powell had ordered the guns off the catwalks but some of the guards had threatened union action. They said the prison wasn't safe. Keeping the guns was one of the few concessions he had made to the guards. He refused to supply ammunition, but word had gotten around that guards were bringing it from home.

It was otherwise an ordinary day for guards and cons, but a special day for the new warden. Architects were coming to Deer Lodge that afternoon to show him their drawings for his new prison. He thought of himself as the reform warden, although some people in town didn't agree. They didn't like his arrogant style. It was no secret that some of the bureaucrats in Helena thought Montana needed a new prison. They had hired Powell to make it happen, but Powell left the impression with some of the local folks that he was willing to spend to the stars to get it done. Building a new prison was an unpopular idea because it suggested that punishment no longer was the priority. Most folks thought a diet of bread and water in a ruthless prison was the best course of action for lawbreakers. Rumors spread around town that Powell coddled convicts. It was unfair criticism and stung him. He understood that he had to build public support for a new prison, but he didn't particularly feel inclined to seek the blessings of the people of Deer Lodge.

He would reflect: "The people in Deer Lodge are typical of Montanans, very friendly but somewhat provincial or protective as far as their community is concerned." He saw himself as a higher authority. He was cleaning up this ragged hellhole of a prison in this Montana cow town, and he convinced himself that when they came to appreciate what he had achieved, townfolk would enfold his new model prison and vote him the money to build it. They would know him across the country for having transformed one of the worst state prisons in America into one of the best. He couldn't wait to start.

On this day, convicts streamed from the cavernous cell houses on either end of the dining room. Some were just freckled boys, others graying men. Eager to eat, they bunched into serving lines, galley by galley, doing little to annoy the few guards who escorted them. Their minds were on the food and that was good. This was the most dangerous time in a prison, when so many men assembled at once. Powell knew the importance of providing good food and plenty of it. He thought he should know what they eat, and they should know that he knew, and because of this attention to detail they would be less inclined to complain. He didn't buck the serving line but instead took a tray and waited his turn with the convicts. To them it was a bold move and an unfamiliar one. Some thought him brave. Others figured him careless. He stood alone among them, not unaccustomed to being surrounded by men who had killed and raped and robbed. Powell and his deputy, Ted Rothe, ate at least one meal a day in the dining room, but never at the same time. If Powell ate breakfast Rothe came to lunch or dinner, and if Powell came to dinner Rothe came to breakfast. Each day Powell sat at a different table.

It was a gorgeous spring afternoon. The wind was up, and after entering the dining hall from the exercise yard, Powell reached for his comb to coax his strawberry hair into place. It took a strong gust to disturb it. Like most men of the day, including the convicts around him, he oiled his hair. It was thick like a boy's but graying at the temples and where he parted it on the left. The paradoxical elements of youth and aging showed elsewhere as well. He had cheeks like swollen apples. Child mischief flickered in his eyes. Yet his expanding neck strained at a dark tie and a tight-fitting white dress collar, and his face wore the history of a prison life.

Sunshine fell across rows and rows of tables in the dining hall. When full, the room seated 400 prisoners. Powell navigated his way through herds of them, carrying a battered yellow plastic tray heaped with roast beef and mashed potatoes and sweet corn, steaming and succulent, and strong dark coffee in a blue plastic cup. Lunch was good here, of that he was convinced. He had ordered that each table be supplied with ketchup and mustard and salt and pepper. Rothe's new "Take all you want but eat all you take" policy, proclaimed from a wooden sign mounted on the dining room's south wall, calmed most of the remaining complainers. To Powell the progress in the dining room was another symbol of the prison moving to better times.

The reform warden sat on the hard bench among hard men. He wore a light brown sport coat and a tie that hung to the swell of his belly. He wasn't tall, an inch or two under six feet. His eyes roamed incessantly, a habit that seemed nosy to some and prudent to others. His presence in the dining hall was a calculated risk to improve morale. He knew a prisoner could stab him with a table knife before the few guards in the room could react. He tried to be calm and casual but alert to danger.

On the east side of the room, from inside a gun cage jutting from the wall, a guard watched. Because the gun cage was a secure place, accessible only from a tunnel that led from the main guard tower outside, Powell equipped it with a tear gas gun. Guards usually brought rifles or shotguns into the gun cage, the floor of which was about as high as a man's head as he stood in the dining room. Slabs of steel, welded to the bars, kept convicts from reaching into the cage. Other than the gun cage guard, Powell had little protection. One unarmed guard strolled around the dining room. Another stood vigil in the kitchen, keeping watch on knives and cleavers. Occasionally a third guard came from one of the cell houses.

Powell favored guards who spoke with authority, as long as they didn't show him up. He thought common sense and clear rules worked better with convicts than guns. He decided he would remove the rifles from the cell house catwalks the next week. Let the guards complain. Let them quit over it. Cons with guns could riot.

Powell said little to the men at his table, and they said little to him. To them he seemed preoccupied. Powell was a man of ideas. He aspired to be a builder of brick and mortar. His subordinates would not come to think of him as a builder of consensus. Confident that his way was the right way, he didn't concern himself with whether others might follow. He possessed great energy. He was determined to drag the prison and its people with him, and rarely did he worry that he might be wrong. His ideas sounded truthful and good to him, ideas of a leader.

On this day, April 16, he thought that the men in the dining hall seemed quiet and evasive. Although he was preoccupied with rifles and architectural drawings and other administrative challenges that only a warden could appreciate, he nonetheless recognized a ripple of apprehension around him. Many of the cons turned their eyes away when he looked at them. For a fleeting moment Powell sensed trouble. He had seen fear and mourned its consequences, for in his long career he too had walked the galleys and catwalks and worked the yard where a guard stood alone. Powell had arrived at the age when he no longer doubted his mortality. He had seen too much sorrow. Much like the men who worked for him, and even like the men he held captive, he was tailored from rough cloth and knew a rip at the seams.

Powell gripped his lunch tray and watched. Silence tells a story in prison. A secret coursed around him, and on a different day this con-wise man, who had worked his way through the ranks at Wisconsin State Prison, would have paid more attention.

He and Rothe had heard rumblings of a disturbance. Canaries up and down the galleys sang to the guards about an upcoming blowup. The guards had warned Rothe, and Rothe told Powell what they had said, but neither thought the rumors amounted to much. They didn't know who was involved, or how it might happen, or whether it might happen at all. They respected the canaries, because no prison operated without its informers, but the truth was that in the infancy of their new jobs, Powell and Rothe already had reached a dangerous level of confidence. They hadn't been in Deer Lodge long enough to know the prison well, however fortuitous they had been. By Powell's own estimation before he took the job, the prison failed all measurements of modern penology. He and Rothe considered it a miracle that Montana State Prison had survived the 1950s without a major riot resulting in lost lives. Scores of prisons in many states had fallen to such violence in the post-war decade.

Through the winter Powell and Rothe often came to their offices before dawn. Many nights they worked long after the third shift of guards came on duty and the prison slept. They just didn't think it possible that they couldn't read every mood and notion for themselves. Their indulgence made them less reliant on the other eyes and ears inside the prison.

Powell thought that the biggest beef among prisoners was not his reform attempts, but their anger toward a parole program that wasn't working to their satisfaction. The word from the canaries was that convicts were angry enough that they were talking about beating up parole board members in retaliation for seeming nonchalance. In the fall of 1958, soon after Powell came to Deer Lodge, more than 100 men eligible for parole had waited inside Montana State Prison for their marching orders. He had seen some of them dressed in street clothes, waiting at the main tower for parole officers who never came. It troubled him. Discontent inside the walls made his job harder.

Bad as the parole problem was, the apprehension that Powell sensed around him on April 16 seemed different, maybe worse. He just didn't know. Maybe he didn't worry enough, because it was a good day.

The cell house logbooks showed little activity that morning. In Cell House 1, also known as the 1912 cell house or the "new" cell house, floor officers scribbled cryptic notes, all of them ordinary, about a handful of men. Most of the cons went to their jobs. The prison, being a self-contained town, depended on them to run the kitchen and the power plant and the print shop and other places. The few who didn't work napped in their cells or played cards or read, and some went to the barbershop along Cooks Row. Painters slathered a mint-green pall on the walls in a few cells. Swampers swished wet mops along the flags, or ground floors, of Cell Houses 1 and 2. Before the main line arrived in the dining hall for lunch, the sunrise bakers filed onto their galley and into their cells, their day done. They stripped off white uniforms soiled with flour and coffee. Tomorrow they would wear clean clothes, washed and folded in the convict laundry.

***

Floyd Powell felt good about his progress at Montana State Prison. His deputy warden and his top officers had demoted the con bosses, those prisoners who had been put in charge of their peers in the shops and industries. All of them fell hard, but none worse than Jerry Myles. That man was a riser, prone to trouble. The guards said he stalked young men for sex. To them and even to his fellow cons he was a faggot and a queer, and the kinder term in prison parlance, a wolf.

Myles had made the most of being a con boss, reigning over the garment shop like a king. Until Powell and Rothe stopped him, he had used the shop for sex and, Powell thought, drinking and drug parties. Within a month of having arrived at the prison, Myles had weaseled a key to the garment shop and had furnished it with couches and colorful draperies from the upholstery shop.

Powell didn't know Myles well. Rothe had dealt with Myles and had informed Powell early that winter that he had sent Myles to Isolation in Cell House 2 for breaking rules and insulting guards. On this day, April 16, Powell saw Myles eating in the dining room with Lee Smart, his teenage boyfriend from Cell House 1. The stumpy burglar, tending alternately toward public cockiness and self-flagellation, didn't impress the warden as an exceptionally dangerous man. Myles was conniving, but that was common.

Today, the architects would show Powell the future. He reflected on his achievements at the Deer Lodge prison, which he flaunted in ostentatious letters to the state government folks in Helena. Walter Jones Jr., the new sociologist, had built a sizable body of case files that hadn't existed in Montana State Prison's entire eighty-seven-year history. Father Lynam, once a professor, had brought Catholicism and his academic wisdom behind the walls. Elmer Erickson, Powell's business manager, was helping him plan the new prison, which would be built in the naked foothills west of Deer Lodge, where in the summer meadowlarks preached from the fence posts. And Powell's guards, nearly doubled in number since the "pea riot" of 1957, were learning how to run a prison. Powell hoped the decent lawful people of Deer Lodge appreciated what progress had been made behind these walls. He had visited the Kiwanis and Rotary clubs down at Hotel Deer Lodge and the coffee klatches where town leaders huddled and listened to his descriptions of progress inside the prison. He was a speaker in demand.

Some of Floyd Powell's employees called him "Rehab Red" behind his back, intending the nickname to ridicule his attempts to reform the prison. He had attracted adversaries even in the early months of his tenure at Montana State Prison. Many of the guards and some of the office workers found his brusque manner offputting. They thought him deaf to their ideas. To the contrary, Powell thought of himself as a warm and compassionate man interested in their opinions. Years later, many of Powell's guards recalled that they wanted to know that he cared about them. Powell had a big job to do to bring the prison into modern times.

As he finished his lunch, Powell greeted the sidelong glances in the dining hall with mild curiosity. Rifles and rumors and ruffled feathers wouldn't spoil his day of triumph. He was going to build a new prison for Montana.

Yes, Powell thought, this would be a good day.

***

Jerry Myles had watched those rifles with joyous disbelief. Getting them, he figured, would be easy. Guards walked on open catwalks only feet from the cell house galleys. Time and again, Myles walked beneath that catwalk, calculating the distance. It was too far to jump, but Myles saw a way to climb across. He had seen guards do it many times. He wondered if they knew what they were showing him.

Myles had been at Alcatraz Island in 1946 when Bernie Coy spread apart the bars over the catwalk in C block, using tools he had devised from the flushing mechanism of a toilet. Coy beat a guard and stole his rifle and the show started. What a show it was, lasting for nearly three days. Myles remembered it well, every detail of it, even as he watched Floyd Powell eating lunch in the dining hall. The Alcatraz riot had started on a Thursday afternoon, just like today.

Myles knew Coy. Both worked as cell house orderlies along the corridor known as "Broadway" between C and D blocks, sweeping and polishing the worn floors. They shared other history, such as their love-starved childhoods, but Myles didn't dwell on that. Nor did he care about Coy's violent death that ended the breakout. But it mattered to him that Coy prized the rifles. Coy was the talk of the place long after his death. Word got around that the newspapers in San Francisco, across the bay, had found a memorable quote: "The first hours belong to us. The last, to God and the straightest shot." Nobody cared much about Bernie Coy before he got to Alcatraz. He was famous now. To Jerry Myles, he left in a blaze of glory.

The catwalks in Deer Lodge would be easier. The prison resembled Alcatraz in some ways. It was smaller than Alcatraz but not by much. Many of the 502 cells on The Rock were empty. Deer Lodge had about 400 cells and most of them full. Myles thought the cell houses similar in construction, but unlike Alcatraz the catwalks in Deer Lodge had no bars or wire, and they were close enough to the cells that a con could spit across from the galleys. Myles couldn't believe his luck.

He hated Floyd Powell and Ted Rothe. They took away his boss job in the garment shop, where he taught men to use sewing machines, and sent him to work on the water detail. Every con and all the guards knew that was the worst job in the prison. It had little to do with water. Myles spent most of his time emptying buckets of waste lowered from the guard towers on the walls, and doing the same from the unplumbed cells in Cell House 2. In his mind he was a man of great authority, deserving of more respect, and they had made a fool of him.

In Isolation, a string of cells in Cell House 2, or the 1896 cell house, with nothing but the Bible to read and that did him no good, Myles spent the unbroken days and nights worrying that Powell and Rothe would take the rifles off the catwalks before he got back to Cell House 1. He spoke in whispers to an escapee, George Alton, locked in the cell next to him. Under the pale light bulb, Myles paced in his closet of a cell. When the plan came to him, it was big. He would have cried out in excitement except that he was a wise con and knew how to keep his mouth closed. Dummy up, they called it in the prison.

In early April, when he got back to his cell on Skid Row, as Galley 1 was known in Cell House 1, he couldn't believe his good fortune. A guard walked above him, carrying a rifle. Myles took note of every feature of it, as he had many times before: a lever to jack in ammunition, a hammer that could be pulled back, a sight mounted on the top. It wasn't a long rifle but more like a carbine. Myles knew practically nothing about firearms. He'd had little chance to ever use one, although he bragged to other cons that he had shot and killed men. The ones more familiar with rifles like this said it carried seven rounds, one in the chamber and six in the magazine. They said it was a .30-.30-caliber rifle, a Winchester, a cowboy gun. Myles had seen rifles just like that on TV westerns. He imagined himself in the movies.

He estimated a distance of no more than seven feet between the galleys and the catwalks. A mere seven feet. Powell and Rothe had made much of their new security rules, but Myles thought they were a laugh. He had seen stricter rules in the federal prisons. Alcatraz was tough. So was the federal penitentiary in Atlanta, and that prison couldn't hold him. He had led a mutiny there that he figured they would never forget. They knew he was the kind of man who would do it again, and that's why they had sent him to Alcatraz. Floyd Powell didn't know what he had done in Atlanta, or so Myles thought, and he felt a bigger man for Powell's ignorance.

In Cell House 1, some guards refused to carry the rifle. Myles observed how they left it locked inside a green metal cabinet in the southeast gun cage. Myles knew it was the same in both cell houses. Some guards wanted to carry the rifle and others didn't. It was common in Cell House 2, the older building, to see the rifle propped against the brick wall just outside the gun cage as one guard in particular leaned back in a wooden chair. Myles expected to encounter little trouble in taking the rifles in either cell house. He hated the guards. They were his lost mother and his mysterious father and the pain and regret of his life. As much as he hated the guards, he needed them too. They stood for everything he hated, but without them he was nothing at all.

Just how he would use the rifles to scare the screws was a more complicated matter. Locked in Isolation, he had time to think. He wanted respect more than anything. Powell and Rothe and their lackeys had treated him like a dog. Nobody had loved him, not even his mother. She didn't want him. What did he care? He hated her, just like he hated his adoptive parents for sending him to reform school. So what if they had bought him a Boy Scout uniform, and a violin on which he'd tried to play comforting tunes to forget his sorrowful life? In every prison, and there had been many, people in authority had mistreated him. He hated his mother. He hated all the wardens and guards and psychiatrists who called him a queer and the prison doctors who wouldn't let him bleed when he ripped broken glass across his wrists. He would show them all. They would remember Jerry Myles.

- 3 -

A lost soul

Born by the name Donald Groat to an unmarried mother who didn't want him, Jerry Myles was destined for a loveless life. His long road to Deer Lodge began in Sioux City, Iowa, a snowy clutch of a stockyard town along the Missouri River. Leah Groat was a transient, inattentive mother. Before three months passed she signed adoption papers at the county courthouse. On March 11, Arthur and Lela Miles took her baby. Prison psychologists later would construe Donald's unremarkable birth on January 15, 1915, as the first step in a life of deep guilt. He would blame himself for his mother's unhappiness. He would become obsessed with drawing attention to himself by committing crimes.

In 1918, while Arthur Miles was fighting in World War I in Europe, his wife divorced him. Lela gave Donald to her sister and brother-in-law, Will and Ledama Hunter of Kansas City. They renamed him Richard Arthur Hunter. His early years appeared to be normal enough, as the Hunters involved him in Boy Scouts and other childhood activities. Little is known of the boy's mental state then, but as he approached his teenage years he became suspicious that the Hunters were keeping a secret from him.

He was thirteen years old when he overheard a private conversation between his new adopted mother and her sister. After begging several leads from Mrs. Hunter, he left home to search for his natural mother. He went to St. Louis to find Arthur Miles who told him how he could find records of his birth. He hitched rides on the highway, working his way north through the ocean of cornfields and eventually the broken river bluffs to Sioux City, where he discovered that he had been born in a maternity home. Through courthouse records he traced his birth mother to Greenfield, Nebraska. She no longer lived there but a lawyer found two of her sisters, who housed him for two months while he searched for Leah Groat. They helped him every way they could to find his mother. He learned that she had been working as a team mistress for road gangs on a railroad line stretching from Nebraska to Salt Lake City. A clerk in the office of the road gang told young Dick that she had gone to Arizona. By now no stranger to the open road, he found his way to Arizona on a journey that might have included car thefts. Police arrested him no fewer than four times for loitering and other minor offenses and returned him to the Hunters in Kansas City.

Dick, as the Hunters called him, returned to their home in Kansas City. The relative normalcy they had enjoyed in his youth evaporated. He blamed them for his rejection and became obstinate and told them he hated them. Dick felt anger and confusion and guilt. He stole and again ran away from home. When he was just fifteen years old the Hunters thought him incorrigible. They committed their adopted son to the Kansas Boys' School. His term would last eighteen months and twenty-two days. Years later he would brag to prison counselors of his sexual experiences with boys in the reform school, and would allege that, at the age of ten, adult men raped him in jail. The latter incident seemed suspect, even to prison counselors who heard the story years later, but it was an early sign of his compulsion to degrade himself with sex and dominate others with it.

He was seventeen years old when the reform school released him to the Hunters in Kansas City. He stayed only a few weeks before hitting the road for Wyoming, where he thought his mother had gone. But when he arrived he found she had returned to Nebraska. Finally, in 1933, he found her, but their reunion was ruinous. She hadn't told her husband that she had a child. Young Dick, or Donald in her fading memory, wanted her tender heart. She offered her cold shoulder. Little is known of their encounter except that she impressed on him that he had soiled her life. His stranger-father was lost to the years. After three days the boy drifted from his mother into the arms of crime.

***

In his waning teen years, Richard Arthur Hunter committed a series of burglaries in Arizona and Illinois. He offered multiple aliases to police, usually inventing a mixture of his boyhood names. Never, however, did he call himself by his true name, Donald Groat.

In 1934 he spent two months in Cook County Jail in Chicago awaiting trial for burglary under a $5,000 bond. His criminal record showed that he called himself Jerry and took his first adoptive parents' last name, but changed it from Miles to Myles. He frequently used other names through the 1940s, but he would assume the identity Jerry Myles, the person he decided he had become. He first went to prison on March 29, 1934, sentenced to ten years in Joliet, Illinois. In the subsequent six years Myles found himself in Illinois state reformatories in Pontiac and Menard, and by the time of his parole in 1940, he already embraced prison's hard ways. Five days after his parole, Springfield police arrested him for another burglary. From that day until his life's violent conclusion, he rarely walked a free man.

Throughout the first fifteen years of his imprisonment his disheartened adoptive parents pleaded that he accept their letters, but he asked guards that they be returned unopened. Whether angry or feeling he didn't deserve them, he turned his back. He did carry from prison to prison the violin the Hunters had bought him, occasionally recalling five years of childhood lessons.

There in the solitude of his cell, he played.

***

Ten months before Jerry Myles won his first parole, Mary Elizabeth Smart gave birth to her first child. Lee Olney Smart was delivered early on September 2, 1939, at Sacred Heart Hospital in Spokane, Washington. Mary was a thirty-two-year-old housewife.

Her husband, Levi Olney Smart, was six years older and a salesman for Sears and Roebuck. She was born a McPherson in Minot, North Dakota; he was raised in Dillon, Montana. They taught Lee the Catholic faith. True to his mother's wishes, he would be given all the favors a promising boy should appreciate.

In the sparse weeks and months between prison terms, Jerry Myles roamed the South and Midwest as a vagrant, resorting to thievery and larceny. He lived on the road, ignoring his home at 353 North 31st Street in Kansas City, Kansas. Restless and distrusting, he wandered through one town and then another. In a momentary burst of conscience he registered for Selective Service in October 1940, the same year that Floyd Powell began work at Wisconsin State Prison and Mary Smart enfolded her new baby named Lee.

***

Eleven days before Christmas in 1942, a Tennessee judge sentenced Jerry Myles to five years' close confinement in the federal penitentiary in Atlanta for driving a stolen car across state lines. He was caught fleeing a chain gang in Cobb County, Georgia, where he was being held after escaping from Georgia State Prison at Reidsville. He had served one year of two five-year terms in Georgia for burglary and possessing burglary tools, barely on parole after serving three months for trespassing in Louisiana.

When he entered USP Atlanta he was a twenty-seven-year-old fugitive, running from his past. He had no home, no family, and no love. Already his youthful face showed the wear of the road. His prison photograph at USP Atlanta showed his hard eyes wide open, shock-white and surprised, leaving the effect of a stage actor performing in the glare of Klieg lights. His masculine square jaw seemed at odds with feminine lips, curved and pursed, as if puckered for a kiss. Someone had mashed his nose in a fight, leaving it bent. Except for the presence of predictable prison-tailored tattoos he could have passed for any ordinary white man, albeit shorter than most. Standing barely over five-foot-two-inches, he became known as "Shorty" among fellow convicts, a nickname

26

that would stick. He weighed 156 lbs. Inmate number 62614 had listed "prizefighter" as his occupation, the only trace of such an unlikely vocation in his prison portfolio but a possible reference to his broken nose. His record showed that as a fugitive he had renamed himself Buddy Rawlins and Buddy Robins.

Myles came to Atlanta penniless. Besides his violin he owned one change of clothes, a razor and a nail file. He had completed seventh grade but showed little interest in formally advancing his education. He signed a form to refuse visitors and mail, specifically denying visitation to his parents, William and Ledama Hunter. Myles wrote "yes" to approve any possible visits by his natural mother, but then crossed out the reference. He refused to divulge personal information during his orientation interviews. Chief parole officer E. R. Goodwyn Jr. contacted Myles' former adoptive father, Arthur Miles, in St. Louis. "The only time I ever hear from him is when he is in trouble," Miles wrote back. Goodwyn also sought advice from Warden Joseph Reagen at Illinois State Penitentiary, where Myles had been jailed for most of the 1930s.

The day after the New Year began, Goodwyn received a letter from the Hunters. "This young man you mention is not our own son, we raised him from the time he was four years old, until he left our home at the age of seventeen. We gave him every possible opportunity that his own parents could have given a child," Will Hunter wrote from Kansas City. "He was a very pleasant and helpful child around the home. The only time I have seen him since he was seventeen was a few weeks in the fall of 1940. He is not married, he has no brothers or sisters, and I know nothing of his parents. Would you please write and let me know what his crime was, and how long his sentence will be, as I am very interested in him as he seems like one of our very own. He has also had five years of violin lessons...."

Eventually, some prison counselors blamed the Hunters for an abrupt and mean-spirited demeanor that contributed to their adopted son's growing anti-social behavior. Prison reports alleged the Hunters had taunted and ridiculed him and cast insinuations on his parentage. To the contrary, other reports concluded they at least had given the young man a marginal upbringing that included Y.M.C.A. memberships.

***

At USP Atlanta, on January 15, 1943, Associate Warden T.J. Gough assigned Myles to a "blocked" cell in C Cell house where he couldn't interfere with other inmates. Referring to Myles as a "homosexual psychopath," Gough instructed guard captains to notify his office of any unusual conduct. Myles was considered impulsive and unstable but not inherently vicious. A confidential psychiatric report forwarded from Illinois State Penitentiary showed he had been confined to the prison's psychiatric unit in 1935 after a sexual encounter and a subsequent attempt to cut his arm with broken glass. Two months later he returned to the general convict population, where his continued misbehavior led to solitary confinement, and a pattern of self-inflicted minor injuries. The report said doctors had diagnosed him as an "inadequate personality with homosexual tendencies."

A week later, United States Marshal Lewis Bowen escorted Myles to Alabama to appear in court on charges of interstate commerce violations. Myles pleaded guilty to transporting more than $39,000 in stolen securities from Birmingham to Atlanta. His ten-year sentence would run concurrently with his federal prison sentence in Atlanta. He would be eligible for conditional release in late 1949. Then he would return to Georgia State Prison to finish his burglary term. He wouldn't be sleeping in stolen cars and eating out of garbage cans. Prison was his home, no matter where it was.

A day after Myles was returned to USP Atlanta, the prison classification committee voted to release him into an eight-man cell near the officers' desk where he could be observed day and night, but at least he would be freed from the numbing routine of isolation. "Inmate denies any suicidal ideas and states he simply put on an act in state prison as he knew he could be transferred to another institution," they wrote. Myles denied any intention of pursuing his predatory ways, but a skeptical prison psychiatrist overruled the committee, and Myles stayed alone in his cell.

He didn't mind. Jerry Myles didn't like company unless his visitors were young, male and to him, beautiful.

*****

Jerry Myles was nobody as a free man, but in prison, doctors marveled at this victim of social shock. They drew many conclusions, among them that when Myles revealed feelings of rejection and want of affection, he compensated with potentially dangerous aggressive behavior. When the former Donald Groat discovered his catastrophic early years, he convinced himself he wasn't worthy of living in decent surroundings. He became somebody else known as Jerry Myles, a man supinely accepting of confinement. One might speculate that in a normal upbringing, Donald Groat might have become a law-abiding man. Jerry Myles invited prison, thought he deserved it, and slid deeper into his mind's darkest recesses where he hid from his demons. No one wanted him, or so he thought. He wanted nobody in return.

To understand Jerry Myles as he embarked on that long highway to Montana State Prison, no better tool exists than psychiatric tests administered during his admittance to USP Atlanta. He scored at a level of "superior intelligence" with an IQ of 125. In one report, the psychiatrists wrote:

"This reveals a young white male who enters the examining room quietly. He is respectful and sincere and rapport is easily established to a certain degree. He answers questions alertly, relevantly and coherently. The content of thought reveals no psychotic preoccupations. The mood is under fair control, however, revealing an underlying insecurity and instability. The sensorium is fairly well preserved except in the field of judgment; insight is only on a superficial plane. Personality studies reveal him to be an unsettled and insecure individual who reveal marked feeling of rejection and want of affection. He was thirteen years of age before he found out that he was an adopted child and has been reacting on an insecurity basis ever since; he has been indulging in extensive anti-social behavior, and has a compensatory symptom of aggression which will require intensive individual psychotherapy. He is tractable under supervision, though he should be placed under fairly close observation during the initial period of his incarceration."

When he arrived at USP Atlanta, Jerry Myles had never been to church. He didn't know if he had been baptized. He wanted to attend Catholic mass. He had no work skills except for prison experience as a sewing machine operator, and brief exposure to Will Hunter's trade as a plasterer. He had read magazines and fiction, but not enough to improve his reasoning ability. His doctors agreed his judgment seemed superficial and outwardly manipulative.

Myles came to Atlanta with no history of serious illnesses. Scars criss-crossed both wrists, evidence of suicide attempts. Gingivitis and cavities tortured his teeth. Vision in his left eye was perfect, in his right eye, blurry. He suffered from hemorrhoids and chronic tonsillitis. He denied any history of syphilis.

In a quest to give their new prisoner a sense of responsibility, prison officials assigned Myles to general maintenance in the culinary department. Feeling he was adjusting normally to the convict population, they eased his security restrictions. He moved into a group cell in A Cell house.

In late February 1943, his predatory sexual behavior became common knowledge throughout the prison. Slurring remarks drove him to ask for a private cell back in C Cell house, where special treatment prisoners were housed. He blamed prison doctors for the taunting he was receiving from fellow prisoners. Conversely, psychiatrist Dr. L.J. Zbranek saw Myles' supposed anger as a ploy to arrange a better position for illegal activities.

The dining room officer said Myles had never shown signs of being "queer" while on duty. He said the convict in his role as a headwaiter was polite, agreeable, and showed no favoritism to any convict.

Denied his request for a cell change, Myles stole food. A guard caught him tucking a brown paper package under his arm. Inside were nine freshly fried eggs: "Everybody in the kitchen was busy preparing eggs for Late Mess and Miles [sic] apparently cooked his in the oven as they were very well done," the guard wrote in his report.

Standing before a disciplinary board, Myles offered this insight: "The charge is right. I was going to eat those eggs. There is a slight mistake as to where they were cooked; they were not cooked in the oven, they were cooked in the pan. I did not know how many was there; there was a half pan or a part of a pan. They had been fried for the other mess."

Officers marched Myles into solitary confinement, assuring him the punishment he felt he deserved.

***

Encouraged by fact-finding inquiries from USP Atlanta, Ledama Hunter tried one more time to contact her adopted son. Her April 1943 letter betrayed her desperation: "Dear Dick, I have been thinking about you so much and just wondering why you don't want to write to your Dad and Mother what have we done that you have forgoten us or want to. we have been waiting to hear from you we still love you Dick no mater what you have done what is your truble now I was so in hopes you would be a good boy when you left home the last time if you love us you will answer this letter and if you don't I wont write you any more. love Mother."

A few days later Jerry Myles appeared before the Good Time Forfeiture Board to face accusations in the egg theft. He waived the record clerk's assistance in presenting his case, instead pronouncing himself guilty. He told board members he had thieved all of his life, ever since his boyhood, indicating his youth-height with his hand. With brag in his voice he said that during his childhood, it was just a habit to take whatever he wanted.

Myles didn't want his adopted mother's letter, but he didn't want it returned to her, either. "Relations seem to be strained," the prison's mail officer wrote in a memorandum to a deputy warden.

Myles didn't write Ledama Hunter, and neither did she write to him, ever again.

***

About five minutes before the four o'clock mess ended on the afternoon of May 27, 1943, Jerry Myles seized the water can from the convict who had been serving water and walked up and down the aisle, serving the water himself. At every stop he joked and talked with convicts who were eating, causing considerable disorder. After being reprimanded by the dining room officer in front of other convicts, he resumed work.

A week later, Myles and another convict steward linked arms, entered the dining room elevator and disappeared downstairs into the vegetable room. Guards couldn't start the elevator in motion because Myles apparently had propped the door open. They waited for five minutes. When the elevator returned both men got off. Myles said he'd been told to help the head cook find potatoes, a story that proved to be a lie.

Having been freed from his earlier, more restrictive "Third Grade" status, Myles started flirting with convicts assigned to bakery detail. Guards saw him hugging, pinching and feeling other men. He was caught smoking Camels, which were prohibited contraband, and although he argued he had rolled them himself, a store-bought pack jutted from his shirt pocket.

Associate Warden Gough again sent him to solitary confinement. Angered, Myles stormed around his cell like a caged animal. He threw a faucet handle through the window, shattering glass into shards. He stuck two sharp pieces into his coverall pockets. Five guards surrounded him, ordering him to remove his pants. They wrestled Myles into a stripped cell, where he tried to bite himself in the armpit. "You can't take my teeth away from me," he told the isolation officer. "I'm going to get the blood out and paint the cell red."

Gough concluded Myles had never adjusted to life in USP Atlanta and that he would be an outstanding behavior problem. At

Gough's request, Dr. Zbranek visited Myles, reporting afterwards that Myles had never learned to take discipline and would calm himself in due course. A superficial bite infected his arm. After a few days in the prison hospital, Myles was taken to the neuro-psychiatric ward for closer observation. He admitted he had tried to escape the "hole" many times in the past by hurting himself just enough to secure a transfer to what he called "the nut ward."

But he told more: in times of emotional distress, he could not control his predatory sexuality and had no desire to do so. He labeled himself a "penitentiary homosexual" attracted to younger, clean-cut, athletic men. He had never experienced any real affection for women except once when he fell for a "dainty doll-type girl," as he put it. He had fallen in love with another prisoner at USP Atlanta but had been unable to contact him. He preferred passive relations and when pressed into an active role lost respect for his partner. "It degrades him in my eyes," Myles said. He expressed the same feeling toward women. He blamed them for his inability to find them attractive. The psychiatrists immediately understood the rejection he felt toward his natural mother.

In light of these revelations, Myles transferred to the Special Treatment Unit. Doctors lost hope that he could live in the main prison population. Only intensive therapy, they decided, would help him. He was recommended for transfer to the federal government's special medical center for problem convicts in Springfield, Missouri. But Bureau of Prisons medical director M.R. King objected because of Myles' escape record. "I am inclined to believe that safekeeping and adequate control are the predominating features of this case at the present time and for this reason he should remain in the Atlanta special treatment unit," he wrote. Associate Warden Gough sent Myles confined to a locked room. Myles quit playing music but added an arithmetic course, supposedly to improve his lot in life.

***

Now that he had captured attention of prison administrators, Jerry Myles worked to manipulate them. He grew outwardly conceited, demanding and hypercritical, given to casting his bitterness on fellow inmates and prison guards. He was quick to argue his opinions at length, often in confusing tangles. He refused to operate a sewing machine in the basement of the treatment unit, offering no explanation except that he didn't want to be bothered. Once again the prison's disciplinary board placed him in "idle isolation" and revoked his recreation privileges. A month later Myles relented, and in a handwritten note to Associate Warden Gough, apologized for his behavior: "Lack of exercise is running me down, and mentally, I am not a very good cell partner for myself."

In May 1944 Gough recommended to Warden Joseph W. Sanford that Myles be returned to the general convict population, assigned to work either in the tent shop or the canvas goods shop. He would be given a blocked cell in C Cell house. Finding himself suddenly back at work, Myles requested that of his monthly earnings five dollars go to his commissary account, five dollars to savings until $200 was accumulated, and the balance be available for general spending. He spent two dollars and fifty cents for a Redbook magazine subscription and ten dollars for his hometown newspaper, the *Kansas City Kansan.*

Two weeks after he started his new job in the canvas shop, Myles slipped into the washroom to smoke. When Lieutenant Claude Nelson caught him, Myles tried to conceal the burning cigarette behind him. He later told the disciplinary board: "That's right, I was smoking in the mill. I knew it was against the rules. I will always take a chance, you know that, Cap. I know the penalty and I imagine I will go to the hole, be put in Grade, and I also would like to go back to the S.T.U. unit."

He got what he wanted, at least in part: a trip to segregation, demotion in grade, and a loss of thirty days' good time. The disciplinary board refused to return Myles to treatment. That's what he had wanted most of all, for a reason nobody suspected.

***

In August 1944, at his request, Myles met with Associate Warden Ben Overstreet to plead for more oversight of his behavior. In a rambling discourse, he told Overstreet: "I can't make it out there any longer, boss. No sir, it is not the work that I do not like, I just can't make it in the population. I don't want to lose any more good time or go to the hole anymore. You know that I am a thief and that I am a queer, need I say more. ... For the past three weeks I have broke every rule in the institution and I just haven't been caught. I don't want to be caught for I can't stand that hole. I have stole every thing that I could get my hands on and I just haven't been caught and I don't want to be. I don't think that I have been cool since I have been in here. I have been hot ever since I came in the door. Boss, you know that I don't have any trouble with any convicts. Nobody is after me, boss. ... I may be queer but I'm not a sissy. ... I have got too much freedom and I can't stand it. As long as I have this freedom I am going to break the rules."

In the presence of several people, including a stenographer, Myles described his sexual encounters in detail. He had never had a woman to love; before he agreed to sex he must truly love his man. "It is apparent from his statements and reaction that he is fighting against overwhelming homosexual urges which have him in a near panic," concluded prison psychiatrist H.R. Lipton, who advised that Myles be returned to the special treatment unit.

***

Jerry Myles marveled at his influence. First he had arranged to leave the special treatment unit; now he was going back. He had leveraged the prison administration's fear of his sexuality to disguise his real intentions. Seen as a lovelorn psychopath unable to follow basic regulations, he was really much more: a shrewd manipulator wise to the ways of prison power. Privately he mocked them. Didn't they wonder why one psychiatrist measured his intelligence at a seventh-grade level, while another classified him in the superior range?

During his months living in the general prison population, Myles stole moments inside the carpenter shop, where he found a machine that wasn't locked. He began grinding steel on the emery wheel. Little by little, two knives appeared from orange bursts of sparks and fury. He cut seams between the heels and soles of his shoes and slid them inside.

Soon those screws would worship him.

- 4 -

'Shorty' and a mutiny

They would call it a "mutiny," what Jerry Myles was about to do, which would imply he had a reason and a plan. When a man riots for his personal pleasure, or something that at least appears to be that, his goals unclear but his ego tickled as more men join his cause, words like "mutiny" and "revolt" attach some legitimacy to a relatively private dalliance.

Impulses bounced in his mind like rubber balls. It seems fair to conclude that Myles might have grown weary of his impulses because in prison every day is a bouncing ball. Sometimes it becomes important to stand for something, anything. Prisons are places where molehills become mountains. That's the result of a compressed society of men who dwell in limited geography, barren of privilege. To this quotient add the magnified distortions of a criminal mind, a hidden bewildered place that labors over trivia. Jerry Myles knew little about life except what prison defined for him. He felt inclined to make a lot out of that little.

On December 4, 1944, Myles walked onto the recreation field during evening stockade to meet two friends, Jack Floyd Adams and George Cecil "Slim" Hollingsworth. Seven times a day inside the Special Treatment Unit, guards had frisked Jerry Myles. Each time he stood patiently in his petite shoes atop steel sharpened to deadly points. Shoe polish disguised slits that hid his knives.

Now, he decided, the time had come. He slipped one knife from his shoe and handed it to Hollingsworth. When the whistle sounded for recall, meaning the recreation period had ended, Myles and Adams trailed the other convicts into the treatment unit. Once inside

37

the door, Myles handed his other shiv to Adams. When Officer Pittlekow started to lock the door, Myles stepped close to tell the guard that convicts were taking over the entire building. Pittlekow edged away. Myles pushed his finger against the guard's back to simulate a knife. Myles had decided in advance that he would try to subdue Pittlekow without a weapon. He didn't know why because he expected a fight; Pittlekow was a rough man and the prison grapevine had it he was skilled in the martial art of ju jitsu. But Pittlekow stood watching him. Myles reached down and grabbed his keys.

Meanwhile, Adams waved his knife at Officer R.H. Townsend, the other entrance guard. In response, Townsend slumped. Thinking the old guard might be suffering a heart attack, Myles braced him with a thick arm. The guard hung onto Myles for support, and together they climbed the stairs toward the guards' office. Meanwhile, Hollingsworth backed Officer Orlin Harper onto a landing. As Hollingsworth wielded his shiv, the guard hid his keys behind his back and, as he yelled and protested, Myles approached him from behind. Again Myles feigned his finger as a knife. Harper dropped his keys. At the front of the building they caught another guard, Officer Jackson.

Myles and his partners herded their hostages into cells 43, 44, 45 and 46 on what was called 24 Range for Negroes. Adams pulled a lever, locking the doors. Then Myles ordered other convicts into their cells. One refused. Myles wrestled him into a cell and locked it.

They went back downstairs to the Quarantine floor, barricading front and back doors and taking more hostages.

Myles opened a window. A guard stood in the cold twilight of the exercise yard. Myles shouted at him to call for the warden. While he waited, he went to a locker where he knew guards kept razors. There on a top shelf he found two cigar boxes full of razors and shears. Four new convicts sat inside the room, two white and two colored. Myles offered to lock them into cells but they hadn't been assigned any. They asked to be left alone, scared at the scene they saw unfolding before them. Myles told them to yell for help at the windows if shooting started or if guards shot tear gas at the building. An hour later, Warden J.W. Sanford arrived in the company of several guards. As Myles watched through a broken window's jagged panes, wiping blood from fingers he had cut when he smashed the glass, convicts began opening cell doors because in their first reckless impulses they wanted to find men they could sacrifice like lambs. In the midst of world war, even convicts insulated from duty or combat felt outrage that they were housed with German prisoners. Myles later recalled:

"Our intention wasn't to use the officers. Germans, yes; rats, yes. We were going to use them one by one as fast as we could use them. We would have made the steps as slippery as glass with blood but not the officers' blood. There was an officer brought downstairs tied, Mr. Townsend. I blowed my top. Now this is the difficult part of me telling the story, but this time there had been men taken out of their cells to be used. Some of them came, as I say, because they wanted to come, because they wanted in on it and some came because we told them to come, that it would not be healthy for them to stay in. We used some Germans and some rats, and later we used some Negroes. We didn't want Negroes out at first because we were afraid they would get their throats cut, and they were too. They were scared to death."

Myles had handed one razor to Adams, another to Hollingsworth, and shoved the remaining two into his pocket. His four guard hostages protested being locked in Negro cells. Myles moved them into cells that had been occupied by white prisoners, then handed them pencils and scraps of paper. They wrote notes to their wives. Myles told a convict to drop the notes through a window to the ground outside. Into the night he rotated his hostages at the front door as a defense against a rush that didn't come.

***

On Tuesday morning four convicts smashed into a cabinet that held psychiatric records. They dumped them onto a galley and, sitting there like schoolchildren, read them loudly to one another.

Folders marked "strictly confidential" attracted the most attention. Myles read his own file that contained documents that made a great deal of his sexual emotions. He slammed them to the floor and stomped on them, while other convicts threw shredded records into the air, watching them flutter like snowflakes.

That curiosity satisfied, they unlocked a cell containing prisoners' personal property, and on the assumption it belonged to Germans, they tore into bundles and suitcases, stealing whatever they fancied. Myles found an expensive watch, guessing its worth at least $250. Marveling at his discovery, he tried to fit it over his stout wrist but broke the straps. As other convicts marauded through cases of cigarettes, Myles selected a white shirt and a pair of trousers. He also found a red dressing robe. He stroked its soft texture and felt inclined to take a bath. He so adored the robe that after his bath he refused to change out of it. He paraded through the cell house like a king.

Before the first day had passed, Myles and his fellow ringleaders lost their riot. Their orders to keep other convicts locked in their cells went unheeded except among Germans and Negroes. Convicts smashed cabinets and stole medicine. One particularly dangerous inmate rushed from cell to cell, calling himself "Doctor" and offering to administer drugs. Others fell into stomach-churning stupors after drinking hair oil and shaving lotion. A double wedding took place, uniting lovers in a sacrament contrived on a moment's notice. If Myles was one of the dearly betrothed, he never admitted it.

Convicts rampaged through the chapel, stomping and urinating on a priest's vestments and smashing the altar stone. They burned Protestant hymnals.

***

When Warden Sanford arrived outside to negotiate, Adams tried to persuade Myles and Hollingsworth to give up. Myles and Hollingsworth overruled him, reminding Adams of their early agreement that they must stand together.

Myles assembled at least twenty convicts. Passing out slips of paper, he asked them to write their grievances. He read all the notes, throwing some away and scratching out passages on others. Convicts compiled what was left on two typewriters in a guard office; when one typewriter broke Myles summoned a convict from the cell house to fix it.

***

Seeing Myles, Adams and Hollingsworth in charge, most convicts sensed an escape plot. Still, other convicts seized the moment, taking advantage of the chaos to intimidate their enemies, ordering them to destroy their personal possessions. Scared Germans thrashed inside their cells in fits of vandalism. It was either that or death, or so they thought.

Myles recalled: "I am 'geared,' I am little, I don't have much force. Slim is tall; a lot of people are scared of Slim. Jack is young, a lot of people are scared of Jack. As far as physical force, I would have no force; as far as mental power, I would have no force." But Myles had two straight razors, a knife, and temporary command of the Special Treatment Unit.

For weeks preceding the takeover, Myles pried information from convict Jack Winn, veteran of a similar takeover in Illinois State Prison at Springfield. Little by little, Myles got what he wanted: facts on how it was accomplished and how guards reacted. He also researched the building itself, and when he learned about tunnels from a convict nicknamed Pegleg Coleman, he delayed their plans until he figured out how to blockade the openings. A stream of screws could charge through those tunnels. Coleman's information cost Myles a carton of cigarettes.

***

On Wednesday morning, a local newspaper published the convicts' grievances. Guards passed copies through the barred windows. Myles, Adams and Hollingsworth, in the company of their four guard hostages, read the article and then discussed surrender. Myles elected to free Officer Townsend. He liked the old man and admired that never once had he raised his voice. Myles suspected Officer Bacon of partially supporting his cause. He too, Myles mused, should be let go.

All morning they sat in the office, debating an outcome. Convicts brought a pan of scrambled eggs, potatoes and bread for breakfast. Myles laid his razors on a desk. Officer Harper tried to shave himself with one.

Myles took Officers Pittlekow and Bacon on a tour to inspect damage. He showed them that Negroes and the informants he called rats were unharmed, and when they came across a large colored man named Robert "Fat" Cutchins whom Myles recognized as a barber, he asked to be shaved. Myles went first, then the guards. Sandwiches waited when they returned to the office. That was all that remained of the commissary food, including eight candy bars stolen from a hiding spot in Myles' cell. While Myles watched, his hostages ate all the sandwiches.

***

Myles hurt all over. He hadn't slept. His legs ached; he hardly could climb stairs. News from the chapel troubled him. Even as a weak Catholic, if that, he couldn't stomach desecration of a priest's vestments. He also suspected time was running out. Guards would assault the building with a violent ending. He sensed trouble that others didn't, if only because since the robe incident he had spent more time worrying than celebrating. A debate that involved just a few people grew into a wide argument involving more and more convicts. Fearing they would persuade Adams and Hollingsworth to persevere, Myles called for a vote of the entire cell house, including Germans and Negroes. This democratic gesture was uncharacteristic of Jerry Myles, but as time would show, typical of his talent to prolong a prison drama.

They convened in the upstairs dining room: ringleaders, hostages, Germans, Negroes, rats. Myles remembered it as a touching scene. Convicts of different persuasions spoke passionately about their will to live, certain they eventually would be overcome and shot or hanged.

Myles fretted over his hemorrhoids. They blistered and drained, stinging him with hot needles of pain. Even surgery a year earlier hadn't ended this nuisance. If prison doctors couldn't fix his hurting, then medical treatment was lacking. Myles rioted over conditions just like this. He didn't get paid enough working in the mill. He was forced to stand with Negroes in the food line. They even handled his food. He hated Warden Sanford and Associate Warden Gough. Nothing made sense to him. Nothing, except his will to make himself the center of attention.

***

Guards knew more than convicts realized. Soon after the disturbance began, a public address system inside the treatment unit broadcasted convict conversations, unknown to them. Nicknames like "Dive Bomber" and "6" and "Jughead" could be heard, but Gough took note special note of "Shorty," the nickname Jerry Myles hated. Gough wrote down several comments, including: "Shorty, did you get your hand fixed? Is it hurt bad?"

Gough also knew that Myles had recruited two intelligent older convicts as consultants for what he called his Board of Advisors. He brought them together in a quiet cell, visiting them at least eight times for advice. Before the disturbance he had entrusted only Adams and Hollingsworth with his secret. He knew how prisons buzzed with information. Great power grew from the grapevine. He kept his circle small.

***

Being a better-than-average tailor, Myles skillfully sewed a razor blade inside one of his shoes. As he and his co-conspirators removed the barricade at the front door and surrendered, guards grabbed Hollingsworth. Quickly, Myles turned to Adams, pointing to his departing lover. "That is the end of everything, we are being separated right now." Myles had loved Hollingsworth for at least eighteen months. "It is there for him and he can have it any time he wants it," he later told Gough.

Myles, Adams and Hollingsworth had made a suicide pact.

***

In the wake of this mutiny, a rebellion that afforded Jerry Myles consequential training for his eventual culmination of power in Deer Lodge, he found himself in a one-to-one interview with none other than the director of the Federal Bureau of Prisons, James V. Bennett, who had come from his office in Washington, D.C., to see in person this distressed manipulative man.

Only in the twilight of his twenties, Myles already was turning heads. Psychiatrists at USP Atlanta considered him a rare case. Myles could force people in authority to react to his temperament and they feared his potential for violence. He was a little man who made big waves, and he knew it. Bennett's presence was just more proof of that. Myles made the most of it. The important man from Washington asked Myles why he hadn't pressed for reform before taking violent action. "I am used to dealing with the man I am in front of, the man that deals out punishment," Myles told Bennett. "I deal with him one way or the other; if I can't deal with him decently I go to extremes. I am a rebel at heart, both sexually, morally and mentally. I am not vicious – I don't think I am – but well, it was one of those things. I am willing to do time, get that; I am strictly willing to do time; I know I broke laws outside, when I play a game I play it for everything it is worth." Bennett described at length his work to improve living conditions and medical care, among other things. Unimpressed, Myles replied:

"You can't deny the medical assistance was bad; you can't deny we had absolutely no church services at all; you can't deny we didn't walk in line with Negroes. I know you didn't see that ... you can't deny we were in there with Germans and the men we should hate, we were being taught to hate by the papers and by every magazine, and we had to see them over there every day. If you are trying to improve us, make us better citizens, don't tell us lies and don't let your men treat us as you want us treated ... and don't make us be hated by the free people by putting [us] in there [with] the German intake and the Negro intake."

Portions of Myles' testimony, like the above, seemed reasonably lucid for a man with barely a fifth-grade education. Intelligence testing showed him certainly smarter than he behaved, but Myles tended to ramble in his conversations, stringing together unrelated, incomplete thoughts. Tired of these nonsequiturs, Bennett flatly stated, "I don't get what you're driving at."

***

Swathed in the familiar darkness of the Hole, convinced that guards would come to beat him, Jerry Myles reached into the special fold inside his shoe for the razor blade. He tightened and twisted his arm until a vein popped to the surface. After a quick slice with the blade, blood pulsed down his arm.

On that night of December 16, 1944, Evening Watch Lieutenant Frank Browne made his rounds inside the Isolation Building. Peering through the glass opening of Cell 6, he saw Myles lying on a mattress in the far corner. When Myles realized he was being watched, he pulled his blanket over his shoulder. Browne entered the cell. He jerked the blanket away to find Myles lying naked in a pool of blood, some of which had already soaked into the mattress. Myles stared at him through glassy shocked eyes. Browne called for a doctor, and then he called Associate Warden Gough at home. Left alone with Myles for a few minutes, isolation officer J.J. Sluder heard him whisper, "Have they sent Hollingsworth off? Is he here?" Sluder said he didn't know, to which Myles responded: "They are not going to kill me like they did the other boy."

Four convicts from the prison fire station carried Myles to the hospital on a stretcher. His wounds were small but deep. Already he had lost two pints of blood. Myles wept as Dr. Saul Korey stitched his left arm. He confided to the doctor that guards said Jack Adams was dead and that he was next. He also said that Hollingsworth, who had earlier answered his signal whistle, now failed to respond. Myles wrongly took that to mean that Hollingsworth had been killed.

On the last day of 1944, Myles and Hollingsworth resumed whistling and calling out to each other. They then cut their arms with broken glass in their separate cells. Hollingsworth jammed scraps of paper into the cell lock. When guards gained entry, he had weakened and fallen. Myles raged in his cell, scooping his fingers through pools of blood and flicking it at the guards. They stopped his bleeding with a tourniquet. This time Myles and Hollingsworth didn't get the pleasure of a hospital stay. After medical treatment they were handcuffed to waist restraining belts and returned to their cells. A day later, Myles asked to speak to Gough. "If he stays around me he will lose all that manhood," Myles said of his friend. "You know what I mean when I say that." Gough removed Myles' waist belt, replacing it with a special canvas jacket intended to prevent self-mutilation.

Then Myles asked to be quartered with Hollingsworth, to whom he wanted to devote his fondest attentions.

***

Later, Gough would interrogate Jerry Myles about his desire to escape, although Myles hadn't decided what he meant to do. Inside intelligence showed he had considering trying to flee through existing tunnels. Thinking that improbable, Myles then considered digging a new tunnel. Myles knew Gough knew, but he denied having considered such a plan. His escape attempt had fizzled for lack of direction and planning. Gough persisted: "Myles, I want you to tell me honestly and frankly whether or not you, yourself, have any complaints to make about the treatment you have received in this institution or the treatment that has been given you."

Myles: "Honestly? No. ... You know at the time we took the building over we thought our beefs were great big mountains and all that but now that I think about them, they were not so big."

Gough: "The truth is, you did not have a beef, did you?"
Myles: "No."

***

Warden Sanford cancelled Jerry Myles' subscription to the *Kansas City Kansan*, citing administrative reasons. He also cancelled Myles' *Redbook* subscription, for which Myles received a refund of eighty-four cents. The warden paid for the stamps himself.

Throughout the winter, Myles continually defied orders to keep quiet, whistling to Hollingsworth and yelling profanities to other convicts. One day he whistled to Hollingsworth seventeen times, receiving a warning each time. "I admit I have been whistling back there since I was told not to whistle," he acknowledged. Unable to do anything else, the disciplinary board revoked his smoking privileges.

***

In March 1945, Myles petitioned Warden Sanford to meet with Adams, Hollingsworth and convicts William H. Sanders, James D. Douglas and Myron G. Hinds. All six had been indicted for conspiracy, mutiny and assault on federal employees. On Sanford's approval, and with Gough present, they met in a cell Sanders and Douglas shared.

Myles took charge, asking each convict in turn which lawyer had been appointed to defend him in court. Myles then said no lawyer could be trusted, urging the others to plead guilty and throw themselves on the mercy of the court. They bickered over strategies that would lessen sentencing on Sanders and Douglas. "Well, we know we are all guilty," Myles told them, and each man nodded in agreement.

Adams tried to persuade the others that being forced to work and eat with Negroes would bring sympathy from a southern jury, and that having to live with Germans would strike a patriotic chord. Myles objected: "If you plead not guilty for the purpose of smearing the institution the prosecutor and these people here will certainly smear all of us and you know exactly what I mean." Gough presumed Myles referred to his sexuality because the group laughed at Myles. They still wanted to plead innocent.

***

In late March 1945, Bureau of Prisons director James Bennett advised U.S. Attorney Neil Andrews to accept guilty pleas from Myles, Hollingsworth and Adams, and to dismiss indictments against the others. "I hope the court will be fully informed of the dangerous character of these men and the serious manner in which they have disrupted the institutional discipline," he wrote.

A month later, Myles returned from court convicted of conspiracy to mutiny. Arrogant, demanding and vile, he was forcibly taken to the neuropsychiatry ward where guards stripped and searched him. He screamed profanities into the night.

Finally, USP Atlanta officials had had enough. Considering Myles a detriment to the security and discipline of their prison, a committee of four supervisors recommended his transfer to maximum security at the United States penitentiary on Alcatraz Island, noting: "On admission, this man tested as having superior intelligence. He was diagnosed as neurotic criminalism. His adjustment has been poor; during his incarceration he revealed psychopathic traits. The prognosis for adjustment here is poor."

Keeping Myles in USP Atlanta, they concluded, would threaten the entire prison. Considering him an outstanding agitator and escape risk, they revoked 1,151 days of good time for good measure. Then they waited to hear from the U.S. Bureau of Prisons. Alcatraz, "the Rock," was the only answer. He was not a man for a lesser prison. Everyone agreed that without close custody where discipline was legendary, in a prison like Alcatraz, Jerry Myles would lead a riot.

- 5 -

Jerry and Alcatraz Island

On May 8, 1945, as the Allies stormed across Europe, federal marshals transported Jerry Myles to California. Booted from the federal penitentiary in Atlanta for his mutiny, Myles now found himself in the company of some of America's most legendary criminals. Moved with him were his fellow Atlanta ringleaders, Jack Floyd Adams and George "Slim" Hollingsworth.

Identified as inmate number 692, Myles was locked into solitary confinement in Cell 1, D Block, for his first nine months on The Rock. So little was known about his family background that most of his Alcatraz registration sheet was left blank. It mentioned only his adoptive parents; his birth mother wasn't listed at all. Under the heading "Other Relatives" the intake officer wrote, "not known." On advisement from Warden Joseph W. Sanford of Atlanta, Warden J.A. Johnston impounded Myles' meager bank account to help pay for damage he had done to the Special Treatment Unit at USP Atlanta. That cost was assessed at $77.37. More trouble followed him from Georgia. The Cobb County Public Works Camp in Marietta filed a detainer at Alcatraz, asking for sixty days' notice before his release. Myles had served less than a year of a five-year burglary term in Georgia before his escape.

At Alcatraz, classified as "idle," Myles sat inside his cell around the clock, denied even recreation privileges, tracing his finger across a peacock tattoo on his left wrist. With the addition of twenty months for conspiracy to mutiny, his federal sentence would expire in early 1954.

The day after he arrived at Alcatraz, psychiatrist Romney M. Ritchey evaluated his mental state: "He has been given to episodes of emotional excitement and aggressive conduct for many years and was held in an Institution for [Criminally] Insane for 5 yrs in 35 to 1940. He was again under mental observation while at Atlanta and made statements there that he should be considered a 'psycho' etc. He has no sense of responsibility to others and is highly unstable emotionally. He is at present well mannered during interview but is highly egotistical and self centered." Ritchey's diagnosis: Jerry Myles was an "emotionally unstable, psychopathic personality."

On Censorship Form No. 14, Myles on May 29 wrote a letter to Bureau of Prisons director J.V. Bennett, convinced Bennett had ordered his solitary confinement. "I would like a chanch [sic] to show that I can conduct my self as the other Inmates do. You know I am not perfect. I am a Thief. I am a 'convict'. But at least I am a truthfull [sic] one. I am not going to give you a line of 'Bull.' I have about 10 years to do and I want to do it as easy as I can."

Concerned that Myles, Hollingsworth and Adams had been given discriminatory treatment not meted out to other new Alcatraz convicts, Bennett asked Warden Johnston to investigate. Johnston informed him by Teletype that other men – Stroud, Groves, Darlino, Parnell and Embry – had been placed in D Block on arrival at Alcatraz. And Myles had been troublesome during the trip from Atlanta to Alcatraz, warranting his punishment status. When he cooperated with prison rules, he would be given privileges.

In late July 1945, USP Atlanta deducted $66.06 from Myles' prison bank account, and then forwarded the remaining $11.31 to Alcatraz.

***

Early in 1946, Myles again petitioned for leniency. He asked for a transfer out of D Block. He complained of nervousness and failing health. Forced idleness had made him fat. "I have tried to show you by my action's and behavior, that I expect to get along. I shall show my appreciation, if transfered, by my future action's and behavior," he wrote. The prison disciplinary board decided to risk moving Myles into the general prison population. He was assigned to Cell 190 and given a job as cell house orderly in C Block.

In September 1946, after a dispute over mint rolls, guards returned Jerry Myles to solitary confinement. He had been sitting at Dining Table No. 11 when he took two extra rolls during breakfast when seconds were served. He then tried to persuade a convict waiter to pass them to a friend sitting behind him. Senior Officer James J. Comerford cited him with a violation. That morning in the Tailor Shop, Myles warned Comerford to leave him alone and then refused to work. Accused of insolence, Myles went to solitary confinement under orders from Associate Warden E.J. Miller. Myles asked for a tablet to write a legal brief, and for a pipe to smoke.

***

Through 1947 Alcatraz officers struggled with the convict they described as a "persistent offender of regulations." Myles frequently tried to be assigned to kitchen detail to get closer to Hollingsworth, who worked there. Recognizing Myles' motives, Associate Warden Miller denied his requests. During a contraband inspection, guards found tin foil wrapped around Myles' cell light globe, and a stash of used violin wire. When asked why he did not abide by cell house rules, Myles replied that he would never get along with anybody. While going to the main gate one day, he was told to button his collar and roll down his sleeves. He ignored the first order. Laughing at the guard in the presence of other convicts, Myles responded to the second order. That night, after being allowed to see a movie, he went to another convict's cell without permission from the cell house officer. Standing before the disciplinary board the next day, he complained in response to the first offense that his shirt was too big, and in explanation of the second, that he went to another cell to get some magazines. Reprimanded and warned, he said he was sorry.

While Myles fought his private and often trivial battle against authority inside Alcatraz, U.S. District Judge Marvin Underwood dismissed a civil action against the Bureau of Prisons in which Myles, Hollingsworth and Adams tried to sue for $5,000 in punitive damages.

By early 1948 Myles had compiled six disciplinary citations, most of them related to small matters that demonstrated his desire to break rules. His work record was spotty and inconsequential; he sometimes changed jobs two or three times in a month. From the fall of 1947 through the spring of 1951 he worked in the laundry thirteen times, the hospital twenty-five times, the mattress shop once, the glove factory four times and the tailor shop three times. He worked as a painter three times, a cell house orderly ten times, a kitchen floor polisher three times, and a general laborer once. He was classified as "Idle" thirteen times and spent four stints in solitary confinement or segregation.

In his work as head washer in the prison laundry, Myles' civilian laundry supervisor scored him "average" in his work aptitude, "quiet" in his disposition and "obeys instructions" in his attitude. Chief Medical Officer R.S. Yocum described Myles as a "constant caller at sick line for multiplicity of minor complaints."

Of the fifty letters Myles mailed in his first three years at Alcatraz, all but two went to lawyers, judges and other justice officials and organizations. The remaining letters went to the *Kansas City Kansan*, which he considered his hometown newspaper, and to the Library of Congress.

In April 1948, Officer A.G. Bloomquist found Myles drunk on homemade beer in the laundry, too intoxicated to make coherent replies. He was sent to solitary confinement, known as the "Hole," for seven days with a full loss of privileges. Then he spent four weeks in D Block, and after that, was locked in a regular cell around the clock.

Alcatraz officials had lost their patience with Jerry Myles. In a special progress report written in the summer of 1948, Myles was assessed as "rather unstable" and prone to self-centered behavior. Chaplains wrote: "Reads quite extensively in detective and realistic fiction. No study courses but lead musical playing in chapel for over a year. Has some musical ability and is intellectually capable. Tends to be a non-conformist. Cooperates well if diplomatically made to feel some authority. Has somatic complaints which are no doubt products of an inferior attitude of mind." The cell house officer reported Myles kept an untidy cell, that he liked to "play around" and that he failed to make his bed according to rules. He was considered friendly with co-workers, clean in personal habits and inclined to complain, but had not been heard agitating other convicts on the job.

By the close of 1948 Myles incurred three more disciplinary violations: insolence in the dining hall, refusal to work, and disrupting the cell house by banging on his cell door with a board and a tin cup and shouting profanities. For this last offense, his most serious and characteristic of his occasional but unpredictably violent tantrums, he again went to the Hole, this time on a diet of bread and water.

In February 1949, staff psychiatrist Leon J. Whitsell and Chief Medical Officer Yocum examined Myles, who had been a hospital patient fourteen times since October 1946. Myles had continually complained of skin rashes and nervousness. He told the doctors of his four previous pseudo-suicide attempts. Now thirty-four, he offered glimpses of his personal life: his allegations of early homosexuality, that he never had a close friend, and that between prison terms he lived in Y.M.C.A. hotels. Fellow D Block prisoner W.A. Hull, hoping to influence Myles' appeal to the classification committee, wrote on his behalf that Myles played whist and bridge and went to the exercise yard every chance he got to play handball. Myles spent some cell time reading, and sleeping in the afternoons. Hull said Myles bathed and shaved regularly and kept his cell in good condition.

In the spring of 1949, Alcatraz released George Hollingsworth. Myles flew into a rage in his cell. Guards took him to the hospital where he started a tirade against Catholics. He yelled again and again: "Oh! You dirty Catholics took my 'Flocko' out and shot him." He interspersed his accusations with hysterical screaming.

Four days later, near midnight, he cut his left wrist and right ankle. An orderly bound his superficial wounds. In late April new Alcatraz Warden E.B. Swope interviewed Myles, concluding: "I discussed with this subject his failure to adjust. He stated quite frankly there was no question of doubt in his mind he was responsible; that he did not fully cooperate, and had abused the Associate Warden in a profrane [sic] and disrespectful manner and it was his intention to apologize. He desired to be placed on some assignment other than the laundry. He refused emphatically to go to work in the laundry, claiming it affected his health...."

Myles wrote his letter of regret to Associate Warden Madigan: "This is a hard note for me to write, because I've got to admit I was wrong. But worng [sic] I am, and sorry I am for the thing's I said to you in fits of anger. (or should I just say 'fits') I have never given you much reason to believe I wanted to get along. and I cannot expect you to believe that I have changed in any way. Perhaps I haven't, time can only prove that. But at the present time, and I hope for a long time to come, my thoughts and hope's are to get along. You may say to your self that you Doubt that. Well! Mr Madigan, I do too. But I am still going to try.

"I would like to have an Interview with you, so that we can talk this over and to work out some sort of plan that will help to keep me from making another dam [sic] fool of myself. And if possible can this interview take place somewhere else besides the front end of the cell house at noon where you always seem busy, and I can never feel at ease. R.A. Myles Cell B331."

Still, Myles longed for Hollingsworth. For the first time in his entire prison life, Myles requested permission to correspond with a woman who lived in Oklahoma. Coincidentally, Hollingsworth had been discharged to Oklahoma authorities who held a detainer against him. "Inmate Myles has pursued no correspondence during his incarceration here and it appears to us that it would be therapeutically helpful for him to have such an outlet, but we are also desirous of avoiding any questionable cultivations," Alcatraz chaplain Byron Eshelman wrote to Oklahoma City probation officers. Officer Charles R. Paine replied that the woman was a married mother of two and was Hollingsworth's sister. She had never heard of Jerry Myles. "She surmised that Miles [sic] wanted to write to her only for the purpose of ascertaining what the state authorities in Oklahoma did with George Hollingsworth," Paine wrote. Associate Warden Madigan denied Myles' request.

In October 1949, Myles got reprimanded again when a guard caught him fondling another convict in the exercise yard. At his disciplinary hearing Myles said this wasn't sexual perversion but horseplay. That was the only recorded misconduct between his special progress reports of 1949 and 1950. His April 3, 1950, report read in part: " ... this inmate has the faculty of ingratiating himself into the good graces of officers if possible in order to get all possible freedom for himself. He needs close supervision at all times; however, he takes direction and criticism very well and can easily be handled. This man is open in admitting that he probably will be in institutions all of his life and at no time ever seems discouraged over his plight. If he can be watched closely enough and handled properly he does his work well and does not get into much difficulty."

In May 1950, Myles accumulated his eleventh violation when he refused to report to work, supporting his fellow convicts in a strike. He claimed no knowledge of the strike or of a dining room disturbance a few days earlier, although officers had watched him participate in both. Five days after the strike, convict Gazie Penksa tipped his dining table over, knocking food and trays to the floor. On cue other white prisoners did the same as Negro prisoners sat and watched. Myles had refused his ration of macaroni but had opted for a dish of dried prunes. When his table tipped he pressed against the wall and watched, in sympathy with the gesture because of poor food quality.

Four months later, while on a work detail dismantling an old machine shop, Myles suffered injuries to his left arm when another convict dropped a case of motors across his bicep. He couldn't move his wrist and complained of numbness in his fingers.

By May 1951, Alcatraz officials recommended a full year of good time be restored to Myles, citing noticeable improvement in his behavior and work performance. Approved personally by Bureau of Prisons Director Bennett, the report concluded: "Reports indicate that this prisoner has made a 'right-about-face' in his prison adjustment. Foremen and officers, supervising his work assignment, state that he is a diligent, cooperative and industrious worker in the Laundry. He has demonstrated over a one-year period, his willingness to abide by regulations, and obey the instructions of supervisors. His attitude has changed to a marked degree; he is friendly, cheerful and is desirous of improving his prison record...."

Myles no longer practiced his violin. He didn't attend school or church. He limited his yard recreation to bridge games. At thirty-six, his interests had narrowed even further. "An ingratiating, fairly sophisticated individual, Myles does not appear resentful of the close supervision accorded in view of his 'reputation,' " his special progress report of 1951 read. Even discovery of contraband butter and fudge candy in his cell during a routine shakedown didn't allay the Alcatraz disciplinary board from commending Jerry Myles for his turn-about. Relieved at his apparent newfound willingness to follow rules and his successful camouflage of his predatory sexuality, they restored his cigarette privileges for two weeks. Jerry Myles, they believed, was being rehabilitated. Shortly before Thanksgiving 1951, citing his "diligence, spirit of cooperation, and obviously genuine determination to conform to the program he abused earlier in his institutional career," they restored another 100 days of good time. It was Christmas. They felt in a giving mood.

On November 29, 1951, Bennett approved a transfer for Myles to the federal prison in Leavenworth, Kansas. Good time had moved his conditional release date to May 1952. After more than twenty years of prison life, this was Jerry Myles' best year.

***

He came to Leavenworth on January 8, 1952, in the company of four other convicts. He had packed his only possessions: two boxes of dominos, one envelope of personal papers, a pipe, a Parker pen, a

chess set, a guitar in its case, and his violin in its case, including a tuner bow and two picks.

Now classified as Inmate Number 68396, Myles quickly assimilated into his new home. On a form intended to list relatives or friends to be contacted in event of injury or death, Myles wrote "No One," and stated his parents as "Unknown." Nobody's name appeared on his list of approved visitors. He listed as his occupation "sewing machine operator." Achievement testing showed an age equivalent of 12.7 and an education equivalent to midway through seventh grade; another test showed his IQ at 125. Prison officials assigned Myles to close custody, a grade between maximum and medium, and upgraded his conditional release date to March 9, 1952. "I don't know what I'm going to do after I get out, and it doesn't make much difference anyway," he told Leavenworth's chief medical officer, Dr. H.A. Storrow. The doctor concluded: "Evidence available indicates a dismal social prognosis, but in favor of at least a marginal social adjustment at some time in the future, is the fact that this man seems to be gradually settling down as he advances in age."

Having spent his entire adult life in reformatories and prisons, Myles could envision nothing else. He knew of no siblings; he was now even denying his natural mother's existence. He had no labor background of any consequence. His prison record listed "Georgia chain gang" among his work accomplishments.

With his Leavenworth release in clear sight, Myles decided late one night to cook stolen food in his cell. Officer Albert Ohme, on rounds in F Ward, smelled smoke. He found a pitcher of hot coffee near Myles' bed, and in his locker, a cup that contained jelly, butter, toast and an egg. Myles would spend seven days in isolation.

In early 1952, United States District Judge Arthur J. Mellotz of Kansas City ruled that Myles be released no later than March 3 on the grounds that he was being illegally restrained. Legal skirmishing over how Atlanta and Alcatraz had computed his good time and aggregate sentences paid off. His total federal penitentiary term would be eleven years, nine months and five days, a total of eighty fewer days than his captors had intended. His federal parole supervision would end two years after his release from Leavenworth.

Sent to the prison storehouse for his discharge clothing, Myles was fitted with a double-breasted suit, size 46; a white shirt with a size sixteen and half neck; a size 38 belt; a size 44 overcoat; a pair of shoes sized five and a half; a straw hat, and new underwear. When Jerry Myles walked to Leavenworth's front gate at nine o'clock in the morning on March 3, the local sheriff took him into custody to await an escort from Georgia's state prison.

***

Jerry Myles spent nearly three years in Georgia State Penitentiary, much of that time locked in Segregation Unit 4. He began exchanging letters with parole officers in Tennessee, asking if he could be released to Shawnee, Oklahoma. "I'm broke on segregation and its [sic] a rough skufful," he wrote in May 1953. And a few days later: "The Government also owes me train fare which you can check on and forward here. I can use it to buy smoking, stationary, and stamps. Its hell to be a poor man." And finally, angry that parole officers wanted to see a detailed plan from Myles before released him to Oklahoma: "The fact that you interfered in my gaining my release by threats of slapping me on the wrists if I don't bow to the Gods indicates your whole-hearted intrust ... I'm holding my breath."

Released from Georgia State Prison on January 20, 1955, Myles inexplicably moved to a rooming house in Indianapolis, Indiana. On February 28 police arrested him on suspicion of burglarizing Henry J. Richardson's law office at 157 North Illinois Street after his stolen getaway car broke down on a state highway. In late May he was convicted and sentenced to two to five years in Indiana State Prison in Michigan City for second degree burglary. He served three years.

Before Myles won his release in late May 1958, prison psychologist Michael E. Holtzleiter wrote of him: "The subject has been in trouble for the better part of the last twenty-five years. Much of this time has been spent in prison in various parts of the country. It would lead one to believe that a career in crime has become a pattern and way of life for him. Also he is rather a disturbed person. He has always had feelings of rejection and these have become more pronounced in his actual rejection by his mother and other members of his family."

So intertwined was Jerry Myles' criminal behavior with his early quest to find his natural mother that it launched him on that longer road that brought him face to face with Floyd Powell at Montana State Prison.

"Feelings of rejection are complicated by actual rejection by his natural mother...," wrote John Stanfield, another Indiana prison psychologist. "It seems as though he attempts to gain attention through overt actions and exhibitionistic attitudes." Holtzleiter came to a similar conclusion: "He likes to attract attention and he has by acting tough in other prisons but his record here other than three minor disciplinary reports has been rather good. So perhaps he is not as bad as he likes to make himself out to be." In a strange foreboding, Holtzleiter wrote: "The subject has no particular parole plans at this time but claims that he can find a place to live and work when he is released."

Indeed, Jerry Myles heard of another place where convicts ran the prison. In that place, "con bosses" managed the prison industries. In that place, the warden and the guards and anyone else in authority would learn to respect him. He would boss them as he pleased, and they would marvel that he didn't bow to their gods.

The source of his information remained a mystery, although circumstantial evidence suggests it might have come from his old friend from Atlanta and Alcatraz, Jack Floyd Adams. Myles had lost track of George "Slim" Hollingsworth and left him in the past. Adams, however, served a year for petty larceny in Montana State Prison under the alias of Vern Stoehr. He was released in August 1957. Somehow, Adams and Myles must have made connections, because Myles bought a bus ticket to Butte, Montana, less than an hour's drive from Deer Lodge.

Getting into a prison was no problem for Jerry Myles.

Warden Burrell and the 'hell hole' in Deer Lodge

Driven to crime by America's oncoming Depression, thieves began swelling Montana State Prison's convict population by 1930. Of the 702 prisoners held in the summer of that year, more than two-thirds had committed grand larceny, forgery, robbery and burglary. Overcrowding reached crisis proportions. The Montana State Crime Commission estimated the prison's two cell houses could safely accommodate 350 convicts between them. The river of thieves drove the inside count to 550, resulting in "fish" living with hardened cons one metal bunk atop the other in cells six feet by eight feet, with ceilings seven feet high.

"That condition coupled with the fact that about 450 of the 700 prisoners are permanently idle, spending their whole time in their cells, makes the prison a crime school where the vicious offender teaches the tyro the secrets of the criminal's trade," the commission concluded.

Just as before World War I, the convict population remained older, but more than forty percent by 1930 were repeat offenders, nearly four times the number of repeat offenders inside Montana State Prison since the turn of the century.

***

In 1930, as an angry and dejected Jerry Myles began his prison career more than 1,000 miles to the east, the Crime Commission decried Montana's prison as a riot risk and town firetrap. The big walls hid from public view a melting pot of wayward men, many of whom lived in subhuman filth. Buckets served as toilets for almost half the prisoners. Overcrowding and unsanitary food preparation led to rampant sickness.

Unsafe ramshackle wooden buildings, including the 1871 Federal Building, butted against newer brick structures. The Federal Building linked the 1896 cell house with the 1912 cell house. On brittle wood floors beneath a timber roof, thirty convicts worked in the license plate factory and the tailor, carpenter and shoe repair shops. The tailor shop, which during Myles' tenure would be known as the "garment shop," made prison clothing and supplied work for other state institutions. In 1929, those men produced 585 dozen shirts, 337 dozen overalls, seventy-three dozen sweaters and sixty-eight dozen nightshirts. In the tin shop, convicts made pails, cups and plates for prison use. Despite these big numbers that implied factory-like production, far too few prisoners worked in these shops. Most sat locked in their cells around the clock.

The Crime Commission commended Warden Austin Middleton for his efficient management and sound discipline: "He has the prison plant in as good repair as is possible with the means given him."

Considered most dangerous among the prison's many buildings was Cell House No. 2, misnamed because chronologically it was the first cell house of any size and distinction constructed at the prison. Built in 1896 in the southeast corner of the six-acre prison yard, Cell House No. 2 housed 174 men in 152 cells in August 1930. Although barely more than thirty years old, the building suffered for lack of repair and modernization. It had no water or sewer connections; it lacked suitable light and ventilation. Any enterprising convict with a sharp instrument could carve brick away from cell doors in chunks. And then there was the promise of human tragedy: Sheet iron covered a wood roof; wood runways flanked cells on the upper three galleys. Each cell unlocked individually. Locks were badly worn; keys did not always catch. If the Federal Building caught fire, Cell House No. 2 might quickly succumb to flames. Guards would have to enter those wooden runways to unlock cells one at a time. It was presumed most convicts would roast in their cells before they could be saved.

Fearful of a calamity that would kill dozens, possibly all the men in the cell house, Warden Middleton and Crime Commission members recommended a sweeping building program that would include renovation of Cell House No. 2. Middleton was the eighth Montana warden since the prison opened in 1871. He started his job in March 1925, just four years after Frank Conley's departure. Being familiar with how extensively Conley had employed convict labor for institutional building construction, Middleton saw an opportunity to put hundreds of men to work. He offered to dismantle the block of cells, which stood in the building's center, then build new cells against the four walls and add another eighteen for a total of 170. A set of catwalks in the middle would give guards commanding views. Middleton would install a fireproof roof, reinforce outside walls and cover outside windows with steel bars. He envisioned running water and sewer pipes. New modern locks operated by outside levers would open and close cells in unison, just as was being done in the newer, 1912 cell house.

Middleton also wanted to abolish the Woman's Ward, a dark hovel housed inside an enclosure 100 feet square attached to the outside west wall of the men's prison. Calling this building a "disgrace," the Crime Commission said its "enforced intimacy under which the women prisoners live is entirely indefensible." Here, in this seven-room brick cottage, nine women dwelled in squalor. Their tiny exercise yard prohibited a good stroll; it was, at least, a courtyard of sufficient size to stand and smoke. A single door leading through the big wall into the main prison provided their only means of escape from fire. Middleton wanted to build a safe secure building for his female convicts and the matrons who guarded them. Then, he said, he would replace the cottage with a maximum-security building for his most degenerate male convicts.

***

Keeping with its tradition of hard labor, Montana State Prison in 1930 had no school. Rehabilitation was a word yet to be invented, at least in Montana. Most convicts came untrained in any trade or vocation. Many were entirely illiterate. After spending their time doing nothing productive, they became disinclined to the task of earning a living in honest fashion. Within weeks of parole, many of them returned to Montana State Prison.

The Crime Commission warned: "... the enforced idleness gives men time to brood and to plot. It tends to make them more anti-social in their attitude. They spend their days thinking over their fancied wrongs and planning to beat the law as soon as they have the opportunity. Warden Austin Middleton has used every possible opportunity to keep men at work. Whenever any job is available, it is apportioned out among the men to the widest extent possible. But it is still impossible for him to employ more than a small portion of the men under his charge at any useful occupation."

And nearly three decades before Floyd Powell's hiring, the commission recommended an innovation for the time: "... to remove the Warden's office from the list of political appointments, and that an experienced and capable officer be assured of permanent tenure, regardless of changes in administration.

"We believe the job is too important and too complicated to make it advisable to be continually changing officers merely because of political changes in the State administration."

Finally, the commission recommended sweeping reform in Montana's parole system, contending colossal failure in deterring men from committing new crimes.

***

Twenty-seven years later, when a disturbance in July 1957 would bring to public attention a deteriorating and dangerous state prison, little had been accomplished. Cell House No. 2 remained much the same. The Woman's Ward had become a bonfire waiting for a match. The only significant physical change was the razing of the Federal Building in 1932 to make room for a fireproof Inside

Administration building that housed several prison industries, a kitchen, a dining hall, a barber shop, a fingerprinting room and the deputy warden's office. Considered far safer than its predecessor, this concrete-and-stucco building featured sturdy grill doors and steel-barred windows. It became the prison's heart of operations.

In 1957 Montana State Prison still lacked a decent school. Convict bosses, not civilians, supervised the manufacturing shops, creating a tyrannical labor structure where only influential prisoners with money or favors got jobs. Paroled convicts were escorted to the front gate in their prison-made clothing, given $25, and told to leave Deer Lodge. They got neither hats nor underwear. Many of them hitchhiked south on Highway 10 to Butte, where they found company with other ex-cons in shacks and shanties along East Park Street. Their familiar black coats and blue shirts attracted stares in cafes, bus depots and rooming houses.

Middleton left the prison in 1937. Had he been given money for reconstruction, Montana State Prison might have been a different place twenty years later. Four other wardens came and went at the whims of Montana's governors before the Korean War ended. Politicians quickly forgot the Crime Commission's recommendation to remove the prison administration from political influence.

***

New guards started their careers at Montana State Prison working night shift, known as "third shift," then graduated to afternoons or "second shift" as positions came open. The lucky ones eventually worked days, beginning their shifts at six o'clock in the morning. In 1958, guards often worked seven-day weeks, for which they received no overtime pay, and worked most if not all holidays. Supposedly they got time off to compensate for extra days worked past their standard forty-eight-hour week, but a state investigation in early 1958 discovered no guard had received this time. Some had accumulated twenty-five days of leave time.

Old guards wanting to earn retirement income were at the heart of Montana State Prison's custody force. Arthritis crippled some.

Others could barely see. One guard well past eighty years old caused a stir among tower guards when he made his nightly rounds in the yard. He was a feeble man and failed to follow common safety rules; watching from above, his fellow guards feared he would fall and hurt himself. Most of the guards older than seventy had been employed at Montana State Prison since the Depression, and a few even since the close of World War I. Well past their prime, they had been relegated to jobs requiring little physical ability, as most of them couldn't have protected themselves against convict assaults and many had trouble climbing stairs. To the other extreme, younger guards came and went with alarming frequency, unable to support young families on the prison payroll and unwilling to risk their lives inside a prison run by convicts.

Most guards of any age considered their jobs temporary, subject to four-year terms much like gubernatorial appointments of their wardens. To guards, lack of job security was one of the greatest disadvantages of working at Montana State Prison. Each time Montana voted for a governor, more guards quit, thinking they would be fired anyway. "I worked there about six months and am one of the very few guards that were not fired," L.K. Palmer of Butte wrote Attorney General Anderson. "The warden does not want to keep anyone on down there for any length of time that he considers intelligent and will *catch on*." As guards began to seek other employment they paid less attention to their work at the prison.

***

To qualify for employment, a guard candidate consented to an informal oral interview, which might include questions about his past. No written tests were given. All applicants were escorted up the winding stairs of Tower 1 at the southeast corner of the prison yard, then told to "walk the wall" all the way around. Metal handrails, nothing more than pipes screwed together, extended outward from each tower for only twenty-five feet. About twenty feet from the railing's end, the wall rose another two feet. Here the applicant paid special attention as he climbed three steps only twelve inches wide. One misstep and he would stumble. With nothing to grab for support, he shuffled along high above two sidewalks, one skirting outside the big wall and the other separated from the inside wall by a grass strip. The same rise and fall of steps appeared on the west wall, while the north and south walls remained level tower to tower.

Should they become guards, applicants would change towers during their shifts, sometimes three or four times, and even in winter on ice and snow and often in stiff wind. Convict workers kept the walls shoveled best as they could, or at least as much as they felt inclined. It was of no worry to a convict that a guard might fall.

***

In 1953, Governor J. Hugo Aronson appointed a new warden from Ravalli County. He was Fay O. Burrell, a former grocery clerk and bank teller who ran a two-cell jail as Ravalli County's sheriff. Burrell had been a baseball player, trapper, a cowboy, and a U.S. Navy veteran on minesweepers in World War I, but by most accounts he knew nothing about managing a prison.

The strong athletic man kept mostly to himself. Few Deer Lodge residents recognized him on the street. Reportedly, only a few convicts knew him by sight. An astounding lack of influence aggravated his fleeting physical presence.

Inside the big walls, where Burrell rarely appeared, convicts accused Deputy Warden Vern Lockwood of leading a campaign of cruelty that included extortion and beatings with blackjacks and iron pipes. Parolees came forward with tales of some convicts being tear-gassed in their cells, others hung Christ-like from bars in 'The Hole' where handcuffs chaffed their wrists until they bled. In this dungeon, men lived in the dark around the clock on bread and water diets. Stories got out that in some cases they got a surprise meal of pork, but purposely soaked with salt. Thirsty men cried out for more than two cups of tepid drinking water allotted them.

In the dining hall, convicts marched to breakfast, tin cup and spoon in hand. Ruled by the prison's "silent system" that was imposed for lack of staff supervision, anybody who talked didn't eat. Men stood at their tables until everybody from their galley arrived from the food line; then they waited for the morning watch lieutenant's command to sit. Unsuspecting visitors misinterpreted this system as a well-disciplined regimen. The prisoners, hungry and angry at the same time, felt ready to explode.

Breakfast consisted of a cornmeal mush with occasional biscuits and rolls from the prison bakery. For lunch and dinner, it was watery soup and lima beans, or butter beans and watery soup, and usually served cold. Each day, each convict got a three-ounce piece of pork fried to a crisp. Each table had one saltshaker and one vinegar bottle. Milk came pale blue but generally cold, coffee a weak tan and occasionally hot. Each convict got one tablespoon of sugar a day. In a strange contradiction to this regimen, convicts with pocket change could order food of their own from downtown Deer Lodge during a staff grocery run each Monday. In absence of vouchers or coupons with monetary value, strong convicts robbed their weaker counterparts of their cash. Privileged prisoners who worked in the office freely embezzled convicts' savings accounts, usually transferring money to other accounts in return for favors.

Between those meager meals in 1957, convicts sat in their cells, either sleeping or trying to read in light that wasn't bright enough to illuminate a page. Exercise consisted of one daily walk on a sidewalk near the hospital. Convicts were promised fifteen minutes' yard time on this sidewalk but often were sent back to the cell houses after eight or nine minutes. Back in their cells they sat, either reading or sleeping, waiting for another meager, germ-laden meal that would further breed their discontent.

***

In March 1955, a young hood named Edward Wayne Edwards broke into the home of Glenville Potts in Akron, Ohio. He stole a clock radio he later sold for five dollars. Exactly a year later, Jailer

Ray Pope led Edwards into court to face burglary charges. Edwards shoved Pope aside, bolted from the courtroom, and ran down the police station steps to the street. Police prosecutor Paul Lombardi chased Edwards to the Palace Theater Arcade, where he disappeared.

Weeks later, after four successful holdups of service stations in western states, Edwards decided to try again in Billings, Montana. He stole $63.70. Police caught him inside a motel that night with his wife, packing their bags. He gave up without a fight. Edwards, a shorter, bespectacled man, bragged that he had forty-two outstanding warrants pending against him in seventeen states. He decided to plead guilty to the Montana charges. The judge sentenced him to ten years. How bad could life be where mountains reached the sky?

Edwards was just twenty-three years old and although a wise guy, he was a bit naive in the ways of tough prisons. He pictured Montana State Prison as a woodsy campus with panoramic views (it's true that Mount Powell and the rest of the Flint Range loomed beyond the west wall towers), sequestered from town by rows of trees. The night before he left for Deer Lodge, he talked with another prisoner in the Yellowstone County jail in eastern Montana. Years later, he described the conversation:

"How much time did you get?" the prisoner asked.

"Ten years," Edwards replied.

"Ten years! I was at Deer Lodge once. I'd shoot myself dead before I'd go back there."

"You were at Deer Lodge? What's it like?"

"Buddy, all I can say is, you'll be one sorry guy."

Edwards, also known as James Garfield Langley, came to Montana State Prison on a dreary March morning in 1956. When he saw the prison's bleak unsmiling face he thought of a Frankenstein movie. Deputy Warden Lockwood met him between two locked doors below Tower 7. Their voice echoes in the cave of stone sounded like the cries of lost spirits.

Edward Wayne Edwards learned right away that convicts in Deer Lodge relied on a black market as a means of economic survival.

They bought and traded all their possessions, even toiletries and blankets. It was his impression that only those convicts who could afford to buy privileges could live safely, and in doing so, acquire influence and power. Edwards insisted, even years later, that he even paid Lockwood to look the other way. Penniless convicts worked at the behest of their moneyed peers, running errands, standing watch during beatings and drug transactions, and falling to rapes because they couldn't pay for protection.

Some corrupt guards, driven to prison employment by their quest for food money, supplemented their meager earnings with convict payoffs. From the fingerprinting room to the garment shop to the hospital and the blocks, the convict grapevine kept a running count of which guards were bought. Honest guards found themselves in a constant turmoil, fending off manipulative convicts while trying to get along with peers on the take. If a con didn't have money, he was nobody. Edward Wayne Edwards didn't want to be nobody.

Anxious for stature and influence, he started selling leather goods out of his cell. Edwards would claim that as many as twenty-five convicts eventually worked for him. They stole hides of leather from the prison shoe shop to make purses, belts, wallets and other gifts, then bought influence. In a matter of months hundreds of dollars worth of leather intended for convict shoes disappeared into the black market. Edwards alleged his payoffs included guards who, in return to his money and gifts, smuggled letters to his wife.

Prisoners didn't make much money, but the more resourceful ones had ways of getting cash when they needed it. Razor blades, food, tobacco, soap and even toilet paper became hot commodities in a prison where filching an extra minute of fresh air and sunshine meant fifteen days in the Hole on stale bread and water. Work time, intended to shave days off a prisoner's sentence, was poorly computed and often not recorded at all. "You never knew if you were coming or going or standing still," one convict complained.

***

None of these conditions, had they been publicized in Montana's mostly Anaconda Company-owned daily newspapers, might have grievously concerned anybody. Montanans, an independent breed, felt prisons were for punishment. They saw no harm in operating an 1880-era territorial prison in post-world war prosperity. Deer Lodge wasn't a rich town. The few families who had reason enough to be snotty hid their wealth well. It was, rather, a working class place, one point on a blue-collar triangle that included Butte and Anaconda. All three towns had glorious theaters and reputations for historical significance, but it was no accident that together they made for Montana's toughest pocket. Icons of this rough culture pointed skyward: Butte's mining head frames, frowning from their pockmarked hill like Sunday morning drunks; Anaconda's towering smelter stack, a phallic reminder of the town that ore built; and Deer Lodge's prison turrets poking into the dry mountain air. Never mind that family farms and ranches quilted the Deer Lodge Valley from its south end near Anaconda to its north end at Garrison, or that influential railroads coursed through Deer Lodge like mighty rivers. Deer Lodge was the prison, and the prison was Deer Lodge, and in a long chain of events that led to a collision between Jerry Myles and Floyd Powell, Montana State Prison was a third man personified. Without him, without his rock face and his tattered clothes and his pockets turned inside out, without his quick fists and his vile talk, Myles and Powell would find little reason to fulfill their destinies in Deer Lodge. It was a case of threesomes, then. Mines and smelter and prison made one triumvirate, Powell and Myles and the prison made the other. What a pivotal place the prison, a keeper of men on both sides.

***

Appointed to Montana State Prison after the 1953 Legislature appropriated money for the coming biennium, Fay Burrell didn't write his own budget until 1955. Reform-minded legislators gave him what he requested and sometimes more, but by the summer of 1957, a curious pattern emerged. The new warden wasn't spending money dedicated to salaries, staff development and much-needed plant improvements. Still, he accused the Legislature of not giving him enough money to run the prison.

For 1955-56 he requested $700,498.14; the Legislature gave him $708,265. Included in that budget was money for a bunkhouse, shop building, water plant and slaughterhouse. Burrell hadn't asked for money to build a slaughterhouse, but the Legislature gave it to him anyway. For 1956-57, he requested $513,295.50. He got $505,675, a cut of about one and a half percent. For 1957-58 he got $619,442, compared with his request of $638,042. At the beginning of 1957 the Prison Industrial Revolving Fund had a balance of $25,764.69; this amount, added to the appropriation, totaled about $6,000 more than Burrell had requested. In 1958-59, Burrell requested $613,362. The Legislature gave him $613.572.06.

Had this money been spent for what it was intended, Montana State Prison in the mid-1950s might have been a safer, less crowded institution. Appropriations for a medium security building, the slaughterhouse, the shop building and the water plant became available on July 1, 1955, but practically none of that $176,000 had been spent a year later. In that fiscal year Burrell spent $125 of the $105,000 that was appropriated for a medium security building to relieve serious overcrowding in the cell houses. That money went for a sand and gravel washer. Records show that he spent less than $11,000 of the $40,000 devoted to the water plant, less than $3,000 of the $26,000 intended for the slaughterhouse, and none of the $5,000 for the shop building. No further expenditures on the medium security building were made until May 1957, nearly two full years later. After two years, less than $9,000 of the $105,000 medium security building appropriation had been spent. Burrell, meanwhile, boasted of his cost-saving efficiency.

***

Hugo Aronson, when campaigning for governor in 1952, demanded a get-tough attitude at Montana State Prison. "Why should Montanans have to sleep with guns under their pillows?" he asked. Aronson contended, and ridiculously, that convicts were permitted to go fishing, frequent taverns, possess liquor on prison property and walk at will around Deer Lodge and Powell County. And he warned: "The people of Deer Lodge, where two convicts have been charged with rape, have reason to worry about the safety of themselves and their children."

This political bluster had little to do with the real problem, the degeneration inside the walls that would worsen with Aronson's appointment of Fay Burrell and bring Jerry Myles to power. Aronson, however, was a populist legislator from the oilfields of northern Montana, and when he defeated Democrat John Bonner to become governor, his get-tough messages on crime and criminals resounded with many Montanans. The man nicknamed "The Galloping Swede" was not a reformer but like Floyd Powell, a self-made man. A brakeman kicked him off a freight train in Columbus, in eastern Montana, after Aronson had emigrated from Sweden in 1911 and worked his way west. He dressed tools for oilrigs, then built his own rigs before starting a trucking business to haul oil equipment from one site to another. It was fitting, then, that he had an oil-derrick face, tall and hard at the edges.

Legend had it that Aronson earned his nickname when he was working in the oil fields, carrying timbers on his shoulders. He ran everywhere he went. A crew boss who saw him running with a twenty-foot timber balanced on his shoulder, a magnificent timber that was eight inches by twelve inches, yelled at him to stop. "Take five, Aronson!" the boss told him.

"Take five, hell!" Aronson replied. "I can hardly carry one!"

Every governor dreads a prison riot because it makes unpleasant news and invites investigations. Montana's prison in the 1950s had been operating on borrowed time, overdue for reform. Aronson's political nemesis, Attorney General Forrest H. Anderson, soon would challenge the governor's benign neglect of the prison.

- 7 -

The 'pea riot' of 1957 and other bad omens

Eunice Taylor hadn't heard about the disturbance at the prison until a neighbor knocked at her house at seven o'clock. By then, her husband Art had been held hostage for nearly four hours. She ran toward the prison. When she reached Main Street she stopped short. Montana State Prison loomed before her like a backwater Bastille. In the shadows of the great walls, she sobbed, "My God! My husband's in there!"

In Deer Lodge, where the locals joked about rolling the streets up at dusk, there were few strangers outside those walls. Eunice's sobs electrified the crowd around her. It was perhaps the largest assembly this generally uneventful dot on the map had seen in even an old-timer's memory. Such excitement was rare to the routine that these small town souls regarded so dearly. The swelling crowd watched Eunice and the rest of the drama in coarse whispers. The prison, and all it hid, became the subject of much discussion. They examined with almost child-like curiosity something they had taken for granted. Perhaps they wondered for the first time who might be looking back.

News reporters rushed to Eunice, looking for a good quote. She didn't disappoint them. "I pray and hope that they do not harm him," she told them, explaining that she'd had a premonition he would be taken hostage. "I knew when I heard that there was a riot that he would be one of the ones who were being held hostage," she told *United Press*. As she cried and stared at Cell House 1, friends tried to calm her. Finally, her father led her around a corner across the street. Her whimpering faded as convicts jeered from the windows.

***

Much had been said around Deer Lodge and Helena about powder kegs and matches, but finally it was peas, not fire, that set in motion Montana's prison disturbance of 1957. Powder kegs and peas don't by themselves make a riot. Men who feel tinder dry in the brain and hungry in the stomach, who feel happier playing their music than harvesting their detestable garden, find reason to erupt, and when they erupt at once in a united cry of protest they erupt not over peas or a garden, but over the entire menu of their lives.

On July 30, 1957, Deputy Warden Lockwood commanded the prison on behalf of Warden Burrell, who had traveled to Indiana to retrieve a prisoner who had escaped seven years earlier. Burrell's absence on an assignment that should have fallen to a rank-and-file officer later was judged akin to leaving the prison unguarded, but it was typical, his critics would say, of how he ignored operations. On duty with Lockwood that day was Captain Everett Ripley, who showed the wear after twenty-six years at the prison. Ripley had been a guard even before the Great Depression had reached its full head of steam, and even through that and World War II and the Korean War, Montana State Prison remained a place unchanged by events around it.

About 3:30 that afternoon, the big and forbidding Lockwood instructed the prison band's twenty-two members to shell peas. They turned to him slowly, their concentration interrupted. They objected to this distraction because they were practicing for a concert they would perform in August. Many of the band members didn't have much use for Lockwood, whom they considered a tyrant on the take, or for that matter most of the other guards. They preferred to be left alone in their musical dreams, lost in happy places beyond those big walls and the drudgery of prison life. Lockwood couldn't see what they saw, nor did he care. He judged the worth of a prisoner by how fast he blistered his hands. The deputy warden kept a sap tucked in his belt.

On this Tuesday afternoon, 380 convicts felt the mid-summer heat of Montana's mountain country. The sun had scorched the spring-green hills surrounding the Deer Lodge Valley into a lifeless brown carpet. In the heat of the day the cattle on the prison's big ranches stood silent in the shade and even the gophers stayed low in their holes, and the valley fell quiet.

Tension had been building inside the prison since spring, when convicts at the behest of their captors once again planted a vast vegetable garden that consumed most of the open space between the cell houses and the west wall of the prison yard. It required watering and weeding but was no picture of hard labor like the grunt of toil known by their prison-building predecessors who had built a creation of sandstone and granite that would never fall down. We might think of those vegetable garden convicts of 1957 as dallying in green leaves all day and hating it. But green leaves hide insects that eat at them. It was a garden, but a Garden of Eden where the pea became the sin, and convicts loathed that garden as a symbol of all that was wrong with the prison, which was plenty by standards of most anybody who lived or worked there.

They wondered aloud where all the food went because they didn't see much of it on their tables. Their outrage included matters of physical scale: Save for sidewalks and some bare ground, no room remained for outside recreation. Convicts who can't exercise are hot-tempered men.

Lockwood yelled at the band to get into the garden, anger rising in his voice. One convict told the deputy warden what he could do with the sap. At Lockwood's command, guards dragged him off to "The Hole," the dark clammy assortment of rooms beneath Cell House 1. At this display of force, other band members begrudgingly set aside their instruments and waded into the garden.

For a precious minute the beast within them held its breath. It was a ripping hot day and on such July days in Montana tempers flare well in dry air. It was the snorting from the beast, deep from its belly, and on that day everyone inside the prison could sense it coming. The disturbance, as it would be called at first, started humbly enough. A trumpet player flicked a pea at the trombonist, who flicked one back. In seconds the entire band began raining peas at one another.

The defiance spread quickly, like a fire in dry grass. Convicts erupted across the prison yard and inside the cell houses. Ignoring armed guards on the towers, they marauded into the garden, trampling vegetables and ripping them from the soil. The few guards inside the walls ran from the horde, but convicts seized Ripley and seven other officers. One of them was thirty-four-year-old cell house guard Art Taylor, a former professional musician, who had worked at the prison only a month. They also grabbed guards Lester Blankenberg, Russell Chamness, William Lloyd and Paul Peterson, and two others: Raymond Hoy, forty-eight, who had been a guard since the previous January, and Garnet L. Cole, sixty-two, who had started in March. They locked each guard in separate cells in Cell House 1.

George Green, a civilian worker, was installing equipment in the license plate plant at the north end of the prison yard when the disturbance broke out. Prisoners had no beef with him. They escorted him to a tower gate.

Inside the kitchen in the daylight basement of Inside Administration, they ransacked coolers and cupboards and carried loot to their cells where they built small cooking fires. They had seen none of the bounty from the vegetable garden. Trusties who worked on prison ranches passed along stories of cattle herds, hog and turkey farms, and enough chickens to feed every man several times. At Burrell's house across the street from the prison, trusties who worked there had seen sumptuous meals. A good meal is a deserved pleasure of free men, but as penologists would attest in the aftermath of this disturbance, it was foolhardy to deny it to men in captivity. Hungry men become angry men who riot over peas, and vegetable gardens become symbols of stupidity.

***

In 1957, Montana State Prison employed only fifty guards to watch a total convict population of nearly 600, a ratio of twelve to one. Guards didn't often trust each other, like each other or even know names, but at the first trouble they raced for guns to protect their kind. And so from those early moments it became an armed standoff at least from their point of view. While convicts ruled the prison's interior, enjoying their element of surprise, which was their only true weapon, outnumbered guards with pistols and rifles crowded into the six castle-like turrets atop the prison wall. Had the horde felt compelled to spill over the big wall in those first frantic moments, it couldn't have been stopped.

Lockwood, seeing that he had lost control, summoned help. Within the hour, commander Richard C. Kendall assembled and armed twenty National Guardsmen from his Deer Lodge battery. They hurried from the city pavilion in pieces of their uniforms; a riot wouldn't wait for a well-dressed soldier. Some were just boys and looked unsure about what they might be asked to do. In Missoula, forty guardsmen waited on alert, and by seven o'clock units in Anaconda, Bozeman and Livingston stood ready. Volunteer fire departments in Deer Lodge, Racetrack in the Deer Lodge Valley and Meaderville in uptown Butte sent trucks in case convicted arsonists fell into their old ways. Dozens of peace officers from Butte, Anaconda, Helena and Missoula swept into Deer Lodge. It made for an odd standoff: a virtual army assembling outside, a joyous unarmed sea of nameless faceless convicts inside, and the big wall serving its purpose on both counts, keeping them in and keeping them out.

There was a lesson here, visible for all who cared to see it. Fortresses hold the line regardless of who's in charge. A big prison wall divides good and bad, but it's also a symbolic line that defines men, as it did in 1957 and would again in 1959.

Neither Jerry Myles nor Floyd Powell had yet seen Montana State Prison, although when they did, one truth was already known. When the balance of power shifts, lightly armed men on the inside can resist an army on the outside, at least for a while. Myles, who knew the rigors of inescapable Alcatraz, would admire the big wall for permitting him to command the world within it. Powell would see in it his vision for a new prison. The big wall gave each of them power, defining their lives in ways ordinary people wouldn't understand. It was the kind of power that promised a warden's job for Ted Rothe, and made Lee Smart somebody. Walter Jones Jr., the student-turned-sociologist, would find real convicts more dangerous than theories in college books, and George Alton, a small-time burglar in minimum security, would discover he had greater influence when his captors put him back inside the big wall with the bad boys after his escape.

***

That very afternoon, Governor Aronson and other members of the State Board of Examiners had met in Deer Lodge to inspect National Guard gunnery damage to a prison ranch. From time to time the Guard drove tanks and artillery some sixty miles over back roads from their Helena armory to practice on the state-owned land west of Deer Lodge, where the foothills met Mount Powell's thick forests. The explosions from the big guns kept residents on edge. The men in the tanks fired round after round, rattling windows in Deer Lodge.

Late that afternoon, Aronson and the others were driving back to Helena on Highway 12, a ribbon of blacktop curving through the bluffs and ranch meadows along the Little Blackfoot River, when they heard the whine of a siren behind them. A highway patrolman stopped them near the hamlet of Elliston, about forty miles from Deer Lodge. He came hurriedly to the governor's car with news of the disturbance. Someone speculated that the cons intended to embarrass the governor, or at least to capture his attention while he was in the neighborhood. It was a good educated guess. The Swede told his driver to turn the car around. In the larger picture, the riot was more about policy than peas.

In Deer Lodge, the scene outside the prison became, in a way, celebratory. A wave of gleaming Fords and Chevys, and an occasional Studebaker, choked Highway 10, the only paved road entering and leaving Deer Lodge. Where it became Main Street at the south edge of town, hundreds of onlookers from Deer Lodge and elsewhere swept onto the boulevards for three blocks, pointing to guards who occasionally stepped onto the wall from stone towers. At the southern end of the prison, outside the main prison walls, Alton and other trusties played an impromptu softball game behind a wire fence. Some 100 yards from the northern cell house where rioters kept their hostages, other trusties made butter.

A white bed sheet hung from east-facing windows on Cell House 1. Somebody had painted its stark message, "We Want Rights," in red paint. A pigtailed girl standing beside her mother pointed to the sign and spoke in awe. "Mommy, that looks like blood," the reporters heard her say, making good copy if not good truth. Dozens of amateur photographers and news cameramen recorded the image as the banner fluttered in the waning light.

The excitement grew when tar-black smoke poured into the darkening sky. Shouts of "Fire!" rang out. Tower guards told firemen on the street that a fire had started in Lockwood's office inside the administration building between the two giant cell houses. As fire trucks jockeyed closer, dozens of police officers and sheriff deputies pushed spectators a block distant. The Deer Lodge fire crew, some wearing loafers and some still in business suits, lifted a hose over the wall to arch a stream of water onto the roof of Inside Administration. Prisoners extinguished the fire on their own before volunteers made much of a difference. Still, the crowd cheered the heroic effort. Tower guards, from their vantage points, verified that little damage had been done.

Just before dark, several men wearing badges and uniforms walked around the prison in a show of force. Rioters watched them from the cell houses. They were an impressive assemblage of guns and glitter and stern faces: Highway Patrol Captain Alex Stephenson; Lieutenant Colonel Ed "Bus" Ellsworth, the Deer Lodge National Guard commanding officer; Richard Kendall of Deer Lodge; Police Chief John Wilson and Highway Patrol Sergeant Bill Benson, who would become acting warden in 1958. As the cell house lights came on, about fifteen rioters pressed against the barred windows to watch the command post across the street. Most of the other convicts, giddy with their conquest, played like schoolchildren in the ruins of the vegetable garden.

***

Inside the walls, word got around that Art Taylor's wife was sick. Friendlier convicts invited him to write her a note. He penned the words, "Everything's O.K." Hours later, moments before midnight, they freed him just twenty minutes before they let the others go. "They told me my wife was in a state of shock because of the riot," he said after he walked through Tower 7 to the free side. "When I was leaving the cell door some of the prisoners wished my wife well." In a lucid moment, they also asked Taylor to become their new band director. They were neighbors, in a way.

***

Throughout his eight hours of captivity, Everett Ripley spoke quiet assurances through the bars. He was the man, Warden Burrell later contended, who stopped the disturbance from becoming a full-blown riot. Shortly after the takeover, convicts freed guards Chamness and Blankenberg through the prison's back wall after Chamness became sick. At sixty-six years old, Blankenberg was the oldest hostage. To the remaining six hostages, convicts supplied tobacco, coffee and sandwiches. They watched with curiosity as the guards sat behind the bars, chewing their food and smoking. The prisoners felt like guards and the guards felt like prisoners. It was a benign disturbance, more like a social gathering. Convicts expressed their concern for guards' families and talked about their own. Several of them apologized to their hostages for what they had done. Later that night when the guards left the prison, unharmed and well fed, a convict handed Ripley a cloth bag containing a ring of cell house keys.

As hostages met the applause of their welcoming brethren in the street, lights in Cell House 1 came on. On the upper galleys, convicts could be seen filing into their cells. It seemed too quiet, too nice. The disturbance wasn't over. Nobody on the outside felt like going inside to investigate.

A cowboy from a ranch in the Deer Lodge Valley stood on the street corner, brushing the brim on his Stetson with a hand scarred from barbed wire. "This thing's been a warm-up," he said. "You don't have to be inside the walls to feel it."

***

A few hours after the disturbance began, Governor Aronson met with Alex Stephenson and other men of high distinction on creaking chairs in the warden's office across the street from the prison. People ran past the windows toward the prison, as if racing for a carnival midway. Aronson and the others hurriedly discussed a plan to regain the prison, talking fast to the tick of a big wall clock.

At daybreak, a strike force of about 200 National Guardsmen and eighty peace officers carrying unloaded but bayoneted rifles would invade the prison grounds. Prison guards atop the walls would have live ammunition. "We are going to have to do this very carefully," Stephenson told his troopers later that night. "If someone makes a mistake and fires a shot not called for, we are liable to set the whole thing off." He instructed everyone to return to the prison three hours after midnight for a final briefing. Before that happened, convicts listening to a radio heard a report of a pending invasion that someone had leaked to a news service. The plan was ruined.

It was the dead of night. Most of Deer Lodge slept, even with the hubbub at the prison. If not for the riot, it was the kind of soft night where the last thing heard was the bump of a neighbor's screen door and the click of his porch light. A rude demand from the prison shattered the silence. Over a microphone wired to amplify sound, a rioter shouted out this grim message from inside Cell House 1: "In the past these things have been won by staying outside and throwing artillery inside the walls. The minute this happens one guard will be killed to show we mean business." The rioter repeated: "Can you hear us all right?" He was heard for blocks.

Disgusted at the turn of events, Aronson stormed to his car to return to Helena to call an emergency meeting of the prison board. Minutes after he left Deer Lodge, cruising under the stars toward the capital city, Attorney General Forrest Anderson arrived at the prison. Their cars had passed on the dark highway. To anyone who knew them well, this was symbolic of the political differences between them, and a signal of things to come.

Anderson was serving his first term as attorney general. He also was a member of the Board of Prisons and began negotiating with the ringleaders right away. He might have done it to spite Aronson, who he regarded as a political enemy, or to showcase his mounting frustration with the prison administration. He was a shorter, slight man, far smaller than the hulking Aronson, and unlike the Galloping Swede he had no colorful blue-collar stories trailing in his dust. He was a legal mind, having been an associate justice of Montana's Supreme Court, and he had political aspirations that eventually would take him to the governor's office. Anderson had fire. The governor wouldn't intimidate him.

Two convict negotiators, escorting a near-blinded prisoner squirted in the eyes with fire extinguisher foam, emerged from the prison. They let go of the stumbling man before walking across the street to join Anderson and Lieutenant Governor Paul Cannon in the warden's office. People all around stared with curiosity reserved for sideshow freaks. The convicts, unaccustomed to walking the free street, stared back. One of them was Harold Goff, serving a life term for the 1940 murder of Butte service station attendant George Kilmer. The other was Butler Perriman. Shackled and smoking, they perched on a wooden bench in front of Anderson looking sometimes animated, sometimes bored, like pouting schoolchildren sitting before their principal. A third convict stood at a wall telephone talking with other rioters inside the walls. At one point he told his listener on the other end: "We give you our word that this will be in the papers and on the radio. You have to realize that it will take a little time."

Anderson listened while Goff and Perriman listed their demands for improved conditions, including the firing of Benjamin W.

Wright, director of Montana's new pardon and parole system. Then Anderson got on the telephone to talk with the rioters. Newsmen in the room heard him say: "I will do whatever possible to right any of the wrongs which exist within or without the walls of the prison. You can be assured that a great number of your demands, after listening to your spokesmen, are of considerable concern to me...." The attorney general outlined an eight-point program that would secure more privileges, better food, better mail service and various investigations.

Aronson got all the way to Helena before he learned what Anderson had done. Furious, he issued a statement: "I have made no concessions to any of the convicts. I will be happy to give consideration to any matters presented to me through the proper channels of the prison, but I firmly believe that the Montana State Prison must be run by citizens on the outside without coercion from those who have been sentenced for crimes against the public."

Anderson paid little attention to Aronson. Neither had much tolerance for the other, particularly on prison matters. On Wednesday afternoon, Anderson went inside the prison. He talked for forty minutes with cheering prisoners who interrupted him four times with applause. Satisfied their demands had been heard, they returned to their cells.

When Anderson emerged from Tower 7, somebody asked if prison guards could enter. "As far as I am concerned, they can go in right now," he replied. Prison guards, National Guardsmen and law officers streamed into the prison. An unarmed detail of twenty uniformed men combed grounds and buildings with metal detectors. They found knives, clubs, scissors and other weapons concealed under garden soil and in hiding places inside various buildings. In the scorched deputy warden's office, convicts had smashed furniture and windows. In the adjacent garment shop, a heap of benches, fabric and other flammable material awaited a match that hadn't been lit.

Meanwhile, Aronson, Anderson and Secretary of State Frank Murray, the prison board's third member, met with newsmen outside the prison walls. The convicts had won – and so had Anderson.

***

With reform in mind, Anderson persuaded Aronson and Murray to summon Kenyon J. Scudder from Los Angeles to investigate conditions. Scudder was considered one of America's top penologists. He was a former warden of California State Prison at Chino and a past president of the American Correctional Association. He also was the California field director for New York-based Osburne Association, a private nonprofit organization that appraised prisons' physical plants and administrations. Just before the outbreak at Montana State Prison, he had investigated riots at prisons in Michigan and New Jersey.

Scudder arrived in Montana on August 3, four days after convicts relented. This was his second visit. Early in 1956, he had come at the state's request and recommended numerous improvements, most of which Warden Burrell had ignored. The prison had deteriorated since his first visit. Scudder wasn't happy. His subsequent report to the prison board would show the depth of his displeasure.

After a Saturday night meeting with the governor in Helena, Scudder drove to Deer Lodge to spend Sunday with Burrell and his staff. For the next three days he investigated conditions at Montana State Prison. Happy convicts applauded his presence. When he stepped into the theater, the same convict band that had rioted over peas played four songs for the white-haired man from California.

Painstakingly, Scudder reviewed each of the convict demands. Meanwhile, Burrell denied comment to news reporters waiting outside his office. "I have instructions that all reports be issued by the Board of Prison Commissioners. In other words, I cannot give anything to the press from here." His statement reinforced the impression of a Helena-led prison. Republican Governor Aronson and Anderson, his Democratic nemesis, asked Scudder to return to Helena for a Wednesday afternoon meeting.

Scudder proposed the immediate hiring of forty-five employees at a cost of $132,000 for the first year, including two associate wardens, a business manager, a clinical psychologist, two institutional parole officers, and four journeyman supervisors of prison industries. The latter would replace con bosses, the prisoners who supervised their peers in the shops. He proposed adding thirty-five more guards to bring the undermanned guard force to eighty-seven. Guards currently making $175 a month would earn $200 a month the first year, $240 a month the second. This upgrading of staff, Scudder told Aronson and Anderson, was only the start of a necessary commitment to bring the prison into modern times, and to avoid a more serious riot.

This shouldn't have been news in Montana. Prisons all over America had fallen to riots, many of them more violent than the pea riot, in the throes of reform. In comparison, what happened in Deer Lodge in 1957 was a picnic. It was a lark, people said. Scudder knew it might have been different if a hardened con, a leader, had taken over.

For two hours he detailed his recommendations, most of them in line with prisoner demands from the July disturbance. The state should put more convicts to work and allow more of them to earn "good time" credit to reduce their sentences. It should improve food handling; remove female prisoners from the main prison grounds; eliminate the convict boss system in which convicts supervised other convicts in offices and industries; build a medium security prison on the state's Deer Lodge Valley ranch; build bigger and better hospital facilities; start a hearings process for prisoners sent to solitary confinement; eliminate bread-and-water no-blanket treatment in The Hole; eliminate the silent system in the main dining room; improve visitor privileges; allow two letters a week and eventually three instead of the current one; post regular library fund audits; replace twenty-five-watt cell lighting with bulbs that would allow reading, and overhaul the prison radio system that despite its ingenuity of the time was a crude method of transmitting music and news into the 1912 cell house.

Montana taxpayers would pay more than a half million dollars a year for these improvements. Scudder warned that the July disturbance could have cost much more: at least $1 million in damages had convicts not policed themselves. He urged the prison board to follow California, Texas and Louisiana and take the prison out of politics, meaning that the state hire a warden who knew what he was doing.

During Scudder's visit, state crews plowed the prison vegetable garden into history. Highway Department trucks loaded with asphalt waited outside the sally port. Convicts would get their exercise yard, but as time would show, little else. Montanans weren't ready for prison reform.

Typical of public sentiment after the 1957 disturbance was this editorial that appeared in the Phillips County News: "These men are criminals ... the people who blow up and shoot up gas stations and take the lives of attendants while they take their money. They are the people who rob banks and shoot down bank employees; who burgle stores, set other people's property on fire and murder citizens who usually have done nothing to merit death except to be in the path of a criminal's bullet. They are the men who rape our daughters. ... They are in prison to be punished, not coddled."

***

One week after Scudder's report, Deputy Warden Lockwood and his two guard captains, Everett Ripley and Harry Berg, gave up. Lockwood said he couldn't work for Warden Burrell, while Ripley spoke more pointedly: "The attorney general gives orders on one thing and the warden changes them. I'm not going to work between two fires for nobody." Lockwood had started his custodial career at Montana State Prison a year after Japan's bombing of Pearl Harbor, as the curtain fell on 1942. He had become deputy warden in 1951. Like other long-time guards, he had seen the prison swing from one warden to another at the whim of Montana's governors. Lockwood packed and left for California to live with his wife and ailing mother. Ripley, a bachelor, moved to Oklahoma.

Two days later it was rumored in Deer Lodge that Burrell had resigned his job, which Aronson had awarded him in 1953. He made himself unavailable for comment. His wife Helen, in his stead, denied the rumor.

***

Most of the convict grievances in July 1957 echoed criticism contained in a report written by three out-of-state wardens the previous February. Invited by Governor Aronson and the Montana Legislature, Joseph E. Ragan of Illinois, Harry C. Tinsley of Colorado and G. Norton Jameson of South Dakota came to assess the need for a new prison. They had found Montana State Prison's food preparation to be an ingredient for sickness. For lack of a civilian steward to plan meals and supervise serving, convict cooks showed favoritism or were intimidated into favoring others. The wardens concluded: "There is nothing more explosive than improper preparation and serving of food."

The wardens spoke out, too, about guard salaries. Montana started new guards at $175 a month. The wardens recommended $259 to start, and up to $300 for experienced officers.

Montana spent $1.56 a day for its convicts; Colorado, by comparison, spent $2.75 and South Dakota, $3. The wardens' study also showed the average Montana prisoner to be 29.6 years old, most often sentenced for burglary.

About 200 trusties entrusted with jobs like fence mending and cattle tending worked on isolated prison ranches over seventy-nine miles of roads in the west Deer Lodge Valley. After Aronson became governor in 1953, he asked the Legislature to make a down payment on land previously leased to the state to build a new prison. The 35th Legislature appropriated $183,826 for a two-year payment on ranch land west of Deer Lodge. When the out-of-state wardens saw the land, they declared it "the finest potential of any location in America" for a model prison.

In Helena, Attorney General Anderson found himself preoccupied with prison events. He made no secret that conditions he had witnessed in Deer Lodge during the pea riot disturbed him. He implored Governor Aronson to fire Burrell. Without a change in leadership, he said, somebody was going to die. Anderson doubted Aronson would act. He openly despised the 'Galloping Swede,' considering him incapable of leading Montana. Anderson held Aronson's prison warden in the same low regard. He stated bluntly that he thought Burrell's administration one of the most inept and corrupt in Montana State Prison's long history, and he faulted Aronson for failing to recognize the folly of his political appointment.

Through the fall of 1957 and the winter of 1958, Anderson peppered Aronson with riot warnings. Anderson pointed out in his memorandums from his State Capitol office that Burrell had failed to act on almost all the recommendations made by Scudder and other reformers.

All of them had encouraged the state to destroy the vegetable garden inside the prison, freeing space for exercise. "There is nothing more important in the operation of an institution than a recreation period to give men needed exercise, fresh air and the opportunity to work off excess energy,'' read the report from the three visiting wardens. "If a recreation period is permitted the prison authorities will find that cell houses will not be as noisy and it is not as troublesome to maintain discipline."

In November 1957, Anderson advised the governor that he thought Fay Burrell should resign at the earliest moment. "I have reached what I consider the unavoidable conclusion that the heart and basic cause of practically all the difficulty which exists at the prison today, and has existed in the past, is the complete and utter ineptitude of Warden F.O. Burrell," he wrote in a private letter. "I believe the warden should resign. Having appointed the warden, I believe it is your duty to ask for his resignation under the present circumstances.

"Being responsible to the people of this state for my every public act and for the faithful discharge of those duties imposed by law, I shall be forced to make my position in this regard a matter of public record in the very near future if Mr. Burrell is allowed to continue as warden of the State Prison."

Possessed with his belief that a worse riot was imminent, Anderson had told Burrell in October that as warden he had more public support for prison reform than any of his predecessors, and that he should immediately institute changes recommended by Scudder and others to prevent future riots.

At Christmas former convict Joseph Hunsinger wrote Anderson that "... you are learning fast about that horrible hell-hole known as Deer Lodge." Hunsinger charged that the lack of rehabilitation made Burrell guilty of treason to American taxpayers. "Would you call it 'defending the people' when, by his own acts, he turns loose upon a naive and gullible public, scores and scores of men not only with mental aberrations, but wild beasts determined to rob, burn, rape, kill and anything in the book to avenge themselves for the beating they took at Deer Lodge?"

Anderson found that Burrell had not been informing Montana's Board of Prison Commissioners of new problems at the prison. On January 20, 1958, Anderson discovered convicts had held a sit-down strike a few days before Christmas, but that no official report had been filed. He went to the prison to investigate. "I found a striking and singularly ominous parallel between conditions at the prison prior to the July 30th riot and those that exist today," he wrote Aronson. "Precisely the same elements that gave rise to the riot have again been allowed to develop, some of them in sorely aggravated form."

In late January, Burrell asked Anderson to define the legality of allowing newspaper, radio and television reporters inside the big walls. In a letter dated January 24, Anderson advised: "In the face of the grave problems within the prison walls I hope that the time you spend in publishing the nice things about your administration is not used to the disadvantage of the State of Montana."

***

On Monday morning, January 27, convicts staged a sit-down strike as the Montana Council on Corrections toured the prison. For about twenty-four hours they refused to report to work, instead strolling and loitering in the cell house corridors, ignoring orders to return to their cells. Warden Burrell ordered that heat and lights be switched off. He planned to freeze convicts into compliance. Guards helped elderly prisoners to the prison hospital where they would stay warm. Sometime the next morning, hungry cold convicts returned to their cells, ending the strike. They ate their first meal in a full day through the bars. "They just wanted to make a little excitement," one convict reflected. As a result, they were locked inside for the rest of the week and denied mail and "canteen" privileges: candy, cigarettes and so forth. Only convicts working in the kitchen, bakery and hospital left the cell houses.

Anti-Burrell pressure grew. A few days after the sit-down strike the Board of Prison Commissioners asked him to write a report listing all disturbances that might have occurred at the prison between July 1957 and February 1958.

Determined to end Burrell's regime, Anderson contended prison staff had no policies to follow. He alleged that various departments and officials fought among themselves, no clear leadership or chain of command existed, and a dangerous anarchy was evident in disciplinary and custody matters. He concluded that convicts were caught in a web of uncertainty, unknowing what behavior was expected of them. He also found evidence of abundant narcotics trafficking that appeared beyond the control of prison authorities.

"The signs are all too clear for anyone who wishes to read them," Anderson wrote. "Further trouble, of a far graver nature than any we have experienced, is inevitable at the prison if the present situation is allowed to drift and deteriorate. At the heart of this perilous situation is not lack of funds, not shortage of plant or equipment, not inadequacy of subordinate personnel, all of which admittedly exist to some degree. The core of the trouble today, as it has been for some time, is a warden totally unfitted in personality and ability to fulfill the demands of his important and presently precarious position. ... I therefore again respectfully urge that you reconsider the advisability of allowing Warden Burrell to remain as head of the prison, keeping in mind that thousands of dollars of state funds and many lives will be lost by inaction or wrong decision."

Attorney General Anderson warned that if Warden Burrell failed to reform the prison, "in my judgment and in the judgment of the experts who have visited the prison, the state prison is in for more trouble, probably more serious than that already experienced."

Montana State Prison had no functioning training officer. Assistant Warden Lester Acord had been hired as training officer, but he appeared to be operating as Burrell's second-in-command after Deputy Warden Lester Blankenberg, Lockwood's successor and a hostage from the 1957 disturbance, resigned in early February. Blankenberg contended he had "too many bosses" and in the wake of his departure, Acord seized the moment. He was a thirty-eight-year veteran of Statesville Prison at Joliet, Illinois, but guards didn't see evidence that he had learned anything there. Forty guards, including a lieutenant, submitted a petition demanding he stay outside the walls. They figured convicts would try to kill the much-despised Acord if he came inside, and that they would be hurt trying to save him. Wrote Eugene Kimball, director of the Council of Corrections, who had interviewed guards in February 1958 during the waning days of Burrell's administration: "He seems to spend most of his time, or at least he did before he was precluded from coming inside the walls, in standing around with a note book making notes, looking at people and not talking to the officers or men and created a general air of uneasiness among both the personnel and the prison population."

Few officers knew the chain of command. An associate warden said he wasn't sure if he reported to Warden Burrell. Kitchen help reported directly to the business manager, but the storekeeper, who specialized in business matters, reported to Burrell. The business manager also was required to transport prisoners and conduct prison tours for guests.

Custody officers found dispute with rehabilitation staff and vice versa. Only hearsay alerted guards to dangerous events that occurred on other shifts because Burrell had no formal method of communication. Convicts wanting to talk with Burrell or another high-ranking official wrote a "kite" that was merely a note they dropped into a box. Guards supposedly carried these notes to an associate warden outside the walls, but they had every opportunity to filter what they didn't like. Still, Burrell relied on this system of "inmate espionage" for his information.

Finally, in late February 1958, Aronson asked Burrell to resign. The governor had tired of Anderson's criticism and Burrell's incompetence. Burrell resigned February 20, but he agreed to stay at the prison until Aronson found a successor. The next day Burrell lamented that nobody recognized his abilities as warden despite his "efforts to do an honest and sincere job." He told Editor J.O. "Owen" Gehrett at the weekly *Silver State Post* that Anderson had "consorted with the ringleaders" during the pea riot. Gehrett, who took little caution in disguising his Republican orientation, wrote in a bare-knuckle editorial: "The prison is now a political battlefield experiencing the ravages and destruction of a political war – which is perhaps the only type of warfare and battlefield with which the attorney general is personally familiar."

It was clear that the longer Aronson took to replace him, the more Burrell would use the prison as a pulpit to prolong his departure. Among the many state legislators who had lobbied Aronson for Burrell's dismissal was Representative M.K. Daniels, a Powell County Democrat. Concerned that the traveling Aronson would procrastinate, Daniels implored him in a March 6 letter to make an immediate change: "It is understandable that the governor has many important places to go but it is respectfully urged that during one of his fleeting trips to the State of Montana he makes such appointments."

Louis Krainock of Billings, representing the Montana Public Employees, said on March 11 that a union was needed at the prison. "There is unrest, grave unrest at the prison," he said. "There is fear in the registrar's office [across Main Street from the prison], fear among the correctional officers in the prison."

Some improvement in the guard force had resulted from the investigations after the pea riot. Only sixty-five employees, about fifty of them guards, worked at Montana State Prison at the beginning of 1957; at the end of the year, there were 107. However, sixty-six of them had quit or were fired.

On February 28, 1958, the prison had 124 employees, of which eighty-five were guards including six sergeants and five lieutenants. This ratio of about seven and a half convicts to one guard was greatly better than the ratio of twelve to one a year earlier, a benefit that resulted from the 1957 disturbance and investigations that followed. Better pay resulted as well. In the fall of 1957 a starting guard earned $200 a month, or about $1.04 an hour if he didn't work more than six days of eight-hour shifts a week. In 1958 a guard's starting salary was $245 a month, or about $1.28 an hour. After six months, he could earn $25 more. After a year, he could earn $300 a month. Sergeants could make up to $325 a month; lieutenants, up to $360.

Not until April 4 did Aronson hire Bill Benson, a highway patrol officer, as temporary warden. Benson would start work April 15. He was forty-eight years old and a Fromberg, Montana, native. Being a World War II combat veteran, he instantly won praise from guards for his no-nonsense approach to discipline. Immediately he clarified lines of authority and, unlike Burrell, visited inside the walls. "I am hopeful the new man, Benson, will be able to hold the prison together thru [sic] sheer strength of character and tight discipline until a qualified man is selected," Attorney General Anderson wrote Edward L. Fike in Lewistown. "I gather from talking to the governor that he actually intends to appoint such a man, not make Benson a permanent warden." Privately, Anderson feared Benson's tough law-and-order approach might provoke another confrontation behind the big walls.

Embittered at the outcome, Burrell persuaded some of his oldest guards to consent to be interviewed for a newspaper story. One of them had worked there forty years. Another had worked for six wardens. Their illustrious portrayal of prison conditions made Burrell sound like one of the most progressive wardens Montana had seen, but their motivation was clear. Being in their seventies and eighties, none of these men could hope to survive a new warden who might impose physical qualifications. At the same time, a petition was being forced on employees in the State Registrar's Office across the street from the prison. Almost all of them were female clerks, none of whom had been inside the prison. "Here is something for you girls to sign," came the warning. Most of the women, fearing for their jobs, signed the petition in support of Burrell's reinstatement, but few knew anything about him.

Investigators were appalled at the staggering lack of morale among the guards. Kimball wrote: "Some do not wear uniforms at all, some have the pants and a jacket of their own and even those with the regulation pants and jackets are allowed to wear shirts of any color and ties of any color. It is not unusual to find a man with a bright green shirt and orange tie for instance, with the air force blue uniform, also, the guards, some of them are not shaven, walk around with their hands in their pockets and there is a very noticeable lack of any kind of a militaristic attitude among the correctional force there."

Few rules and regulations guided guards in their work. Burrell had compiled a loose-leaf notebook of various memoranda he had written apparently on the recommendation of visiting penologist Raymond Wham in October 1957. Lacking any overall security procedures, the notebook contained orders written to transportation officers, afternoon custodial officers, watch lieutenants, cell house guards, morning watch sergeants and tower guards. Another small book called "Rules and Regulations for Officers" contained mostly general common sense rules. It advised guards not to take keys from the prison, not to permit unauthorized people on the walls and gun towers, not to loiter around shops and work details when off duty, and not to write news releases. It also instructed guards when and how to clean tower rifles.

Guards had no written instructions on how to react to trouble. One guard said that if he heard the prison siren, indicating a riot, "we have ways and procedures for getting rid of our keys. Now, for instance, we are supposed to throw our keys outside of the cellblocks and over the walls." But he also pointed out the obvious flaw in this plan: how did guards know to whom they threw their keys?

If Warden Burrell had a riot plan, he hadn't shared it with his custodial force. Each guard held a different idea than another. Guards who had worked during the previous summer's disturbance knew first-hand that convicts could riot on the flip of a pea.

***

In a parting shot, Burrell told the *Silver State Post* that since becoming warden in 1953 he had nearly doubled the prison's cattle herd to 1,810 and tripled hog production. As an apparent testament to his foresightedness, Burrell also noted that under his leadership the value of drugs held in the pharmacy had increased from $750 to $47,819 during his tenure. He didn't elaborate on whether drugs from that growing stockpile ever had been dispensed for the medical benefits of his prisoners.

Burrell was gone, but more problems loomed. Attorney General Anderson had told Benson to make no changes that would risk inciting a riot. Within two months, Benson fired William James Lloyd, his associate warden in charge of classification and treatment. Lloyd had been promoted to his position in the wake of the 1957 disturbance. Lloyd was a retired lieutenant commander in the United States Navy and, seeing some potential in leading the prison, he drove to Helena to test for the warden's job. Benson demanded Lloyd's resignation on the premise that he hadn't granted permission for the Helena trip. Lloyd fired back: "Inasmuch as I am certain your sole reason was to eliminate the Office of Classification and Treatment thereby putting the Prison on a concentration camp status, your reason was probably as assinine [sic] as any other you could have dreamed up."

Lloyd accused Benson of mocking investigations by penologists Kenyon Scudder and Raymond Wham, superintendent of custody at Men's Colony Institution of California, and of being in collusion with Burrell to ignore cries for reform. "It is my firm belief that your policies will eventually lead to grief for all and give another 'black eye' to the State of Montana. It has never been my intention to resign my office knowing that my doing so would be detrimental and not in the best interest of the institution."

Benson himself had taken the warden examination after promising when appointed that he would not be an applicant for the permanent job. "To the uninformed this may seem insignificant, yet just this move alone could cause internal strife at the prison and could lead to a recurrence of the July 1957 riot," Anderson wrote Governor Aronson.

Benson's fate was cast. He scored 29th in the examination, far behind a reform-minded Wisconsin associate warden named Floyd Powell.

8

Reform, Warden Powell and 'Lil' George

This was Montana State Prison in 1958: A territorial fortress reeling from scandals and uprisings, populated with angry rebellious convicts, guarded by men barely trained in custodial security and inmate psychology. Reform was but a glimmer in the eyes of dreamers – such as Floyd Powell, who became warden in late summer.

Earlier that year, the nonpartisan Montana Council on Corrections got a grant from the Ford Foundation intended, in effect, to bring historic change to the prison. Acting Warden Bill Benson's successor would be professionally selected after a nationwide search, breaking the pattern of political appointments that had plagued Montana State Prison for most of its eighty-eight-year existence. Attorney General Forrest Anderson said his research of the law showed that someone outside Montana could be hired to be warden. By mid-March the seventeen-member council, chaired by Randall Swanberg of Great Falls, had agreed with Governor Aronson on a hiring plan. The council's role in this decision displeased the *Silver State Post's* Owen Gehrett, a bald and scowling man who wore black suits and undertook his role of government watchdog with a vengeance. He was a punishing wordsmith, hawkish both in appearance and in vitriol. He alleged that the council was a tool for "purely private undertakings" of the National Probation and Parole Association. Outsiders, he said, were stealing Montanans' constitutional rights. "All too often this type of high sounding association or committee is nothing but a figment of imagination and dream of grandeur in the mind of some ambitious empire builder," he wrote.

The pea riot of 1957 had hastened the appetite for reform. Despite the negative reviews the prison received from out-of-state penal consultants who visited at the state's invitation, it hadn't been an uncommonly violent place since 1908 when convicts killed Deputy Warden John A. Robinson and wounded Warden Frank Conley during an attempted breakout. In the melee Conley shot prisoners Frank Rock and W.A. Hays, then clubbed them with his gun butt and a chair. They survived, only to be hanged inside the prison walls.

In 1922, guards shot and wounded prisoner John Fink when he bolted from Warden W.M. Potter en route to the county courthouse for a hearing on another break. In October 1941, a free-for-all fight among prisoners resulted in several injuries. In August 1949 came a three-day hunger strike. Convicts complained about poor food, demanded radios, and smashed windows in Cell House 1. In May 1953 trouble broke out in the women's section when three female convicts tore open a temporary wall and lodged themselves in the corner, slashing with a knife at anyone who came close. Finally subdued, they were taken to the county jail.

***

When prison reform swept the United States in the 1950s, Montana State Prison remained outdated, much like scuffed shoes serve their purpose but draw attention at the big dance.

Twenty years before Montana gained statehood, and seven years before Lieutenant Colonel George Armstrong Custer died at the Little Bighorn, Deer Lodge broke ground for its new territorial prison. In 1869, local construction superintendent A. H. Mitchell started work on a ten-acre federal land grant site. To celebrate, citizens fired five 100-gun salutes.

The new federal prison was one of seven the United States Congress commissioned in 1867 after Territorial Governor James M. Ashley asked for money to build a prison when the Civil War ended. Given $40,000 for construction, Mitchell and his crew built a fourteen-cell, three-story structure that opened July 2, 1871, and operated as a federal prison until 1889 when Montana became a state. Montana officials, left with a decrepit physical plant surrounded by a collapsing board fence, commissioned a new firm named Conley and McTague to reconstruct the prison. What they had built beginning in 1892, including both cell houses and a wall built of sandstone and later granite, remained much the same in 1958.

Even before the pea riot hinted to Montanans that something was awry in their prison, attempts at reform in other states led to a wave of violence in state and federal prisons. The riots had a common thread. When prisons began hiring civilians to replace convicts in the shops and industries, they upset the power equilibrium. Criminologists would conclude that this shift of power broke a truce of sorts in which wardens had depended on con bosses to keep order. The director of the U.S. Bureau of Prisons, James V. Bennett, had seen it coming. In 1948 he wrote of a "paradoxical scheme" of running prisons, meaning the clash of punishment and rehabilitation: " ... our ideas and views regarding the function of correctional institutions in our society are confused, fuzzy and nebulous."

An unprecedented period of violence began in 1951. In February at Louisiana State Prison in Angola, thirty-one convicts slashed their heel tendons with razor blades to draw attention to brutal treatment and "subhuman living conditions." (In the late 1950s in Deer Lodge, prisoners who had served time in the South bore scars on their wrists and ankles from being shackled.) Major riots broke out in the spring of 1952 in New Jersey at Trenton Prison and the State Prison Farm at Rahway. At the same time, one of the worst riots of the era began at Jackson Prison in Michigan. In that mega-prison of some 6,000 convicts, rioters held Cell Block 15 until state troopers drove them out. In October 1952, rioters at Menard State Prison in Illinois took several hostages, and at Ohio State Penitentiary, 1,200 convicts rioted until the state's National Guard stopped it. By the end of 1953, other riots began in Pennsylvania,

California, Oregon, Minnesota, Washington, Massachusetts, Colorado, New Mexico, Idaho, Kentucky, North Carolina and Georgia. In the period from 1952 to 1955, forty-seven riots had been counted in the United States. Most of them had happened in the fortress-type prisons of the northern and western states.

In 1953, the American Prison Association (APA) appointed a commission to study causes of prison violence. The wave of nationwide violence fueled a frantic debate, at least among criminologists, about how prisons should be run. It was generally agreed that the lack of classification standards in American prisons – the practice of mixing convicts of various crimes and ages – begged for trouble.

The APA renamed itself, becoming the American Correctional Association, and urged its members to refer to prisons as "correctional institutions." On advice from the commission it had appointed, it revised the authoritative "Manual of Correctional Standards," which in its original 1946 volume had contained fifteen chapters but by its publication in 1959 would contain forty-eight chapters, many of them driven into print by the violence-saturated decade. The section on rioting would contain warnings of the "alertness to detect and report any signs of unrest or tension," and a companion concern, the "early recognition and control of agitators." The book urged prison wardens to adopt a "Master Riot Plan" that would clearly explain who does what during an emergency. And it warned that wardens and other leaders should not rush to the scene of the action because of the danger of being taken captive and even killed.

This book was printed in August 1959 and would become the quintessential handbook for prison guards. More than 120 prison wardens and state corrections officials compiled its 600 pages. The manual wouldn't arrive in Deer Lodge in time to stop trouble.

Despite the reform nationwide, few Montanans came to view their state prison as a monument of neglect. Even the pea riot, although a warning, tended to provide the public more entertainment than concern. In the late 1950s when law-abiding folks went to bed in their post-war prosperity and slept on clean sheets the convicts of Montana State Prison lived in a stink that was as much politics as it was buckets for toilets.

Prison might be a worse fate than death for some men. For others, it was life and the only real life they knew. Like Jerry Myles, they found a home in the wreckage of humanity around them. Almost all of the men who lived there, and a relatively few women confined inside the stockade behind the prison, were a forgotten story. They were nameless and faceless, lending a supernatural aura to the tons of brick and mortar. Ghosts always tickle the imagination.

***

Floyd Powell wanted something more out of life. He considered ending his career as associate warden of Wisconsin State Prison in Waupun. He knew how the pea riot had greased the way for reform, and for hiring an out-of-state warden. His investigation of the prison's turbulent recent history began when he read an advertisement inviting applications for the job.

He was not a man accustomed to radical change, having spent his entire career at one prison. It was his style to instinctively march through his life with deliberate steps, typical in prisons of the time. He held his ambitions close. He dreamed, yes, but he was not a dreamer in the artistic sense. Powell planned his life in orderly rows. He did his best work inside a web of rules and regulations from where he could command his subordinates. Like many prison officers, he had a military background, having served in the Army Air Corps in Colorado during World War II.

Floyd Powell had ascended to a position of some enviable authority in Wisconsin. As he anticipated adding more worth to his own human potential and conversely, at middle age to see the limits of his mortality, he had begun to wonder what other riches his life could bring him.

And so it came that in 1958, as a hopeful beneficiary of the unrest in 1957, Powell pictured himself as Montana's next prison warden. In a way that granite and brick and steel bars and other hard elements of a prison superstructure identify a man's worth, he saw in Montana's gothic prison a place for his unflappable ambitions.

We know of life's myriad roads that lead to their own fateful conclusions. Powell chose this one, seeing ahead an opportunity to succeed in what others had failed to do. He didn't underestimate the challenge before him. Prisons hid many secrets. How could he anticipate a collision with a stranger named Jerry Myles?

***

In Wisconsin, Floyd Powell tore open an official envelope, and there it was: on the strength of qualifications alone, and references who knew his firm relentless demeanor, he emerged second among seventy-one candidates. That would be good enough for an interview in Montana.

When he went to Deer Lodge for a tour of the prison, he observed what out-of-state prison consultants had told Montana legislators more than a year earlier: Guards didn't know how to take control. Many were afraid with good reason. Some were much too old to be supervising dangerous convicts. Guards who couldn't see and couldn't run were a liability and potentially a casualty.

Convicts moved freely inside the prison. A few of them commanded industry programs through a "con boss" system that put a privileged few in charge of their peers, and even in charge of inmate records. Most of the convicts remained unemployed. Without jobs, they had plenty of time to start trouble.

In the auto shop, Powell found a car engine donated by the Ford Motor Company. He didn't disapprove of that, but a few of them had written a manual that tutored their fellow inmates in the various methods of starting the motor without a key. It seemed that everywhere he looked in the prison, convicts did as they pleased.

Records that Warden Burrell provided legislative investigators in January 1958 claimed only ten convicts idle in a count of 625 men. On closer scrutiny, these investigators discovered at least forty percent of those men counted as having jobs worked no more than a few hours a day. Much of their work was repetitive and unproductive, improvised to provide an illusion. "The dangers of this condition were dramatically revealed to the people of Montana by the July, 1957 riot," investigators concluded in their report, referring to Kenyon Scudder's description of idleness as a "curse." They quoted this passage from the American Prison Association: "The enforced idleness of a substantial percentage of able-bodied adult men and women in our prisons is one of the great anomalies of modern prison administration. It militates against every constructive objective of a prison program. It is one of the direct causes of the tensions which burst forth in riot and disorder."

Reported numbers of employed convicts in 1958, while inflated, showed more diversification than average citizens might expect. Inside the walls: bakery, dining room and kitchen, forty-eight; tag plant, twenty-two; shoe shop, twenty; garment shop, twenty-four; tailor shop and dry cleaning, twelve; laundry, twenty-three; toy shop, four; wood finishing and upholstery, thirteen; carpenter shop, five; electrical shop, two. Outside the walls: ranches, seventy-three; slaughterhouse, four; construction, twenty-four; garage, two; outside carpenter shop, three; laundry, three. Additionally, both inside and outside the walls: band, thirty-one; typing class, thirteen; water crew, twenty-three; potato crew, twelve; state Registrar of Motor Vehicles, seventeen; segregation or isolation, thirty. The prison listed 207 "miscellaneous" workers.

Numbers reported to state government in Helena exaggerated the truth. Many of the men didn't have real jobs. In Powell's estimation, the combined problems inside the walls made the prison even worse than its reputation, and he left Deer Lodge wondering how the prison had avoided a violent riot.

***

After a round of comprehensive testing and interviews unprecedented in Montana prison history, Governor Aronson offered the warden's job to Wisconsin Deputy Warden Ray J. Stoffel, who had placed first in the examination. Stoffel declined, citing sudden health problems in his family. Aronson then offered the job to Powell, his second choice. Powell didn't consent right away, remembering the admonition of a California candidate who had told him: "Now that I've been here and seen the prison and the situation, I wouldn't take this job for $100,000 a year." Feeling suddenly unsure, Powell wanted two months to think about the offer. The challenge was tailored to Powell's ambitions, but secretly he was having second thoughts whether he could find support, financial or otherwise, to bring the nineteenth century prison into modern times. Aronson pressed for an answer. He needed his new warden to help plan the upcoming budget and Powell took the job. He would earn $7,500 a year and receive a rent-free state-owned house and a food allowance. "It was not much remuneration for taking on what was considered to be one of the toughest institutions of its kind in the United States, and certainly in the worst condition of any," Powell later would write. "I was to wonder many times why I accepted such a challenge...."

Montana's new prison warden took command on August 25, 1958, after working more than eighteen years at Wisconsin State Prison, which when he left had 1,543 convicts and more than 300 employees. Waupun had eluded the riot frenzy of the 1950s. The latest disturbance there had been in 1947 when sixty-nine convicts seized the laundry and held guards hostage. Otherwise, the 1950s had been a time of relative peace in Waupun, much like Deer Lodge except for the pea riot.

Other similarities became clear. Several buildings at the Waupun prison, notably its cell houses, resembled those at the Deer Lodge prison but were far older. The original cell houses had been built in 1854, the administration building in 1855. Those buildings remained in use. Both prisons had stone walls, and both prisons had been built with convict labor. Privately, Powell would think of the Deer Lodge prison as a newer one. He would recognize that the fortress-type construction did not set Deer Lodge apart but was common among prisons in the north and the west. In a way, the Deer Lodge prison gave him comfort because in appearance at least it came close to his practical experience.

At Waupun, Powell had learned everything he knew about prison administration. He started there as a guard on February 27, 1940, before his military service. In the summer of 1948 he was appointed assistant to Deputy Warden Stoffel, the very man who would enable his employment in Montana.

The second of Ray and Edna Pearson Powell's six children, Floyd Powell was born just before World War I on a dairy farm near LaValle, Wisconsin. It was a trinket of a town, near nothing of any commercial consequence, and as a boy he rode horses on the 140-acre farm and learned how to hunt and fish in the splash of empty country around him. He played baseball and became good enough that the Chicago Cubs tried to recruit him, but his family needed money. When he was a young man he left the farm to spend more than four years as a senior foreman for the Civilian Conservation Corps in logging camps, but he was destined for prison work. His younger first cousin, Fred Alden Powell, remembered that Floyd liked the interpersonal nature of custody and, like most guards, related salacious stories about real men behind bars. Floyd once told Fred that he had arranged surgery for a prisoner who had a congenital deformity known as a harelip and tried to hide it. Floyd said that the surgery corrected the condition to the point that the prisoner's personality flourished, making him a talkative, gregarious man. Fred and his younger brother Dan, who lived near Floyd when they were young, thought of him as a personable but not a hard-fisted man, and recalled that people spoke well of him at the prison. To Fred, Floyd was friendly and intelligent, and flashed a big trademark smile that reminded Fred of a trustworthy town sheriff in the western movies. Dan, nearly thirty years younger than Floyd, thought of him as a hero. When Dan was about nine years old, Floyd took him squirrel hunting, showing him how to hold and shoot a rifle. After giving Dan a chance, Floyd shot the squirrel.

At the prison, Floyd doggedly worked his way through the ranks, becoming administrative assistant to the warden after conquering a progression of college criminology courses that added value to his high school diploma. Because he talked rather slow, in what Fred Powell described as a soft pleasant masculine voice, he feared getting his point across when talking to larger groups of men. To overcome that, he drove to nearby Fond du Lac to take speech classes.

***

A few months after Jerry Myles entered Montana State Prison, Floyd and Dorothy Powell chugged along State Highway 212 through Minnesota, towing an overloaded U-Haul trailer behind their car. They had sold their home and said goodbye to their daughter Judie, a nurse at Milwaukee General Hospital. Powell loved Wisconsin. He was taking the biggest risk of his life.

In Deer Lodge, one of America's sorriest state prisons awaited his leadership. Before he left Wisconsin he had searched records for convicts there who had served time at Montana State Prison. He found eighteen and interviewed each of them. Some offered extensive descriptions of beatings and black marketing; they even named guards they claimed were responsible. Although within a year his critics in Deer Lodge would say he was inclined to see the worst in anybody who worked for him, Powell took care not to accept the convicts' allegations at face value. Some of them, he knew, might be trying to settle a grudge.

On the first day, the Powells drove to western Minnesota, where the forests and hills and rhythm of blue lakes passing the car windows gave way to a treeless tabletop of farms. The next day they drove across North Dakota to the prairie isolation of Baker, Montana, where they stopped at a family motel dependent on a large single-cylinder generator for its electricity. All night it hammered, keeping them awake. That morning they left for Helena, Montana, feeling almost as tired as when they had arrived in Baker. The mountains came in great heaves. The Powells chugged up winding strings of blacktop through one high valley and then another. Floyd found himself wondering why men would forsake their freedom in such wild beauty to live behind bars. All custodians of such men struggled with this question.

On the fourth day the Powells crept upwards to MacDonald Pass, their car radiator boiling, and over the summit downward toward Deer Lodge, brakes smoking to brace the load against the steep decline. After fifty-eight miles they arrived in Deer Lodge on a bright morning.

The town was in no hurry. Battered farm trucks and long family sedans meandered up and down Main Street, a wide brim of asphalt between rugged frontier buildings where on Saturday nights cowboys drank and fought and, in earlier days, had taken their whores. Old men talked away the morning on benches outside the saloons and the town's shoe shop, the stink of spilled beer and a pleasing aroma of new cut leather colliding around them. Store clerks unfurled awnings as the high sun began to stare into their window displays. The air was clear and dry and it was a lazy summer day in western Montana.

Acting Warden Benson waited for Powell at the prison office outside the walls. Benson felt deep disappointment at not being considered for the permanent job, but he greeted his replacement warmly. Here was the man from Wisconsin hired to wrest the prison from state politics. Here was the man who would bring a broad new vision to this ailing prison, a man who would lead it into an era of reform. As they shook hands, they sized each other up. Benson knew little about Powell but he felt uneasy. Benson later would tell his son that Powell talked of his desire to build a new prison even before he inquired about the people who would work for him. That bothered Benson, who showed Powell around and wished him well. They would meet again under more trying circumstances.

***

The Powells would live across the street in the multi-gabled warden's residence, an eleven-bedroom extravaganza that showed why Montana State Prison's top job had been considered a political plum by county sheriffs and other men who had friends in the governor's office. This splendorous wood frame rambler, built in 1920, looked strangely modern against the prison's backdrop of stone and red brick. Shrubs and flower displays decorated a wide verandah that flanked the south and west sides of the house. Inside, expensive furnishings dressed up large living and dining rooms. The park-like yard, surrounded by shade trees, extended nearly a block to the south, ending at the historic brick building that housed the prison commissary and butcher shop, where guards and their families spent up to forty dollars a month in free food allowance. Within two months, Powell would order that the side of the building closest to his house be renovated into an apartment for new Deputy Warden Ted Rothe and his family.

Behind the warden's residence, trees cloaked a two-story guesthouse. Next to that building, a two-story, two-car garage opened onto Maryland Street. The basement housed a laundry and sleeping quarters for three convict trusties, or minimum-security prisoners. One trustie washed and ironed clothes, one cooked meals in the residence's expansive kitchen, and the other served as the warden's houseboy.

These state-owned grounds consumed the entire west half of the city block. Four private homes inhabited the other half. The warden's house fronted Main Street, which doubled as U.S. Highway 10 and extended north and south. From his living room window, he looked across the road to a prison that loomed against the western sky.

Built of cut blocks of sandstone (and later granite) nestled into place like hand in glove, Montana State Prison's security wall surrounded six buildings and two yard towers in 1958. Work on the big wall began in 1892, when convict crews hauled sandstone by wagon from a Deer Lodge Valley quarry. They completed their work in sixteen months. The rectangular wall stood eighteen feet high in some places and twenty-two feet in others, rising and falling with the ground's contour. Forty inches thick at the top, it was considered impossible to penetrate, but to the guards required to walk atop it, treacherously narrow. Underground it broadened to four feet and was buried six feet deep to discourage tunnel escapes. At each of the four corners, round castle-like towers constructed of the same sharp-cut rock gave guards broad views. The towers measured eight feet in diameter.

Behind the prison, Mount Powell's muscled face stared from the thin mountain air. Even in the summer when its white cap of snow melted away, the mountain looked dreamy, like paint on canvas. The new warden smiled at this coincidence in names. That Deer Lodge was the county seat of Powell County was additionally befitting a man named Powell who hoped to build a new prison at the foot of Mount Powell.

Deer Lodge, a town of some 3,800 residents, had known prisons since territorial days. Three generations of Deer Lodge families sent their men to work there. Houses flanked the prison's looming rock walls to the north. Kitty-corner from Tower 6 on the prison's northeast corner, travelers stopped to eat at the 4Bs Restaurant and to gawk through broad windows at this uncommon sight. Townsfolk rarely bothered to look, even at night when from certain restaurant booths they might watch convicts on upper galleries, silhouetted against pale yellow lights in their cells.

***

North of Montana State Prison, Deer Lodge sprinkled about a mile from east to west. Streaks of train tracks, worn to glistens by abundant Milwaukee Road and Northern Pacific traffic, divided the town into two unequal geographic parts. Following along the tracks was the steady but narrow Clark Fork River, which began near the toes of the Anaconda Company's toxic waste dumps near Anaconda, twenty miles to the southwest. Greater Deer Lodge, including the prison, inhabited land east of the river. To the west, known locally as the West Side, neighborhoods nestled on a bench of land where the foothills below Mount Powell began. The railroad and the river set the West Side apart almost like another town.

Main Street formed Deer Lodge's spine, as main streets tend to do. In recognition of its perseverance as Montana's oldest surviving town, Deer Lodge preserved its grand old buildings along Main Street, including its crowning glory, the historic Rialto Theater. The downtown business district stretched three blocks north and south. Prison, railroad and ranching incomes kept downtown stores and bars in money, although prison guards commonly had to portion out their meager incomes and when the cash ran out, buy on credit.

Deer Lodge wasn't a rich town in 1958, although it had begun more than a century earlier with the promise of fast wealth. In those early days, prospectors searched for gold nuggets in the clear cold streams that coursed into the valley from the mountain snow pack. In 1852, a discovery in a tributary that became known as Gold Creek attracted more miners but little wealth resulted. Mexican miners named the camp Spanish Fork; later, it was La Barge City, named by Missouri River steamboat captain Joseph La Barge who tried to found a city there. In 1864 the town became Deer Lodge, the English interpretation of "lodge of the white-tailed deer," which Indians had named a nearby hot springs where deer came to graze.

The town's strategic location made it a trading center for a large district. Mining camps sprung up in the mountains surrounding Deer Lodge. The Northern Pacific Railroad came in 1892. The Milwaukee Road built its roundhouse and car shops there in 1908. The fertile valley became one of Montana Territory's early farming and ranching centers. Most of these enterprises supplied much of Deer Lodge's annual income, but the prison remained the most visual symbol of its history. There it stood, a stark monument to convict labor, its cell houses visible for miles around. Deer Lodge residents, who accepted the prison as part of who they were, hardly even noticed.

***

In early September, Floyd Powell summoned most of his new staff to the ornate prison theater inside the walls. Clark Theater was a gift from W.A. Clark Jr., son of the Butte copper king. Made of red brick, the theater in 1958 remained a monument to Butte's mining heritage. It was a respectable place to make a speech. As guards and office staff listened from the wooden seats, Powell spoke from the stage about his desire to make the prison a model for rehabilitation. He told them that Montana needed a new prison, built separately from the existing one. He said he wanted the prison to parole "far better men and not a menace to society, as is often the case." Years later, his daughter Judie would relate that he felt compassionate toward inmates and wanted them to function in society as responsible citizens and family members.

Powell came to Deer Lodge with a mandate for reform. Bureaucrats in Helena, tired of the prison's political liability, wanted a fresh face. Powell's out-of-state credentials gave them what they wanted, and in return he hungered to stamp his name on a new prison. He couldn't know that tragedy would arrive in just months.

***

Within weeks of his arrival in Montana, Floyd Powell asked Ted Rothe to be his deputy warden. Rothe felt reluctant to leave Wisconsin, where he had enjoyed a fine career. The thirty-nine-year-old Rothe had been supervisor of Wisconsin State Prison's license plate factory and coordinator of its civil defense program. Powell convinced Rothe that success at tough Montana State Prison would be his career's biggest break, leading in all probability to a warden's job.

In Wisconsin, Powell had been instrumental in Rothe's hiring, and had personally made background checks on him. Rothe started his prison career eight years earlier as a guard. He worked through the ranks to become superintendent of the Twine Plant, ranking first in proficiency testing. When the prison closed that industry, he was assigned to the license plate job. Rothe's formal education was modest, and he knew it, and like many men of the day he compensated for that weakness by working harder and convincing his superiors, including Floyd Powell, of his unwavering loyalty. Rothe, being a deserving and religious man, prayed for a break that would propel him into top prison management.

At first his appointment attracted some controversy. Some Deer Lodge community leaders asked Powell why he hadn't chosen a

Montanan for the job, puzzled why he had snubbed new Deputy Warden Bill McCleery, who had worked at the prison since 1942. Powell said he couldn't find anyone locally who was qualified, and further explained that Rothe's experience in inmate classification at Wisconsin State Prison would contribute to the reform he had in mind in Deer Lodge.

On September 25, 1958, Rothe notified Powell by letter that he would start work in two weeks. "I am planning and looking forward to that day and anticipate a long and pleasant association with the State of Montana and you personally," he wrote. Back home in Theresa, Wisconsin, Ted and his wife Elsie and their teen-age children Phyllis and Jim prepared for their new home on the Rocky Mountain Front.

Rothe had built an impeccable reputation at the Wisconsin prison. "You certainly selected a very capable man to be your deputy," Warden John C. Burke wrote Powell that September. "Ted Rothe, shortly after starting work as a guard, showed evidence of the ability to 'catch on' quickly. He was a 'natural' and, far quicker than most new guards, he showed enough understanding and ability to be assigned to important guard posts. ... He has a very pleasing personality, a fine physical build, and his character is above reproach."

Burke considered Rothe one of his best prospects for promotion. Rothe was a Navy veteran of World War II. He had fought in the battle for Iwo Jima in the Pacific Theater. Now he belonged to the American Legion. His background of limited education and military experience matched many of the men he would lead.

Rothe began work at Montana State Prison four months after Jerry Myles came into the prison, and about twenty-two months after Lee Smart arrived. Myles was five years older than Rothe, Smart about half his age. Powell kept an office in Outside Administration across Main Street from the prison. Rothe, as the operations commander, worked inside the walls. As Powell began publicly campaigning the case for a new prison, Rothe tackled security shortcomings.

***

A month after Floyd Powell arrived in Deer Lodge, he declared war on the rackets inside the prison. He asked administrative aide John Simonsen to compile a list of all men living on Galley 5, known as the "band galley" in Cell House 1 because it housed most members of the prison band. Here, in Powell's mind, was the heart of Montana State Prison's drug-running operation. On this galley, third from the floor on the block's east side, forty-three convicts shared twenty-five cells. Among them were eight forgers, seven burglars, six rapists, five escapees, five thieves, four robbers, three bad check writers, and two murderers.

One of those murderers was Lee Smart. Of the remaining three convicts on Galley 5, one was convicted of manslaughter, another of assault and a third of an undetermined crime. Evidently a man could be held for reasons unknown.

On the day that he hired Rothe, Powell wrote a letter to the Bureau of Narcotics at the U.S. Treasury Department, stating his concern about drug use inside Montana State Prison: "There have been several burglaries in this area recently where it was quite apparent narcotics was the principal loot."

Despite Montana State Prison's fearsome appearance and big walls, civilian visitors and a few dishonest guards smuggled drugs and alcohol, primarily barbiturates, Benzedrine and hard liquor. A lunch pail raised to a guard tower by a convict food worker inside the walls might contain cash that would be replaced with a "goof ball" or a pint of whiskey when the pail came down. Convicts' friends, including parolees, tossed little bags of narcotics over the wall into the exercise yard. Drugs came hidden in kitchen orders of milk and groceries. Sometimes corrupt guards smuggled narcotics through Tower 7 into the prison. Minimum-security prisoners entering the big walls for movies, church, and doctor and dentist checkups brought more drugs. Sunday visitors stashed drugs in restrooms where convict orderlies, in their cleaning duties, pocketed them. Visitors, too often allowed to mingle unsupervised with convicts, became another source.

With Floyd Powell in their midst, convicts who earlier had
bought and sold drugs as a matter of economic survival now traded
with more urgency. His new security procedures squelched much of
their freedom. Stakes got higher, drugs became costlier, and
addicted convicts ran up debts. Rothe intercepted a secret cell house
account list in January 1959 that showed thirty-eight convicts owing
cash balances for their drugs. One of them was Lee Smart, who
owed nine dollars in one case and $19.20 in another. Included were
other names that would mean something in a few months: Jerry
Myles, Donald Toms and Earl Jackson, to name a few. Two men on
their list, Harold Goff and Butler Perryman, had been inmate go-
betweens in the pea riot.

When Rothe began as deputy warden in mid-October, he and
Powell worked twelve- and fourteen-hour days and sometimes
longer to move the prison toward Powell's vision of modern times.
Despite their early determination at reform, they found themselves
confronted with indifference that had beset the prison for most of its
history. In the fall of 1958, they fired a few guards they caught
dealing drugs, but fired even more for common infractions like
failing to come to work, or for coming to work drunk, or for falling
asleep on the job.

Reform overjoyed one element of the prison population. It
infuriated another. Honest guards and convicts just trying to do their
time felt relief; others who had built influence, power and stature
felt threatened.

***

In early 1959, Rothe received a "kite," a snitch letter, that
extensively described cell house drug dealings. Typed in clean
English that revealed the anonymous author's skill with words, the
eight-page letter detailed alleged drug connections between convicts
and staff. References to "Wayne Edwards' connections" alluded to
circumstances Rothe must have understood. Rothe attached a cover
note to this kite with the words: "Warden Powell. Quite interesting
eh what? TJ Rothe."

Edwards, admittedly, seized on the black market as another ready source of income. He bought a sixty-nine-cent product known as the wyamine inhaler, made for asthma patients, that he resold for six dollars or more. This and another asthma inhaler known as Valo could be swallowed, or boiled and injected with a needle, giving a convict a rush.

Various over-the-counter medications like headache tablets and rectal suppositories contained heroin and could be dissolved and injected with a needle. Continued use of them caused jaundice and other health problems, but few cons cared. With drugs in high demand, convicts loaned their needles in exchange for a few smokes. Mostly older men, many of them harboring dark, dangerous backgrounds, populated Cell House 2. Here, needles passed from one convict to another. About fifteen convicts wore the Mexican-American *Pachuco* gang emblem tattooed on their left hand between thumb and forefinger. These men pledged themselves to various forms of strong-arm influence involving narcotics. Other prisoners feared some of these men as being willing to kill for drugs. Like all prisons, Deer Lodge had its share of men who stuck together for protection. Some were gangs, others informal groups.

The snitch letter handed to Rothe contained dozens of names. Painstaking explanations followed each name. Unsigned, the letter nonetheless made references to the author's personal circumstances. It referred to his incarceration at Warm Springs State Mental Hospital after the pea riot, and attempts by other convicts to frame him as instigator of the disturbance.

***

The kite alleged a drinking party in the prison hospital involving patients and fifteen gallons of confiscated "pruno," a vile alcohol fermented from oranges, ketchup and assorted kitchen scraps. The apparent author, Harold Goff, also told of a regular visitor from Deer Lodge who smuggled contraband on behalf of "his golden-haired boys" who provided him sex, a former bootlegging guard "who is always trying to help the bad actors," an old guard known as "Whitey" who took candy to a convict in segregation, and a former guard he described as such: "... was a gutless sort and asked me in plain simple words not to harm him, and thereafter left my cell door open all day to be on the good side of me. It developed that [he] had a relative confined here at the time. ... During the sit-down strike [of 1958] it was [this] officer that was phoning information to radio station KOPR [in Butte] about every move being made. That is how information was leaked out on everything that happened."

On went the allegations: letters appeared on the inside without postmarks, indicating they hadn't gone through the mail or the prison censors; leather goods were given to guards and civilian workers as rewards for illegal activities and then to their daughters, sons and wives; guard-convict friendships grew into smuggling connections; gifts were laundered to guards through relatives in other towns; convicts with influence ran crooked sports lotteries to fleece younger more naïve men; rigged poker games tricked new convicts into losing their money and sometimes their property. One convict "ate pills like they were peanuts," Goff wrote.

He spoke of a gang with murderer Lee Smart and four other men at its nucleus. He also mentioned another man frequently seen in Smart's company: George Alton.

Goff reported seeing Smart kissing other convicts, one of them on "numerous occasions." Powell and Rothe understood how drugs and sex could be intertwined, one being leverage for the other.

Harold Goff had risked his life typing the kite inside his cell in Cell House 1. The letter came to an abrupt halt at the end of page four, at the time he was summoned to a meeting of an inmate committee investigating the parole board. He hid what he had written, then started another page when he returned.

At least before he came to prison, Goff was a disturbed man. He had robbed a Butte gas station attendant of twenty dollars before driving the man to a wooded area south of Helena where he told him to run for his life. Goff shot him in cold blood, and during Goff's trial, his accomplice testified that Goff "laughed like a maniac" as he fired at his fleeing victim.

As a trumpet player in the twenty-two-member prison band, Goff saw firsthand the dispute over pea shelling that led to the 1957 disturbance. In his kite, he wrote that he was not the instigator or the leader of the riot, but that a "gang" that included Lee Smart had done it. Goff said he was a spokesman, "elected by all the inmates" to bargain with the prison administration.

"It is my opinion that I was picked in advance to be the fall guy for the riot," he wrote, and he referred to guns that a gang of inmates had hidden and intended to use. He also wrote that the same gang controlled money in the prison. "I have also noticed while employed in the bookkeeping department that certain ones of that clicque [sic] have made it a point not to have many dealings with transfers and in my opinion that is done to make it appear they have no money, but on the other hand I know and can prove with a lie detector that they have had money for large quantities of pills even though no money transactions appear on their account."

Powell was confident that he was taking the right steps in reforming the prison, but he wasn't sure that everyone understood the depth of the problem. The conditions Goff described showed how much work Powell had to do. In a report to the Board of Prisons commissioners, he wrote:

"At the time when the present warden took over, there was very little discipline. Use of pills and narcotics was rampant, there was little work programs within the institution itself and the inmates wandered in and out of all the buildings at will. The general attitude of the staff was not to do anything that the inmates didn't like. Homosexual activity, gambling, payoffs among the inmates and other nefarious activity was going on constantly. It was, in fact, in a very, very deplorable state. Both myself and Deputy Warden Rothe had been approached many times by young inmates, by new inmates and others to protect them from the pill peddlers, the strong-arm boys and the homosexuals.

"There was no social service program, practically no education program and the parole procedure was not functioning anywhere near satisfactorily.

"To bring about the tremendous change needed to make the Montana correctional system a workable, valuable, efficient, adequate activity is an almost insurmountable job, particularly trying to do it in a grossly inadequate physical plant and with lack of trained personnel."

Montana's prison in the 1950s was in search of reform. Its broken and scarred security wasn't noteworthy to many people except the ones who had been around enough to know the difference. Jerry Myles did. If Alcatraz Island was the Rock, Deer Lodge was the Powder and the Dust.

9

When prison becomes home

Lee Smart's slender form was a sliver against the yawning Montana sky. He puffed on a cigarette barely caught between his lips. The sheriff watched him. The boy stood atop the roadside ditch just yards from crunched grass blackened with Charles Denzil Ward's blood, yet he seemed disinterested, as if he didn't care at all. He looked into the greening fields through curls of blue smoke. Sheriff T.J. Dellwo and his deputy, Emil Schultz, watched their impassive handcuffed prisoner with curiosity. Dellwo waited for the boy to speak but he didn't. He seemed bored and not at all nervous about the murder he had committed twelve days earlier.

In the company of two barbered lawmen in this rambling empty north central Montana countryside populated mostly by scattered ranches, Smart looked oddly out of place: bushy brown hair combed back over his ears, sideburns bunching at his jaw and a wisp of a moustache that accentuated a protruding upper lip. Tattoos mapped his early interests: a skull-and-crossbones and the number "13" marked his left forearm; on his left wrist the words "Jan" and "3 diamonds." On his right forearm, he had tattooed "Lee" and "Judy" and "3 Hearts." Physically, he didn't look much of a threat. His right shoulder drooped. He was thin like a boy needing exercise. He was nearly six feet tall but weighed only 149 pounds. But it was his face that gave him a tragic dangerous appearance. Those eyes, calm and emotionless and cold like death, had made Charles Denzil Ward quake in the last minutes of his life, taking the salesman on a road he had never traveled.

***

When on the road, which was most of the time, Charles Ward liked to look his best. Late on the morning of April 28, 1956, he carefully parted his hair and dressed in a gray business suit before checking out of his motel in Kalispell, Montana. He cashed a $100 check issued by the Thrift Novelty Company of Denver, and after pressing five $20 bills into his wallet next to his hunting and fishing licenses, drove his Chevrolet north into the Flathead Valley toward Glacier National Park.

Selling novelties was no easy job. Charles Ward spent weeks, sometimes months, away from his wife. They had no children. Being a traveling salesman, he lived out of a suitcase. Back home in Colorado he had friends at the Elks Club, but here on the road, conversations were limited to clients and strangers. On this day, for the first time in a year, he planned to drive U.S. Highway 2 past Glacier National Park through Browning, on the Blackfoot Indian Reservation, then down lonely State Highway 89 to Choteau and finally to Great Falls. On Monday he wanted to call on Elmer Neff at Central News and Novelty Company, just as he had for each of the past three years. They were at least fleeting acquaintances. A man of careful habit, Ward always looked forward to a familiar face.

Ward had gotten a late start. Spring snow filled the mountains, and where the highway wound through the fold of mountains along the park boundary, a gloss of ice shone on the asphalt. A flat tire delayed him even more. He hurriedly threw it in the trunk and pressed on. It was mid-afternoon already when the reservation town of Browning disappeared in his rearview mirror. He was determined to make Great Falls by nightfall.

It seemed important to stop. A young man standing beside a stalled green Mercury waved for help. Ward saw the tire flattened on a wheel painted red. Reminded now of his own blown tire in the trunk, he steered his Chevrolet to the highway's edge. Ward stepped out of his car, straightening his suit jacket. The young man might think his distinguished appearance oddly displaced in the dusk.

Ward noticed the Washington license plates right away. Getting closer, he could see this man was younger than he first appeared. This boy was far from home, yet he seemed much too casual and cool. Being a World War I veteran, Ward never forgot danger. But being a man of the road, he felt compassion for his fellow travelers, even if he didn't like unfamiliar faces.

Before him was a teenager evidently preoccupied with Elvis Presley, a hot new rock and roll sensation. Peeking from beneath the boy's black leather jacket was a blue shirt that matched blue trousers and blue canvas shoes. Thick brown hair swept back from his face in ducktail fashion. Pale hypnotic eyes peered from above a ragged early beard. In less than a year Charles Ward would be celebrating his sixtieth birthday, inviting thoughts of retirement and home and the happy conclusion of a traveling salesman's solitary life. The boy's piercing eyes troubled him. He felt afraid.

***

Early Saturday evening a teenager walked into Tim Latham's Phillips 66 station in Choteau to ask for help fixing a flat tire on his 1954 Mercury. Employee John McLaughlin found a tire and rim that he thought would fit the boy's car. They headed north on Highway 89 in the service station pickup. Three miles north of Pendroy, McLaughlin saw a car parked in the dark on an approach road. He started to turn off the oiled highway. Puffing on a cigarette he'd bummed from McLaughlin, the boy paid little attention except to say, "No, that isn't my car. Mine is the next one, I guess."

The tire and wheel didn't fit. They drove into Pendroy, where McLaughlin borrowed a tire from the operator of the Cornet Pool Hall. While the men talked, the boy bought a wristwatch for $20. After mounting the tire on the red wheel from the Mercury, McLaughlin returned to Choteau and the boy followed in his car. Concerned about McLaughlin's delay and his eerie feeling about the boy, Latham started looking for them about 10 o'clock. He met both vehicles driving into Choteau, and together they returned to the station, where the boy paid for a new Goodyear Double Eagle nylon tire and a used tire because he didn't have a spare. He also bought gas and oil. He paid the $38.10 bill with two twenties he pulled from a wad in his pocket. Before he left, he tried to convince them he was a GI from the Great Falls air base, an unlikely story considering his appearance. He said he was driving to Spokane, Washington, to visit his mother.

***

Just after midnight on Sunday, April 29, highway patrolman Henry Helf left Choteau en route to Dupuyer on an accident call. Three miles north of Pendroy he passed Charles Ward's Chevrolet. When he returned two hours later, he saw the car again and stopped to investigate.

Finding the key in the ignition, Helf started the motor. He watched the instrument panel under the pale dome light. The oil gauge didn't register. After briefly searching in the dark outside the car, he drove away, thinking the driver must have gone for help.

Fifteen hours later, retired farmer Russell Frisell and his friend, Jack Wellenstein, left Wellenstein's ranch for Choteau on the gravel road that connected with Highway 89. About 100 feet from the highway, they saw the parked Chevrolet. A jack protruded from fresh snow in the middle of the road. Curious, Frisell and Wellenstein searched around the car. After a few moments they found the cold body of Charles Denzil Ward, looking both formal and forlorn in a business suit, lying on his face in a nearby borrow pit.

Sheriff Tom J. Dellwo and his under sheriff, Walter Magee, didn't know what to think at first. Considering the victim's shattered head, and the proximity of the jack, they surmised a passing car might have struck him as he changed a tire. Dellwo weighed the clues. All four tires on the car were inflated. He found the flat tire, which appeared to have been driven for some distance that way, stowed in the trunk. The lid was closed with the trunk key still in the lock. The key remained in the ignition, just as highway patrolman Helf had found it, but Dellwo didn't know then that the trooper had been there. Ward's suitcases and novelty samples remained in the car, allowing the sheriff to identify the body. The victim's pockets contained $4.85, but his wallet was missing.

The sheriff's hit-and-run theory didn't last long. On Monday, after the snow melted, he found the murder weapon, a bloodstained pair of lineman's pliers that measured about nine inches long, lying at the end of a culvert near where Ward's body was found. Hairs stuck to the pliers matched hairs on Ward's head. Coroner G.L. Banks of Choteau ruled death had occurred sometime before midnight Saturday.

Word got around Choteau fast. Latham and McLaughlin at the service station told the sheriff about the bearded teenager whose car had been parked just a quarter mile from Ward's. Dellwo issued a bulletin describing the Mercury: light green on top, darker green on the bottom, red wheels, and a new Goodyear white sidewall on the right rear wheel. Both service station men remembered seeing red spots on the Mercury that they now concluded were blood spatters. On the front pages of the *Great Falls Leader* and the *Great Falls Tribune*, Dellwo warned readers to watch for a murder suspect who was young, thin and unkempt.

Dellwo pieced together the evidence. Ward had stopped near the Mercury, but after he died the murderer drove the salesman's Chevrolet up the approach road. The murderer then dragged the body into the borrow pit only eight feet from the oiled highway, but sufficiently hidden from passing cars.

In Great Falls, a housekeeper at a rooming house blinked as she read the suspect's description in her newspaper. She could positively identify Charles Denzil Ward's killer. She hurriedly telephoned Deputy Sheriff John Krsul.

On May 3, police arrested the murder suspect's 16-year-old roommate, who confessed to the boys' escape from a Washington state reformatory. After they stole the Mercury they drove to Great Falls, where they found laboring jobs at Fritz Roll Greenhouse. The suspect lost his job the day before the murder.

The same day of the roommate's arrest, Spokane police stopped the driver of a green Mercury for a minor traffic accident. They then discovered he was driving a stolen car and that he had escaped from the reformatory camp in Cedar Creek, Washington. They didn't know about the murder until they contacted Great Falls police to ask about the other boy.

After hearing the details, Spokane detective Robert Piper began interrogating the young man who wore a ducktail haircut and a black leather jacket. The boy admitted flagging down a motorist to seek help changing a tire. He told investigators he had borrowed the salesman's jack and that Ward had tried to fondle him when he crawled under the Mercury to fit the jack in place. The boy said he hit the older man with his fist and knocked him down. Then, he said, Ward stood and swung at him. In self-defense, the boy said, he hit Ward with the pliers. Police doubted his story.

They pressed the boy, who eventually confessed to murdering the suited man and dragging and robbing the body. "As long as I had gone that far I thought I might as well take his wallet," the boy said. Six days after Charles Denzil Ward died on a lonely rural highway, the prosecutor in Teton County, Montana, charged the boy with first-degree murder. For the first time, Montanans heard his name. He was Lee Smart, a 16-year-old juvenile delinquent from a broken home and a troubled childhood.

***

Lee's mother, Mary E. Smart, signed extradition papers. She and Lee's father had separated when the boy was three years old. He grew up unruly and defiant. A month after his sixteenth birthday, Lee and a friend went to Washington's state reform school in Chehalis on burglary charges. In January 1956, they were transferred to Cedar Creek. They escaped April 14. In three weeks they stole two cars, broke into a service station at Chelan to steal candy and cigarettes, then drove east through Idaho to Montana.

Dellwo and Schultz had gone to Spokane to drive the boy back to Choteau, stopping briefly at the murder scene on their return. They arrived in Choteau about mid-afternoon on May 10. Inside Teton County's crumbling jail they fingerprinted him and then locked him behind steel bars smelling fresh with paint. Smart was the county's only prisoner, and historically, one of the youngest.

For all of his outward bravado, Lee Smart feared prison. He told his mother he would rather be hanged than spend his adult life in Deer Lodge. Mary Smart hired two attorneys, K.M. Bridenstine of Choteau and Thomas F. Lynch of Spokane, to defend her son. They entered an innocent plea at his arraignment on first-degree murder charges.

Bridenstine tried to rally a cause that Smart's case belonged in juvenile court. A prolonged legal argument ensued. Montana law said anybody over the age of sixteen accused of murder could be prosecuted in adult court. Bridenstine claimed Smart wasn't over sixteen if he was not yet seventeen; Teton County prosecutor Leo H. Murphy countered that even in being seven months past his sixteen birthday, Smart was over sixteen. So vague was this law that the competing lawyers filled their briefs with arguments of legislative intent and even dictionary definitions of the word "over." Finally District Judge R. M. Hattersley denied Bridenstine's motions, and a trial date was set for October 1, 1956.

Bridenstine then petitioned for a change of venue, arguing that extensive newspaper coverage of Charles Ward's murder would deny a fair trial for his client in Teton County. He peppered the court record with affidavits, quoting even Lee Smart's mother as someone who had visited the county and contended she had seen prejudice. The *Great Falls Tribune* and *Great Falls Leader* caught most of his legal wrath, but he named even the weekly *Fairfield Times* in his court documents, alleging that it swayed jurors with its distribution of 900 newspapers that contained an account of the murder. Furthermore, Bridenstine blamed stories in a nationally circulated detective magazine for inflaming anger against this young Washington hooligan. County Attorney Murphy fought back, including even Sheriff Dellwo in affidavits swearing Teton County had no anti-Smart bias. Judge Hattersley denied the motion for change of venue as well.

Beset by hard evidence against their client, including his confession to Spokane police and upcoming testimony by a string of

witnesses who would link him to the murder scene, Bridenstine and
Lynch asked for, and got, a trial delay.

By November 1956, Smart had been transferred to Cascade
County Jail in Great Falls. Sheriff D. J. Leeper angered Mary Smart
when he restricted her visits. When she discovered her son was
being fed just twice a day with food she considered unfit for a
growing boy, she demanded that Bridenstine intervene. He told the
court: "His teeth are turning very bad, and he is suffering from a
case of trench mouth which is not being retarded. That defendant is
not receiving milk and other healthful foods such as are necessary
for a growing boy of the age of 17 years. That defendant is
becoming very nervous due to lack of proper foods."

Mary Smart had asked Dr. James Gerlach of Great Falls to
examine Lee. The doctor prescribed dietary supplements that Mary
Smart later claimed were denied her son. She also alleged that
jailers refused her son food packages she had sent from Spokane.
Hattersley immediately transferred Lee Smart to the juvenile section
of Helena's Lewis and Clark Jail, specifying Mary Smart be given
adequate visiting hours and that her food packages be delivered to
Lee.

By late 1956, Bridenstine and Lynch had negotiated a plea
agreement. Their client would plead guilty in return for a second-
degree murder charge. On January 14, 1957, Lee Smart entered his
plea before District Judge Charles B. Elwell in Choteau. Elwell
promptly sentenced the troubled teenager from Washington to thirty
years of confinement at Montana State Prison. Again, Lee begged
his mother to tell authorities to hang him. Fellow prisoners in jail
had told him ugly stories about the joint in Deer Lodge.

"I can't live in prison," he told her.

***

From the time Lee Smart entered Montana State Prison, Mary
Smart peppered administrators with letters, seeking favors for her
son. Just seventeen years old, Lee was among the youngest boys
ever sent to Montana State Prison for a capital crime. In her

charming handwriting, Mary Smart implored the wardens to approve special attention for young Lee. At first she seemed particularly interested in his education; his criminal extracurriculars in Spokane had permitted him completion of only the ninth grade. Still, he was better educated than at least half of his fellow convicts, many of whom listed "laborer" and "farm worker" as their occupations. Smart listed "electrician" and "auto mechanic," in fact more of a desire than an accomplishment. A precocious thief, he knew less about fixing cars than he did about stealing them. His mother's efforts to arrange a correspondence course on those subjects failed when Lee needed tools that couldn't be allowed inside the walls. Mary Smart wrote Burrell: "It is sincerely hoped you do not consider the writer presumptuous for making such a request. However, because of the boy's youth and the long sentence if correspondence courses are permitted it would probably do much toward his rehabilitation and preparing him to become a useful citizen at some time in the distant future."

She tried again with International Business Schools of Scranton, Pennsylvania, hoping to start her son on a series of high school business lessons, but Burrell wrote to the school that Lee's enrollment was improbable considering the absence of typewriters inside the walls. However, Burrell did suggest that Mary Smart take advantage of a free correspondence program at Montana State University. Nothing came of that, either.

Smart worked first as a plumber's helper, a job that lasted one day, then joined the prison band. Except for occasional periods of disciplinary action, he played drums throughout his first two years of confinement. To band instructor Art Taylor, the same guard held hostage during the pea riot, the teenage drummer was "a very good man" who rated "exceptional" in five categories: Quality, Quantity, Attitude, Suitability and Habits. That 1957 report was followed by instructor John Malatore's identically praising assessment in 1958. Malatore wrote on April 3, 1958: "Inmate Smart plays drums in band and also helps with the cleaning of theater on his off time, is very good worker."

Smart listed eight individuals and couples on his mail request form. Among them were his parents and his only sibling, his brother John, who was two years his junior. Mary Smart had moved from Spokane to Seattle, and Lee O. Smart Sr., Lee's father, lived in Wenatchee, Washington. Each person listed on the mail sheet received a letter of notification from Warden Burrell. In June 1957, a furious mother in Fairfield, Montana, shot back: "I opened the letter by mistake believing it to be car papers – so you can imagine my shock. Upon questioning my child, who, by the way, is only a child of thirteen, I find that she has written and received and sent several letters to this Lee Smart. Since we live close to the community where he murdered a man, we know all about him. I must confess to you that I can't understand my little girl's interest in such a monster. ... You can understand that this morbid interest ... cannot be tolerated. ... I'm certain that you will cooperate with us in refusing any letter from her – and also not sending any written by Lee Smart. It may sound melodramatic to add that since some children glorify criminals, it is not improbable that she might even try to aid him in anything he might attempt. ... We are certain that she has never met Lee Smart, but just decided on her own that it would be romantic to write to him."

Lee's father, a baker, had remarried before Lee went to prison. He had lost custody of his sons after an acrimonious parting with his wife. Lee Smart Sr. knew little about his namesake son's crime and subsequent conviction. His lawyer wrote Acting Warden Benson with this message: "Mr. Smart is very much interested in the welfare of the boy, and says that whenever the boy is eligible for parole that he will provide employment and a home for the boy." Benson replied that young Smart, whom he called "above captioned subject" in his terse letter, would not be eligible for parole until September 1962. Benson neglected to mention that Lee's cold-blooded murder probably would encourage the parole board to keep him behind bars far longer than that. The father's lawyer reported his client "greatly encouraged" by Benson's response. Lee Smart Sr. promised to send $37.50 every month, beginning May 1, 1958. And Mary Smart, in addition to sending money that Lee could spend at the prison canteen, where he could buy cigarettes and candy and so forth, assembled Christmas packages that included socks and underwear.

Early in 1958, during a routine shakedown of Cell House 1, Sergeant Frank Moody discovered Smart had fashioned a weapon known as a stinger by cutting wire from a set of earphones and attaching the wire to a strip of metal. Moody also found a pair of scissors issued only to convict barbers. As punishment for possessing this contraband, Smart served thirty days in Segregation.

A few months later, on April 12, Smart landed in trouble again for repeatedly refusing to get a haircut. A fan of rock and rollers like Elvis Presley, Carl Perkins and Jerry Lee Lewis, Smart preferred a ducktail style. He combed and greased his brown hair into a singular curl that dangled onto his forehead while in the back, at his neck, his hair shagged over his collar. Sergeant Fred Pruitt sent Smart to Isolation for five days for this misconduct, and for using vulgar language in front of Cell House 1. That wasn't all: Pruitt ordered a "close haircut," resulting in a military-style buzz by a convict barber happy to oblige. More trouble followed on October 4, 1958, when another guard found more contraband, this time a needle-like weapon, in Smart's cell. For that, he got three days in Isolation. Smart now lived alone in Cell 249 on what was known as the "band galley." George Alton, who had been his cellmate, had gone to minimum-security quarters before his escape from the car repair shop. Inside the walls, the men buzzed with the news that Alton was a fugitive.

Mary Smart's strained attempts at saving her son from himself never dwindled. While she rarely visited, she bombarded young Lee with letters, sometimes writing more than a dozen a month. Her mother's love blinded her to the violent psychopath he was. She believed her son wrongly accused. She persisted with her conviction that he would right himself, and that he would survive prison to fulfill her expectations of the man he could become.

***

The day after Floyd Powell started his new job, two young burglars escaped from the minimum-security buildings outside the main walls on the south end of the prison. One was twenty-three-year-old J.B. Sanders, serving a term from Fergus County. His companion was George Alton.

Being a man of some small stature at five-foot-six and 136 pounds, Alton didn't appear dangerous. He was raised in a family that would eventually include twenty-four children born to the same mother and father. George boxed to survive; by age four, he wore his first pair of gloves. As he grew older he made trouble and fought. When he was fourteen the authorities sent him to the state reformatory in Miles City, where he spent more than three years for various crimes including breaking and entering. His life only got worse.

Alton was just a baby-faced eighteen year old when he came to prison on March 19, 1952, after pleading guilty to burglary in his hometown of Culbertson in northeastern Montana. Handsome, blue eyes peeping from beneath his blond hair, Alton looked almost child-like. Scars on his face and knuckles of his left hand, the hand he favored, suggested something different.

Alton paroled in 1953, but almost immediately landed in El Reno Prison in Oklahoma after driving a stolen car across state lines. When he left the federal prison in 1956, he went to work in a Wisconsin broom factory earning about two hundred dollars a month. He ran from new trouble in Milwaukee, drove to Mississippi, then to Williston, North Dakota, where he met a friend. On a chilly October night they drove to Montana to meet two girls. The party that ensued led to a burglary of Hall's Retail in Culbertson and subsequent arrests. Alton pleaded guilty. This time he got a fifteen-year sentence.

On October 27, 1956, Alton returned to Montana State Prison for his third induction into a prison in less than five years. He had grown almost two inches taller. His hair had begun to recede. A square jaw and cold piercing eyes had replaced the baby face. George Alton had the hard look of a seasoned convict.

***

Nobody saw Alton and Sanders drive away from the prison. Nobody except Floyd Powell.

Entrusted with some responsibility, as was the habit with trusties, Alton possessed keys to the sliding gate that admitted vehicles to and from the auto repair shop. In the morning, as the sun washed Main Street with gentle warmth, he pushed the gate open. He drove across the street to the prison creamery where Sanders worked. In view of guards in Tower 1 and the wire cage in front of the minimum-security dormitories, Sanders walked out to the car. Signs on both front doors read, "Registrar of Motor Vehicles." A block north on Main Street they waved at Warden Powell, who stood on the curb in front of his house, waiting to cross the street to the prison. He waved back. Alton drove through back neighborhoods to Deer Lodge's north side. In minutes he and Sanders gunned their stolen car north on the highway through a sea of hay bales and farm fields.

Floyd Powell didn't realize at first that he had waved farewell to escapees. When he learned the truth, the furious new warden demanded an explanation from Lieutenant Raymond Hoy, the minimum-security supervisor. Shaken by Powell's fierce reaction, Hoy offered to resign. Powell had in mind for him something worse: perpetual tower duty. Hoy's family would remember that he was one of the first custodial officers to experience Powell's anger. The new warden, they figured, was not a forgiving man.

Four days later, sheriff's deputies found the stolen car stripped of its license plates and hidden in Missouri River brush near Giant Springs, about two miles east of Great Falls in north-central Montana. They thought Alton and Sanders had abandoned it there, but they were wrong. They didn't know the car had been stolen a second time after they had parked it on the main street of a little town named Scobey, hundreds of miles to the east, and left the keys in it.

Their odyssey from prison had been a remarkable one. Within an hour of leaving Deer Lodge they pried the magnet-held signs from the door, tossing them into a ditch. They waited until nightfall to drive into Helena. Worried that the white stripes running down their pant legs from waist to cuff of their blue denim convict uniforms would alert someone, they prowled a neighborhood in the dark until they found a clothesline. Alton pulled loose a man's clothing and ran into the night. Sanders laughed at Alton, who looked clownish in his new oversized shirt and pants that draped over his hands and shoes.

They drove north to Great Falls, then east to Scobey. Police searched for Alton in Culbertson, his hometown in eastern Montana. Alton, however, had gone west. Within weeks of becoming a fugitive, he got a job in Washington, earning enough money over a few months to buy a 1955 Hudson Hornet. Months later he drove east through Idaho and Montana to Williston, North Dakota, to see his girlfriend. It wasn't the real thing, but Alton felt like a free man.

***

Two years after Lee Smart's crime faded from Montana's newspapers, Jerry Myles drifted into Butte, still a punch-drunk city that had turned its back on underground mining in favor of its new friend, a vast open pit that was gobbling up Finntown, Dublin Gulch, Dog Town, Meaderville and other ethnic neighborhoods on the Hill. Myles didn't know anybody, nor did he care.

Four days earlier, on June 18, 1958, he had been released from Indiana State Prison. Barely twenty-four hours after arriving in Butte, he broke into Gribbens Hardware Store on a dark street in the valley, known as the Flats. It was out there, far from the mines and the crowds on the Hill, across the street from a city park and a funeral home, where a successful burglar could steal and flee into the night as anonymous as he had begun. Instead, Myles waited. His nineteen-year-old accomplice begged him to hurry. Once inside, Myles didn't seem at all inclined to steal money. When police came and handcuffed him he seemed gratified at their presence. Two days later, he appeared in court in uptown Butte. He refused legal counsel and confessed to the burglary. After pleading guilty, he told the judge that he had tricked the boy into the burglary and that he was blameless. "Let's get it over with," Myles said. He welcomed his punishment. He had done a bad thing and for that he shouldn't be a free man. This was a familiar thought, one that brought him comfort. That very minute, Judge T.E. Downey sentenced Jerry Myles to five years' confinement at Montana State Prison.

Jerry Myles, a.k.a. Richard Arthur Myles, a.k.a. Buddy Rawlins, a.k.a. Richard Arthur Hunter, got what he wanted. One of the federal prison system's most rebellious convicts was going home. Montanans wouldn't know that a prisoner from the legendary Alcatraz had burgled his way into their prison. They wouldn't know that Myles had shared cell houses with criminals of some notoriety from the bootlegger era: Bank robbers Alvin Karpis and George "Machine Gun" Kelly. Floyd Hamilton, who had driven getaway cars for Bonnie and Clyde. Robert Stroud, The Birdman of Alcatraz, who lived on The Rock for more than twenty-five years, longer than anyone else.

In Montana, nobody knew Jerry Myles. He was a common thief. Butte had plenty of those. Dozens of front-page stories made Lee Smart an icon of violence. Jerry Myles got a scant two paragraphs in the *Butte Daily Post* describing the bare facts of his crime, with no mention whatsoever of his extensive prison history, or his proclivity to riot. And so it was that he came to Montana State Prison as a blank face, and blank faces hide dark minds.

- 10 -

Jerry, Lee and the con bosses

Jerry Myles found unfamiliar freedom in the garment shop. He decorated a room for himself, furnishing it with draperies and couches. These were the perks of a con boss. Allowed night visits after guards had locked most other convicts in their cells, Myles created his own sexual fiefdom, a near-fantasy world for a convict accustomed to being closely watched in maximum-security prisons. Here, the man described as "a bull in heat" fulfilled his sexual aggressions, often in utter privacy.

Industries operated Mondays through Saturdays. Workdays normally ended by mid-afternoon, leaving one hour for recreation before dinner. When he wasn't in the garment shop, Myles passed his time playing chess, bridge and occasionally ping-pong. His opponents made a handy audience. He talked big of his world, of how the prison should be run and of his influence in Deer Lodge and other prisons. Impulsively he made himself a bigger and taller man and a man of achievement. Characteristic of his impulse to brag beyond the facts, he had listed "Nurse/Athlete" as his occupation during his orientation at Montana State Prison. His state and federal prison records disclosed no evidence of work as a nurse, or of sports. Except for occasional handball matches he preferred quiet intellectual board games. He told other convicts and even prison staff that he had worked as a swimming instructor, although his long incarceration presumably would render that claim bogus.

***

Though sounding like a revolt in progress, the "con boss system" at Montana State Prison was a state-sanctioned arrangement in which older, more experienced convicts supervised their peers in shops and industries. For lack of will or money to hire civilian supervisors, or even professional regard for the perils of putting convicts in charge of their own, con bosses flourished in the 1950s. In the garment shop, the laundry, the license tag plant, the shoe shop, the dry cleaning plant, the upholstery shop and other prison industries, con bosses commanded considerable influence.

In the workplace, obsolete machinery surrounded Jerry Myles. The newest model sewing machine was of 1934 vintage; most were manufactured in 1926. The 1958 Montana Legislative report stated: "The workmanship is not comparable to that found in even the poorest quality merchandise manufactured on the outside." Equipment in the adjoining guard uniform tailoring shop consisted of a single 1915 model sewing machine. Likewise, the dry cleaning plant had little to offer: one brush, a barrel of solvent, two steam irons and, as Warden Powell later would note, "a hand washing plunger as used by our grandmothers back in the 1800s." In the shoe shop on the opposite end of Inside Administration, convict workers made shoes by hand under the supervision of a con boss, or a "straw boss" as some men called him, whose training came from the con boss who preceded him. Although Montana State Prison contracted to provide shoes to other state institutions, their quality was sufficiently inferior to invite rejections.

The tag plant was considered more modern than other shops. It required nearly forty workers at those times of year when Montana needed license plates. Housed on the west end of the one-story hospital building near the north wall, this plant represented a true industry, being the most common type of work available to convicts in forty states. But for the fiscal year 1953-54 (the most recent data that was available in 1958), Montana ranked forty-fifth among the forty-eight states in reported gross income from prison industry sales. For perspective, Montana ranked thirty-seventh in total population in the same period.

In 1958, nearly half of Montana State Prison's more than 600 convicts remained idle. Work paid nothing, but meant "good time" (in rare instances when records were accurate) that would reduce a man's sentence. It also relieved the ceaseless routine that made men crazy. To a convict locked in his cell around the clock, each day lumbered in its slow-motion way, going nowhere in particular. Men shouted from their cells, furious at everyone and no one. The shortage of work forced a supply-and-demand climate where con bosses sold precious jobs for money, alcohol, drugs and sex.

Shops served as clearinghouses for the prison's black market trade. They hid weapons, mostly "shivs" constructed from pilfered utensils, and containers of pruno. Convicts with no interest in trading leather goods were often bullied into buying them, because con bosses or their minions directed nearly every operation inside the big walls. Convict clerks handled office transactions and even inmate financial records, which they doctored to suit wishes of the bosses who ran their lives.

***

Being a tailor of some accomplishment, his skills having grown as he made a home in one prison after another, Jerry Myles maneuvered into the garment shop with uncommon speed. Within a week after his arrival in Deer Lodge, and as word of his federal confinement in Leavenworth, Alcatraz Island and USP Atlanta spread among his fellow convicts, Myles rose in stature. He was not liked well, but likeability held far less sway than criminal glorification and how a man carried himself. When Myles rumbled into the garment shop on June 30, 1958, he already had decided he would own the shop. By July's end he did, and in a matter of weeks, he emerged as one of Montana State Prison's most powerful convicts.

Like most prisons, this one had a convict pecking order. Men who had showed daring or ingenuity in committing their crimes ranked first, earning strong flattery from their subordinates. Jerry Myles qualified for having led a mutiny in USP Atlanta, and for his length of service in state and federal prisons. Lee Smart qualified for his cold-blooded killing of Charles Denzil Ward. George Alton qualified for his daring daylight escape and his fearless fighting skills. Bill Rose, who many on the inside considered the grand sultan of the convict culture, had killed a Montana highway patrolman. And there were others.

Convicts like Myles and Alton who dominated other men either through strength of personality or an element of fear held considerable sway. Myles had built his power and influence as a con boss in the garment shop. Alton was a man who would give trouble to anyone who came looking for it. He considered Smart "bondable" to Myles, meaning Smart had taken a subservient role. Still, Smart's reckless unpredictable nature and his connection to the band gang kept convicts watchful and wary.

Below these men, another tier took its place. These were those men that Alton called "wannabes," men who ranked high in commission of their crimes but didn't possess enough force of personality to claim a higher position. Alton considered these men weak but loyal. They were men who wanted more status but refused to fight for it, men who valued other men's risks more than their own. In Alton's opinion, this group included men like Donald Toms, a burglar, and Jerry Walker, a common thief who sported a "Born to Lose" tattoo below his right bicep.

Falling deep in the pecking order were mentally deficient and retarded convicts. Some were treated as outcasts and shunned. Others found themselves accepted and even protected. Stronger convicts often found their gullibility useful, easily influencing them to participate in unwelcome behavior of many kinds, including sex. Stool pigeons also fell near the bottom. These men tried to secure favor with guards at the expense of other prisoners, trading information for position. Gang leaders and con bosses supplied them with false predictions of trouble and gossip, knowing guards soon would hear the news. This was called "salting the grapevine," which stronger convicts did to amuse themselves or to discredit others.

Ranking at the bottom, convicts jailed for sex crimes worked as servants for their superiors. They performed menial tasks, including running errands on orders from any number of men. These convicts had committed crimes like incest, child molestation, rape and mutilation, and sodomy with animals. Commonly called "rapos," they lived with ridicule and disrespect and often violence, inflicted as recreation. Carl Frodsham, who would figure into Jerry Myles' plans, was one of these men.

Warden Powell concluded that most prisoners floated through Montana State Prison without direction or purpose. Because he lacked much written documentation that would tell him what these men had done with their lives, he learned to study eyes and faces. He saw hollow looks in some, gazes of fire in other.

***

Jerry Myles, long considered a "comparatively disturbed person" by psychologists at Indiana State Prison and every other prison that had held him, took charge of twenty-three men at Deer Lodge. He wasn't entirely without supervision. Guards staffed the garment shop, but they sometimes rotated assignments every two hours. In their comings and goings they didn't watch Myles as carefully as should have been required. Knowing nothing about making clothes, they often deferred to Myles, who seized on this opportunity to impress on convicts he supervised that he bossed guards. This demonstrates how three problems converged to make another: untrained, underpaid guards; a career criminal wiser about prisons than anybody who guarded him; and in the aftermath of the pea riot, ongoing neglect inside the prison. These conditions gave birth to a king boss, Jerry Myles.

It's reasonable to question how this could be so. Why didn't the extensive paper trail that followed Myles through other prisons accompany him to Deer Lodge? For example, psychologist John Stanfield at Indiana State Prison had written: "It seems as though he attempts to gain attention through overt actions and exhibitionist attitudes. I am afraid that he will be an institutional problem and would like to suggest that we employ him ... in a dormitory or cell house where he will not have access to too much material. However, I would like to suggest that he be given maximum housing and a close watch kept over him for at least 6 months."

The answer appears to be that Montana State Prison until Floyd Powell's arrival had neither the resources nor the inclination to collect and manage this information.

***

Walter Jones Jr. had grown up in Butte, a brawling city, where thousands of miners ate away at the ground day and night. His father, a shift boss, had invested forty-eight years working underground in the dust below Butte's checkered surface. Likewise, Walter spent summers pecking away at old drifts on the 4,400- and 4,800-foot levels in the Mountain Con and Steward mines. Down there in the dark stopes, the men fought the chill and each other and the cough came hard and black. Above ground, sunlight lent a yellow feminine-soft accommodation to Butte's man-tough underground city.

Now, just thirty-two miles to the northwest at Montana State Prison, Walter Jones Jr. would prepare for a tougher job. Powell had wanted to hire someone who could research and assemble case files on each prisoner. Powell hoped that work would lead to a classification system that would segregate men by crime and age and social history, preventing the worst of them from mingling with the best.

The general population contained convicts of all dispositions with little or no control over their behavior and influence. Murderers, rapists and robbers mixed with bad check writers and other relatively minor offenders on the galleys, in the yard, in the dining hall and other public places. Even teenagers and new convicts known as "fish" fell into the cell house vice that included rapes, payoffs, drinking parties and extortion. Because convicts weren't classified or graded, meaning they weren't segregated by severity of offense or by level of risk, prison-wise cons like Jerry Myles preyed on weaker naive cons.

It didn't take Powell long to recruit Jones, freshly graduated from college in Missoula. Thinking he had been hired for research, his sociology specialty, Jones delayed his plans to attend graduate school in Washington State. His career goal of working with criminals came sooner than he had expected. Only a year earlier, he had been a research intern at the prison, interviewing prisoners on their social histories to help a parole officer.

Jones was recognizable by his red hair and a hawkish long face chiseled into square corners like the granite formations surrounding Butte. His body was long and hard. His wide shoulders, built over years of competition swimming, looked too broad, giving him a scarecrow-like appearance. He had been a United States Marine and a college judo instructor. Now, at twenty-four years old, his university professors praised him as a man with a promising future. "I have a great deal of respect for his abilities and personal qualities," said his advisor, Professor W. G. Browder, sociology chairman at the school. "He has a real dedicated interest in the field of corrections, which he wants to make his career."

Jones started work on the same day in October 1958 as Ted Rothe and another of Powell's recruits, Father Lynam. It was a busy month for the new warden. Powell was showing that he meant business.

Jones set up a makeshift office in the Inside Administration's south wing, in a space squeezed between the turnkey lobby to the north and the convict laundry to the south. He started with a desk, a chair, and a growing humility, as he comprehended the insurmountable chore awaiting him. Having taken only a few courses in case work, he didn't know where to start. But he had minored in psychology, and that, coupled with his sociology major, seemed to Warden Powell sufficient education for leading a Social Services department.

Powell sent Jones and the prison's new business manager, Elmer Erickson, to Wisconsin State Prison for training. When they returned to Deer Lodge two weeks later, Powell told them to develop a casework file on all convicts. They started with names beginning with A, collecting criminal information from police and sheriff departments and other state and federal prisons. They compiled social histories, work records, military profiles, psychological tests and prison backgrounds. Jones learned about George Alton early in his research.

Jones assembled several convict clerks to work on non-confidential research. He also hired a secretary, Gladys "Babe" Lightfoot, the first woman to work inside walls and whose husband, Buck, supervised prison ranches. Jones and Buck Lightfoot had worked together in the Mountain Con in Butte. The Lightfoots' daughter Marlene was a senior at Powell County High School with Phyllis Rothe, the older of Ted Rothe's two children. Occasionally Marlene and Phyllis walked home from school together, talking about school plays and their forthcoming graduation in the spring.

When Jones and Erickson started their research, the task looked as big as Mount Powell that loomed to the west. The long road that followed, mapped by men new to the prison and unfamiliar with most of its personalities, meant a prolonged discovery. Only over time, probably a year or more, would Powell and his men fully benefit from their investigations. They had to identify their dangerous men before they could isolate them.

Had Powell and Rothe fully understood the dark mind of Jerry Myles they might have guarded him with more authority. They were men seasoned in a larger, more sophisticated prison. More knowing of Myles and his motives, one might conclude, could have prevented him from fulfilling his destiny. But destiny takes its course. Already in the first month of his new job Powell had set the course of his fateful collision with Myles. Even as Powell unfolded the orderly rows from his mind – policy after policy, procedure upon procedure, rules of every kind – Myles kept his reckless pursuit toward power. Both men wanted leadership. Each wanted the prison structured to his satisfaction. Powell hoped to reform his prison into a model for all of America to see. Myles cared little about Powell's mandate to improve the prison, but he saw changes that progressively denied him of influence.

***

Guards felt reluctant to enforce rules among the con bosses, especially those convicts with records of assaults and murders. When Floyd Powell came to Deer Lodge some of the guards told him: "Don't do anything the prisoners don't like or we will have trouble." Powell thought some of his staff to be very much afraid. Some of his guards refused to challenge defiant prisoners. Con bosses had achieved a measure of power superseding that of most rank-and-file guards. As the practice appeared to be a sanctioned one, guards avoided bucking unwritten rules, even when confronted with flamboyant misbehavior.

Before Powell's arrival, the prison kept practically no personnel files on its guards. No documentation existed of previous work, or of types of work a guard performed at the prison. No orientation or formal training was given. Other state prisons required at least two weeks of intensive training before new guards came in contact with convicts. Investigators concluded a large number of Montana State Prison's new guards couldn't foresee or forestall discipline problems, and that untrained guards tended to be timid with convicts. A new guard was on probation for six months, generally provided he came to work sober and on time, but after that time he received no evaluation to determine his job performance, nor did he get any written explanation of what was required of him.

Myles and other con bosses, being in many cases more intelligent and often more devious than fellow convicts, persuaded prison guards that they could be trusted. Being a skilled manipulator, Myles pretended full loyalty to rules and regulations. Succeeding as a con boss meant playing a seductive game of "king of the hill" where he maintained a delicate balance of deception. As long as con bosses produced the required production from their shops and ensured a reasonable behavior among their workers, they remained in good graces. Their influence ensured that any convict who rebelled at taking orders would be punished for refusing to work. Segregation with loss of privileges reinforced the con boss method. Powell wrote: "They, too, were bitter because, for the most part, they were a better class of inmate with more principle than most."

Followers of Myles and other con bosses clung to them for many reasons: a need for belonging, for love, for recognition. Myles surrounded himself with young men, some of American Indian ancestry, who appealed to his sexual desires. Followers enforced their con bosses' wishes with extortion and beatings, fearful of the same happening to them. Lee Smart, an outwardly lonely teenager, came to know Myles in these early months. The older man's influence appealed to young Lee, a fellow psychopath by every clinical definition, who found himself seduced by Myles' constant talk about riots and escapes. The boy wanted out. If he served his full murder sentence he wouldn't be paroled until 1987. To him, that seemed eternity. He would be forty-nine years old by then – an old man, even older than Jerry Myles, the career criminal.

***

Even before Floyd Powell came to Deer Lodge, sexual queens trying to intimidate scared handsome boys into becoming their punks roamed both cell houses, encouraged by a few corrupt guards willing to look away in exchange for money or gifts such as hand-crafted leather wallets and belts. (Known as "fish," these boy convicts often didn't know the rules of the game.) Queens paid those corrupt guards with money or favors to assign their prey a bunk in their own cells. One of their intended victims was a young convict from George Alton's hometown. The boy asked Alton for help. Fearing no man, guard or con, Alton sold him protection for ten dollars a month. Unlike some other convicts, Alton didn't have rich parents. In fact, he received no money at all from outside the walls. "Nobody touches you, nobody bothers you," Alton told the boy. "You get out of line, that's another story. As long as I can take care of it, I will."

Beginning with that boy, Alton built his protection racket. Each ten dollars bought his candy and cigarettes at the prison canteen. He cornered intrusive convicts and fought furiously, pummeling them with swift left hooks. In a fight, Alton never gave up. He would rather die than lose. That was his secret. He won most fights, but when he couldn't, he paid others to finish the job. Alton kept company with other young men. Like him, they hated sexual attacks on boys. In his early years at Montana State Prison, Alton fought for his dignity and eventually his life. Once three stronger convicts jumped him, beating him bloody in the fight that ensued. Alton wasn't going to be anybody's punk.

Among the convicts asking Alton for protection was Lee Smart. He was impulsive and prone to violence, and as a result made enemies. Because Montana State Prison in 1957 had no classification system that would have separated the boy from older convicts, Smart mixed freely. By the time Floyd Powell and Ted Rothe took command in 1958, Smart had become a full-fledged member of the gang that ran the prison drug trade. The pecking order descended from men convicted of murder to a few hangers-on who ran errands for the main members. As a central gang member, Smart enjoyed drug trafficking privileges, sexual opportunities and the regular intimidation of other convicts. By the fall of 1958, the boy had become a rebel again.

In early 1959, after serving time in Isolation for his escape, Alton was assigned to bakery detail. Then he went to the prison band, which practiced and performed in the Clark Theater inside the walls. There he renewed his friendship with Smart, then nineteen. Between band practice and weekend duty running a movie projector, Alton spent considerable time at the theater. Smart asked if he could move into Alton's cell on Galley 7 in the 1912 cell house. In return, he would finance Alton's account at the prison canteen with money his mother sent from Spokane. From Cell 317, high on the block's east side, they watched Outside Administration, Floyd Powell's house, and the lights of Deer Lodge. They respected each other's privacy, taking turns cleaning the sink and toilet bowl and otherwise avoiding personal questions that would be interpreted as prying.

Captivated by the new rock and roll craze, Smart listened to radio music whenever he could. Crude earphones connected every cell to what was known as the radio room in the southwest tower of the cell house. The connection was clumsy but adequate: a loudspeaker wired to a radio relayed music through lines strung through the maintenance portion of the cell houses, called the well. Here, in this steep vertical space about five feet wide that divided the block's two equal sides, plumbing and wiring webbed through the gloom from floor to ceiling. Cell house guards unlocked a grill door at the block's south end to admit convict workers assigned to maintenance detail. Those convicts shared their intimate knowledge of the block's inner workings with other convicts. In 1958 they decided to find a way to tap into the prison's telephone system, using earphone wires to hear official conversations.

Although he was sharing a cell with a murderer, Alton didn't fear Smart. In the band, where he played coronet, Alton had seen first hand Smart's unpredictable and explosive temper. When aggravated, Smart swore and threw his drumsticks. But in his cell he laid quietly on his bunk, his mind tuned to Elvis Presley and cars and the free road. Alton had never seen Smart fight. Alton felt safer in Smart's company than he had with a previous cellmate who attacked him one night with a knife, jabbing at his throat. After Alton hit him with a closed fist, the convict slashed Alton's four knuckles to the bone. Alton didn't report the attack to guards because he was sure it would result in something worse from fellow convicts. He disposed of the knife and bound his bloody hand with a rag. The ache kept him awake but he wasn't going to tell, not then, not ever.

Many days Alton returned to his cell angry about one problem or another at auto mechanics school, where he had been asked to teach. Smart reacted pleasantly and then went about his business. Their conversations included general observations about their upbringings. Having only one sibling, a brother two years his junior, Smart marveled at Alton's large family. A brother and a sister had died in World War II. Alton hadn't even met some of the others.

They talked of other things too. Smart told Alton he had never hunted or even shot a rifle. He said he didn't know how to handle guns. Smart couldn't see well. He rarely wore his glasses, preferring instead to insert little glass discs into his eyes. They made his cold gray eyes look angrier. At night, under a bare light bulb, Smart washed his contact lenses in the basin. Alton had never before seen this invention. Privileges like this, including money sent monthly from Lee's mother, led Alton to wrongly believe Smart came from a well-to-do family. Lee's parents had divorced in 1947 when he was eight years old. His mother, a stenographer, supported him not from wealth but from love.

***

Before he went to Segregation in late 1958, Alton had never talked with Jerry Myles. Alton had heard stories about Myles being in federal prisons including Alcatraz Island. At first Myles impressed Alton as nothing special. Other convicts called Myles a queen, tittering with stories of his sexual liaisons. Alton didn't trust Myles, at least in part because he found such behavior repulsive. In the short time he had seen Myles around the prison before his escape, Alton watched Myles work his way through knots of convicts, entertaining them with his gift of prison gab. Stout and threatening as a bulldog, Myles strutted fearlessly through his new home, spouting a torrent of manipulation from his intelligent and tortured mind. To this uneducated and unsophisticated audience dominated by forgers and thieves, Myles preached his view of prison life accumulated over nearly thirty years of hard labor.

George Alton thought he was seeing a professional convict at work. Being a man who valued freedom over confinement, he felt quite sure he wanted nothing to do with Jerry Myles.

***

From the start, Floyd Powell decided to fire Myles and the other con bosses. "I knew that bringing about improvement, especially in discipline and control, constituted the greatest likelihood for rebellion," he later wrote. His reasoning was in line with conventional corrections wisdom of the time, which held that reform-minded wardens unwilling to tolerate convicts in supervisory jobs would need money and morale on their side to succeed. Guards couldn't rule by force alone, even if they had sufficient numbers to try it.

"And this turning point in the administration of the prison often sets the stage for the tension and discontent which ultimately grow into insurrection," author Gresham M. Sykes reflected in a *Nation* magazine article printed in early May 1959. Sykes, who had authored the books "Crime and Society" and "The Society of Captives," specifically mentioned Deer Lodge and Walpole State Prison in Massachusetts, which had suffered a violent takeover in March 1959, as prisons subject to hopeless internal malfunctions and morbid external fascinations.

"Prison riots depend heavily on the rise to leadership of the more violent, aggressive and unstable prisoners who can fuse the many dissatisfactions of prison life into an organized plan of action. And such men get a chance to move into positions of leadership when the officials start their attempt to tighten up the institution, since the elimination of *sub Rosa* privileges and relaxed routines often carries in its train the elimination of inmate leaders who have been cooperating with the officials to keep things quiet. By precept, example and personal charisma, these men have set the pattern of getting along with the custodians; in addition, they have passed along the benefits of compromise much as a ward boss dispenses patronage. When they fall out of favor, however, as the officials strive to regain a close control, they leave a vacuum of leadership and the wilder, disgruntled inmates stand ready to take their place. In a spiral of agitation, the prison moves toward disaster."

Jerry Myles thought he was simply was too wise to prison ways, too keen on power, to bow to low-class convicts in a small Montana prison.

Myles, in his mind, was a big, big man.

***

Soon after Ted Rothe's arrival in October 1958, Powell and Rothe broke the con bosses. Jerry Myles and the others lost their authority, their ability to hand-pick convicts and look over the "fish" who entered the prison for the first time, their self-established schedules and hours, and extra privileges. They were allowed to continue working in the shops, but only under the supervision of a guard or civilian instructor. A few former con bosses showed gratitude and relief.

Others, like Jerry Myles, fell hard. Dennis Spalding, one of Rothe's five lieutenants, carried the news to Myles. The surly jocker, angry at his loss of freedom started a campaign of agitation among other convicts. "Prison is my home," he complained to Walter Jones, the social services officer. "You're making it a tough place for me to live."

After Myles lost his power, fewer convicts listened to him. He felt humiliated, disrespected and wronged. Even as a newcomer to Montana State Prison, he regarded his short-lived con boss role as an entitlement that reflected his nearly thirty years of incarceration. Only when he occasionally convinced untrained supervisors of his supposed need for more freedom did he get it. Otherwise, as he was told, he taught other convicts to make garments, mattress covers and pillows.

Myles didn't want work. He wanted power. Sociologist N. Eliason had spotted this inclination early. He had written of Myles on July 11, 1958: "He has never held a job for more than three weeks on the outside. ... As for work when he gets out it won't matter as he will be right back in." And then a foreboding of trouble: "He has very high respect for Alcatraz as he feels they helped straighten him out mentally. He likes to deal with problem inmates and feels he can do much more with them than the officials. He feels he and most other men here who are inside are psychotic. ... I feel this man will be a leader among inmates. It could be good but with his vast experience I fell [sic] it should be kept in hand. He plans to start group therapy when the Warden is appointed. He claims he usually gets what he wants while serving time. I feel this man is intelligent and should be watched as he is definitely of leader caliber."

***

In November 1958, three months after George Alton escaped from Montana State Prison in a state-owned station wagon, bragging that he had waved to Warden Floyd Powell as he drove away, Deputy Sheriff Raymond Atol patrolled a neighborhood in Williston. Alton's parents, Charles and Louella, had moved there before his second Culbertson burglary. Police suspected him of having committed several burglaries with a younger brother in North Dakota. They also knew his girlfriend lived in Williston. Waiting in the girlfriend's neighborhood, Atol spotted Alton driving a car with two boys inside and arrested him at gunpoint. Alton didn't resist, but he warned the officer he would have started shooting if not for the boys, one of them his girlfriend's brother.

George Alton spent Thanksgiving in the company of other convicts at Montana State Prison, but back inside the big walls, his minimum-security privileges revoked. Powell and Rothe seemed unsure what to do with him. More than two weeks passed before guards escorted him down a steep narrow stairwell into an isolation cell below the 1912 cellblock. Here he spent thirty days, most of it in darkness. This was the "Hole," the damp cellar feared by convicts who spread stories of being handcuffed high on the bars until only their toes touched the cold floor, hanging there until they shook. Up and down the galleys they gossiped, and sometimes bragged, of being flung down the narrow concrete steps, and of beatings by sadistic guards. Guards, however, said it was never as bad as that. Outside investigators hired before and after the pea riot recommended The Hole be closed but they never told the real story of this punishment, superficially referring to "inhumane treatment" in their official reports.

Down here, George Alton thought of freedom. Accustomed to harsh living, he felt thankful for two meals a day. This was a place that reduced other convicts to tears, but Alton wasn't afraid. Here he could think. He didn't mind being alone. He resolved to escape this prison. Much like Lee Smart, he accepted prison only as temporary detainment. He filled his mind with images of freedom. Someday he would make a break, even if it killed him.

Of the many tiers of convict relationships, George Alton seemed to Walter Jones to be near the top. Jones also thought of Alton as caged and wary, a man who wanted to be free. Unlike many other convicts, Alton wasn't a man who comfortably did his time. Alton, thought Jones, wanted to escape again.

Even before Alton was captured and sent to the Hole, an angry Jerry Myles began a pattern of petty misconduct that eventually came to Deputy Warden Rothe's attention. This was the same type of misbehavior that he practiced in USP Atlanta and other prisons.

Early on the morning of December 10, 1958, having been informed that he was being sent to segregation for repeatedly breaking rules, Myles demanded to see Rothe. Lieutenant Pete Lynch brought Myles through the double-doored vestibule, past the turnkey guards, into Rothe's office. Myles argued with Rothe. When Rothe didn't back down, Myles swore and leaned across his desk, lips curled in anger. "Don't push me into anything here!" he warned.

"Are you threatening me?" Rothe asked, his big body tensing in his chair.

Myles turned to Jones, who with Rothe and Elmer Erickson formed the prison's disciplinary committee. "Jones, does it sound like I'm threatening the deputy warden?" His voice was thick with sarcasm.

Jones met his glare. "Yes, it sounds like a definite threat to me," he said.

"I'll kill you for that someday," Myles promised Jones, and Jones knew he meant what he said. For a moment the room was silent except for the creak of Rothe's chair. Everyone, including Myles, knew a line had been crossed.

Rothe wasn't a man to tolerate threats. He intended to make sure that Myles knew who was boss. Rothe changed the disposition of Myles' punishment to Isolation, where he would stay for an indefinite time. Myles would have a Bible to read, and be given one meal a day. Isolation was a worse punishment. At least in

Segregation, Myles would have had more to eat and reading materials of his choice, which might include *Redbook* and a few other magazines.

***

To some cons, "going to the Hole" meant being locked in the dark cellar below Cell House 1, but this was only one of several isolation areas guards used for punishment. A narrow barred stairway at the 1896 cell house's north end led to another series of dungeons beneath the cell house floor. To anyone inclined toward claustrophobia these rooms would resemble brick ovens; they would remain in use until a convict suffocated there in the late 1960s. At another location, the ground floor tier on the west side of Cell House 2 served as Isolation and the one above it, as Segregation. To some convicts, these too were known as the Hole. On the far corners of Cell House 1, various cells kept troubled convicts apart from others. Called "Siberia" because of their geographic isolation, they became long-term homes for some convicts.

Jerry Myles, thought Walter Jones, should be isolated in Siberia. Jones had met Myles shortly after beginning his new job, and despite his lack of practical experience as a prison sociologist, he recognized Myles as a dangerous man who should be segregated from other convicts. Myles told Jones he had come to Montana because he had heard convicts ran Montana State Prison and he wanted to become a con boss. He also bragged to Jones that he had waited for police during his burglary of the Butte hardware store because he wanted to be caught sooner rather than later.

Had Jones known of Myles' extensive prison history, he might have discerned one significant change sooner: the man they called "Shorty" in other prisons had become a bigger man in Deer Lodge. Myles was taking advantage of Montana State Prison's looser security to find his personal glory. Here was the man who in his past had asked to be punished for minor infractions. Now he had escalated his troublesome behavior. Already in Deer Lodge the guards called him "Little Hitler" and described his preoccupation with young men. Jones heard stories about how Myles, with help from Lee Smart and others, cornered and raped the fish. Still, Myles remained a mystery. Few people knew about his long journey through federal prisons like Alcatraz Island.

Curious about this self-possessed man, Jones asked prison schoolteacher John Storey to administer an intelligence test. Myles scored at 147, a rare IQ that Jones would find unparalleled among convicts at Montana State Prison.

***

When they left Rothe's office, the smallish Lieutenant Lynch tried to escort Myles outside and toward Cell House 2, but Myles accosted Lynch with carnal profanity and stormed away. Several guards caught Myles and wrestled him down the sidewalk and then into Isolation, a familiar environment for a lonely man. He would spend Christmas here. Myles paid little attention to his prison-issued Bible. Night and day he thought of how Ted Rothe, that new man, would pay for what he had done.

The deputy warden didn't relent until thirty days later, when he ordered Myles into Segregation, housed on a different galley on the west side of Cell House 2. Here, in the 1896 block, one unplumbed cell was as intolerant as another. Convicts from the water crew brought one metal container for drinking water and another for human waste. As he served another forty-seven days, Myles had more on his mind than sanitary conditions.

When he arrived in Segregation, he was put in a cell next to George Alton, who had been moved from the Hole. They whispered at length. What they shared was between them and "the gods" that Myles frequently mentioned in his discourses about power and struggles.

Conversations in such places can't be good. Myles had virtually no life outside the walls. Alton thought of nothing but escape. Officer Noel Davidson, a third shift catwalk guard and a newcomer to the prison, watched Myles pace in his cell all night, night after

155

night. Davidson wondered what was tumbling in a man's mind that kept him awake and intense and furious.

On February 27, 1959, after Rothe relented and released Myles from Segregation, guards assigned him to the water crew, one of the least-regarded jobs in the prison. He would be dumping toilet buckets from Cell House 2, and from the guard towers on the big wall. Convicts called it the "shit brigade" and looked down on men who did it.

His fall from grace was complete. He put some effort into his new job, however minimal, because it was the kind of menial labor he knew best. Ted Rothe, seeing this obedient behavior, might have concluded that Jerry Myles had learned a lesson. But Myles wanted revenge. He was primed for the kind of trouble that administrators at USP Atlanta anticipated after his mutiny there, leading to their decision to dispatch him to Alcatraz.

In Deer Lodge, to the great misfortune of Rothe and Floyd Powell and two dozen guards and other staff who would work the day of April 16, 1959, he went back to a regular cell in Cell House 1, where he fell into company with Lee Smart, his young friend.

It was a dangerous combination: Myles, no longer a watched man, and Smart, loving trouble and dreaming of the free road.

George Alton, 1956

- 11 -

Thursday, April 16, 1959

The wind came dry but breathy, setting flight to kites and flags and guards' caps. It brought promise of warmer seasons. First it blew from the west and then from the northwest, sweeping a chill of spring snow from the brows of Mount Powell and the rest of the imposing Flint Range. It was a cool but promising wind. Only by April did spring seem real and alive in Deer Lodge; in March, alternating waves of snow and rain blew off the Flints and turned the roads to mud and got housewives swearing. But this would be a different day. Temperatures edged above freezing in the morning, and there was talk among the guards of the second shift that the mercury would hit forty degrees by mid-afternoon. The sky spit snow but it was clear to everyone that winter had worn itself out.

***

Early that morning, in dawn's pink light, Sergeant William Cox settled at his desk outside Deputy Warden Ted Rothe's office. A pot of coffee brewed on the table next to him. It was six o'clock, barely the break of day, and most of the prison slept. Day shift guards had taken their posts, night shift guards had left for home, and bakers and cooks prepared breakfast downstairs. Soon, guards would be working the galleys, rousing hundreds of men.

Cox had big bones and a jaw of rock. He cut a rugged silhouette against the window behind his desk. Straight across the yard from him, the square hulk of Tower 4 glowered back in the first strain of light. He watched a guard shift positions behind the wide glass. Behind the guard tower, at the back of the prison, the Clark Fork River would be percolating through a tangle of golden willows. Beyond the river, the night-shift machinists would be punching out from the railroad roundhouse, where they repaired locomotives. As the coffee bubbled, as the clocked ticked, as Cox tapped his pencil on a clipboard and wondered what another shift inside the prison might bring, the shadows edged away from the far corners of the empty exercise yard, opening more of it to a new day.

This was a quiet moment for Inside Administration. Before long those heavy grating doors would clang open and shut with the day's business. Bill Cox hadn't expected to come to work until 8 o'clock. Scheduling had been fouled up and he didn't want to be late. He had worked at Montana State Prison for two years and four months. That was a long time at this prison. Many of the oldest guards had left since Warden Burrell's departure. Cox knew the prison for what it was. The real story, he knew, was not out in the open for everyone to read.

On April 16, Cox came to work with the day custody officers, known as the first shift, who would go home at two o'clock that afternoon. More guards would come at 8:30 o'clock. They were guards who supervised convict work crews and other areas that convicts frequented during daytime hours. Cox was Rothe's administrative aide. He put his fingerprints on building keys, disciplinary reports, cell house logs, inmate count sheets and anything else that came into Rothe's office. The outer office where Cox worked also was known as "the captain's office" and "the count office," which meant that most of the guards at one time or another brought their business here.

Cox also dispensed medications kept locked inside a cabinet in Rothe's office. To get their pills, convicts came to the grating door just outside where Cox worked. Through a barred window in the wall between the captain's office and the vestibule, he could see them enter. Throughout the day, turnkey guards had words with a stream of convicts who came to the grating door. Every conversation meant trying to sort serious needs from nonsense.

In these quiet morning hours, Cox attacked his paperwork. He often worked longer hours than he should. He hoped that today he could leave at two o'clock like the other guards who had started work at dawn.

***

Warden Floyd Powell and his deputy, Ted Rothe, decided that very morning that they would remove rifles from catwalks in the two big cell houses within a week. They had been warning guards about the danger of having guns inside a prison. They had done so outside the walls when the first shift waited to enter the prison. They would do the same in the afternoon, when the second shift came to work.

Powell and Rothe had learned at the bigger and more modern Wisconsin State Prison that firearms inside a prison invited trouble, although that hardly was a secret to anybody. According to conventional wisdom, convicts would plot to seize those guns and turn them against guards. Soon after his arrival the previous summer, Powell had confiscated two .30-30 carbines that guards carried on catwalks in the cell houses, but he faced a revolt. Several guards threatened to stay home from work, telling their new warden that it wasn't safe to work inside the prison without a show of force. Powell relented, but he decreed that only the rifle in the older cell house be supplied ammunition because of the presence of segregation and isolation cells on the first two galleys on the west side.

Some of the guards who worked the catwalk in Cell House 1 thought that Powell, by giving them an empty rifle, was inviting them to die. Some brought their own ammunition to work, hidden in their pockets, and jacked it into the rifle when they knew Powell wasn't around. The few guards remaining who had worked during the Burrell years had seen a relative lawlessness when convicts ran prison industries and came and went as they pleased. Now, after Powell and Rothe busted the con bosses and continued to institute policies they had brought from Wisconsin, their guards sensed a growing tension among convicts who lost their freedom. The guards liked tougher rules, but they feared the rip of a shiv.

Many guards distrusted Powell. He came to Deer Lodge educated in penology and more experienced in practical day-to-day convict-staff relationships. That alone wouldn't have set him apart, but they thought he talked down to them, and that he spied on them. They saw him in odd places, trying to observe without being observed. One morning, tower guards watched him walk behind the hospital, where he cupped his hands to shield his eyes from the sun and stared through a back window. Guards saw him on prison ranches with binoculars, watching them from nearby hills. They thought he kept a black book in his desk drawer that, like a diary, contained secrets about various people who worked for him.

By contrast, Rothe found favor with guards. He shared Powell's ideas of rehabilitation and reform, but the men in blue thought of Rothe more as a guard's guard. Most of the time Rothe talked straight with guards and convicts. They admired him for that.

***

On that Thursday of April 16, 1959, few guards had worked in the prison long enough to know a riot up close. Like the men they guarded, they were rough men. Most guards were not educated; many had not finished high school. They wrote their names, addresses and three previous jobs on simple one-page applications in the hiring office outside the prison. Some of them, including men who drifted into Deer Lodge to escape trouble in neighboring Butte and Anaconda, couldn't contribute even that much. Men who didn't know how to write, or didn't want to write, asked their wives or sisters or waitress friends to fill out the applications instead. Rare were the guards who came to the prison with experience. They were like Clyde Sollars, for the most part plain men who heard the prison was hiring. They knew little or nothing about law enforcement or corrections. When they went to work at Montana State Prison, they had neither education nor training to save them.

There were bad convicts and good convicts, and good guards and some bad guards. Some on either side could have traded places. For the most part they swore and smoked and spat alike. On the bar stools of Deer Lodge and Butte and Anaconda drank men who had been either or maybe both, and who was to know the difference? A guard's life wasn't for everyone, even when lumber prices fell and the mines quit hiring. Fear and poverty-level pay discouraged many men from applying at the prison.

A prison administration hungry for guards recruited them even from bus depots, where they slept on scarred benches with a battered suitcase or two and no dream in the world but to find a hot meal. Some even came from the freight trains that stopped across the river from the prison. Occasionally, a recent college graduate or a discharged soldier found his way into a guard's uniform, but he rarely stayed long. To a man like that the prison was on the road to somewhere else. To qualify for employment, a guard needed the courage to walk atop the wall all the way around. Some couldn't stand the height. Occasionally a guard fell.

Poorly trained as they were, Montana's prison guards at least sensed the mortal danger of being taken hostage, of falling to the mercy of the men they guarded. They struggled to manage a dangerous dividing line between owning control and being controlled. The more months a guard worked, the more he wondered why he had survived that long. A year's experience qualified a guard as a veteran. Two years and more made him an old-timer. The newer guards had heard graphic stories about the disturbances in 1957 and 1958. It was the stuff that didn't make the papers. Every day they dreaded the worst because in a practical guard's mind, violence was an inescapable consequence. When they bellyached about the "joint" or the "zoo" they swore heavy and loud. It wasn't long before the typical guard knew and used every vulgarity spoken in the prison.

Sollars, the mail officer, and other officers assigned to administrative duties worked mostly regular business hours. Custodial officers responsible for keys and locks came and went in three shifts. Two hours before Sollars sorted his final mail delivery on April 16, afternoon shift guards awaited orders to go inside. They huddled and smoked outside the prison wall, their conversations evaporating with their cigarette breath in Montana's hard wind. Outfitted in gray-blue wool uniforms made by Jerry Myles and other convicts handy with needle and thread, they no longer looked plain men but men with authority. They felt pride in wearing their uniforms. They showed them off as a reward of the thankless work of being prison guards.

At precisely five minutes to two o'clock, fifteen men of the "second shift" entered the prison through a double doorway at the base of the southeast tower, known as Tower 1 or to the guards, Gate 1.

First through a barred cage in the compound and then through the broad sandstone wall they filed, one after the other in their uniforms, past a barred gate and then a thick oak door held fast by mighty steel hinges. Inside, the blue pool spattered into a raindrop pattern, each guard walking alone to relieve his counterpart on first shift, the breakfast shift. To the catwalks, galleys and flags of Cell Houses 1 and 2. To the hospital, to industries, to dining, to the library, to the garment shop and to the yard itself, where during recreation time convicts outnumbered a guard a hundred to one.

Here they were no longer bachelors and married men with families, but turnkeys and relief officers and the hard-time guards who stood watch in the isolation units where during dreary nights even the toughest convicts with venom for brains sometimes cried and begged for the Lord. Here, the guards walked with the punks and the gopher men and the greasers and the vagina vandals, in a place where every crime and skin color and sexual behavior had a nickname. They moved convicts from bed to table to job and back again. It was repetitive work, fraught with danger. Most guards had been attacked at least once. Except for thirty minutes taken for late-afternoon dinner, including time spent walking to the officers' dining room outside the south wall and back again, these guards mingled with convicts, their only protection being common sense and sheer luck and the supposed authority of the uniform. After they sent the cons to their beds and locked their cells, they waited in relative relief until ten o'clock when the third shift came on duty.

Older men and new men usually got tower work. They endured an excruciatingly dull routine. No reading. No lights. Just watch, listen, and fight the sleep demon. Guards assigned to towers over street entrances at least enjoyed some human contact. They lowered and raised keys and recorded the comings and goings in logbooks, and they got to shout down to small faces on the ground about what was wrong with the world, and being in the throes of a guard's life, they didn't hold back with their opinions.

The ultimate drudgery happened in those towers on the big wall's northwest and northeast corners. Those guards protected no outside entrances; there, except for occasional distractions when convicts got their yard time, guards fought to stay awake. The abbreviated training procedures kept it simple: tower guards must keep their eyes roving the scene before them for anything amiss, any odd movement suggesting trouble. And after the initial sense of purpose wore away, bored guards asked themselves an inevitable question: How long could a sane man stare at brick and mortar?

Over time they told stories of each other's misfortunes, like the one about a tower guard who tried to impress cons with his quick draw antics but lost his grip on the pistol and watched it fall to their feet in the prison yard. In another case, a guard's rifle tumbled to the street when he slipped on a patch of ice outside the tower door. A third guard who couldn't see a foot in front of him, even through thick glasses, walked right off the tower wall, breaking his legs. It was fair to ask how he could have watched for trouble in the yard below.

On that day, on the afternoon of April 16, six guards climbed narrow wooden stairs inside the southeast wall tower. At the top, from where they could see the old cell houses looming right in front of them and the ground around it, the shift sergeant gave his orders. In those days guards frequently walked the walls as a show of strength, no matter the obvious danger that had nothing to do with convicts but everything to do with height. Towers had outside entrances, but walking the wall was common; guards shifted to the next tower every hour or two. On trembling legs these guards of Thursday's second shift stepped onto walls without rails, staying low against the gusts off Mount Powell, scuffing their shoes along the gray-brown gravelly surface that measured precisely forty-one inches in width.

Now walking twenty-two feet above the ground, these tower guards witnessed an oddly dichotomous scene. On the free side, Deer Lodge's pastoral neighborhoods marched away in orderly grids. The entire little town looked but a paint drop on this sprawling valley, where vaulted foothills melted into the grandeur that surrounded them: Flint Range to the west, Deer Lodge Mountains to the east, Pintlers to the south and Garnets to the north, all topped with caps of snow. Looking outwardly from this wall you could see heaven. But to the inside, that was as close to a hell as a man would see in his waking hours. That's how the guards saw it. Inside this wall was Montana's criminal city, populated by hundreds of felonious men guarded by a few dozen officers distinguished less by professional demeanor than by convict-made uniforms and brass keys as big as soup spoons and monthly paychecks that barely set a table. In some cases, not even that after a few nights of hard drinking in the saloons in downtown Deer Lodge.

Most guards who put down roots and paid their bills found that their neighbors respected them. On warm days they mingled on the sidewalks downtown, catching up on the town talk. It felt good to be relaxing in the free air.

Inside the prison at the other end of Main Street, they coped with conditions that stretched the limits of human dignity. To many convicts they were hacks and screws, fodder for manipulation, parent figures forced to react to every primal need. These poorly paid servants of public safety felt some pride in their jobs, although it was a self-inflicted pride and not the kind that came from administrative rewards of a job well done. Their pride grew more from a basic human dignity and from the eventual reasoning that they knew more than anyone on the outside about how the convicts played out their pecking order of power in the daylight and sometimes, cried like babies at night.

The guards knew more about Montana's felons than the lawyers or parole officers and even the warden, and most certainly the public. To the newspaper reader and the radio listener, criminals who made headlines were churlish cartoon characters. Guards saw those same men as real people.

Savvy guards found allies among the cons, striking cautious unspoken relationships of trust that in return for fair treatment, a con would protect the guard from assault. They were rough men against rough men. No amount of supposed authority could save a guard who cons saw as weak or confused. In the final analysis, for lack of anything else that would substantially change the equation, it was how a guard could talk with cons, if he could speak their language and laugh off their bad business. On any shift cons outnumbered guards more than thirty to one.

***

Like other second-shift guards on duty April 16, Victor Baldwin would come to regret his substandard training. In July 1958 he quit work at the smelter in Anaconda, where men labored at furnaces hotter than crematoriums and sniffed and gagged at the black dust that choked their lungs and they wondered how long it would take to die. Baldwin came to Deer Lodge and walked the wall. A prison, if nothing else, was cleaner air. Hours later he was assigned yard duty, working for Sergeant Andy Holmes. It dawned on Baldwin as he stood in the prison yard with no protection at all from the criminals around him that if death couldn't get its fingers into you one way, it would find another. He felt the cold stare of a hundred eyes. He felt their curiosity, their silent warnings, and their measuring-up of his every step. He didn't know if the prisoners held within these imposing walls did that to all the new guards or just to him. He never shook the feeling, even as summer turned to winter and the snow fell into April. He knew a wiser head would have seen trouble coming.

Most of Victor Baldwin's fellow guards felt the same way. A single noise, or a word, or a forgotten unlocked door could determine whether they lived or died. This wasn't high drama, or flirtation with bravado. That's just how prison was. Baldwin felt the tension. Before April 16, 1959, melted into night, it would become a defining day in Montana prison history.

***

The Winchesters kept on catwalks in each cell house were identical Model 1894 lever-action types. Serial number 1555124 was kept in Cell House 2; 1555730 was logged to the 1912 cell house. Most guards knew firearms, and knew the buck of a .30-30 when it fired. Many of them hunted in thick timber that lined mountain canyons, and in the alpine meadows far above the Deer Lodge Valley. Nobody, not even military-trained guards, knew when to shoot a convict. Weapon training at Montana State Prison in 1959 was minimal. The Winchesters comforted the guards, or least most of them, but it was a shell game. Did convicts know which gun was loaded? Did they think both guns were loaded, or neither? They wondered: did convicts know which guards might shoot and who might not?

Warden Powell never doubted that the rifles, if left on the catwalks too long, would invite violence. The catwalks were open and unprotected. Powell suspected that some guards would hesitate to shoot if attacked. He and his good friend Ted Rothe, a man Powell considered a most promising prospect for prison leadership, decided to take a stand. They decided the morning of April 16 that they would leave those rifles alone for just another week before removing them. They hoped they weren't waiting too long.

They had felt tremors of unrest. At the end of January, Rothe had squelched an uprising during dinner when convicts protested how their food was served. Rothe stood on a table in the dining hall and spoke in a loud and authoritative voice. "Men, here's the way it is," he said, and on the spot he enacted a "take all you want but eat all you take" policy that quieted most of them and led a few weeks later to a convict-painted sign that adorned the wall, reiterating Rothe's message. Some cons remained angry over Rothe's discipline as he took over the prison. But under his leadership most convicts felt safer, and they observed in Rothe an unfamiliar fairness. Considered outspoken, decisive and fair by a growing number of convicts, Rothe started hearing grievances, which gave official voice to cell house rumblings. He walked among the cons, eager to show concern for their welfare.

Outside the walls, Ted and his wife Elsie had moved their family into their new home beside the prison commissary. It was handier than their apartment on Milwaukee Avenue near downtown, and it was newly redecorated. Elated, the Rothes decided to buy new furniture. They wanted to look their best in a town where they would enjoy high visibility.

Forever a man who worked long hours, Ted nonetheless found time to join Kiwanis and Toastmasters. His children, Phyllis and Jim, had made friends in school. Phyllis won third place in a talent show sponsored by Key Club and Future Homemakers of America. She performed a pantomime entitled "Love Me To Pieces" on the auditorium stage at Powell County High School. She also had been mistress of ceremonies at "Wheels of Fashion," the home economic department's annual fashion show. Jim, although just a sophomore, played on the varsity basketball team. Decades later, the 1950s would be remembered as the golden age of basketball in Deer Lodge. That year, in 1959, the Wardens of Powell County High School placed second in the state Class B tournament, losing the championship game to Fairfield, 66-53. The Rothe children's notable achievements extended to academics as well; the local weekly newspaper reported that both Phyllis and Jim made the A honor roll for the six-week period ending in February.

The new deputy warden liked this town. He was a city boy, born in Lincoln, Nebraska, but raised in Milwaukee, Wisconsin, from a young age. In those days the Rothes never had much money; his mother worked as a janitor in a department store. He found in Deer Lodge a homespun civility that matched his humble roots. He celebrated his fortieth birthday in Deer Lodge on March 9, 1959. Ted liked this new beginning. His family, he said, would stay there forever.

***

From sociologist Walter Jones' research, three convicts emerged as men to watch. One was Jerry Myles. Another was Lee Smart, the pimply-faced teenager who impressed on Jones his willingness to follow Myles. Jones, like others on the prison staff, figured Smart for a reckless killer who could kill again. More and more, Smart passed his time painting violent pictures. One showed an arrow ripping through the breast of a nude woman.

Jones also observed the quiet firm influence of a third convict, George Alton. They were the same age but otherwise a study in contrasts: Jones, tall and brawny; Alton, short and wiry. Jones, an overachiever; Alton, a petty burglar. Jones, a gifted intercollegiate swimmer who lettered his way to public recognition; Alton, a gifted boxer who fought his way through reform school in Miles City and who tattooed fighters with swift punches in prison boxing rings. Known as a square shooter, Alton attracted a substantial following of convicts who detested rape, extortion and other violent acts. Alton kept much to himself, preferring company of a few good friends. Lee Smart, his close friend and cellmate, stood for much of the trouble that Alton seemingly opposed.

***

A couple of hours after Bill Cox started work on April 16, officers Gus Byars, DeForrest Thompson, Clinton Fowler, Erwin Seiler, Robert Wyant and Marvin Wallace entered the prison from Tower 7, the main entrance. Cox handed out their keys and wrote on the log what he had done. It was most important to keep track of the keys. The guards moved quickly through the vestibule, some after hurriedly pouring cups of coffee, because their convicts would be waiting for work detail.

Thompson headed to his normal assignment at the theater. Byars, one of the most experienced guards working that day, went to his teaching job in the auto mechanic school in the theater's basement. Fowler went to staff the library, a small place sandwiched between the hospital and the tag plant. Seiler would supervise a yard construction crew. Wyant, a former Anaconda smelter worker who had worked at the prison only six weeks, walked north to the hospital where he would watch a convict nurse and three convict patients all day. Part of his job was keeping pills and other drugs locked away from pilfering hands. Although a sleepy place, the hospital needed careful attention.

***

When Floyd Powell became warden, most of the prison's original wall remained, and all of it sturdy after nearly seventy years. It was a prison of modest size compared with prisons in more populated states: from north to south, it measured 585 feet; from east to west, 270. Eight structures, including two yard towers, inhabited the nearly four acres inside the walls. The two brick-and-stone cell houses stood along the east wall. While built sixteen years apart, they resembled each other in size, design and ambition. Cell House 2, on the south end, enclosed 160 cells. The newer Cell House 1, on the north end of the prison, had 200. Each place had a four-tier block of cells at the interior's center with all cells facing either east or west windows. In Cell House 1, guards locked cell doors with a sophisticated lever mechanism secured behind steel panels at the block's south end. The Pauly Jail Building Co. of St. Louis, Missouri, owned the patent to this invention of interlocking grating doors. Guards could open all doors on a galley at once, or just one, or even two or more cell doors not adjacent to one another.

Catwalks skirted interior walls in both cell houses. One guard stood watch on each one. At least one floor guard, and often two, worked below the catwalk guard to watch for trouble the best they could. All the cells in the newer cell house and those on the east side of the older one had double bunks. Cells had bars as fronts. In addition, floor-to-ceiling gates of bars isolated the blocks of cells from the lobbies that led outside. In Cell House 2, the 1896 block, each convict got a washbasin and two buckets: one for human waste, the other filled with water for drinking and washing.

Custodial work in the cell houses was often the most dangerous. Working from small battered wooden desks, guards coped with endless human problems, many of them contrived. They had no telephones and no protection except good common sense and the threat of a rifle shot from the catwalk. Here, in their living quarters, convicts traded cigarettes for favors. When the guards weren't looking they traded drugs, brewed pruno or its cousin, "applejack," and stalked weaker, younger convicts for sex. The guards, being too few in number, couldn't prevent all the beatings and rapes.

In the dining hall, double solid steel doors at either end were kept locked from inside both cell houses until meal times. When guards swung the doors open, convicts entered the dining hall to sit at four long rows of tables facing west. Each row seated 100 men at twenty bench-style tables, five of them to a table. Gun ports along the east wall gave guards a wide view of the dining hall, as did the gun cage in the southeast corner. Midway on the west side of the dining hall a door opened to a short flight of steps that led to the prison yard.

The top floor of Inside Administration, where Rothe and Cox and other guards worked, was the hub of prison commerce. Here was the mailroom from where Clyde Sollars would hear what he thought was a board falling flat, and an inmate receiving room and a storage room. A visiting room, chaplains' offices, attorney interview rooms and the social services office filled out the remaining space.

Only one door entered the building from the east. On the west, three doors opened from concrete steps to the yard: the center one into the vestibule near the deputy warden's office, and the others into prison industries at either end. North steps led to garment and shoe shops. South steps entered dry cleaning and the laundry. The top floor could not be entered from inside the cell houses.

Underground passages led into gun cages and catwalks inside each cell house. In the 1896 building, guards entered the northeast corner. A similar entrance at the 1912 building opened from the southeast corner. It was a complicated matter entering the gun cages from these steep dark shafts, where metal ladders, attached to concrete walls, stretched perilously into the gloom. Guards changing shifts on the catwalk in Cell House 1 found a faster way to get down by scrambling across the bars separating the cells from the lobby and the door that led outside. They did this unthinking of the ample breach of security they were demonstrating to Jerry Myles and Lee Smart and the other men they were guarding. Details like that, while practically meaningless by themselves, conspire in the big picture to give fate its weight.

Corner towers on each cell house contained various rooms linked by steep narrow stairs. In Cell House 2, doors at floor level led to stairs that wound through the darkness to circular towers used primarily for storage. Those towers, about twelve feet in diameter, extended above the roofline of the cell house. At Cell House 1, rectangular towers at each corner with parapet-style roofs reached high above the roof. Each tower had four rooms, one above the other, reached through a stairwell that climbed from room to room. Over the years these rooms had been used as guard living quarters, isolation rooms, quarantine rooms and classrooms. Cramped, tomb-like and feebly decorated at ceiling height with wallpaper-like patterns painted over thick concrete, they resembled larger versions of custody cells. A steel door on the northwest tower's third floor opened to the catwalk inside the cell house. In 1958 and into 1959, Jerry Myles watched this door night and day. He intended to use it. Once again, such small details take on meaning in a prison.

The remaining structures faced each other from opposite ends of the enclosed yard. At the north end, near the newer cell house, a white one-story building housed the hospital and the automobile license plate plant.

On the south end of the prison yard was the majestic Clark Theater, the heart of prison culture. Bands performed. Artists painted. Community groups danced and sang for convicts. And convicts, like George Alton, boxed. To the west of the theater, near Tower 2 and the sally port with its castle-like doors that opened beneath it, was a small greenhouse.

This, then, was the complete view of Montana State Prison in 1959, as seen from the air: Two gigantic cell houses, linked by an institutional-white administration building, stretched all the way from south to north in the prison yard; a building housing a hospital on one end and a tag plant on the other filled the remaining space on the north end; the theater and a small greenhouse completed the south end. Convicts used the remaining pool of open land for running, boxing, shuffleboard, basketball, softball and weightlifting. This was ground formerly occupied by the vegetable garden where the pea riot had begun.

***

Down in the Bitterroot Valley of western Montana, nearly a year before Floyd Powell appeared in Deer Lodge, an unemployed former cafe owner heard of job openings at the prison. Everett Felix's family had moved to Corvallis from Minnesota when he was a year old. Except for seven years he spent working on an Air Force base in Alaska, and his military service in World War II that included the D-Day invasion, he had lived all of his life in Corvallis, a sleepy high-country town where early risers awoke to a canopy of stars.

The prison warden was Fay O. Burrell, Ravalli County's former sheriff. He owned a ranch near Corvallis, and when he came home to visit, word got around that he was looking for guards. Felix knew little about the prison, but he drove to Deer Lodge to walk the wall.

In October 1957 he started working night shifts. Like all new guards who rode the river of nameless faceless people into Montana State Prison, Felix felt bewilderment in his strange new surroundings. He was a plain man, rail-thin and balding and unadorned by title or reputation. He now had a steady paycheck, however small it was, and he moved his family into an apartment building that in its heyday had been one of Deer Lodge's best mansions, replete with a ballroom on its top floor.

Autumn nights grew colder. Felix worked from a yard tower outside the entrance to Cell House 1. He came on duty with the third shift at 10 o'clock, and while convicts slept, secured behind locked cell doors, Felix and other guards passed away the night smoking cigarettes and playing cards on wooden benches in a round yard tower. Once an hour they prowled the cell houses with flashlights where they walked each galley's full length, counting the men in their beds. Their lieutenant, usually Pete Lynch, logged their totals on a count sheet to make sure nobody was missing.

Night shift guards roused the kitchen crew at four o'clock. These "short line" bakers and cooks slipped like ghosts from the sleeping galleys into the dining hall below the administration building. When "main line" convicts started for breakfast shortly after dawn, an aroma of fresh bread filled the cell houses.

One officer patrolled the dining hall floor, watching for misbehavior. Sometimes another guard watched from a gun cage in the southeast corner of the rectangular room. To get there, he climbed through a trap door inside Tower 7, the main gate, before entering a tunnel that connected to the dining room. From inside the gun cage, built four feet off the floor in a semi-circle of inch-thick iron bars, he could see the room's full length.

Normally the gun cage guard carried a rifle, but it wasn't always loaded. Convicts quickly and accurately spread this information. Boldly, and with increasing frequency, they started food fights, throwing mashed potatoes, utensils and whatever else they found handy. Felix and other guards watched the prisoners' increasing attention to the rifles in the gun cage and on the catwalks in both cell houses. They didn't feel safe without the rifles. It was that kind of prison.

Convicts hounded Felix, as they did with every new guard. The bold ones stepped within hearing distance, their voices inaudible to anyone but him. Did he know someone was brewing intoxicating drinks in the kitchen? Did he want to stay home to avoid tomorrow's riot? Did he want protection in exchange for a favor? The gentle cafe owner from Corvallis didn't know how to react. His kind face, framed between oversized ears, showed the strain. Many days he walked home shaken by convict ridicule.

Their mastery troubled him, as would an undercurrent of discontent that rippled the river's surface now and again. This river of broken humanity haunted the man who knew restaurants and star-spangled skies. Fate would assign him a role in tragedy, as it would to Jerry Myles and Floyd Powell, Ted Rothe and Lee Smart, Walter Jones Jr. and George Alton, and all the others.

Two supporting casts numbered in the hundreds: poorly trained guards on one side, nameless faceless cons on the other. In 1959, few of these plain men in uniforms of blue on either side of the bars cramped their minds with the poetry of life. It had been this way for nearly ninety years. Montana State Prison was still the joint, still a place that broke men.

Everett Felix never could unload the psychological burden. Even in the closing year of his life, speaking aloud about an event that riveted his life to Jerry Myles, he wept.

***

Captain Everett Felix started his day shift at 8 o'clock on April 16. He too worked in Rothe's outer office, the busiest small room inside the prison. Felix hadn't planned on being captain of custody. He had worked at the prison only a year when he heard that Rothe intended to hire a new captain. The captain's job had been discontinued several years earlier, but now, with attention to reform, it was reinstated.

Persuaded to apply, Felix took the test. By early 1959 he found himself with new stripes on his jacket, promoted from officer to captain in one fell swoop. Lieutenants from each of three shifts reported to him. Felix reported to Rothe. At least twice a day, Felix walked outside the big wall, stopping to talk with each tower guard. He walked through each cell house, the women's prison attached to the west side of the main prison, and trustie dormitories and shops. It was Felix's job to know what was going on, and to make sure guards clearly understood orders. Felix liked working for Rothe and Powell. He remembered how things had been a sorry mess, in his words, when he had come to work under Burrell.

Shortly after Felix started work, George Axtell passed through Inside Administration on his way to the typing rooms in the 1912 cell house. An older, slight, bespectacled man, Axtell worked for the state Bureau of Motor Vehicles in the same building across

Main Street that housed Floyd Powell's office. Normally he taught general typing. On this day, his convict class would type automobile registrations. At Cell House 1 he entered a washroom in the southwest tower. From there he climbed stairs to bunker-like concrete rooms on the second and third floors where sixteen convicts would clack away on battered typewriters. Arriving too late to help Lee Smart as his mother envisioned, the typewriters had been brought into the prison when it became clear that prisoners could provide a measure of help to the clerical pool in the state offices across the street. Some who wanted to type couldn't read or write. Axtell taught them how to find letters on the keys.

On this day, he didn't have a full class. A runner brought notes from cell house guards that excused two of his typists for being sick. They would spend the day in their cells. One was Carl Frodsham, a Butte man convicted of child rape. Guards assigned to cell house custody recognized him by his artificial leg, which had been fitted to him after a car accident. They knew him, if not by name, as "the con with the wooden leg."

Walter Jones started work first thing in the morning, too. He dressed in a sport coat and tie, more administrative in appearance than anybody in the blue uniforms that surrounded him. He was a man who stood out: A shock of red hair, a craggy face, his scarecrow shoulders. While convict Carl Jensen and other carpenters constructed his new office, Jones set up temporary quarters inside the athletic office, a small room inside the yard entrance to Cell House 2. His new secretary, Gladys "Babe" Lightfoot, had a desk in the area where the carpenters worked. Other than female convicts housed inside the compound west of the prison wall, and matrons who guarded them, Lightfoot was the only woman who worked inside the prison. She wasn't bothered, although she brought paper towels from home to cover the toilet seat. One day a convict came close to her desk and whispered that in the event of trouble, she must grab her purse and leave without hesitation. She wondered what he meant.

***

175

Floyd Powell wanted a prison that looked like it meant business. Soon after he came to Deer Lodge, he had colorful draperies torn away from cell doors, believing they disguised frequent sexual encounters. Enterprising convicts who traded for paint and brushes through the black market had decorated their cells however they fancied. In the years before Powell's arrival, convicts and some guards pilfered maintenance parts and equipment and other supplies. Convicts stocked cells with stolen goods that would have been considered contraband at most prisons. Lacking suitable training or written policies, few guards could define contraband. Rare and often predictable shakedowns gave convicts comfort. They hid just about anything without concern about being caught.

George Alton, the Culbertson burglar, worked in the auto mechanics school where Officer Byars taught. Alton's father, a coal miner, had taught him how to repair car engines. Several days before April 16, Alton poured a few ounces of gasoline into a small bottle that he tucked inside his pants pocket. He was foremost a thief, and good at it. On his walks from the school beneath the theater at the south end of the prison yard, Alton avoided the few routine shakedowns by conning his way past the guards. Inside their cell, Alton and his cellmate Lee Smart constructed a cardboard shelf with a hollow middle. Each afternoon after work, Alton poured gasoline from his small bottle into a larger jar that they hid inside this shelf. By April 16 he had filled the jar.

Three days earlier, Smart asked Alton to come with him to Cell 19. Jerry Myles lived in that cell, which was on the same side of the galley, facing east, and two levels below the cell that Smart and Alton shared. The cell house grapevine contended Smart and Myles were lovers. Smart and Myles had celled together after Alton's escape, but Everett Felix and other guards split them up, hoping to end whatever was going on between them. Felix decisively called them "homosexual lovers" and knew them as constant companions. He sent them to different galleys in Cell House 1.

Alton, however, felt certain that nothing of the sort had gone on between Smart and Myles. He valued Smart, whom he called "Lee," as one of his best friends, but he referred to Myles by his last name or as "the queen." He couldn't believe that his friend would get mixed up that way with an old jocker like Myles.

Now Myles celled alone on Skid Row. This suited him just fine. Myles liked the company of young men, and his sprawling criminal past made testimony to that point, but he liked being alone even more. After nearly thirty years of prison life he was accustomed to solitary living. He could find a boyfriend whenever he pleased. Until Powell and Rothe took command he had enough freedom to romance men of his choosing. He liked Lee Smart, in fact thought he might be in love with him, and resented the guards for laughing.

Jerry Myles fumed over his decline in prestige and power. This wasn't his home anymore. However brief his stay in this prison had been, he already attached great importance to himself as a man who deserved more respect. Spalding and Rothe had humiliated him in the garment shop. Walter Jones warned young men to stay away from him. Now he couldn't live with his lover.

To any convict who would listen, Myles pontificated about his "gods" who wished on him "guts" to seize his destiny. For that reason convicts up and down the galleys felt the tremors of a forthcoming riot, causing a combustible reaction to what George Alton called the "wannabes" who had neither courage nor intellect to plan such a thing themselves but felt compelled to participate no matter the motive or outcome. Those forces churned and conspired. In 1959 they took names like Donald Toms and Carl Frodsham and Herman Cardinal and Jesse DeWeese. Jerry Myles, the loner and ringleader, had a supporting cast without asking.

This lonely man distrusted men around him, yet he wanted their trust in return. And so it was that in a private huddle with Lee Smart and George Alton inside his cell, Myles outlined his plan to escape the prison, although he didn't tell them that he had entered voluntarily. They would subdue guards, dress in their uniforms, and walk out Tower 7, which Myles and the others referred to as "the front gate." Myles spoke vaguely about fleeing to Argentina. He lied to Smart and Alton, telling them that wearing guards' uniforms had been his ticket out of USP Atlanta, and that it would work in

Deer Lodge. He neglected to tell them that he had given up without attempting to escape.

Back in their cell, Alton tried to discourage Smart. Alton said Myles was crazy to think such a plan would work. He distrusted Myles. Smart held fast, and Alton began to see that Myles held some power that resembled hypnotic influence over Smart. Unable to persuade Smart to see the folly, Alton decided to stand by his friend and cellmate, thinking he could protect him. But Alton, like Smart, tasted freedom. He remembered the exciting wild ride from Deer Lodge in a stolen state car just seven months earlier. Thinking about it made his heart pound.

***

No stranger to custody matters, Floyd Powell nonetheless reeled as he looked at the convict community he had inherited. When he assumed command in late summer, Montana State Prison housed about 540 convicts, ranging in age from sixteen to eighty. Only eleven of them were women. In this melting pot, nobody was separated by age or offense but only by gender. Because of this absence of classification, stronger, tyrannical offenders exploited younger, weaker ones. Convict leaders evaluated new prisoners as they arrived. From the moment a fish stepped into an induction room that was largely run by convicts, he was being assessed like property on an auction block. There, he was fingerprinted, then stripped, weighed and measured. Standing nude, he was inspected as a potential lover for the highest bidder. An examiner carefully noted tattoos and scars. The new prisoner was given new a blue shirt and trousers, socks and underwear, brown lace-up leather shoes and a coat, all made by one-time con boss Jerry Myles and his convict tailors.

The fish was assigned a number that would stand as his principal identification. Holding that number before him on a slate, he first looked ahead, and then turned to the side, as a convict photographer snapped his picture for the prison "big book," a chronological record of prisoners as they made their acquaintance with Montana State Prison.

News of a fish's arrival spread quickly, and because convicts saw most of their fellow prisoners' records, they bought and sold intimate details intended for confidential documents. Con bosses had the influence to collar particular fish for work in their industries, or for placement on their galleys. Sexual predators like Myles had humiliated some younger men to the point that they convalesced at the state mental hospital at Warm Springs, about thirteen miles south of Deer Lodge.

***

Floyd Powell came to Montana State Prison with a vision for rehabilitation. He wanted to do more than to bring order. He wanted to build a flagship prison, and from the start, he preoccupied himself with plans to build a new physical plant west of Deer Lodge. Construction had already begun on a new minimum security building on a treeless bench of foothills. The homely face of this plain cinder block building resembled progress, but it was a modest beginning to Powell's ambitious plans to relocate the entire prison in a spanking new state-of-the-art complex on that site. In his mind, Powell already had abandoned the territorial prison. After all, he was the reform warden, and men of such vision dwelled not on what was, but what could be.

Only weeks after his arrival in the summer of 1958, Powell met with news reporters to alert them to his intentions. Owen Gehrett of the *Silver State Post* and representatives from *United Press International, Associated Press*, and newspapers in Butte, Helena and Missoula came to the prison. He informed them that he planned to move the prison to the state-owned 33,000-acre ranch west of Deer Lodge, an intention he further confirmed in early December when he said he would recommend a $6.5 million building program to the Legislature when it convened in January. He eventually asked for about $1 million less than that, but Gehrett, who had concluded

Powell was not representing the people of Deer Lodge but his own ambitions instead, started a campaign of words against him.

On January 9, 1959, the *Silver State Post* reported: "The $5,243,755 budget request of Warden Floyd Powell for operation of Montana State Prison for the coming two years tops the list of all other state agencies – elective offices, administration departments, higher educational units and custodial institutions – by asking for a 319 percent increase in funds for the next biennium."

In an editorial that day, Gehrett called for a state investigation into Powell's administration, questioning both his motives and his competency. He called Powell a man of contradictions: alleging the warden knew little about farming (Powell had grown up with farming) but wanting to invest heavily in it; giving conflicting positions on removing the state Registrar of Motor Vehicle office from Deer Lodge (a political hot potato considering it was one of the town's larger employers), and not promoting his guards through the ranks as he had promised but hiring new guards for day shift, or first shift, and leaving guards of his predecessor on night shift.

A week later, Gehrett thundered again: "Already, from within the prison walls, are heard rumblings of unrest both from prisoners and from employees. Can such a situation be effectively controlled when a prison warden – given to errors of judgment, and to a lack of suavity, or perhaps tact, in his handling of personnel – does not answer directly to the will of the governor, the state board of examiners, or the people of Montana?" Gehrett, the Republican, was not a man without an agenda. Gehrett and Powell despised each other, but Gehrett owned the ink and a printing press. Powell later alleged that he silenced Gehrett by persuading some of the town's business owners to pull their advertising from the weekly newspaper. It was unclear who that might have been. Several guards petitioned the newspaper on Powell's behalf.

On April 10, 1959, the editor calculated twenty-one escapes from the prison over five years of the Burrell administration, but twenty-four more in the year since he had resigned. He wondered in print why the Legislature was considering a $900 annual pay raise for Powell.

Gehrett would not give the man he called "the Wisconsin expert" a moment's peace.

***

As Floyd Powell ate lunch with convicts on April 16, 1959, he relished his afternoon meeting with architects from Knight and Vantylengen, a Great Falls firm retained by the state Board of Prison Commissioners to develop plans for a new prison. They would be listening to his novel ideas. He would tell them that in less than eight months, Montana State Prison under his leadership had made great strides toward becoming a modern penal institution.

Despite what Powell and Rothe had accomplished – steps toward achieving a radical reform by historical measurements in Montana – they were years away from building the type of prison Powell envisioned. As leaders they saw the prison as it should be. Rank-and-file guards saw it for what it was.

In Wisconsin, the average length of service among guards was eleven years, eight months and twenty-three days. In Deer Lodge, it had been less than eleven months. The churn guaranteed that many of the Deer Lodge men were too new to know policies and procedures. Some guards who came to work on April 16, 1959, couldn't pronounce their fellow officers' last names, or didn't know their names at all. Some guards were too new to know convicts like Jerry Myles who had reputations for trouble. Those with lesser experience knew little about anything or anybody outside their immediate areas of responsibility. They hadn't been sufficiently oriented to fit pieces into the whole. Guards often traded shifts, and because of rampant sickness, absenteeism and walking off the job in the guard ranks, new faces frequently appeared.

Jerry Myles counted on confusion. He knew more about the guards than many of them knew about each other. He told Smart and Alton that he'd heard of the disagreement over the rifles, and that there was no better time to seize the prison. To him, the prison didn't look that secure. It was no Alcatraz, for sure.

He'd been watching the rifles, and the catwalks, and the new guards trying to learn their jobs. This was the time, he told Smart and Alton. The confusion would help them, as would a good plan, and Myles had one of those.

- 12 -

Jerry's Riot

They knew him as the best gopher man in the joint. Nobody could pick locks like Harold Laureys, inmate 17570. During the summer of 1958, Jerry Myles pestered Laureys to stand ready for any escape attempt that might come along. Within two months of his entrance into Montana State Prison, Myles joined with Lee Smart, Carl Frodsham, Jesse DeWeese and others to plan an escape on Thanksgiving. They had heard that Warden Powell had taken the rifles away from cell house guards, but when they saw a guard carrying a rifle as he patrolled the catwalk one day, they abandoned their plans, uncertain of whether the gun was loaded.

Myles suggested they delay their plans until springtime. He warned Laureys to be ready to pick the locks on doors below the Tower 7 leading out of the prison. Not wanting to get involved with Myles, Laureys confided to Deputy Warden Rothe that he was being pressured into trouble. Rothe moved Laureys to a trustie dormitory outside the big walls.

Laureys took advantage of Rothe's good graces and escaped. In March 1959 he spent fifteen days in isolation as punishment. The day he got out, Myles and Smart cornered him in the exercise yard. Myles said he and Smart had found a forty-five-caliber pistol they would use in a break. He said the gun had come into the prison hidden in a delivery truck, and that it was buried under a pipe beneath the floor in Old Siberia, a couple of isolated ground-floor cells on the northeast corner of the 1912 cell house. Myles didn't explain how he planned to retrieve the gun, because Old Siberia was fenced from the rest of the prison, but he promised to kill anybody who got in his way.

On April 9, a convict came to Laurey to tell him that Myles and Smart wanted to talk. Laureys went to Myles' cell on Skid Row, where he also found Donald "Tommy" Toms. Just twenty-three years old, Toms already in his young life had served prison terms in Virginia and Florida. Now he was doing five years for robbing sixty dollars from a man in Yellowstone County, Montana. Of Irish descent, Toms had flaming red hair. He spoke Spanish. He was a follower but quick to act behind another man's leadership, especially if that man were Jerry Myles. Toms looked fully involved. He spoke with passion about joining in an escape attempt. This time Myles talked about scaling the north wall between the hospital and the northwest cell house tower. He said they had a rope and would steal a ladder from the theater.

Laureys was unclear what they wanted of him. They didn't need a locksmith. A twenty-two-foot wall, barbed wire and a likely barrage of fire from armed tower guards would confront them, even if they escaped guards inside the walls. Myles had mentioned that someone would be waiting outside with a car, but he wouldn't say whom. Toms warned Laureys to stay silent about what he was hearing. Laureys replied that he doubted they would try to escape anyway. Myles said he was boss and Laureys could expect to follow his orders when the time came. Agitated, Myles threatened to cut Laurey's throat if he talked.

Early on the afternoon of April 16, soon after Warden Powell enjoyed his lunch in the convict dining room, Myles and Smart came to visit Laureys in his cell. Myles said the break would happen that afternoon. He told Laureys to stay inside his cell until further notice. An hour later, Laureys received an unsigned note from a convict runner. Later that afternoon, he was told, the cell doors would open, and when they did, he was to report to the desk on the flag, awaiting further instructions.

***

Jerry Myles was a big wheel. That had been evident to anyone who watched him operate. Fellow convicts felt naturally drawn to his force of personality. He was smarter than most of them. He could have put his intelligence to use as a teacher or a poet or a musician. He could have been a champion for improved conditions. He might have led men to better, more justifiable decisions about their lives, or even imparted that wisdom to himself and earned parole and lived a lawful life. Had he employed his intelligence for the public good, he would have been a bigger man than he had dreamed.

Walter Jones, until late 1958, knew little of Jerry Myles. They rarely spoke; Myles never came to Jones for counseling, nor did he seem outwardly conversational during chance meetings.

Jones interviewed Myles as part of his routine to build case files on all convicts at Montana State Prison. Concerned by inferences from that short interview, Jones wrote letters to other prisons where Myles had served time. A troubling profile emerged. Psychiatric evaluations of Myles as a "homosexual psychopath" stopped Jones cold. To Myles, sex was a weapon. Myles was inclined toward rape as a means of feeling superior to other men. Deprived of that, he reacted violently. If isolated, he would punish himself. If not, he would punish others. Jones recognized the potential of this violence and had concluded from the first reports mailed from other prisons that Myles was more dangerous than anybody in Deer Lodge realized.

That wasn't all. When the prison's disciplinary committee met in December 1958 to hear the complaint against Myles that led to his subsequent confrontation with Ted Rothe, another dimension of the man became clear. His strong intellect came across, as did his temper. When Myles threatened Ted Rothe, Jones felt certain he would act on his threat. Jones recognized Myles as an intelligent leader. At Deer Lodge and other prisons, he created problems to overcome his feelings of inadequacy. Once he felt wronged, he would use his abundant mind to find a way to command respect. That's why officials at USP Atlanta and Alcatraz Island had kept him isolated much of the time. He had little respect for the welfare of others. Being a self-possessed, antisocial person, he thought only of himself. Given the chance, he would create his own world, a world to his liking.

When Rothe decided to release Myles from segregation in late February, Jones implored him not to do it. "You're making a terrible mistake," Jones told the deputy warden. Rothe was unmoved. He told Jones that he and Floyd Powell believed that convicts should be treated equally and that Myles had been punished sufficiently. Jones argued that Myles had both the ability and the mental condition to lead a violent riot, but Rothe refused to compromise. Myles, he said, would be returned to Cell House 1. He would be given the same privileges as other convicts.

The psychopathic mind of Jerry Myles was not an uncommon one, although psychopaths, Jones would know from his college studies, could be polar opposites: law-abiding citizens or killers. Most of them shared fundamental characteristics, among them egotism and selfishness to the extreme, emotional detachment from other people that precluded feelings of guilt, and a tendency toward boasting and impulsive behavior. Not all psychopaths committed crimes. Jones would come to understand that business chief executives who closed entire divisions of their companies to get richer, destroying careers and livelihoods of hundreds of people without conscience, displayed psychopathic behavior. But so did Lee Smart, who killed a traveling salesman without remorse.

As his conversations with people in authoritative roles showed, Myles' glib and superficial charm was a common psychopathic trait. His self-deprecating notes to prison officials after his outbursts seemed to untrained observers to be light-hearted attempts to apologize and promise a more obedient course of action. To Jones, this behavior represented other traits of psychopaths: conning and manipulative thinking, lying, impulsiveness and shallowness toward consequential behavior. When he could get an audience with a prison official, and the higher in rank the better, Myles loved to pontificate about rules and regulations. It was clear he hadn't taken the time to understand them, but he felt inclined to complain about them anyway. His meetings at USP Atlanta had shown that, and his promises at Deer Lodge that he could put into practice what he learned at Alcatraz Island showed arrogance that was typical of psychopaths.

Jerry Myles never thought of parole as a privilege to be earned. He had no long-term goals nor did he care. His juvenile delinquency was a common psychopathic trait. He lacked a father in his life, which was another. He distanced himself from the Hunters, the only people who professed to love him. It seemed that because Jerry Myles didn't have a natural family, having been rejected by his natural parents, he didn't want any family at all. Prison was his family, if for no other reason than to make him feel worthy and powerful. That was the purpose of his existence.

***

In the days preceding April 16, yard officer Victor Baldwin watched convicts walk laps around the yard in perplexing patterns. In twos and threes they huddled close, intense in conversation. They frequently changed partners, continuing their walking pattern until recreation period ended. Baldwin didn't know what to think. He'd had but a little guard training since he left his smelter job in Anaconda eight months earlier. Watching these convicts as they walked, he realized he didn't know many of them, nor was he sure what they were doing. He recognized some men talking with other men they normally shunned. Rivals didn't mix.

At two o'clock on April 16, Lieutenant Charles Brown brought his second shift of custodial guards through the door at the base of Tower 1, from inside the minimum-security compound. A hulking bachelor in his mid-thirties, Charlie Brown wore the irreverent look of a schoolyard bully. Guards kidded him about the comic strip and the hit song by the same name. He felt some pride with that.

Like several other guards who hadn't married, Brown lived in the Guard Quarters a block down the street. He had earned his seniority. Responsible for prison operations until ten o'clock as second-shift lieutenant, Brown supervised the closing of shops and offices, and the activities that followed: short line and main line dinners, evening recreation and cell house lockdowns. It was an important job because guards of this shift had to watch convicts all over the prison. When Lieutenant Pete Lynch and his third shift officers came on duty at ten o'clock, they would guard a quiet, peaceful prison until the early stir of kitchen staff off "Cooks' Row" in the wee hours of April 17.

Twelve men assembled with Brown outside Tower 1: Officers Fred Dawson, Larry Cozzens, David Hinton, Lawrence Backman, James "Little" Jones, Vernon Kelpin, Chris Pletan, Ralph Knutson, Murry Giles, Thomas Stanford, George Schaffer and Ray Quilici. Dawson and Cozzens went to Cell House 2. Dawson worked as a relief officer, covering any shift when a regular officer had the day off. Today he would work as catwalk officer, with Cozzens as floor officer. Hinton, Kelpin and Pletan went to the 1912 cell house, where Hinton would walk the catwalk and Kelpin and Pletan, the floor. Jones, a turnkey, went to the lobby outside Deputy Warden Rothe's office where he would open and close steel security doors. Schaffer and Quilici went to the kitchen, Knutson to the nearby dining room. Giles and Backman, both relief officers, would go where needed; for Backman that meant Cell House 2, and Giles would spend much of his shift on bunkhouse detail in minimum security. Stanford, the yardman, walked a beat around the yard.

Among the guards entering towers was Harold Phillips, assigned to Tower 1. Everett Swecker assumed command of Tower 4, the large tower midway from north to south on the west wall.

***

Early on the afternoon of April 16, as Jerry Walker left his job in the prison laundry, Jerry Myles stopped him on the sidewalk. In a low voice, Myles told Walker of a "storm" planned for that afternoon that would include an escape attempt. Walker, convicted of grand larceny in Park County, was still just a skinny kid. He had served nearly a year of his three and a half year term. Although Walker had heard that the pea riot in 1957 started as a spontaneous response to conditions, he hadn't been there to witness it. Now

Myles was telling him this new riot was over conditions, particularly food, and Myles ordered Walker to help. "I'll help you to a certain extent and that's all," Walker later would relate to investigators, who reacted with skepticism.

Montana State Prison buzzed with rumors of that "storm" for several days preceding April 16. Everybody could feel the tension. Some men reacted with fear, others with giddiness. Myles, Smart and Alton had confided in certain men, carefully excluding others. Convict Charles Carlson later would report that Myles had said to him: "There is going to be some excitement. My boys are going to be in on it."

Despite what he preached about rioting over conditions, Myles didn't believe his own words. He couldn't train his thinking on a single plan because his anger toward Powell and Rothe tore at him with sharp monster claws. He knew only that he wanted trouble. They would remember Jerry Myles for what would happen on this day. He was certain of that.

In the privacy of his mind the plot grew bigger and better. He told different stories to different men, and offered more information to some than to others. He convinced Smart that to make an escape plan work, they needed to recruit more convicts to help them. Myles knew from his experience in Atlanta that he could widen the circle of involvement by lamenting prison conditions, even in ways that under close examination didn't make sense. He could stir up other convicts simply by blaming Floyd Powell and his staff for "taking things away" without having to be specific.

Myles needed George Alton, also known as "Little George," to pull it off. Respected as a straight talker, Alton enjoyed a wider following. Myles felt both power and resentment at knowing that. Alton's involvement would lend credibility to Myles and Smart. When trouble started, Alton would keep other convicts in line because he wanted more than anything to taste another wild dash into Montana's free air.

He had told Lee how it felt to escape, how it filled the heart to see nothing but open road ahead, gunning the motor on the stolen car and hearing it roar and riding that horsepower into the cool night. To see not bricks and stone, but blankets of trees blue as campfire smoke, and turning the radio dial to find more than one station (the music you like! Alton told him), and then turning it louder to hear it over the wind rushing through the open windows. This was what Lee Smart wanted to hear. He kept parked in his mind the stolen green Mercury with the red wheels that he had driven in northern Montana. It was a toy on the shelf, waiting for him to play.

Myles counted on these fantasies. Alton's previous escape had spoiled his judgment. Driving a state car out of the motor pool was one thing; taking hostages and escaping from inside the big walls was another. Still, Alton was a wiser man. Smart was a fool. He was a kid looking for a fling. He didn't need to understand the consequences. He only needed to be reminded that time was passing his teenage years away. He was forgotten by most of his family and friends and probably all of the rest of the world. He wanted to hit the road. He would follow Myles, and Myles knew it.

As Myles preached about poor conditions to those men on the periphery – men he decided would work in supporting roles – he told Smart and Alton that the intent of his plan was escape. Once he seized the inside, Myles told them he needed only to persuade the Tower 7 guard to lower a key to open the thick oak door beneath the tower. Myles remembered how the key drop worked when he entered the prison ten months earlier. After nearly thirty years in prisons, he took mental note of details like that. If they could get both outside doors open, they would be free men.

Myles told Smart and Alton that he had decided to include Toms and Walker to help them subdue the guards. Once dressed in their uniforms, they would huddle behind Ted Rothe, using him as a shield. To a clear-thinking man this plan would seem illogical and even ridiculous. If they held Rothe hostage the uniforms served no purpose. Smart listened to Myles like he was a genius, and Alton cared less about the details than the result. Both men, crazy with desire for the free ride, acted like bucks in rut.

Myles felt the power. It filled his senses with a familiar nicotine-like rush. He didn't care that he had lied. He didn't even know that he had lied. People listened to him again. He was the king boss.

In the summer of 1958, no more than a month after he entered Montana State Prison after his burglary conviction in Butte, Myles had told his new friend, Bo Sherman, about a so-called escape. He described in detail what he would do, and how he would capture the warden or deputy warden to lead him out. Sherman wondered why a man who committed a crime just to get into prison now wanted to get out. He took Myles' philandering to mean that he wanted to put on a show. Myles was trying to get noticed. Sherman saw it in a flash; in prison, a man hears a lot of con talk and mostly it's just that. As he got to know Myles, hearing more of that long prison history and his bold promises, he knew this swaggering short man, built like a bull, might throw his weight around someday.

On the day the riot would begin, Myles and Sherman didn't talk much anymore. Sherman distrusted Myles. In mid-afternoon, Officer Cozzens gave Sherman a pass in Cell House 2 to visit a parole officer in the fingerprinting room near Deputy Warden Rothe's office. When Sherman returned, Cozzens had left for dinner. Sherman went to his living quarters, Cell 7, the fourth cell from the corner on the east side and south from the floor desk where Cozzens, and now Victor Baldwin, kept vigil. Sherman slid into a rocking chair, facing away from the desk, to watch four of his cell house mates play a furious game of dominos.

Myles told Smart and Alton the riot would start about 3:30 when guards started taking turns for dinner. Myles knew they left the main prison to eat; their dining room was inside the minimum-security dormitory outside the main prison's south wall. The ringleaders rightly recognized this as a weak link in custody because the inside guard force dropped to fewer than ten in the comings and goings. Guards less familiar with certain convicts and various custody rules took over for thirty minutes.

The window for revolt was a small one. At 3:50 as usual, floor officers would order convicts onto their galleys and into their cells. In Cell House 1, Officer Erwin Seiler would pull levers that would close doors on all twenty-five cells on each of eight galleys in one clatter. Shortly after that, acting sergeant Chris Pletan would return to feed the "short line," releasing protective custody convicts for their evening dinner. After their return and lockup, Pletan would open other galleys for main line.

Inside the older Cell House 2, at 4:10, runners would bring meals for isolation convicts. For two hours, convict cooks had prepared the evening meal under direction from Assistant Steward George Schaffer. Officer Quilici watched kitchen workers and Officer Knutson supervised waiters who set tables. Soon they would stand in the midst of hundreds of prisoners. A beef aroma drifted into the cell houses.

All the shops had closed. Convict Jim Gaines Jr., the prison's head painter, had two men working in the new wing, another in the kitchen. In the old wing, Clifford Amdahl painted floors inside two cells before quitting for the day. One convict crew after another checked tools with guards, who took inventory, locked the tools in cupboards and returned keys to Sergeant Cox in the captain's office.

In Cell House 1, men played ping-pong along Skid Row on the east side. One of them was Carl Frodsham, a man of Swedish-Irish ancestry. The twenty-three-year-old Butte native and former ranch hand had served more than six years for forcing a six-year-old girl into oral sex in 1953. Sentenced to forty years, he ranked near the top in cell house seniority but because of his crime, at the bottom in the prison pecking order. A car wreck near Butte had ripped off his right leg eight inches below the knee.

On the afternoon of April 16, Frodsham borrowed Jerry Myles' chess set for a game with friends, and after returning the set to Myles' cell, played ping-pong with Donald Toms and Roger LaVe.

George Alton had known Frodsham since they were kids at the state reformatory for boys at Miles City. Now, as adults, they stayed mostly separated, observing unspoken rules. "Ray-po" was what Alton called Frodsham. Myles and Alton planned to use Frodsham during their break, but they hadn't told him anything. As he battered a ping-pong ball, Frodsham didn't realize what was about to happen above him.

On the west side, barbers clipped away in their little shop between Cooks' Row and the outside wall of Cell House 1. Up and down the galleys in both cell houses convicts played cards, dominos, chess and checkers. Some of them slept, others read. In the 1896 cell house, except for two galleys of isolation and segregation cells, other grating doors stood open, allowing men to move from galley to galley and cell to cell.

Both big cell houses rang with loud talk, whistles and catcalls. In this community of hard men, they consummated the day's business. Favors exchanged hands. They settled grudges, nurtured new ones. It was a buying and selling atmosphere. They bet cigarettes, bartered belongings (pinups of nude women being a thing of value) and promised cash for protection and retribution. Men met their friends and avoided their enemies. It was a time for relaxation and a time for being careful, and in prison it could be both at once.

Inside the theater across the yard, Harry Walks On Top boxed inside the ring on stage. Walks on Top looked forward to his next fight against an outside boxing club. Training was serious business. He planned to return to his cell house, the new wing, before four o'clock.

Most everybody that afternoon knew trouble was in the air, but they didn't know it was imminent. Harold Laureys and other designated helpers for Myles, Smart and Alton mixed quietly in the hubbub, watching for a signal. They waited nervously, wondering how it would start. They knew Floyd Powell and Ted Rothe to be unforgiving men when wronged. An angry reaction from the czar and his top man scared them as much as Myles and Smart and their reckless disregard for the consequences.

At 3:15, Officer Fred Dawson stood on the catwalk on the west side of Cell House 2, in the doorway that separated isolation cells from the remaining cells to the north. He saw Lee Smart and another convict enter the cell house. They ran up the stairs and out of view. Convicts from Cell House 1 weren't allowed in the older block, and Dawson recognized Smart by appearance and knew he didn't belong there. Employed eleven and half months to the day, Dawson knew most convicts on sight. Suspicious, he walked down the catwalk to the north end and then to the northeast corner above Cozzens' desk. He dropped a note of warning to Cozzens as he watched Smart walk down Galley 7 on the east side.

Cozzens climbed the block to look for Smart, but he found only a young convict named Don Lee Smith. Dawson returned to his post near the door to isolation, on the south end of Cell House 2, awaiting Lawrence Backman to relieve him for his dinner break. At dinner, Dawson and Cozzens talked about Smart. They both wondered what he was doing and where he had gone.

***

At 3:15, carpenter Ira Barnes put down his tools at the south end of Inside Administration, where he was helping remodel an office for Walter Jones. He went to Cell House 1, climbing stairs to his cell on Galley 5 level with the catwalk. His cell, 215, was eighth from the south end. Barnes didn't see anything unusual. He got clean socks, underwear and a towel and then went for a shower. From his vantage point beneath open showers on the ground floor's north end, Barnes saw Officer David Hinton standing above him in the catwalk's northeast corner, watching convicts below him.

At 3:30, James Braby left his job at the garment shop and returned to Cell House 1, where he asked a floor officer for two aspirin before going to Cell 238 on Galley 6. He saw Officer Hinton climbing to Galley 6 from the catwalk across steel bars that stretched from floor to ceiling.

These "monkey bars" screened the entire cellblock from the flag, or lobby, that led outside. Grating doors opened onto each galley from a zigzag of metal stairs on the south side of the block. Supposedly guards entered the catwalk from doors inside the gun cages, but instead they took shortcuts by climbing across those tall bars. In Cell House 2, guards entered the catwalk from a door that opened outside at the southeast corner near Tower 1. Only occasionally did a guard permit a convict to step onto a catwalk. That was only for cleaning. As Braby watched Hinton climb the bars above the barbershop, he also saw Officer Byars standing outside the gun cage in the southeast corner. Hinton, he knew, was going to dinner. Byars would spell him.

Shortly before 3:30, Herman Cardinal, a convict plumber, went to work in the "well" between east- and west-facing cells in Cell House 1. Carrying wrenches and other tools, he faded into the dark web of pipes that ran water up and down the galleys. He heard the grating door that opened onto the flag slam behind him; a key turned in the lock. A former Anaconda smelter worker, Cardinal built a reputation as a habitual criminal. In 1955 he robbed an Anaconda man of his keys, money and bus tickets. On July 30, 1957, on the morning of that summer's disturbance, he escaped. Caught a week later in Ogden, Utah, Cardinal waited for a guard to drive him back to Deer Lodge.

Officer George Morris, fifty-two years old, got the job but he was sent alone. When Fay Burrell was warden it was standard practice to do this and all the guards knew it wasn't safe. Morris was expected to round up Cardinal and two other escapees. Ten miles west of Drummond, in western Montana, his escapees asked to relieve themselves. When Morris stopped his car, they threw him to the ground. After stealing his thirty-eight-caliber revolver, his wallet with thirty dollars and a sport shirt, they left him handcuffed and leg-ironed in an old cabin near Maxville, south of Drummond, and fled in his state-owned car. Morris crawled back to the highway where he flagged a motorist. Police caught Cardinal a week later in Los Angeles, and after a brief parole the following summer, he beat somebody up and was returned to prison. No stranger to weapons or to impulsive acts, Cardinal was a man to watch.

Meanwhile, Officer Marvin Wallace closed various shops. After taking his keys to Bill Cox, he hurried into Cell House 1 to relieve Officers Pletan and Kelpin for their dinner break. Officer Sieler, who had worked outside with the yard crew for most of the day, was already there, sitting at the scarred wooden desk on the flag below the gun cage.

In Cell House 2, a convict shouted to Officer Dawson where he stood inside the gun cage on the southeast corner, asking when Officer Backman would relieve him for dinner. Dawson looked at his watch, noted it was 3:30, and shouted back to the convict that he expected Backman soon. Dawson thought nothing of it. Catwalk guards kept a running dialogue with convicts on their galleys. He watched the convict turn around the corner of Galley 5 and disappear. A moment later, Backman appeared, and Dawson took the stairs leading to the outside door and hurried away. He and other guards had only thirty minutes for dinner, and that included their walking time through the wall beneath Tower 1 to the minimum-security compound.

As Backman took Dawson's place, Cox walked into Cell House 2 in search of convict Edsel Dodson, who had failed to come to the Deputy Warden's office for his medication. Cox was scheduled to leave at two o'clock, but he decided to stay until Deputy Warden Rothe returned from his meeting at Warden Powell's house across the street. He didn't know exactly when Rothe would come back inside, but figured the deputy would arrive in time to eat dinner with the convicts. As Cox looked for Dodson, Officer Baldwin relieved Officer Cozzens for his dinner break. Cozzens knew Baldwin well. Baldwin was married to his sister.

At almost the same instant, Officer Clinton Fowler locked the library and went outside to relieve yardman Tom Stanford. In a matter of minutes, six guards assigned to Lieutenant Brown's meager afternoon shift had left the main prison.

Jerry Myles watched them go.

- 13 -

Jerry, Lee and the torch

Roger LaVe, waiting on the flag with Carl Frodsham to play ping-pong, happened to glance upward. Outside the last cell on the north end of Galley 5, two men he knew as Jerry Myles and Lee Smart stood like lords, surveying the crowd below them. It was a busy time in Cell House 1. Men occupied all the galleys. Some talked with friends. Others leaned on the railings, locking shoes on the bottom rung, and stared through the windows at the sprinkle of residential streets and the blue mountains behind the town. Unlike the men around them, Myles and Smart hinted a sense of purpose, as if waiting for something to happen.

They made an odd couple to anyone who cared to notice. One swaggered along on short feet, his body built like a panel truck driven on tires too small. The fray and wear of middle age showed in his dark arresting eyes and on the gray flare of his temples. Despite his mashed nose and his balding pate and a drooping belly, he looked strong as a bull. By comparison, the younger man strutted on crane-like legs in an air of youthful nonchalance. He walked like he knew where he was going. He wasn't much of a physical specimen. His drooping shoulder and faint chin made him look weaker than he was. In blocky prison clothes he was a fencepost, all straight up and down. The crack of his butt winked over his sagging overalls.

As different as Myles and Smart looked from one another, they shared a deep malevolent mission that was something more than a sexual attraction. Men who knew Smart's penetrating eyes saw

197

something terrible behind them. It came from something ugly within him, or it wasn't him at all. Myles had a saner look about him, maybe only because he was smarter and wiser. He was old enough to be Smart's father. For all their physical differences, they shared a haunting aura of psychotic disturbance, unfettered by social conscience. They were much the same man.

***

Carl Frodsham lived in Cell 41 on Skid Row, several cells north of Myles in Cell 19. Each side of the new block had four galleys of twenty-five cells each. The third level, Galley 5, started with 201 and ended with 249, where Alton and Smart had bunked before Alton's escape. Even-numbered galleys and cells on the west side started with Cell 2, the first on Cooks' Row near the barred door that led to the flag. These 200 cells housed more than 300 men on April 16.

Galley 5, where Smart and Myles waited at 3:30 that afternoon, was level with the catwalk on the east wall of Cell House 1. The catwalk ran 236 feet from north to south, and forty-nine feet on the ends. On the northwest portion of the catwalk, across from Cell 248 on Galley 6, a steel door led into cell house tower near an isolation room that guards and convicts called the "TB Ward," a place where tuberculosis patients once had been quarantined. That door, like every other door in Cell House 1, was locked. It was welded shut, too.

Myles realized the security shortcomings of this catwalk right away. It was much too close. It wasn't enclosed with bars or wire. Only a horizontal metal-pipe railing lower than a man's waist, similar to galley railings, separated the guard from his potential captors. It was common practice to store soap inside the gun cage, often called the "soapbox," and for catwalk guards to toss the soap to convicts on the galleys. Myles and Smart had watched this happen many times.

A guard pointing his rifle at someone standing across from him would fire point-blank, but in such close quarters he needed to make every shot count. Convicts had watched the ease and speed with which guards climbed across the "monkey bars" grating from the catwalk to the galley. Nothing prevented them from doing the same. Nothing, maybe, except a catwalk guard who would shoot his rifle.

Being a careful student of prison mutinies, Myles in nine months had already calculated every security weakness at Montana State Prison. In his mind, he knew more than every other man, including Powell and Rothe, about timing and surprise. Myles saw around him a sea of buffoons unschooled in sophisticated breaks. That was the prison world according to Jerry Myles. He would show them. Jerry's riot would be bigger and better. It would grab more headlines. He wanted revenge, too. Ted Rothe had embarrassed him in front of other convicts. He felt wild with excitement at the prospect of humiliating Rothe.

***

Myles remembered clearly the most famous prison mutiny at Alcatraz Island. He had watched it from his cell. On May 2, 1946, longtime federal inmate Bernie Coy seized the main cell house with help from five men who were serving a total of 283 years plus three life sentences. Coy arrived at Alcatraz in 1937 to serve twenty-five years for Depression Era bank robbery. He was a Kentucky hillbilly and, reputedly, a crack shot with a rifle. His sharecropper parents treated him cruelly. He first did time at Kentucky State Prison, then at USP Atlanta. Myles didn't know Coy especially well, but he knew of his background. In some ways, they were similar men. Both men broke laws by stealing, but neither, at least on record, had killed anyone or assaulted a police officer. Both had artistic leanings; Coy painted Kentucky landscape scenes, Myles played the violin and wrote tortured poetry. Having both been confined at USP Atlanta and Alcatraz Island, they belonged to a rare fraternity of dangerous and agitated convicts. From the time Alcatraz opened in 1934 until it closed in 1963, only 1,576 men lived there.

At Alcatraz, Coy waited for lunch relief before climbing to a catwalk where he pried apart the bars. He squeezed his slight body through a narrow opening before surprising the catwalk guard and taking his rifle. Myles and other Alcatraz convicts marveled at how he accomplished that feat. Knowing what Coy had done at Alcatraz, Myles looked across to an unprotected catwalk at Montana State Prison and laughed.

A month earlier, in February, Smart fretted about how they would subdue a catwalk guard. Smart asked how, even at a short distance, that they could catch the guard before he escaped into the gun cage. Towers 1 and 7 on the big wall loomed outside broad windows above the east catwalk. They saw guards out there wearing holsters, sometimes holding rifles or shotguns. Smart asked Myles what unarmed convicts could do against a show of force like that. Without hesitation, Myles spoke one word: "Fire!"

***

Within a minute after Officer David Hinton left the catwalk for his dinner on the afternoon of April 16, Officer Gus Byars walked northward from the gun cage, and as fate would have it, stopped across from Jerry Myles and Lee Smart on Galley 5. Byars, a husky man with keen eyesight, turned away to open a window to the spring wind. The air in Cell House 1 felt stuffy. From where he stood, he could see city streets and the Deer Lodge Mountains rambling through the background. In the mid-afternoon sunshine it was a pretty picture.

Somebody called him by name. Then came a moment of fate. Such moments come without warning and inside a prison thousands of those moments and transactions constitute a routine and routine feigns innocence and that's where trouble begins. Even routine can be dangerous, as Byars knew and every other guard knew, but he turned impulsively, and as he wheeled toward Galley 5, gasoline splashed into his face. Blinded, he groped for the railing. His eyes burned with a fury. Gasoline soaked through his shirt, stinging his chest.

A young man's voice called to him, and although Byars couldn't see who spoke, he recognized Lee Smart's words. He knew Smart well. The boy was one of Byars' best students in the auto school. He had done his work without complaining. Smart's quiet agreeable behavior surprised Byars because around the cell house, Smart acted like a punk.

Smart surprised himself. He figured Byars would notice what they planned to do and run, but unexpectedly, Byars stopped at the window. Pitching George Alton's stolen gasoline, Smart hit Byars squarely in his face and chest. In his psychopath's mind he felt no remorse at assaulting his teacher. He felt nothing at all. Myles had told him what to do and he did it.

As Smart threw the gasoline, Myles struck a match. He lighted clothing wrapped around a mop head and leaned from Galley 5, pushing the torch toward Byars. Myles and Smart hadn't planned to set Byars afire but to scare him into surrendering. They didn't care, either, if he burned. They felt no emotion about it at all.

Instinctively, Byars tried escaping north on the catwalk, his left hand gripping the railing for guidance, but through his clouded eyes he saw flame in front of him. He wanted to break loose and run to where he could toss his keys through a window. He remembered that much from his limited training. Like many guards, Byars had worked at Montana State Prison for less than a year. In fact, he had worked there only nine months. A few lectures hadn't prepared him for a real riot. Stiff with terror, he now realized he could become a human torch.

As Myles waved the fire to discourage Byars from running, George Alton helped Smart set fire to a broom, which Smart threw onto the catwalk. Through his clouded eyes Byars saw fire on either side of him. Farther down the galley, Alton jumped onto the grill bars. He swung across to the catwalk in a matter of seconds. Myles handed his torch to Smart and ran down the galley to follow Alton. Convicts standing on the galley below them, including James Buckley, saw the action up close. Buckley, who minutes earlier had entered Cell House 1 after a day's work with the yard crew, stood in front of Cell 149, below the cell that Smart and Alton once shared. He saw the stick of fire and watched Alton scoot across the monkey bars to the catwalk.

Convicts who had gathered around the ping-pong table on Galley 1 smelled gasoline. They looked up to see Alton leap onto the catwalk and run north toward Byars. Myles propelled his stocky frame across the grill to the catwalk and, a knife visible in his hand, stomped after Alton. Before Byars could kick the broom torch off the catwalk, Alton grabbed it. Waving it, he demanded that Byars surrender his keys to the gun cage.

"Don't burn me!" Byars pleaded, sensing a second man's presence on the catwalk. All three men now played out their drama across from Cell 245. Balls of fire waved on either side of Byars. Myles wanted the rifle. He leaned close to Byars' ear. "You might as well give it up," he told the frightened guard. "I have a very sharp knife and I'll use it." Byars fumbled in his pocket to find his keys. He felt someone jerk them away. Alton tried to open the gun cage in the southeast corner but he couldn't find a key that would fit the lock. From down on the floor, several convicts watched Alton turn and run back to Byars, twist his arm behind his back, and take another set of keys.

When Alton opened the door, he went straight to the metal cabinet at the back of the cage. He couldn't find the right key and called to Smart, who threw down his torch and crawled across the grill. They found a key that fit the cabinet. Myles, meanwhile, led Byars down the galley nearly to the gun cage door. Alton emerged with a rifle. When Smart crawled across the monkey bars back to Galley 5, Alton threw the rifle across to him.

They had subdued Byars within two minutes, exactly as Myles had foreseen. Prodded by knives and threats of death, Byars climbed onto the grill and struggled across, his unseeing eyes stinging and hot.

***

When Jerry Walker saw Smart throw gasoline at Byars, he and another convict, Mike Maciel, crept behind Officers Sieler and Wallace where they sat at the floor desk below the gun cage and opposite from the west-facing yard door on the south end of Cell House 1.

Sieler had watched Byars replace Hinton on the catwalk. Sieler had come first to relieve Officers Pletan and Kelpin. Wallace showed up minutes later after closing the garment shop, the carpenter shop and the laundry, all of which he supervised. Wallace had spent six weeks working in towers. Except for convicts who worked in his shops, he didn't recognize many faces. But he did know Walker, from the laundry crew. Sieler sat behind the floor desk. Someone asked for socks. Sieler reached into a drawer for a pair. Wallace took a chair at the corner of the desk. From where they sat, Sieler and Wallace could watch all entrances including stairs leading to all eight galleys, the locked double door to their left that led into the dining room, and in front of them the large door leading outside.

Another convict approached Wallace, holding out a cloth bag that he said contained radio equipment. He asked for permission to take it to the radio room in the cell house tower. Wallace looked into the bag. Distracted for a second, he didn't see Maciel behind him. Maciel grabbed Wallace by his hair, jerked his head back, and pressed a knife against his neck. With his face aiming upward, Wallace's eyes locked on the clock, which said 3:35. At the same instant, a knife flashed in front of Sieler's face. "There's a riot, give me the keys," Walker told him.

Watching Walker, Sieler didn't realize Wallace was being held at knifepoint. Sieler stood up. "You're fooling, put that knife away," he told Walker. Maciel pressed his knife into Wallace's skin, deep enough to cut, and Wallace called out to Sieler. "It's no use in fooling. He's got me here by the throat. Give him the keys."

Sieler fished in his pocket. He had two sets, but handed just one to Walker. This ring included a key that unlocked the door to the Hole under the cell house. This seemed to satisfy Walker and Maciel; they didn't ask for other keys. Convicts who carried hammers, clubs and homemade knives appeared, as if on cue. They steered their hostages toward the Hole, entered through a single door in a corner of the flag. Concrete stairs descended into humid, stale tomb-like rooms, an area familiar to all cell house guards. To the left was a dark cell.

Minutes later Sieler and Wallace smelled gasoline. Byars came down the stairs. Fumes from his drenched hair, coat and shirt filled the unvented enclosure. Within five minutes, Jerry Myles and his crew had seized Cell House 1.

The riot had begun.

***

Isolated inside the typing room, where no windows or doors opened from the tower into the cell house, George Axtell had no idea of trouble. He excused his class at 3:30 as usual. It had been a routine day, except for some peculiar absences.

Ten minutes later Axtell walked down the stairs, carrying a sheaf of completed motor vehicle registrations. A squat graying man he didn't recognize, but whom he later learned was Jerry Myles, stepped in front of him. "The boss wants to see you in the cell block," Myles told him. Thinking Myles meant the sergeant on duty, Axtell stepped into the cell house. Just as the door swung shut behind him, someone struck him in the middle of his back, knocking him to the floor. Axtell, a thin and frail man, tried to stand. Someone hit him again, and then kicked him, and he heard a low voice: "Get down the stairs." In front of him, the door to the Hole stood open. He felt a push. He stumbled and rolled down the stairs, pain and gasoline fumes jarring his senses.

At 3:35, Lieutenant Brown passed time with a few convicts in Cell House 2 before going to dinner. Behind him, he heard a voice: "Brown, they want to see you down in the new cellblock."

Brown didn't know who had spoken, but his job required him to move around the prison solving problems. It wasn't unusual to be summoned to one building or another. And so it was that Brown walked outside on his fateful journey toward Cell House 1 on the long sidewalk. Halfway, he met Captain Felix, who was leaving his office in Inside Administration to make his rounds.

Minutes earlier Felix had talked on the telephone with his wife Amy Lee. She called him "Guff," like "don't give me guff," and it seemed a fitting nickname for a man who worked in a prison. She was at the bank trying to secure a fifty-dollar bank loan. The Felixes owed a tax debt because the prison hadn't withheld enough money from his paycheck. The bank clock, she remembered, said 3:30; she had timed her call to catch him before dinner began in the prison. As Brown approached, Felix stood at the foot of concrete steps outside.

"I was called down to the new cell house. What's wrong down there?" Brown asked Felix, who didn't know either. Together, the two highest-ranking officers inside the prison at that moment walked to Cell House 1 to investigate.

From his post on Tower 4, Officer Everett Swecker watched Brown and Felix walk north. Better than other tower guards, Swecker could see entrances to both cell houses: one framed by the theater to his right, the other, by the hospital and tag plant to his left. Straight across the recreation yard from his tower stood the chalky face of Inside Administration. It was Swecker's job to detect unusual behavior. A minute before Brown met Felix, Swecker watched four or five convicts playing catch with a baseball near Cell House 1 remove their gloves and go indoors. To Swecker this seemed a bit strange. On warmer days convicts stayed outside until the guards, like perturbed parents, told them to quit.

From Swecker's vantage point everything else seemed fine. Earlier he had watched Officers Hinton, Kelpin and Pletan leave Cell House 1 and walk south along the sidewalk that sliced between Cell House 2 and the theater, toward the Tower 1 gate that led into the compound to the guards' dining room.

Nearing Cell House 1, Brown didn't notice anything unusual, other than a recreation field empty of convicts. He and Felix strolled into Cell House 1. Once they stepped through the entryway, prisoners with knives surrounded them. In front of them, Lee Smart stood near the levers that opened cell doors. He pointed a rifle at them. Alton approached with a knife. He searched Brown, taking his keys. Felix felt two knives. Myles pressed from the left, Frodsham from the right.

"This is a riot!" Myles informed him with some urgency, and Felix could see a flush of excitement in his face. "Don't try anything and you won't get hurt."

Myles stopped Brown at the doorway to the Hole. Brandishing a linoleum knife sharpened to a shine, he stepped close and pushed his knife against Brown's belly, just below his ribs. "Charlie, tell me where those shells are for that gun," he said. Brown tried to fool Myles and replied that he thought guards kept shells in Tower 7, on the big wall.

"Don't lie to me," Myles warned him. "Don't make me have to kill you." Brown told him again that the rifle didn't have shells. Myles looked at Brown curiously, as if a new thought occurred to him. "You bastard, you know that the rifle in the old wing has shells, don't you?"

Brown tried to stall him. "I don't know about the old wing," he said. Myles pushed him into the stairwell to the Hole with a parting comment that chilled the lieutenant: "If anyone comes in we've got gasoline and we're going to burn you up. We have three gallons of gasoline." Felix, meanwhile, saw Officer Byars and found his pale appearance disturbing. He comforted a dazed and bruised George Axtell. Shaken by the quick turn of events, Felix barely noticed Sieler, and he didn't remember seeing Wallace at all. Now six men fumed under a single light bulb's feeble light.

About the time Felix and Brown appeared in the Hole, Assistant Steward George Schaffer left a storeroom beneath the kitchen. This storeroom butted against the Hole, but a locked metal door separated these rooms, and none of the men heard each other. The kitchen, bakery and dining hall consumed all the space in the basement of the Inside Administration building. When Schaffer climbed the steps from the storeroom, the kitchen looked normally busy. His convict helpers were ready to open the short line. As he walked through the kitchen door into the dining hall, he felt a sharp prod in his ribs.

Donald Toms, pressing close to him, told him to give himself up. Unsure what was happening, Schaffer shot back: "Get that shiv out of my ribs." Waving to the aisle that led to Cell House 1, Toms growled, "I mean it. Upstairs!" As he turned into the aisle, Schaffer came face to face with Lee Smart, who shoved a rifle barrel against his chest. Schaffer became the seventh hostage. Toms escorted him to the Hole.

At 3:30, Officer Clinton Fowler, relieving Tom Stanford, began walking a beat around the exercise yard. A few minutes later he walked into Cell House 1 where he saw Gus Byars standing on the east catwalk halfway between the north and south ends. Officers Wallace and Sieler sat at the desk under the gun cage. Byars hollered down to Fowler that he had forgotten his uniform jacket in the auto mechanics school beneath the theater. Fowler volunteered to retrieve it. His walk to the theater and back took less than ten minutes. When Fowler walked into Cell House 1, Myles and Alton grabbed him at knifepoint.

From where Officer Ralph Knutson stood with his back turned to the kitchen, he hadn't seen Toms capture Schaffer. Minutes earlier, about 3:45, Carmen Jack Linton, Deputy Warden Rothe's runner, left Rothe's office with three other convicts to eat dinner on the short line. Officer Jones opened the inside grating door for him. The outside grating door stood open, unlocked. After descending outside steps to the yard, Linton turned to his right and took a shorter flight of steps down to the dining hall. This was the only yard entrance to the dining room. Linton, a forger serving his second sentence, got his tray and went to the serving line. Before he got to eat, Lee Smart appeared from the kitchen, carrying a rifle. George Alton followed him with a knife.

About five minutes had passed since Linton left Rothe's office. The short line had opened, right on time. It was 3:50, the time when convicts in both cell houses would be locked in their cells except for those designated to eat in the short line. And most of them were, except that Myles, Smart and Alton, hoping to avoid chaos that would tip off their intentions, had done the locking.

Being a new officer, Knutson didn't know many prisoners by name, even though he had seen hundreds of them eating at orderly rows of tables. Knutson's growing family included a kindergartener, his oldest child; his wife was pregnant and due soon. He found it hard to be gone from home in the evenings but the clatter and rush of dinner at the prison passed time quickly.

As Knutson turned to watch convicts work their way through the short line, Ramon Gonzales, who worked in the dining hall, thrust a shiv against his stomach. "This is a freeze," Gonzales said. Not understanding the man's words but comprehending his wild-eyed look, Knutson stumbled backwards about fifteen feet, trying to put distance between them. Gonzales signaled other convicts to join him.

For the first time, Knutson saw somebody at the first table by the front door through which Linton had entered. This man, a pimply-faced teenager that Knutson later learned was Lee Smart, sat quietly, staring at him. It was the kind of stare that portended danger. Defeated, Knutson surrendered to Gonzales who led him northward toward the front serving counter. Alton searched Knutson before Gonzales forced him into Cell House 1, where a gamut of armed convicts shoved their ninth hostage toward the door leading into the Hole.

It was nearly 4 o'clock when Sergeant Cox, on his return trip from Cell House 2, saw Myles, Smart and Toms standing outside the entrance to Cell House 1. They called to him to come talk. No, Cox yelled back. If they wanted to talk they could come upstairs. Convict Dodson followed Cox up the steps into the vestibule. Officer Jones let Cox through the inside grating door and locked it. Dodson stood outside, waiting for his medicine. Cox handed Dodson his prescribed three pills through the grating door and then Dodson left. Cox sat down at his desk outside Rothe's office.

***

Warden Powell at that moment ended his afternoon meeting with the architects who were designing Montana's new prison. They had come to his house where they could spread drawings across Powell's big state-owned dining room table. While Powell and Business Manager Elmer Erickson walked across the street to their offices, Ted Rothe went to Tower 7, where he unclipped a brass key lowered on a rope by a tower guard standing on the wall. Rothe disappeared into the prison. He wanted to finish some paperwork in his office before he went to the dining room for dinner.

- 14 -

Hostages, like dominos

When Ted Rothe decided to return to his office inside the prison, most officers assigned to Charlie Brown's second shift had finished their suppers in the guards' dining room and had re-entered the main prison, taking the key from Officer Harold Phillips in Tower 1.

In nearby Cell House 2, Victor Baldwin sat at his brother-in-law's desk. From there, in the northeast corner, he could see the outside door to his right and in front of him, the east galleys. Behind him were the locked double doors that led to the dining hall. The key to open them hung from the ring that Larry Cozzens had given Baldwin. Kitty-corner from Baldwin and hidden from his line of sight was the gun cage that Officer Lawrence Backman occupied. It was positioned high in the corner at the junction of the south and west catwalks.

Cell House 2 measured as wide as the newer one at forty-nine feet, but forty-eight feet shorter, 178 feet from north to south. Jammed doors and general neglect rendered some cells unusable, although overall it was a formidable cell house. About eighty men celled in Cell House 2 on any given day, counting convicts in isolation and segregation cells.

Among its longtime residents was Paul "Turkey Pete" Eitner, a wisp of a man with a honking nose who killed a man in Miles City, Montana, in 1918. Turkey Pete earned his nickname while tending the prison's turkey farm near Galen, south of Deer Lodge. Fellow cons also called him "Champ" because he liked to slip between the

211

ropes of the boxing ring to tell the fighters a thing or two. He had lost his mind somewhere in the past and didn't know where.

Eitner wrote checks for spectacular sums on dummy accounts he thought were real. By 1959 he thought he owned the prison. Most of the guards and convicts treated him like a king. Jerry Myles craved reverence, but not that kind. Turkey Pete enjoyed compassion, even pity, and he got the respect that old cons deserved. Friends even made check blanks for him in the prison's print shop. There was no evidence that Myles resented Turkey Pete, who was nearly forty years older.

Nearest the yard door, below the Isolation and Segregation galleys, the floor-level row of cells facing west housed an upholstery shop. Cell doors stood open. Furniture in various stages of repair and construction, mingled among piles of upholstery backing, cluttered the galley floor.

Baldwin expected to see Cozzens soon. It was nearly 4 o'clock. When Cozzens returned, Baldwin would go for dinner. That's how it worked. One guard relieved another. Guards couldn't leave the prison grounds to eat dinner. In the guards' dining room, at the back of the minimum-security bunkhouse, they ate fast but with satisfaction. The food was good, even substantial. Convict cooks made sumptuous meals from the riches of the prison farms and dairies: fresh beef and milk and vegetables, pork and ham, and other deportments of a hot dinner: fresh-baked bread, fresh-brewed coffee, pies still steamy warm. This was a comfort to a guard's life, particularly for bachelor guards who lived in their military-style rooms in the Guards' Quarters across the street.

At the floor desk in Cell House 2 where Baldwin sat, a stack of yellow bank statements became popular a few minutes before Cozzens returned. Convicts used the statements to draw money from their prison-held accounts for various purposes. To Baldwin's dismay, one prisoner and then another asked for a statement until men in blue clothes surrounded him. Baldwin stood. Spreading his hands in an appeal for silence, he told them to return to their cells and later ask Cozzens for help. They left without comment, which aroused Baldwin's suspicion. A floor officer grew accustomed to complaints and arguments. They went away too quick, and it wasn't right.

When convicts surrounded Baldwin, blocking his view, three men slipped into the cell house through the main entrance to his right. Jerry Myles, Lee Smart and George Alton hid inside open cells in the upholstery shop. Robert Griffin, a convict in Cell House 2 who was walking outside to watch a basketball game, passed Smart in the entryway. Griffin saw Smart carrying what appeared to be a roll of leather. It was about as long as a rifle, he would conclude later.

Within minutes, at about 4 o'clock, Officer Cozzens returned to his desk, accompanied by Tom Stanford, the second shift yardman. Stanford came inside Cell House 2 looking for Clinton Fowler, the guard who had relieved him while he ate. Not finding Fowler, Stanford left Cell House 2 and walked to Cell House 1. It was a pleasant walk in the afternoon sunshine. The yard seemed unusually quiet. The convicts of Cell House 1 would be going to dinner soon.

Stanford didn't see Fowler. He waved to the tower guards and they waved back, and it seemed business as usual and that's why in a prison a guard never knows what might happen next. Stanford entered the roomy entrance to Cell House 1. When he opened the inside door, someone grabbed his arm. Stanford saw Harold Laureys holding what he thought was a pearl-handled switchblade. In front of him stood at least six convicts wielding various weapons, including a meat cleaver. Stanford willingly entered the stairwell to the Hole, which seemed a safer place.

In Cell House 2, Victor Baldwin got up to leave; now it was his turn for dinner. He handed Cozzens his keys, then walked through the entryway and onto the front steps of Cell House 2. There he met Officer Murry Giles, who was walking north toward Inside Administration. They talked for a moment, taking notice of cloth lying on the ground. Giles would remember it as an inmate jacket, Baldwin as upholstery fabric.

They hesitated, each cussing at the other to do something about it, the way guards would do. Baldwin said he would take it back inside and then Giles said he would, and finally Baldwin scooped it up and walked inside Cell House 2 to hand it to Cozzens. Convicts surrounded Cozzens, but with his mind on dinner, Baldwin paid little attention. He walked right past them, and after handing Cozzens the cloth, turned to leave. Baldwin felt a hard bump. A shorter man with receding blond hair stood beside him. George Alton held a knife against Baldwin's stomach. Baldwin flinched and Alton, thinking Baldwin might try to fight back, warned him: "Don't try it. Behave yourself and you won't get hurt."

Surprised, Baldwin blurted, "What kind of a dumb stunt is this?" Then he heard another man order, "Come on!" and turned to see an impatient Jerry Myles. Near him, he saw two convicts holding knives on Cozzens. Back toward the entryway leading outside, Lee Smart stood in the shadows, his rifle leveled and aimed at Cozzens. Both guards looked around and felt scared. As fear comes, the body goes limp.

Myles pulled Baldwin's wallet and keys to his car and house from his pocket. Baldwin had five children at home including twin daughters. He had built a home for his family on Oregon Street, a new road on Deer Lodge's West Side. He wondered at that tense moment if he would go home, ever again.

Myles commanded Cozzens to open the door leading down into the dining hall. Cozzens fumbled with the lock, nervously watching the array of weapons around him. Myles grabbed the keys, turning the lock with a clunk that seemed to echo in the cell house. He warned Baldwin and Cozzens not to make trouble or they might be attacked. He prodded them across the dining hall and all the way up the stairs into Cell House 1. Many of the prisoners standing around them held meat cleavers and butcher knives pilfered from the kitchen. Some clutched hammers, others wielded clubs of wood and iron. The new captives wondered in bewilderment where they had found all those weapons. Minutes after Stanford's capture, Victor Baldwin and Larry Cozzens descended into the Hole. At least a dozen nervous faces, barely illuminated under the dim bulb, stared back.

A low voice came from somewhere in the shadows. "What the hell?" it said.

***

When Officer David Hinton entered Cell House 1 from his dinner break he saw an empty guard desk at the base of stairs leading to the galleys. Curious, he started up the stairs. A convict he didn't know met him with a knife. To a second convict he gave up his wallet, which contained a Canadian nickel he kept as a keepsake, and his car keys. Behind Hinton came Officer Kelpin, taken hostage as he walked into the cell house. A small, dark-complexioned convict held a knife on Kelpin while robbing him of a self-winding wristwatch and his wallet, which contained two twenty-dollar bills and one dollar and ten cents in change. Carl Frodsham, following orders from Myles and the others, pushed Kelpin into the Hole at knifepoint. Hinton followed, prodded along by two or three convicts who acted like they didn't care what happened next.

Myles yelled to them to stop. "I want that man!" He pulled Hinton away from the doorway to the Hole. Knowing Hinton as the regular catwalk guard, Myles asked where he could find ammunition for the rifle that the guards usually carried up there. Hinton told him that he hadn't been given any. That wasn't the answer that Myles wanted. Enraged, he summoned Lieutenant Brown from the Hole. "We're taking you over to the old wing," Myles told him, thrusting a knife against the officer's back. Myles paraded the taller man down the steps from Cell House 1 and through the dining hall, pushing him from behind. Alton trailed, carrying a knife. They stayed close to Brown, watching the gun cage. As they neared the stairs leading to Cell House 2, they met Lee Smart, who told Brown, "We're going to use you, Charlie. We're going to use you to help us go through the front gate." But Myles also threatened to kill Brown if he didn't find ammunition.

***

Within minutes after the capture of Cozzens and Baldwin, Officer Backman walked east on his catwalk, along the south end of Cell House 2. Officer Dawson hadn't returned from dinner.

Backman walked until he could see the floor desk at the north end. It was empty. Backman thought Cozzens had gone to Isolation, on the west side, to start feeding convicts there. He turned and walked back to the gun cage in the southwest corner, his rifle in hand.

Just as Backman entered the gun cage, a convict he called "the purse peddler" stepped out of hiding inside a doorway in the southeast corner. A new mop slung over his shoulder, Jimmy Hubbard approached Backman on the south catwalk.

Occasionally Hubbard had been allowed onto the catwalk to clean, but Backman knew he didn't belong there this time. Backman caught Hubbard on the catwalk about two weeks earlier when he was leaving the gun cage after relieving the regular officer. He told Hubbard to get off but he didn't watch him leave. Later, it would dawn on Backman that Hubbard had climbed across the grating bars to the catwalk. He didn't report the incident, presuming the regular catwalk guard would do so.

Convict Eugene Howe saw that earlier incident. He thought it unusual that Hubbard would be on the catwalk in the afternoon because he and other galley swampers did their cleaning in the mornings. It was almost like Hubbard was finding out how easy it was to get onto the catwalk, and how Backman would react if he did.

Now, on the afternoon of April 16, Hubbard appeared again and he looked in the mood for taking chances.

"What the hell are you doing up here?" Backman called to Hubbard.

"Well, I'm going to change this mop head," Hubbard replied, giving an excuse that didn't make sense. He moved closer than he should have dared. His gold front tooth glistened in the afternoon sunlight that streamed through the high windows. "You ain't got any damn business up here," Backman told the slighter, smaller man. "Get off."

Backman jacked a shell into the chamber of his lever-action rifle. The metallic click of it sounded loud and desperate. In a flash, Hubbard jumped forward. He grabbed the rifle barrel with one hand and pulled a knife from his pocket with the other. "I will kill you,

you son of a bitch!" Hubbard warned Backman. For a second they stood staring at each other, still and breathing hard. "You will never kill me with that knife," Backman said. "I'll guarantee you that, because it is going to take more than that."

Hubbard swung the knife, cutting Backman's hand. Backman tried to strike Hubbard with the rifle. He lost his balance and fell backward, losing his cap. Backman wanted to shoot Hubbard but the little convict was too quick. From where he fell outside the gun cage door, Backman glimpsed Jerry Myles below him, holding a knife to Charlie Brown. It all seemed strange and improbable. Backman thought they were both watching his fight with Hubbard. He could see that the other guard was in trouble. He let go of his rifle. He also gave Hubbard two keys on a leather strap. One of those keys opened a locker in the gun cage, where Hubbard found more cartridges for the rifle.

Backman knew the convicts now had seventeen rounds of ammunition.

***

Clifford Amdahl heard the commotion. It sounded different from the normal cell house clatter. He peered from Cell 208, where he had gone after finishing his painting work. Along the catwalk above him, he saw Hubbard chasing Backman down the galley, pushing and striking him. Many times Amdahl had seen Backman sitting in a chair on the catwalk outside the gun cage, his rifle leaning against the wall about three feet away. Practically every convict in Cell House 2 felt teased at seeing that rifle. Backman, some of them decided, would never shoot. Scenarios tumbled in their heads. It didn't take long for word to get to Lee Smart that Backman was the guard they wanted on the galley when the riot began.

Amdahl had painted handrails on the catwalk several times. Getting up there had been easy. As he painted, he jabbered with Backman and other catwalk guards about the weather and sports and women and everything else. They were just regular guys having a conversation.

217

Now Amdahl and his fellow Cell House 2 convicts watched Hubbard wave the rifle at Backman's back as the guard trudged ahead on the west catwalk, about thirty feet from the grating bars. Men on both sides recalled the rumor racing through the cell houses that Powell and Rothe wanted to remove the rifles the following Monday, in what Backman later described to prosecutors as "Rothe's new setup."

Hubbard's fight with Backman and his surrender had lasted less than two minutes. The man with the gold tooth told Backman to hurry. "We want to get this under way," he said. Below and behind him, down on the floor, a young man Backman mistook for George Alton called to Hubbard.

"How are you doing, Jimmy?" Lee Smart yelled.

"I'm doing alright. I got the gun!"

"Where are the shells, what have you got?"

It had been Smart's mission to plan the takeover of Cell House 2, but Myles was the mastermind. He couldn't have planned it better. He laughed and called to Hubbard from down on the floor. Hubbard indicated he had ammunition. Lieutenant Brown felt sick. Why, he thought, didn't Backman shoot?

"What should I do now, go back?" Brown asked, his voice full of resignation. Myles told Alton to lead Brown back into the dining room. "Alton, which lane do you want me to go in?" Brown asked, referring to aisles between rows of tables. "This one, this one," Alton pointed. Slowing his pace, Brown shot back to Alton: "What's your trouble, what do you want?" Alton said they wanted better conditions, but to Brown he seemed agitated like he wanted something else. Alton didn't mention an escape.

"Just take it cool," Brown told Alton. "Don't get nervous. Hang onto yourself there. You're pretty nervous, George." And Alton replied, "I'm not nervous. We're not going to hurt any of the officers."

Back in Cell House 2, Hubbard forced Backman to climb across the grating bars, just as Alton did with Officer Byars in the 1912 cell house. One galley down, Earl Jackson, an Oklahoma bank robber, stood watching. Guards regarded Jackson as one of Montana

State Prison's most treacherous convicts. Like Myles, he came to Deer Lodge with a dark, crime-drenched past, but his crimes had been more violent. Jackson's tough aura kept other convicts at bay. A stoic, deliberate man with a haunting long face, Jackson left an indelible impression that he was capable of more trouble than he revealed.

Backman climbed across the grating to Galley 6. Prodded by Hubbard, he turned through the grating door onto the stairwell that led to the flag where Baldwin and Cozzens were captured. Jackson stood waiting for Backman, and before the guard could defend himself, Jackson punched Backman in the face. Backman reeled. Blood splashed onto his shirt and dripped onto the galley stairs. Backman pressed his handkerchief against his smashed nose and torn lips. Jackson stepped back, clenching something in his hand.

Myles waited for Backman at the dining room door. He didn't seem much concerned at what Jackson had done, and while Backman tried to wipe his pain-watered eyes, Myles hacked away at the guard's belt with a butcher knife to remove a key attached by a leather strap. Backman didn't want to give it up because it opened a drawer in the garment shop where he kept personal items.

Myles knew Backman from his days as a con boss in the garment shop. He had seen Backman use the key. He didn't know what the drawer contained, but he wanted a look. Another convict robbed Backman of his pocketknife and fifty-three cents. Habitually, Backman brought enough change to buy a newspaper when he left work at night.

Smart took the second rifle from Hubbard. When Alton returned from Cell House 1 after securing Brown in the Hole, Smart handed him the empty rifle, the one he had seized from the gun cage after subduing Officer Byars. Smart kept Winchester Model 94, serial number 1555730. He saw that it was loaded and he cocked it and uncocked it and then cocked it again, making a game of it. He marveled at how a simple twitch of the finger would fire the gun. Wary at times of potential danger around him, because Smart had lived in prison long enough to distrust most everybody, he amused himself with this dramatic turn of events. Here he was in prison, holding a rifle that could kill men.

***

From Tower 1 on the southeast corner of Montana State Prison's big wall, Officer Harold Phillips watched portions of the Cell House 2 catwalk through windows that stretched along the east and south sides. Closest to him and in front of his round wall tower, about thirty feet away, was the cell house corner tower. The symmetry of these towers, one in sandstone gray and the other in red-brown brick, intrigued picture-snapping tourists who stared at the juxtaposition of architecture from the street.

Inside the cell house tower, stairs led to the catwalk. When he left for dinner, Officer Dawson entered this tower from the catwalk and emerged from a door at the base of it. He would return the same way. This was the shortest outside walk any guard would make, lasting no more than ten seconds to the gate beneath Tower 1 that led through the big wall into the minimum-security compound.

A few minutes after 4, Phillips watched a man approaching on the catwalk, walking south along the east windows. He couldn't discern a face, but when the man disappeared behind the corner tower and then emerged into view again walking west on the south catwalk, Phillips noted a convict's numbers on his back. All he could recognize were two numbers, "1" and "7", before the convict disappeared from view. All convicts wore their five-digit prison-assigned numbers on patches sewn on the back of their shirts. Phillips didn't know whom he had seen. Jimmy Hubbard's number was 16762. Lee Smart wore 17950 and George Alton, 17852. Harold Laureys wore 17570. Phillips tried immediately to connect with Deputy Warden Rothe's office on the new intercom system to warn of trouble in Cell House 2. He couldn't get it to work. All that week workers had been installing it; apparently it wasn't hooked up right. Phillips couldn't get an answer. He tried the telephone, but that didn't ring through either. He wondered if somebody tampered with the phone lines.

When Dawson appeared below Tower 1 on the compound side, Phillips yelled a warning that he had seen a convict on the catwalk. Dawson took the key drop. After he passed through two sets of doors into the main prison, he hurried back into the southeast tower of Cell House 2 to investigate.

When Dawson stepped onto the catwalk he first saw a chair and water bucket overturned in the gun cage. He looked down toward where Cozzens sat at his floor desk but saw no one there. Convicts lined the east-facing galleys. Dawson raced to the gun cage, where he found Backman's officer hat lying upside down on the floor. Rifle and ammunition were missing. As one discovery led to another, Dawson heard metal banging on metal. Below him, both grating doors that opened onto Isolation and Segregation galleys stood open. He watched one convict slam a hammer against the lock of another's cell until it opened. The freed convict stepped onto the galley.

This was the moment guards fear. Danger comes fast to the human mind, but comprehending its purpose takes longer. And so Dawson hesitated, looking again. He glanced downward toward the main door that opened into the yard. Nothing. His troubled eyes scanned the galleys but he saw no guards among the unblinking convicts. He saw no guards anywhere. And where was Officer Backman, whose hat lay abandoned as if knocked from his head?

As genuine understanding dawns, thus does a quest for survival. Dawson tore back across the catwalk and out through the corner tower into the yard, where he shouted to Phillips on the tower. "All hell has broken loose!" he informed him. "Throw me those keys!"

***

Minutes before Officer Phillips saw a convict on the catwalk, he admitted Officer Chris Pletan through Gate 1. The looming hulk of Cell House 2 prevented Phillips from seeing much of the prison grounds except what was right before him, but he watched Pletan walk west along the sidewalk between Cell House 2 and the south prison wall, toward the theater. At the far corner of Cell House 2, just below the inside gun cage where Backman had been captured, Pletan turned north out of view, walking between Cell House 2 and the theater. Close as they were to each other, Cell House 2 and the theater created a blind alley that couldn't be seen from any of the six wall towers.

Walking with his back to Phillips, Pletan saw movement at the corner of Cell House 2 at that alley across from the theater, and then just for a second, glimpsed convict James Randall peering at him. Accusers would say later that Myles recruited Randall as a lookout. In lengthy court proceedings that followed, Randall maintained that he was going to and from his job as a janitor at the auto mechanics school in the theater basement. Officer Baldwin, when stepping outside Cell House 2 before his capture, had seen Randall watching him from about forty feet away at the flagpole in front of the theater. When Pletan rounded the corner he watched Randall running toward Cell House 1.

"That's funny," Pletan thought to himself. "I wonder what he's doing out here running like that." He also noticed that except for the running convict, the yard was empty and uncommonly silent. When Pletan approached the first door into Cell House 1, he again saw Randall, who this time peeked out at him and appeared to be hiding. Pletan ignored him. Convicts played games all the time. When he pushed open the second door he first saw a cabinet knocked over, its contents strewn on the flag. Like other guards, Pletan was taken hostage from behind with a knife. A convict cook ordered him into the Hole. Seeing another convict in front of him gripping what appeared to be an axe handle, he didn't argue.

***

Both cell houses loomed above Deer Lodge's modest skyline, but their castle-like architecture hid any clue of a disturbance. Deer Lodge residents were accustomed to seeing the prison but not the people inside. In the first half hour of his riot, Jerry Myles and his accomplices took fourteen hostages. They now owned both cell houses and the entire bottom floor of Inside Administration. They had escaped detection from tower guards as they plucked one unsuspecting officer after another from his rounds.

That Captain Felix and Lieutenant Brown didn't reappear from Cell House 1 might have inspired sufficient curiosity among west wall tower guards to sound an alarm, but it didn't. Brown customarily went to dinner at 3:30 and for him to walk into Cell House 1 at that time suggested a change in routine. Neither cell house had telephones. Guards either had to call from Captain Felix's office or walk close enough to a tower guard to shout. Myles hadn't expected to catch Felix. The captain's chance encounter with Brown below the Deputy Warden's office was a lucky break. Now Myles held both high-ranking officers in seclusion, stuffed into a suffocating cellar lacking windows, telephones or any other method of escape or alarm. For years guards had enjoyed punishing convicts in this awful place called the Hole. Now they were victims of it.

From a growing stack of brass keys they plundered, ringleaders took stock. They couldn't tell from the jumble which keys opened which locks. Several convicts, driven by personal motive to open certain doors, yelled down the stairs into the Hole to ask advice. They had captured keys to both cell houses. Having keys to open dining room doors at both ends allowed them to move between the cell houses without having to go outside in view of guard towers.

Their arsenal included more than thirty weapons, possibly as many as fifty. Convicts smashed kitchen drawers and cupboards, arming themselves with knives and meat cleavers. From beneath bunks and inside toilet bowls, they retrieved their homemade knives. Constructed from silverware, nails and other pilfered metal items, these shivs were sharpened to lethal points, affixed to handles constructed from wood, leather and medical tape. To a Montana State Prison convict, a shiv meant survival. Even convicts who opposed the riot desperately tried to arm themselves for protection from their enemies. Old hands knew that before long, rioters would find pills of all descriptions. They would start brewing potent batches of pruno, the homemade prison alcohol. When that happened, they might try to settle old disputes.

Myles, Smart, Alton and their helpers herded convicts into their cells. They worried that noise from the growing celebration would alert tower guards. Most convicts, hundreds of them, went to their cells voluntarily, not wanting to get involved. Some laid on their bunks, straining to hear news of the riot from down on the flags. Others joined their friends and tried to ignore the commotion by playing checkers and cards.

The newest convict, Larry Nelson, a nineteen-year-old salesman sentenced to life for murder, didn't know anybody. He had entered the prison that morning after Cascade County Sheriff John Krsul and Deputy Francis Baker drove him from Great Falls. The law officers had declined an offer from Floyd Powell and Ted Rothe to tour the prison. They returned home only two hours before Smart splashed the gasoline on Gus Byars. Arliss Allen, a forty-two-year-old laborer, was the other new arrival that day. He came from Anaconda on a four-year sentence for child molestation.

Armed with cleavers and other daunting weapons, Carl Frodsham and other helper convicts roamed the galleys to keep order. In Cell House 1, Myles pulled the operating levers that closed cell doors, locking most convicts inside.

Myles toppled Lieutenant Charles Brown's second shift at its weakest points. His careful organization paid off. Better than he had imagined, he and Smart and the others captured guards at pivotal moments, disguising one capture from another.

Had even one guard seen unusual activity, he could have sprinted into the yard to raise an alarm. But Myles knew guards hurrying to get their dinners didn't pay attention to details. As they relieved one another, and as other day shift guards criss-crossed the yard from one building to another, they sometimes didn't notice when somebody was missing. Myles seized on this activity. His lookouts supplied him information on the whereabouts of various guards. He knew Fred Dawson got away but the other guards returned from the outside dining room in staggered rhyme, one after the other. To Jerry Myles, this was music to his ears.

Still, Myles hadn't found Walter Jones. He hated Jones. He wanted the social worker but couldn't find him. Jones must have left the prison. He was a big man and hard to hide. Myles wanted Ted Rothe most of all. He dispatched runners to the grating door outside the deputy warden's office to watch for his return.

Through a window imprudently positioned in the concrete wall that separated the vestibule from Rothe's office, any convict could look through the captain's office to Rothe's desk. Other convicts permitted through the grating door for work detail overheard conversations. The deputy warden was meeting across the street but he was expected back inside for dinner. Myles fretted that Rothe might not return in time. Soon, somebody would notice the missing guards. If anybody discovered his riot before Rothe's return, he could negotiate. His hostages ensured that. Myles needed Rothe for his supposed break to Tower 7, but he hated Rothe.

Torn between trying to appease Smart and Alton with escape talk and his personal outrage toward the man who dared to dishonor him, Myles lost his concentration. He filled with rage, and when a messenger breathlessly reported that Rothe had entered the prison, Myles prayed to his gods.

At the moment Rothe returned, a fateful moment that fit into the takeover as if Myles wrote a script for it, a prisoner appeared at Babe Lightfoot's desk. "You must leave, now!" he whispered to her. Sensing alarm in his voice, she reached for her purse. Without looking back she walked to the east grating door, where Officer James Jones let her into the sunshine below Tower 7. Babe promised herself that if something terrible happened, and she was certain it would, not even in her dying breath would she reveal who warned her away.

- 15 -

Jerry, Lee and the deputy warden

Close to 4 o'clock, about twenty-five minutes after the capture of Gus Byars in Cell House 1, the bunkhouse guard left his post inside the minimum security compound to take his latest bed count to the captain's office. Officer Murry Giles had worked at Montana State Prison for fifteen months after selling cars in Columbia Falls, "up in the Flathead," as he liked to tell it. Like most other officers he brought no background for prison custody, but he worked close and personal with convicts and already had become familiar with most posts a guard might work.

In the bunkhouse, a jail-like building to the south of the big prison wall, a guard worked alone except for occasional appearances by the compound sergeant. Taking count was weary work. It meant continually reporting new bed assignments as trusties, as they were called, came and went, and to account for their whereabouts. Giles frequently worked the compound, and when he worked second shift he spent the evening hours in their midst as they hung around the bunkhouse, swapping stories and playing cards and catching a few hours of television. Giles, a thin man with receding black hair, had a knack for rough talk. Like most new guards, he was learning how those conversations could ease tensions or foreshadow trouble.

At Inside Administration, James "Little" Jones opened the grating door, and Giles stepped into the captain's office where Sergeant Cox worked. He didn't see Captain Felix, which wasn't unusual. Felix frequently was out making rounds. Giles logged his

227

count. Then he went to the medicine drawer inside Deputy Warden Rothe's office to get aspirin for his headache.

Giles stepped back into the lobby from the captain's office. He met Ted Rothe, who had just entered the prison through the east grating door at the far end of the lobby. They made small talk. Then Rothe, saying he had something to do before he went downstairs to the dining hall, walked into his office.

Jones unlocked the west grating door for Giles to leave. Giles heard Jones slam and secure the door behind him, and as he walked outside he met three convicts he knew were trouble. Jerry Myles came first, followed by Lee Smart and then Donald Toms. Smart carried a long roll of leather. Convicts carried leather all the time to make belts and wallets and other items. Leather craft was a principal hobby in the prison, and every guard had become familiar with the long rolls.

All three of them pushed past him. "What are you doing in here?" Giles asked of them. Myles swung around. "Get the hell out of here!" he growled. Giles knew something of Myles as a con who liked to throw his weight around, but they had never been at odds. Myles had migraine headaches too, or so he said, and they had talked about that a few times. It had been nothing involved. Giles ignored the comment, and thinking Sergeant Cox would sort out whatever Myles had on his mind, he walked back to Tower 1.

Something about what Myles had said needled him. Guards heard sass from convicts all the time. His tone of voice had sounded more like a warning than a threat. What were Myles and Smart and Toms doing together? What did they want?

***

Officer DeForrest Thompson followed Murry Giles into the captain's office, arriving from the theater just a minute or two later. His day shift had ended. He planned to go home after he checked his theater keys with Bill Cox. Thompson was a happy man. His family called him "Frosty," a nickname that stuck in his younger years. Some of the children in the Thompson family even knew him as "Uncle Faud," another nickname that originated with his uncle by the same name. DeForrest, it seemed, was just too hard to say. In his youth his family lived in southern Montana where the highway climbed over high and mighty Monida Pass into Idaho.

Like many men Frosty came to the prison for a steady paycheck but he was not without other talents. Down in the Centennial Valley country, where the Thompsons knew everyone, he played his guitar for old country dances, the kind where people moved out the furniture and rolled up the carpets and danced until dawn and went home filled with good home-cooked food and true appreciation for their neighbors. To his younger sister Phoebe, who was married to Carl "Bill" Parish who also worked at the prison, Frosty did no wrong. She thought of him as an idol, a big brother who protected her from trouble, and in turn she fretted at the thought of him working inside the prison with convicts all around.

With his keys secured, Officer Thompson heard Ted Rothe's big voice in the lobby. Then Rothe entered the captain's office, and Thompson greeted him, and they talked briefly. Thompson stepped into the lobby to the west grating door. Rothe went into his office to the chair behind his desk. In the outer office, Cox saw Myles and Toms through the window, standing in the vestibule.

The window, although it had bars, was big enough to allow a view of Rothe sitting at his desk. Guards had questioned the wisdom of that arrangement. A convict could know too much, and they often knew more than the guards or Rothe knew, or thought they did. It was the conniving that was dangerous. Nobody knew what was spinning in a convict's mind until it came tumbling out in some trouble, and that was hell in a guard's life. Always it was a game, and the wise guard never believed what they told him. Keeping the edge was hard, just too hard, and it was dangerous to trust a con at his word. Most guards who did paid for it later.

Cox went to the grating door. Myles said he had come for his headache medication. On record as a sufferer of migraine headaches, Myles was allowed to come to Rothe's office for pills whenever he needed them. Doctor's orders limited him to a weekly maximum of six, and two at any one time. Cox asked Toms and

James Randall, who he saw standing behind Myles, what they wanted. They asked to see the deputy. "Do you have passes?" Cox asked. They said they did. He told them to wait until he fetched Myles his pills. Cox didn't remember seeing Smart.

Officer Thompson, who had waited for Cox to talk with Myles, now stepped forward to the grating door. "Ready to go home?" Jones asked, his key clunking in the lock. Jones swung the door open, even as Myles stood only feet away. In the second or two that followed Jones must have understood his mistake but it was too late. Myles jumped forward, Toms behind him. They pushed Thompson backwards through the door past Jones. Myles pulled a knife from his shirt. He wheeled Thompson around, and pressing the knife against Thompson's back, pushed the guard into a lavatory a few feet away. Toms menaced Jones with a cleaver, backing him into the lavatory behind Thompson. Within seconds, Toms closed the door behind them. The guards were too stunned to yell for help.

Cox hadn't seen or heard anything unusual. He was inside Rothe's office to ask the deputy warden if he should give Myles two pills. "Give him just one," Rothe said. Cox unlocked a desk drawer in a corner of Rothe's office. As he reached for a pill bottle, Myles rushed past him brandishing a butcher knife. Cox hesitated only a second as he tried to comprehend this surprise. He started after Myles, who already leaned against Rothe's desk.

Myles was in a rage. Flopping strands of his graying hair, usually oiled in place, framed his red face. He swung his meaty arms. "You big son of a bitch, I'm going to kill you!" Myles screamed. He slashed at Rothe, who jumped to his feet. The deputy warden grabbed a plywood letterbox from the corner of his desk to protect himself. As Rothe shielded himself with the box with one hand and reached for the knife handle with the other, Cox lifted an oak office chair high above his head, intending to crash it down on Myles.

***

Warden Floyd Powell abided by a philosophy that fewer rules give convicts fewer reasons to break them. But for his staff, he had begun writing an exhaustive manual of policy and procedures. Each person got a loose-leaf binder Powell hoped would eventually include memoranda on everything from schedules to personal appearance to professional conduct.

To ensure that guards treated these binders with value, Powell required each of them to sign a receipt. Anyone who left a job at Montana State Prison either surrendered the manual or paid a fine deducted from a final paycheck. Powell reasoned in one of his many memos on custody responsibilities: "We as staff must protect every inmate as much as possible from adverse or negative influence of the more sophisticated criminal who made his criminal specialty a way of life and attempts to influence as many as he can to follow his pattern of living." He reminded guards that they must be careful to hide differences of opinion between themselves and their superiors. "Never give the impression that we don't know what we are doing or why we are doing it," he instructed them.

Shortly after he came to Deer Lodge, Powell initiated a pass system for convicts. It worked like this: Any guard summoning a convict sent a pass form by runner to the guard in charge of that convict, whether it be a work detail, hospital, cell houses or somewhere else. The second guard wrote the departure time on the pass and sent the convict as requested. The receiving guard added the time of arrival to the pass. When he was ready to send the convict to his point of origin, he recorded time of departure. Intended to curtail convicts' free movement from building to building, the pass system in actuality wasn't fully observed, or so Powell thought.

Contrary to rules, at least four consecutive security breakdowns combined to allow Jerry Myles a face-to-face armed confrontation with Deputy Warden Rothe. That Myles could charge into Rothe's office defied every rule of security. In this cataclysmic turn of events, the man believed Montana State Prison's most dangerous psychopath by sociologist Walter Jones stood toe-to-toe with the man hired to reform custody. They were now just plain men. Only a wooden desk separated them as they struggled. In this extreme passion of life and death, with Myles trying to kill and Rothe trying to live, whatever distinguished them before as opposites melted to this final and terrible reality.

Rothe had listened to Jones' warnings, but he hadn't agreed. Driven by his quest for fairness and even compassion, Rothe couldn't isolate the one man who, by all accounts, had never in his life felt he belonged. Myles, the loner, now attacked the man who wouldn't send him to live alone in a remote corner of the prison they called Siberia. In the seconds that he countered Myles' vicious knife thrusts with the only defense he could find, the plywood box, Rothe would have struggled to understand. He had spent all day reviewing plans for a new prison. Hadn't Rothe and Powell and their new caliber of guards reversed decades of decline and mismanagement? Had their work been in vain?

Four sad failures in quick succession gave Myles easy admission to Rothe's office. First, the outside grating door stood open. This door, on the vestibule's west end, led into the yard. Weeks later, in the aftermath, an additional guard would be posted inside the vestibule. The outside door would be locked, creating a kind of chamber. But on this day Myles walked right through the open outside door.

This is where the second violation occurred. By being together, Myles, Smart and Toms defied Warden Powell's order that only one convict could enter the vestibule at a time. On the third count, Sergeant Cox asked Myles if he carried a pass. Myles lied that he did, but Cox didn't ask to see it. Barely more than a half hour earlier, Myles had seized Officer Byars, then the others. No guard remained to sign a pass.

The fourth lapse came when "Little" Jones opened the grating door for "Frosty" Thompson, even as Myles stood before him. Jones had opened and closed those doors again and again as officers and prisoners came and went. Convicts waited for permission to pass through, but Jones couldn't have known what was churning inside Jerry Myles' mind. Jones was perhaps too trusting, maybe weary from opening those doors hundreds of times a day, week after week. In a more circumspect moment he might have told Myles to get back outside before opening the door for Thompson.

On this day, at this moment, the only door separating Jerry Myles and Ted Rothe stood open.

***

Everything happened so fast. In the millisecond before Sergeant Cox tensed to slam a chair into Jerry Myles, a crazy thunder filled the room. Ted Rothe buckled and fell quiet as if the angels waited for him. It was that quick. Cox stopped, stunned at the noise, and looked to his left. Standing inside the captain's office, several feet from Rothe's desk, Lee Smart held a rifle. At that instant Myles whirled. Pushing away the upraised chair with his left hand, he slashed Cox high on his left arm, leaving a gash from elbow to armpit. The chair clattered to the tiled floor.

Myles stuck his bloodied knife against Cox's stomach, forcing the sergeant to the window against a table where the prison's failed new intercom system rested. Cox didn't realize he was hurt. He was trying to put the pieces together. Rothe lay quietly on the floor behind his desk, his big shoes visible from where Cox stood. His fury somewhat defused as he looked at Rothe, Myles warned Cox to be quiet and to stand still and he wouldn't be hurt worse. It was deadly quiet and for a moment, Myles appeared uncertain what to do.

"Let's go," Myles told him. When Cox stepped into the outer office, Smart backed across the room. Cox saw in the kid's eyes an unemotional calm but he saw that the boy was afraid of him, at least for a minute. The boy watched Cox's rugged chiseled face, holding the rifle up and ready. Neither wanted to get close to the other. Outside the captain's office, in the lobby, Donald Toms stood guard at the lavatory door. Trapped inside, Officers Thompson and Jones wondered aloud how Myles had gotten a knife. Within fifteen seconds, they heard a fight and then a gunshot.

Just a few feet farther from Toms, Officer Clyde Sollars emerged from the mailroom, curious about a noise he heard that sounded like a board falling flat to the floor.

***

Sorting letters inside the mailroom as he ended his day, Sollars decided something had gone wrong. From where he stood, back inside his cubbyhole room, the noise didn't sound like a gunshot at all. He thought the noise had come from carpenters working in the administrative area across the lobby. Still, he decided to investigate. Sollars first saw Cox. Then more urgently, his eyes locked on Jerry Myles, who held a bloody knife, and Smart, following with a rifle. He felt like a man about to die.

As Sollars stood at gunpoint, Toms shook down Cox, but didn't take his watch, his cigarettes or his lighter, the only personal possessions he carried. Toms pushed Cox into the lavatory, then Sollars. In the gloom of the lavatory, they heard the ragged breathing of shaken men.

"They shot the deputy," Cox told his fellow hostages, and then fell silent. Numb from his fight, and from Rothe's murder, Cox still didn't realize he was hurt. Somebody reached for the light switch. The others saw blood coursing from Cox's severed bicep. Sollars tried to bind Cox's arm with a towel he found on the floor.

***

Entering Montana State Prison from below Tower 7, John Simonsen heard a noise. To Simonsen, as to Sollars, it sounded like a falling board. Simonsen had heard that sound many times as carpenters worked in the building. He wondered how he could detect such a sound through the closed outside door of Inside Administration, deciding it had come on the lips of a brisk wind from the northwest.

Simonsen climbed the steps leading to the wooden door, kept closed except on summer days. He sounded the buzzer to alert the turnkey of his presence. Nobody came. Peering through a little window on the door, Simonsen saw the opposite grating door standing open. He also saw Sollars walking into the lavatory. Being bright outside and dim inside, he couldn't see anyone else.

Simonsen buzzed again. Still nobody. As he turned to leave, the outside wooden door opened.

"There's a gun in front of you," Jerry Myles told the startled office worker, who stared through the grating door at blood smeared on Myles' face and hands. Standing behind Myles, about halfway across the forty-foot lobby, Lee Smart swung his rifle point-blank. Simonsen wanted to run but his feet felt like lead.

Myles left to find a key to open the grating door. Simonsen couldn't see where he went because a steel plate surrounding the lock blocked his view. Simonsen flirted with the thought of fleeing. The sight of a stoic Lee Smart armed with a rifle froze him. Hoping to attract attention of the Tower 7 guard, Simonsen raised his hands shoulder high. But the tower guard, only thirty feet away behind a broad window aligned with where Simonsen stood, didn't see his appeal for help. Fearful Smart would shoot, Simonsen fought his impulse to turn and run. Myles opened the grating door and pulled him inside before closing both doors. Toms stole Simonsen's wallet before leading him to the lavatory.

***

Myles heard Rothe's phone ring while he dealt with Simonsen. From Tower 1, where he had joined Officer Phillips, Officer Fred Dawson waited frantically for an answer. Rothe's phone rang again and again. Guards had given up trying to use the intercom. Now that they had finally gotten a connection from Tower 1, both guards expected somebody to answer. At least one officer, "Little" Jones, should hear the phone. They wanted to tell Rothe about Backman and the missing rifle in Cell House 2. Something was terribly wrong.

Inside the lavatory, Simonsen helped Sollars press towels against Cox's arm. It bled freely, soaking one towel after another. They sat cramped on the brown tile floor. The air was damp and salty and smelled vaguely like stale urine. The door opened again. Myles took Simonson to Rothe's office where he told the young man to call Warden Powell. "Tell him there's trouble inside, and he had better get inside, and then hang up," Myles told Simonsen. "Do as you're told, or you'll end up like him," Myles said, pointing to Rothe on the floor.

Simonsen recoiled. Rothe lay on his back, his head tilted toward the northeast corner of his office between his chair and a coat tree. Simonsen didn't know if he was dead, but he didn't look good.

Simonsen called Powell in his office. "There has been a knifing in the prison," he told the warden on Myles' instructions. "How serious?" Powell asked. "I don't know," Simonsen replied. "You better come over if you can." Detecting Simonsen's nervousness, Powell probed for more information. "Is it between an officer and an inmate or two inmates?" he asked.

Simonsen, standing at Rothe's desk with Myles pressing his knife against him, wanted to end the conversation. "I don't know any more yet. I think you better come right over." Simonsen hung up. Powell puzzled over the call. Why was Simonsen, not Rothe, making this call?

The phone rang just after Simonsen placed the receiver back in its cradle. He looked at Myles, who gestured toward the phone. Simonsen picked it up. Officer Giles, calling from a phone in the compound, warned him of trouble inside. Giles had compared stories with Phillips and Dawson at Tower 1, and now the three guards were feeling anxious. "I know it," Simonson replied, confirming their suspicions, but standing beside Rothe's body, he was too rattled to comprehend much of what Giles was saying. After Simonsen finished talking with Giles, Myles grabbed him by the shirt and led him back to the lavatory door. He noticed blood on Simonsen's clothes. 'That's too damn bad," he said. "Smart was going to wear your suit out."

The phone rang again. Myles escorted Simonsen to Walter Jones' phone, connected to the same line, in the construction area on the south end of Inside Administration. When Simonsen got to the phone the line was dead. They started to the lavatory again when the buzzer sounded at the grating door on the Tower 7 side.

***

236

From Tower 1, Harold Phillips and Fred Dawson looked north down the wall to Tower 7, and to the sidewalk between the tower and the east steps leading to Inside Administration. Phillips tried to call the outside prison office to caution Floyd Powell. Again, the phone wouldn't work. When Dawson escaped through the gate below Tower 1, he first saw maintenance supervisor Carl Parish, who said a convict near Cell House 2 warned him that he should get out. "They're tearing hell out of things in the old wing," Dawson told Parish. He told Parish that Officer Backman was missing from the catwalk, but he forgot to mention the stolen rifle. Dawson went to join Phillips in the tower. When he stepped through the door, Phillips looked at the clock. It was 4:15. Ten minutes earlier, more or less, he had watched Ted Rothe enter the prison.

Parish ran down the sidewalk outside the big wall to meet Warden Powell and Elmer Erickson, the business manager, crossing Main Street from their offices. "Something's wrong," Parish told Powell, but in the excitement, he failed to relay what Dawson had told him about Cell House 2.

Powell, Erickson and Parish entered Tower 7. When they emerged on the prison side, in the courtyard leading to Inside Administration, Dawson and Phillips couldn't believe their eyes. While Phillips dialed the Tower 7 guard again and again without success, Dawson ran onto the wall, shouting at them to stop. Even at a distance of about 100 feet from where he stood, the three men didn't hear him. Wind blasted into Dawson's face, carrying his words away from the men he was trying to save.

Officer Giles, meanwhile, dialed the telephone from inside the compound until he got a connection. Finally, someone responded in Outside Administration. By that time, Powell, Erickson and Parish had climbed the steps and buzzed for entry into Inside Administration. When the buzzer sounded, Lee Smart slipped behind the visiting screen to the south of the grating door, to Floyd Powell's left as he stood outside. Smart kept his rifle level and ready. He had shot one man and would shoot more. Outside, Parish stood between Powell and Erickson. Dawson, frantic that they couldn't hear him, thought they looked like three men waiting for execution.

John Simonsen opened the outside wooden door.

"There is a gun at my back," he whispered, but the three men did not appear to understand. Hiding to the side of the grating door, Myles told Simonsen to open it. Louder now, Simonsen repeated his warning, just as Powell stepped through the door. Suddenly seeing the danger, Parish and Erickson jumped back. Powell disappeared, yanked by his coat into the dim lobby. Parish got a fleeting glimpse of Jerry Myles.

Erickson heard the curt announcement, "You are a hostage!" In the instant that he contemplated what to do next, he saw a rifle. He jumped over the side railing, falling about six feet to the ground. Parish slammed the wooden door and held it shut as Erickson waved and hollered at the tower guard. They couldn't see him through reflections on the tower window, and they feared they would die or be taken captive before they could attract his attention.

When the guard finally saw them, he ran onto the wall. He didn't bother with the rope drop but threw the keys to them. Parish leaped over the railing beside Erickson, who issued a command to the tower in a voice thick with emotion. "You cover us while we go to the door and unlock it and get out of here!" As the guard poised with his rifle aimed at the doorway of Inside Administration, Erickson and Parish escaped through Tower 7 to the safety of the street.

Telephone records show that at 4:24, Erickson placed a call from telephone extension No. 467 in Outside Administration to Governor Hugo Aronson's office in Helena. Erickson didn't talk with "Swede" Aronson, who was driving from Great Falls to Helena, but minutes later Erickson broke the news to Attorney General Forrest Anderson that convicts again took over Montana State Prison – the second time in less than two years – and that Warden Powell had been taken hostage. Anderson told Erickson to call him with the latest information every hour on the hour, even through the night.

***

Warden Powell glimpsed Erickson jumping off the steps before the door closed behind him. Powell saw four men: Myles, Smart, Toms and Randall. They eyed him warily, and for a moment, it was quiet. Myles had left Alton in charge of the cell houses and the hostages in the Hole. Powell had no reason to know yet how much he had lost.

Myles couldn't believe his good fortune. He couldn't remember when a warden had come into a prison during a riot. He hadn't expected this to happen. Powell looked edgy. For a moment they looked like fighters in a ring, each appraising the other before the first punch. "Take it easy and you won't get hurt," someone cautioned.

Simonsen leaner closer to Powell: "I think Ted is shot." Myles took Simonsen back to the lavatory with other hostages. Then he searched Powell, stealing his wallet with fifty-five dollars cash, his wedding ring and his wristwatch before handcuffing him. A fifth convict, Carl Jensen, watched from a distance. Jensen had been working as a carpenter in the office remodeling when he heard the rifle shot. Earlier, Jensen witnessed Toms rustle through Rothe's clothing at Myles' order. "He's supposed to have a gun," somebody said. Jensen sensed some presumption that Smart shot Rothe for this reason, because of a rumor that he carried a pistol under his coat, and now he laid dead. It was murder in cold blood.

Seeing Jensen, Myles told him to return to his cell house, and Jensen departed through the outside grating door. Powell tried to reason with Myles and Smart. "I shot Rothe," Smart said, showing no emotion. Powell told them they were making a big mistake. He figured the convicts knew as well as anybody how he and Rothe had been trying to reform the prison, and how a riot would set them back. "There's no use in being foolish about it and getting yourselves more seriously involved," Powell told them. "Call this thing off."

Myles got angry. "You don't call the turns in this!" he screamed at Powell. He drew his knife across Powell's throat, drawing a trace of blood, and threatened to cut him wide open. Powell stared back, his eyes wide. Myles turned and opened the lavatory door to make

Powell join the other hostages, but then changed his mind. Myles, Powell could see, was acting on impulse. Powell glimpsed at least five men, most of them wearing guard uniforms. Whatever Myles had accomplished was bigger than Powell first thought. "Let these men go. I'm the only one who's valuable to you as a hostage," he told Myles.

"I'm giving the orders," Myles snapped. As if in defense of his lover, Smart aimed his rifle at the warden. Myles stepped closer to Powell. "Call the governor and tell him to get over here and that he will meet our demands or you're dead," he warned. And then he asked Powell: "Do you have any definite setup to cover a situation like this?"

The warden knew Myles was asking about a riot strategy. "No, I had no plan," he told Myles. "Both Rothe and I were working on the theory that by dealing honestly with you, then you would deal honestly with us."

One guard remained free inside the prison even after Rothe was shot, and Powell was taken hostage, and Erickson had called the governor's office. Even tower guards on the west wall didn't realize a riot had begun, because if they had, they would have alerted Officer Robert Wyant when he left his post at the hospital after the evening meal arrived for his three patients. It was a few minutes before 4:30.

Despite the turmoil in the dining room, convicts had delivered food on time. Wyant saw or heard nothing unusual. Just as he did as each working day ended, he collected medical reports that listed pills dispensed throughout the day and walked from the hospital south to Inside Administration, where he would store his reports in the mailroom. In view of the tower guards he walked down the sidewalk past the entrance to Cell House 1, where Brown and Felix and several other guards had been seized over the past hour. He climbed the steps to Inside Administration, and as he entered, he wondered why the inside grating door stood open.

Inside the lobby he first saw Jerry Myles and Warden Powell. Mutually surprised, Wyant and Myles stood staring at each other. Wyant considering bolting back outside to alert the tower guards but

Myles got between him and the door and pushed him into the lavatory with the other hostages. It was now a full hour since Sieler and Wallace, and then Byars, had been taken hostage in Cell House 1.

Myles and Smart marched Powell to the telephone in Rothe's office. Aghast, Powell's eyes locked on his friend lying on the floor. Powell could see most of Ted Rothe's upper body. Blood soaked the right side of his white dress shirt. Detecting no movement, Powell feared his deputy warden was dead.

Smart pressed the rifle barrel behind Powell's ear while Myles whispered into the other. "We have every screw locked in cells, and tell the governor that if he doesn't go along with our requests we'll soak every one of you with naphtha and watch you burn," Myles said. Naphtha was a solution used for dry cleaning. Its use was restricted because it could catch fire and burn, fast. Every con in the joint knew that.

Powell looked up Governor Aronson's private telephone number in a little book he kept in his shirt pocket. At 4:31 he tried the call but an operator told him that number was busy, and that someone would call him back. Powell then pleaded with the convicts standing around him that they help Rothe. "If we can get some blood into him, he might be saved," Powell told Myles and Smart. They ignored his pleas.

For five painfully long minutes, Powell stood waiting for the phone to ring. Finally, at 4:36, he tried again. The line was still busy. At 4:42, the phone rang. Myles pushed close, listening. Somebody named Mr. Coover from the governor's office spoke. "The governor is out of town," he told Powell. "He's en route." With Myles' ear pressed close to the receiver, and Smart capable of shooting again, Powell decided to take a risk. "Will you have him call me at Number 8 when he is available?" Powell asked. Number 8 was a secret code Powell and Rothe had arranged with Governor Aronson months earlier. Powell knew that rioting convicts often tried to place calls to high-ranking officials from prison telephones. They had agreed in advance that if Aronson ever got a call from

Number 8, he must not return that call. "Yes, I will," Coover replied, and they hung up.

Myles said he would wait for Aronson's call, a call Powell hoped would never come. If Myles got a direct line to Aronson, he would have a big show. Powell pressed Myles to do something to save Rothe. Finally, Myles relented. "All right, if you'll get an ambulance and a doctor up here to the gate, we'll get him out of here," he said. Powell asked the telephone operator for St. Joseph Hospital up on College Hill. It was a three-story dark brick building at the corner of St. Mary's Avenue and Dixon Street, staffed by nuns from the Sisters of Leavenworth convent. Somebody there could help.

***

Inside the crowded lavatory, Bob Wyant found six other men. One of them was teacher John Storey, seized when he entered Inside Administration after ending classes for the day in his modest schoolroom in Cell House 1. Fellow hostages had bound Cox's arm with dirty towels. Still, he bled. Wyant stared into his ashen face, looking for signs of shock. He found the door to be unlocked and opened it, calling for Myles to send someone to the prison hospital for sterile bandages. Myles told him an ambulance was coming for Cox and the deputy warden and to shut the door.

"How bad is he hurt?" Wyant asked his fellow hostages of Rothe. Nobody knew. They wondered if he would live. Myles opened the door to ask about Cox. "You're going to have to take that bandage off," Wyant said to Myles. "It's saturated with blood. You'll have to change it again." Myles refused, but he did find them more towels, which Sollars tore into strips to make a tourniquet. Wyant asked Myles if he could help Deputy Warden Rothe. "No, it's just a flesh wound," Myles lied.

It seemed forever before help came, but maybe only minutes. Powell hollered out an open window at the Tower 7 guard that Myles had agreed to give a stretcher crew free passage to carry Rothe out. "He is badly hurt," Powell yelled. Weak but alert, Cox

242

stumbled outside and through Tower 7 to safety and a waiting car. A guard sped him to the hospital, six blocks to the northeast. Meanwhile, George Alton arrived from Cell House 1. He and two other convicts carried Rothe into the lobby.

"Cover his face," Powell said, sure his old friend had died. The prisoners complied. Ted Rothe, who had looked forward to a long and pleasant association with Deer Lodge and its people, was gone.

The warden falls captive

On the afternoon of April 16, Robert Foster slept in Cell 217 on the east side of Cell House 2. He hadn't heard the disturbance on the other side of the block where Jimmy Hubbard had taken Officer Backman. Foster was doing five years for grand larceny. He worked nights in the radio room inside the southwest tower of Cell House 1. Shortly after 4 o'clock, dayside radio room worker Delmer Ayers woke Foster.

"Rothe's been shot," said Ayers, who was playing shuffleboard when he heard the news. Foster, who slept soundly, had missed the excitement. He washed and dressed in a hurry. "If it's who I think it is, do what they tell you. They'll kill you in a minute," he told Ayers. Foster went over to Cell House 1. On the flag he met George Alton, who carried a rifle. Alton told Foster that he didn't want broadcasts of news reports, and to turn off the radio and play records instead. As soon as Foster started playing records, Alton reappeared and told him to switch back to the radio. It made no sense, but Foster knew better than to argue.

***

All day, sociologist Walter Jones had visited with convicts in one building and then another. With his office under construction, he made do. He continued to interview convicts for their case files. Earlier that afternoon, he had worked in Cell House 2, left for awhile, and then came back. Behind a closed door inside the athletic office, near the door that opened to the yard, Jones didn't hear anything to warn him of trouble.

After Cell House 2 fell, Jerry Myles fretted that he hadn't caught Jones, who he thought had left the prison. Myles held Jones responsible for his demotion from con boss to the water brigade. To Myles, Jones was a do-gooder who, like Rothe, had wrecked his home. Jones had been walking inside the prison from place to place when the riot began, but he hadn't noticed anything unusual and Myles and the others didn't see him. Jones entered Cell House 2 about 3:45. He glimpsed a guard's blue uniform at the floor desk as he turned into the athletic office, a small room near the outside entrance. He closed the door and he sat and talked with a convict about his polygraph test results.

When Myles and Smart had gone to Rothe's office, Alton stayed downstairs to keep order. He carried an unloaded rifle. Frodsham, who had been assigned protection detail, stuck to Alton, just as Toms followed Myles. The ringleaders knew they couldn't trust their fellow convicts. Some prisoners opposed the riot. Others would lose their wits on pills and pruno and start trouble. Some men would attempt to seek retribution for past wrongs. On patrol, Alton encountered two convicts with knives. They told him they had found Jones and would take him hostage. Fearful of the outcome, Alton took charge. "I don't want nobody hurt," he said.

At 4:30 Alton burst into the athletic office, armed with a rifle. Raising his hands in surrender, Jones stepped into the foyer where armed convicts closed around him. Alton told Jones to drop his hands, with the admonition: "Don't try anything foolish and you won't be hurt. Just do as you're told." Alton appeared nervous. He held the rifle at his hip with the barrel pointed at Jones.

The sociologist felt sure Alton wouldn't shoot out of meanness, but he might from excitement. Distrusting him, Jones stood still. He noticed Alton didn't have his finger on the trigger, but that Jimmy Hubbard was armed with a knife. Earl Jackson searched Jones, taking his keys and his wallet. Jones couldn't tell if Jackson took anything from his wallet, but the convict stuffed it back inside a side pocket of Jones' coat. The prisoners led Jones through the dining room into Cell House 1 and then to the Hole.

It had been a full hour after the takeover began, and at least twenty minutes since Lee Smart had shot Ted Rothe. The Hole was dark and stuffy and full of men and fear.

After Alton took Jones to the Hole, he went into the dining room where he met Richard Walks-On-Top and other runners assigned to keep him informed of developments in Rothe's office upstairs. News had come minutes earlier of Smart's slaying of Rothe.

Alton fumed. He wanted to escape, but Smart, his friend and cellmate, ruined their plan. Murdering a deputy warden was heavy business. Now Myles, he heard, had captured Warden Powell. Alton decided to go upstairs to see for himself.

***

From his vantage point on Tower 4 on the west wall, Everett Swecker watched convicts staring at him from the doorway of Cell House 2. As he watched Cell House 2, his phone rang. A woman he knew only as Eleanor, calling from the outside switchboard, warned him of trouble inside the Deputy Warden's office. She didn't know the details.

Minutes later, Swecker saw two convicts hurry up the stairs leading to Inside Administration. Two more followed. Swecker and the Tower 5 guard yelled at them to stay out of the office. One convict turned and left but the other went inside. Swecker recognized one of the men as Walks-On-Top, who appeared to be running messages from the Deputy Warden's office to the kitchen and back.

Earlier, Swecker had watched Officer Wyant leave the hospital and walk along the main sidewalk to Inside Administration. Everything had seemed quiet. Swecker tried to call Ted Rothe. The phone wouldn't work. About 4:50 a convict emerged from the dining hall, just below the steps leading to Inside Administration. He waved to Swecker, asking permission to go up the stairs. Before Swecker could answer, he turned back inside, and a shorter blond man carrying a rifle raced past him toward the stairs leading to

Inside Administration. Swecker later identified him as George Alton.

Seeing the rifle inspired Swecker to action. In a flash his mind put together the pieces. He didn't know Ted Rothe was dead. Miraculously for Myles and Smart, none of the tower guards had heard the rifle shot that killed the deputy warden. Light from the fading sun washed the windows across the yard, and although Tower 4 was even with the deputy warden's office, Swecker hadn't seen the struggle. Now it was clear something was terribly wrong. He took aim. Alton saw him do it, and as he ran up the stairs, Swecker fired from about 200 feet away. A slug smashed into the concrete wall just above Alton's head. He ducked inside, out of sight of the guard who had shot many a running deer in the mountains. It had been a good shot, and close.

When Myles saw Alton and comprehended what had happened, he looked for an instant like he wanted to start killing guards. "You'd better tell that son-of-a-bitch to stop shooting," he told Powell, and the warden saw the will in his eyes. Powell went to the outside steps where he waved his arms at Swecker in a stopping motion. Back inside, Smart handed some shells to Alton, who knelt down and fed them into the magazine of his rifle. Heeding Myles' threat of killing hostages, Powell called Elmer Erickson in Outside Administration. "Tell the wall guards not to shoot," he told Erickson. "They can't accomplish anything and might do a lot of damage."

Until that call, Erickson didn't know if Floyd Powell had lived or died.

***

Ralph Filcher, Deer Lodge's ambulance driver, also worked for Beck Funeral Home, the town's only mortuary. He had taken the frantic call from St. Joseph Hospital that somebody had been shot at the prison. He telephoned Police Chief John Wilson, who often helped Wilson with the ambulance, and told him that it might be Ted Rothe.

Less than a minute after Filcher arrived at Tower 7, Dr. Leonard Benjamin, one of three medical doctors in Deer Lodge, pulled up. Taking the key the tower guard lowered to them, they unlocked the outside door and went inside. Filcher secured the door behind them, clipped the key to a rope suspended through a chimney-like tube in the ceiling, and waited. Another key appeared. This one would open the inside door. As Filcher reached for the second key, the tower guard jerked the rope back up. His voice rattled down the tube but neither Filcher nor Benjamin could make out his words.

Peering through a small window in the Tower 7 door, and through the grating door atop the steps of Inside Administration, Filcher saw feet and legs of an unmoving body on the floor. He couldn't distinguish anyone else in the gloom.

The silence bothered them. Again, the key came down, and again, the guard jerked it back before they could grab it. Filcher and Benjamin decided it was too dangerous to go inside. They returned to Main Street, where they conferred with the others. Two prison guards and Ralph Beck, Filcher's boss and Powell County's coroner, volunteered to rush inside, where they found Rothe lying on the floor. Myles held Powell in a back room, but the rescuers saw Smart and Alton with the rifles and other milling convicts looking for trouble, and they hurried. Alton helped them lift the deputy warden onto a stretcher, which they wheeled out of Tower 7 and into the street.

Dr. Benjamin, at first glance, knew he couldn't save Ted Rothe.

***

Marlene Lightfoot, Babe's daughter, stayed after school that day for a meeting of Thespians, the drama club at Powell County High School. She remembers that her friend and classmate, Phyllis Rothe, did the same. Marlene and Phyllis would graduate in June. The Lightfoots and the Rothes had become fast friends. On Christmas Eve in 1958, Ted and Elsie had come to visit Buck and Babe at their home on Kentucky Avenue. In turn, the Rothes invited Marlene and her parents to their house for dinner. Marlene thought of Ted Rothe as friendly, talkative, competent and secure in his knowledge about the prison. The dark-haired deputy had a brooding long face but a happy disposition, smiling and joking with everyone. To Marlene, Phyllis seemed to take after her father. Tall and attractive and involved, Phyllis swept into high school activities and made friends in her new town.

Marlene remembers that on the afternoon that Ted Rothe died, Phyllis discussed an upcoming play with Isabel Eaton, a language teacher who doubled as drama coach. Both girls loved the stage. Marlene had just returned from Billings, where she had competed in a drama tournament in the starring role of "The Twelve Pound Look" the previous Saturday. School had ended for the day and the halls were empty. Marlene and Phyllis thought about walking home when they were summoned to the principal's office where Police Chief Wilson and another city officer waited for them.

The chief didn't say much. The girls felt scared. Riding in the back seat of his patrol car, they asked what had happened. "We'll see when we get to the warden's house," Wilson replied. He knew already that Phyllis' father might be dead. He also thought Marlene's mother might be trapped inside the walls.

At the warden's house, Phyllis and Marlene scrambled out of the car. They stepped onto the boulevard and turned to look across the street at the ambulance. The grating door leading into Tower 7 opened. The girls watched prison guards push a stretcher feet first, its occupant covered with a sheet. Forty years later, as Marlene revisited that spot on the boulevard, she recalled the shock of that scene and how her eyes went to two big black shoes sticking out. The girls hoped it was no one they knew.

***

All over town, an awakening came. Off-duty guards began arriving soon after Elmer Erickson and Carl Parish made their break for freedom. Minutes earlier, high school senior Bert Gangl, unaware of a prison riot, cruised Main Street in his 1952 Ford. It was his birthday. At the prison he slowed for guards who ran across the street to Tower 7, the main gate. He wondered what the commotion was about. Minutes later Gangl heard a radio report about the riot. Before long the police had blocked off Main Street near the prison. Gangl quit cruising the drag and drove to his house two blocks north of the prison.

The women at the switchboard of the Deer Lodge telephone exchange felt the urgency as again and again they were asked to connect to homes of men they knew were guards. By 5:30, two or three armed guards occupied every wall tower. Guards had locked minimum-security convicts in their bunkhouse inside the compound. In the foothills leading to Mount Powell west of Deer Lodge, more guards reinforced Montana State Prison's vast cattle ranches, where a relative handful of trusties lived in bunkhouses with little supervision. With Ted Rothe dead and Warden Powell, Captain Felix and Lieutenant Brown held hostage, business manager Erickson took charge of operations with help from Lieutenants Dennis Spalding and Pete Lynch, among others, and experienced sergeants and rank-and-file guards. Erickson contacted the National Guard, the state Highway Patrol and law officers in nearby Butte and Anaconda. Guards joined with city police and sheriff deputies to encircle the prison.

Nobody was exactly sure who was held hostage, save the warden and those officers Cox had seen inside the lavatory. The day's duty roster wasn't accurate. It included names of guards who didn't work that day, but excluded names of men who did. And Erickson didn't know if convicts held just parts of the prison, or all of it. In the growing confusion, as guards ran from place to place, it got harder yet to account for everybody.

By 5:30, Deer Lodge people started to talk about a riot. Nobody remembered hearing a warning siren, but anyone who had seen the ambulance at the prison fed the grapevine. John Richards, who owned the John Deere implement dealership on Main Street, several blocks north of the prison, had watched a sheet-covered body being loaded into Ralph Filcher's ambulance. Soon after, Richards knocked on Amy Lee Felix's apartment door on Missouri Avenue across the street from the high school. Amy Lee already knew something had gone awry because her husband hadn't come home from work. After hearing Richards describe what he had seen, she asked her friend, Helen Sollars, to come stay the night. Amy Lee and Everett had a two-year-old son, Curt, and Amy Lee would be giving birth to another child in five months. Neighbors cooked dinner for these hostage wives. They appreciated the gesture, but they couldn't eat.

At home on College Avenue, across the street from Walter Jones' apartment and just a block and a bit from where the National Guard would bivouac at the old school gym that night, Gert Knutson lived close enough to Montana State Prison to see it. She only needed to cross the junior high school's front lawn to the hill overlooking the football field where the high school Wardens played. Meanwhile, teachers at nearby Central School decided that, at recess Friday, students couldn't play on the school's prison side.

Like many wives of guards held hostage, Gert didn't know about the riot until she switched on the 5:30 television news from KXLF in Butte. She first heard the words, "A guard has been stabbed...." She thought her husband Ralph would be nearing the end of dinner duty, and because nobody from the prison called or came to the house, she expected Ralph home shortly after 10 o'clock as usual. Now in those first frantic moments, she wondered if she would see him ever again.

***

About 4:55, Myles and Alton decided to take Floyd Powell and their other hostages downstairs into the dining hall. Powell leaned close to Lee Smart. "Your mother called this week saying she was coming to visit on Saturday and Sunday," he said, watching Smart's features soften just for a moment, then convert into a hard mask. The boy spoke bitterly. "She won't come. She never has." He practically spit his words.

Powell knew the story all too well. Mary Smart had written the warden many times promising visits to Deer Lodge. Each time, she asked that her son be informed of her intentions. And each time, she failed to appear. Powell knew Lee loved his mother; he had heard him say so. The boy claimed he didn't know his father's identity. To Powell, Lee Smart seemed lost, consumed with feelings of abandonment. Powell wondered if that explained why human life meant nothing to him. Now, at the age of nineteen, he had murdered again.

The few convicts who thought the supposed escape plan might succeed knew Myles ruined their chances when he attacked Ted Rothe. Myles blamed Smart, calling him "trigger happy," but everyone knew that if Myles had asked Rothe to surrender, Smart might not have fired. Myles had talked about using Rothe as a shield. To pass through Tower 7 they needed an element of surprise. That's how Alton had it figured. They would lock up all the guards, then bluff their way through the main gate. They were close, so very close, and now Myles and Smart had done this boneheaded thing.

From the window near the east grating door, Myles watched a growing force of uniformed men fortify the towers. He seemed less perturbed toward Smart than did Alton. "What the hell did you shoot the deputy warden for?" Alton demanded of Smart, who shrugged. "I thought he was reaching into his desk for a gun," Smart told Alton, whose earlier doubts returned. Alton, distrustful even more of Myles, thought he had persuaded Smart to shoot.

Myles called Wyant and Simonsen, the latter of whom he called "the white collar worker," out of the lavatory. Toms handcuffed them together. They were led into an adjoining darkroom used by convict photographers to process pictures of new prisoners and guards. Next came Sollars and John Storey and then Jones and Thompson, handcuffed in teams. The hostages didn't know why they had been taken into the darkroom, but minutes later their captors led them in a line back into the lobby. Warden Powell stood before them, his hands now secured behind his back.

Myles choreographed a strange parade. Powell came first. Myles huddled close to the warden, pushing a knife against his back. Toms and Randall pressed hostages on either side of Myles to protect him from rifle fire if one of the tower guards decided to ignore Powell's order not to shoot. Alton and Smart followed. Thinking they should disguise their rifles, they draped coats over them. From Tower 4, Officer Swecker watched them emerge from Inside Administration. They shambled down the concrete steps like a clumsy caterpillar, all packed together and trying not to trip. At the bottom Myles steered Powell downstairs into the dining hall.

All around them, convicts carried knives and cleavers. Officer Wyant estimated as many as thirty men mingled in a state of confusion; some armed, some not. Myles pulled Powell aside to a table that had been set for the evening meal. Wallace "Buzzy" Bear, wearing a guard's cap, took charge of Simonsen and Wyant. He escorted them into Cell House 1 where, before locking them into cells on Galley 2 along Cooks' Row, he removed their handcuffs. Simonsen went into Cell 4 and Wyant went alone into another cell, where Lieutenant Brown would join him later. Sollars, as he entered the dining room, saw Earl Jackson wielding what he estimated to be a slicing knife more than a foot long. Bear waved to Sollars and Storey to follow him onto Galley 2. Alton unlocked their handcuffs. Bear pushed Sollars into Cell 4 with Simonsen. Storey went into another. Cons ordered Little Jones and Frosty Thompson, still handcuffed together, into the Hole. One of Myles' boys followed and unlocked their handcuffs.

These new hostages found the prisoners' cells comforting after seeing the show of force in the dining hall. Anybody could have attacked them; they had no faith that Myles and Smart and the others would protect them. Another round of storytelling began as hostages compared experiences. A hush fell when hostages from both cell houses heard from the new arrivals that Ted Rothe might be dead.

***

After the 1957 pea riot, workers built an emergency door from the Women's Compound that led through the base of adjoining Tower 4 to a service road behind the west wall. A second door opened from the compound into the main prison yard. At meal times, sergeants and lieutenants supervised crews that brought food to the women from the prison kitchen. They entered through two reinforced wooden doors and a steel grill door that opened at the foot of the big wall, about midway between Tower 4 on the middle of the wall and Tower 5 on the northwest corner. Otherwise, this entrance was rarely opened. Female guards like Helen Sollars, called matrons, led their prisoners through the newer door under the tower to work, medical appointments, church worship and other activities. It wasn't wise to walk the women through the men. On the afternoon of April 16, the main door into the men's prison remained locked.

Matron Eleanor Meyer, working the evening shift inside the Women's Compound, felt that afternoon that something had gone wrong. Her nine prisoners looked worried, said little. Finally one told her in confidence that the men planned a riot. She couldn't understand how they knew. "They were more worked up about it than I," Meyer later told a news reporter after she spent twenty-three consecutive hours with the women. "Some got sick to their stomachs. They liked some of the guards, especially Charlie Brown. One of the girls felt awfully bad about it. She got down on her knees and prayed for him."

***

Left behind as convicts took their newest hostages to Cell House 1, Warden Powell sat alone at a table in the dining hall. Powell hoped that by now guards were watching through the gun portals lining the dining room wall.

Walter Trotchie, apparently assigned to guard Powell, stood close beside him, a butcher knife in plain view. Alton and Smart sat a row back, clutching their rifles. They talked with passion about how they still might escape, gesturing to Myles like they were trying to persuade him. The warden, still handcuffed, asked them to surrender. "Your situation is pretty helpless," he told them. "Give up before you get into deeper trouble. You've killed Ted and some of you are going to hang for it. We don't want more lives lost before this thing is settled." Powell hoped to create disagreement among the ringleaders, but they ignored him and continued talking.

Out of earshot of Myles and the others, a convict Powell knew only as Buckman bent toward him. "Warden? Would you like a cup of coffee?" Trying to keep a clear head, Powell nodded. "I sure would," he said. Another older convict brought Powell a slice of cake, which he ate. "The condemned ate a hearty meal," Powell told him. Tears showed in the convict's eyes. Some of them had the wits to know what was coming. Others made a party of it and kidded and exchanged bold threats. Before long arguments broke out. They seemed incapable of agreeing with each other on the serious matter of conducting a riot.

Myles disappeared. Walter Trotchie and others led Powell into Cell House 1, where they left him standing alone on the flag for nearly ten minutes. Powell didn't speak to anyone, and nobody spoke to him until Carl Frodsham appeared with a knife. Froth flecked his mouth. He weaved, high on pills or drunk or both. Powell thought he looked like he was dying to cut someone up. "You're no longer in charge. You're going to die!" Frodsham teased, thrusting forward as if to stab Powell in the stomach. Another convict struck Frodsham and shoved him away.

At 6:20, several convicts led Powell outside and back upstairs to the offices. In the gathering dusk, guards watched from their towers. Somehow thinking Governor Aronson would call at 6:30, Myles planted Powell in a chair at Rothe's desk. Earl Jackson, who had struck Officer Backman, came upstairs. He now seemed to be trying to restore the peace. He told Myles and Smart: "You boys made a mistake when you killed that man."

At twenty minutes to seven, Powell looked at the clock. "The governor is going to be late with his call," he told his captors. Powell tried to talk Myles into releasing Captain Felix, knowing his wife was pregnant and thinking she was an emotional person and would suffer. He also wanted his captain available to organize the guards outside. If he could free Felix, he might use the same persuasion to release more hostages. He kept talking about how Felix needed to be with his wife, and for a moment he thought it was working. Toms and Jackson seemed sympathetic. "I got a couple of daughters," Jackson said. "I was married, up in Canada," Toms offered. But the others refused to release Felix.

Somebody wanted coffee. "There is a place in the back room where they make coffee. Why don't you rig that up?" Powell suggested. Walter Trotchie, dressed in a white uniform, saved them the trouble. He and another bakery worker brought a kettle of coffee, plates of cake and a stack of cups to the captain's office outside the office where Ted Rothe had died less than three hours earlier. A gunpowder odor hung in the air.

Once again, Montana State Prison's warden drank coffee and ate cake, this time joined by his captors in an incongruous, illogical moment that resembled a social, except nobody smiled.

***

When they finished, Myles, Smart, Alton, Hubbard, Jackson and a few others left the room. Powell sat alone, unsure what to do. He heard them arguing in the lobby about who should kill him. Someone even went into detail about how to cut a throat. They would hang his body in a window. A sign attached to his coat would read, "Only the first."

Powell felt like a condemned man. He thought of a picture of Christ that he admired; he wished he had been more diligent in attending church. He regretted not buying more life insurance. Powell had fretted about losing twenty pounds. Now, he thought, it didn't matter. "Get everybody out that could be a witness to it," Powell heard somebody say. They seemed to be disputing who should get the honor of killing him. He hoped some of them argued against it. As their argument grew louder, a convict burst into the lobby, calling for help to quell a fight in the dining hall. Everyone but Trotchie ran downstairs.

Designated to execute Powell by cutting his throat, Trotchie reluctantly entered Rothe's office. He was a burglar, not a murderer. A medium-sized man, he was twenty-six and a native of Havre, Montana. He came to prison in December 1957 after breaking into

Sutherland's Jewelry in Great Falls. He had escaped in April 1958 but got caught a few weeks later. Powell didn't know Trotchie particularly well, but as the convict came closer, a knife in hand, Powell could see "Lois" and "Josie" tattooed on his forearms.

"You know damn well why I'm here," Powell heard him say. "I'm going to kill you." Trotchie hesitated, then cried. "I can't do it. I can't hurt you." He struggled to unlock one side of Powell's handcuffs. Powell took the key from him to unlock the other. Trotchie surrendered his knife. Powell slipped it into his hip pocket under his coat. Jackson, watching through the barred window through the captain's office to Rothe's desk, had seen Trotchie leaning over the warden. He ran into Rothe's office with an upraised meat cleaver. "Don't do it, Walter!" he yelled, thinking Trotchie was preparing to kill Powell. "I like you and all that, but I'm not going to let you harm the warden."

Trotchie winced at seeing Jackson. Cons knew Jackson as a "lifer" who had a sharp edge about him. Jackson's record showed twenty-nine convictions in twenty-five years for crimes ranging from vagrancy to grand larceny in towns from Fort Worth, Texas, to Anchorage, Alaska. He had done time in three state prisons and one federal penitentiary. His first arrest was in Fort Worth for vagrancy on February 9, 1934. His next arrest brought a three-year term in the Oklahoma State Prison at McAlester for car theft. He escaped from there and was next arrested in Bisbee, Arizona, for passing counterfeit money. He served two years in the federal prison on McNeil Island. He later served two years at Texas State Prison on an incest conviction. His record showed arrests for assault with a deadly weapon and violations of the alcohol and narcotics acts.

Jackson had come to Deer Lodge from the southwest Montana town of Dillon, where he had committed grand larceny. Carl M. Davis, Beaverhead County's prosecuting attorney, recalled a story Jackson told when he was sentenced June 21, 1957, to eight years at Montana State Prison. Jackson said he had once stolen a refrigerator, but when he learned the victim was blind, he insisted that he be allowed to return it.

Trotchie pulled a snapshot of his wife and three young children from his pocket. "You know damn well I'm not going to harm him," Trotchie told Jackson, shoving the picture at him. "Now I'll never see them again. This is what going along with these people is costing me."

Trotchie turned to Powell. "I want to walk out of here," he told the warden.

"Well, why don't you?" Powell asked him. The warden volunteered to shout from the window to keep Tower 7 guards from firing. As they talked, more cons appeared from the dining hall, including Buzzy Bear, who no longer wore a guard's cap. Another convict, John Fiddler, walked into Rothe's office to look at the blood. He emerged pale and sick. By now at least five convicts encircled Powell. Some of them wept. For them, it was a short-lived rebellion. They were not desperate men.

"Why don't all of you go before you get yourselves involved here?" Powell asked. "If these fellows will let you go, I'll go to the window and tell them to pass you on through and they will take you down in the Compound and lock you up." Toms, back from the dining room, told them to go and Jackson agreed. Fiddler and Trotchie asked if they could take a friend, Joe Williams. "Hell, yes. Go get him," Powell told them. In a minute, they returned with Williams. A fifth convict, Jimmy Gaines, stepped forward. "I've done six years and two months in here and have only eighteen days until my discharge and now I'll never get out," he told Powell, who invited him to leave. All the men relinquished shivs and socks full of rocks. "Let's go!" someone shouted, eager to leave before Myles returned.

At the lobby's east end, Powell raised a window. "There's five fellows in here that don't want any part of it," he shouted to the guards on Tower 7. "Tell Mr. Erickson to let them out and put them down in the Compound and lock them up." Before they left, Powell turned to Jackson, who prepared to open the grating door. "Why don't you get out of here? You're in this about as deep as you can get. There is no use of you getting in any deeper." Jackson stared back at him. "Warden, if I leave they'll kill you." Powell didn't hesitate. "Then I'll go too," he said. Jackson handed Powell a cleaver and a knife, and a key to the door where Powell had been taken hostage several hours earlier.

"Toms, the same thing goes for you," Powell told him. "You're in this deep enough already." Powell unlocked the grating door and started down the steps with Jackson. Toms stopped at the top of the steps, then turned back inside with his parting words: "To hell with you guys, I'm sticking with my buddies." He locked the grating door behind him.

"Pass the key down, I'm coming out," Powell told the guards on Tower 7. Powell knew Toms would inform the ringleaders of their escape. Fearing a gunshot from behind, he hurried to fit the key. He hit it with the first try. When he swung the door open, the guard inside pointed a shotgun at his face, unaware of what was happening. One of the convicts screamed a warning. "Don't shoot! It's the warden!" As Powell pushed the six convicts into Tower 7, glass broke behind him. He slammed the three-inch oak door shut just as a rifle barrel, aimed at his back, protruded from the window of Inside Administration.

Warden Powell, center,

outside his office after he fled his captors.

Courtesy Old Montana Prison Archives

- 17 -

Jerry and the hostages in Cell House 1

Floyd Powell's emergence from the prison in the company of six convicts startled the crowd. Associated Press newsman Jack Zygmond raced toward the convicts to interview them, but a prison guard leveled his rifle. "Stop or I'll blow your head off!" the man commanded. Zygmond knew he wasn't kidding. It was an emotional moment, full of threats and desperation. The guard told a nearby highway patrolman to confiscate the newsman's notebook, but Zygmond convinced the law officer otherwise.

Surrounded by a cadre of guards, Floyd Powell's freed convicts waded through law officers, onlookers and newspaper and television reporters. In minutes they disappeared into the minimum-security compound to the south.

The warden emerged from the riot a spent man. Flashbulbs and the unforgiving glare from spotlights mounted on cars bleached his normally ruddy face, and the people stared at him. Powell saw his wife and his daughter Judie, who just had quit her new nursing job in nearby Helena and was preparing to return to Wisconsin. After hearing about Ted Rothe, they had expected the worst for Floyd, but there he was back on the street.

"I'm glad to be out," he said simply. Wives of hostages stormed him, seeking news of their loved ones. Powell tried to reassure them, but privately he knew a rescue would be risky and dangerous and might cost lives. After the hair-trigger impulses he had seen inside the walls, any convict could have killed him as recklessly as Smart had killed Rothe. Powell felt like the beneficiary of a miracle. When the news reporters swarmed him on the lawn of his house, he spoke in platitudes, as public officials in crisis are prone to do. He wouldn't tell them what he already knew about the rifles and the hostages and the mood. The truth would be too dangerous.

Once he regained his composure, Powell telephoned Governor Aronson in Helena. It was about 8 o'clock. Aronson was relieved at Powell's escape and told him to direct National Guard and Highway Patrol personnel however he needed them.

Aronson refused to come to Deer Lodge, believing his presence would please Jerry Myles and worsen the danger to hostages. But another problem plagued the governor. For most of his time in office, public reports of Montana State Prison's inadequacies haunted him. Attorney General Forrest Anderson and other reform-minded people had forced Aronson to hire a professional out-of-state warden. Now the prison was enduring its most violent takeover ever. News of this riot already was being reported on radio and television broadcasts across the country. Reporters and citizens alike clamored for more information. Aronson wanted to leave the riot in Powell's hands.

***

Below Cell House 1, deep in the Hole, hostages cried out for fresh air. Some of them felt faint. Now numbering twenty in all after Officers Jones and Thompson joined them, they pressed together in suffocating closeness, wondering what fate awaited them. Would Myles shower them with gasoline, as Smart had done to Officer Byars, and then toss a torch down the stairs? Myles, furious that Toms and others had let the warden escape, felt mean enough to do it.

Counting the four hostages locked upstairs in cells on Galley 2, and Warden Powell before he escaped, ringleaders held captive a total of twenty-five men. Sergeant Cox, the twenty-sixth man, might have bled to death had he not been released and whisked to the hospital. Donald Toms told Harold Laureys that two other guards escaped, prematurely alerting reinforcements outside the prison. Toms referred either to Officers Fred Dawson and Murry Giles, who escaped through the southeast tower gate, or to administrative managers Elmer Erickson and Carl Parish who fled when they saw Warden Powell grabbed at Inside Administration.

Toms told Laureys that Myles believed tower guards to be armed with machine guns. In those opening hours Myles felt good to be getting so much attention. It made a man feel important.

Walter Jones and other hostages locked in the Hole fretted over Officer Backman's broken nose and smashed lips. The blood ran and ran. Jones shouted up the narrow concrete stairs for help. Harold Laureys opened the barred door at the top. "Bring that officer up and we'll see if we can do anything for him," Laureys yelled back. Concerned with Backman's clouded eyes and his semi-delirious state, Jones asked to help stop the bleeding. Backman kept talking about the convict with the gold tooth. "I could have killed Jimmy Hubbard," he muttered. "I could have killed him deader than hell." Meanwhile, Alton instructed fellow convicts Leroy Wentz and John Ahilbin to fix sandwiches and drove them at gunpoint toward the kitchen.

Jones and Backman went into Cell 2, the first on the west. Backman lay on the bunk. Jones placed a towel under Backman's neck, tipping his head back, and soaked another towel with cold water in the sink. He folded that one over Backman's face. Frodsham stopped outside the cell. "We aren't doing any good," Jones said. "We can't stop the bleeding."

Frodsham returned with George Alton, and Backman heard Frodsham talking to Jones. "He's allowed to go over to the hospital, but he will have to go by himself," Frodsham said. Backman asked for his uniform jacket, which he had left in the Hole. Harold Laureys went to retrieve it. "Take Axtell, he's hurt too," Captain Felix advised Laureys, who said he would return. Axtell's body ached, particularly in the small of his back where Myles punched him. Frodsham unlocked the cell door, helped Backman slip his jacket on, and led him to the door to the yard.

"Once you get out that door, you're on your own. We're not responsible for you after that," Frodsham told Backman, who stepped into the yard in the fading daylight, raising his hands high above his head. Nobody spoke to him from the towers, nor did he encounter any convicts. At the hospital, two convict orderlies attended to his bleeding until it stopped. They fixed him soup and coffee that he inhaled through smashed lips. A convict Backman knew only as "Bull" offered his own bunk. Backman fell asleep.

After Backman left, convicts locked John Storey, the schoolteacher, inside Cell 2 with Jones. Laureys returned to the Hole for Axtell, who told convicts standing on the flag that he had lost his pipe and playing cards when Myles knocked him down. Raymond Schurch, who worked for Axtell in the typing room, gathered them from the floor and handed them to Axtell. Laureys took Axtell to the outer door of Cell House 1.

"We don't want you. Walk out with your hands up," the convict said. Axtell walked to the hospital, a distance of about a hundred feet. The wind continued to blow from the northwest. A chill settled over the prison yard. The man named "Bull" unlocked the hospital door for him. Inside, Axtell saw three elderly convicts from Cell House 2 and several inmate patients. Bo Sherman and Jimmy Gaines had taken these older men, one of whom was "Turkey Pete" Eitner, to the hospital for safekeeping after Cell House 2 fell to the ringleaders.

Back in Cell House 1, Walter Jones took stock. He figured Myles, Smart and Alton for the ringleaders, with Myles leading the riot. Myles and Smart were likely prospects to start a mutiny, but Alton didn't fit. He wasn't reckless like the other two, nor did he have a history of violence except in self-defense. He had committed crimes against property, not against people. Jones knew Myles would covet Alton's reputation as a straight shooter among fellow convicts, but Alton would need powerful motivation to get involved with Myles. Jones could only surmise that Alton sincerely believed he could escape. Alton couldn't do hard time. Jones thought Alton's loyalty to Myles and Smart would last only as long as he thought they would help him flee into the free world.

From where he sat inside Cell 2, the cell closest to the flag, Jones heard convicts shouting to each other. The voice of Jerry Myles rose through the din. "I hear we got Jones!" he heard Myles exclaim. Jones heard both jubilation and danger in the ringleader's tone. Jones whistled Myles to his cell, hoping to learn more about the riot. His captivity thrilled Myles, who thought that Jones had escaped being taken hostage. Myles gleefully badgered his much taller and younger prisoner through the bars of Cell 2.

"I'm going to kill you!" Myles bragged to Jones, and his voice came hard and loud along Cooks' Row.

Myles revealed a list of men he planned to murder. He told Jones he had compiled it before the riot: Floyd Powell came first, then Ted Rothe, then Jones and finally Elmer Erickson, the business manager. These were the men Myles perceived as ruling Montana State Prison, men who had ruined his standing as a con boss.

Myles staggered Jones with his brag of killing Rothe. It was like the deputy warden's slaying didn't disturb Myles at all. Jones found it hard to believe that his friend, mentor and boss was dead, but earlier in the Hole, Officers Little Jones and Thompson broke the news, relating Sergeant Cox's eyewitness account. Myles strutted around Cell House 1, full of himself, and nobody dared to get in his way. Walter Jones took Myles at his word. He knew the convict's psychological profile and his long and dangerous prison background. Myles would kill Jones out of revenge, or maybe just to pass the time. Motive held little distinction in a psychopath's mind.

Nine months earlier Jones had graduated from college. Now he faced a ringleader who promised to kill him, and probably would. If only Rothe had listened, Jones thought, he would have lived. But Rothe had rejected Jones' warnings that Myles be sequestered in the isolation cells known as Siberia, perhaps thinking Jones in his college idealism overreacted to the textbook nature of Jerry Myles' dark side.

Now Jones, almost disbelieving that the terrible developments he feared earlier now had come true, watched Myles recreate himself. This must be the Jerry Myles who had taunted prison officials at

USP Atlanta. This must be the Jerry Myles who the government had sent to Alcatraz Island's close custody unit.

He had been a chameleon of a man, seemingly meek and apologetic at times, yet few people who watched him work felt convinced of his sincerity. He could pull from within himself some kind of fury. From his dark belly a different Jerry Myles found the light, or was he the same man? That other man didn't come forth in great bursts of madness that made him creepy and insane, but in a measured way, as if his insides contained great volumes of criminal knowledge that he wanted to spill out as he felt it was needed. He seemed intent on taking full command of everyone around him.

Jones watched as Myles commanded with such natural leadership that other men fell into line without question. Jones suspected he was watching the beginning of a longer drama. Myles would relish each tragic and dangerous moment. Those moments would be building blocks, and after he had constructed a monument to himself that stood high and public and sated his deepest desires for glory, and after the streets of Deer Lodge filled with onlookers and all the papers wrote about what he had done and hostages wives cried and he could feel anguish of his captive guards in the heavy cool air of the cell house, he would commit murder before his monument toppled. Two dozen hostages waited to die.

Jerry Myles succeeded in overthrowing a prison. He had loaded guns to protect his domain. Never in his life had he enjoyed such power. As little as Walter Jones knew about Jerry Myles' checkered life, he knew more than anybody else. Jerry Myles, a psychopathic hardliner, would kill them all.

Scared as he was, Jones knew he must act quickly or die. His Marine Corps training had taught him to think decisively in life-and-death situations. He thought of it now and felt grateful. Myles or Smart might kill him on a lark, just like they did Rothe. Myles seemed to savor the moment as he promised to kill Jones. Knowing that Myles tended to act impulsively, Jones tried to stall him.

"Well, before you do that, I know you're going to want certain things," Jones told him. "You are going to need someone to speak to the people outside, and I'm the natural one for that." Myles appeared to consider the idea. "I'll think about it," he told Jones. For the moment, Jones would live.

***

Ringleaders Myles and Alton decided to lock their hostages two to a cell along Cooks' Row, where they already placed Jones, Simonsen, Storey, Sollars and Wyant. Most convicts were locked in their cells on all eight galleys, except for willing participants in the riot, or men forced to run errands. Fifty convicts or more remained loose. About 7 o'clock, Myles wanted the kitchen crew released from Galley 2. At first the men refused to leave their cells. Myles told them to get out or suffer the consequences.

Disheartened, they filed down to their ransacked kitchen and the remains of their evening meal. In the Hole, Toms instructed the remaining hostages to pair up. By twos, he led them into cells along Cooks' Row while Alton stood guard with a rifle. Laureys worked the levers from the block's south end, opening and closing each cell individually. Frodsham and Toms and others prodded their hostages with knives. Along they came: Felix and Thompson, Knutson and Fowler, Sieler and Schaffer, Pletan and Quilici, Brown and Wyant, Baldwin and Little Jones, Wallace and Byars, Hinton and Kelpin, Cozzens and Stanford. With that done, Alton locked the grating door that separated the cells from the flag with a brass key.

Myles made his way down the galley, making sure the hostages knew who was boss. When he saw Baldwin he stopped. The guard asked if there was any chance they could be turned loose. "No, I'm sorry," Myles said, almost kindly. Someone then asked if hostages could watch a movie. The humor broke the tension, if only for a few seconds. Myles managed a grin. "You know I can't do that," he said. Then he turned to Baldwin: "Lee and I are both dead men right now and we know it."

Pletan complained of an aching stomach. He was diabetic and needed an insulin shot. "Myles, we better turn another one loose," Laureys said, but Myles had no such inclination. "The only way they'll get loose is dead," he informed Laureys.

Kevin S. Giles

***

Soon after Lee Smart shot the deputy warden, Jerry Myles called a hurried meeting of his inner circle near the Hole door in Cell House 1. Harold Laureys, who had been summoned from his cell as Myles had promised earlier that afternoon, listened nearby as Myles outlined a new escape plan to Smart, Alton, Frodsham and Walker.

If they couldn't leave through front or back doors, they would dig their way out. They would tunnel from beneath the northwest tower of Cell House 1 north past the big wall to the street, where they would burrow into a storm sewer that led to the Clark Fork River to the west of the prison. Myles said they would shoot tower guards when they got outside. He also said someone waited to help them on the other side. To Laureys this plan sounded disjointed and desperate, even improbable, but Myles promoted it passionately and it was Laureys' impression that none of the four cons who stood around him objected.

Myles told Laureys, Frodsham and Walker to bring shovels and other tools from the storage room below the gun cage in Cell House 2. Myles didn't have a key; Laureys would pick the lock. Laureys objected, asking to be returned to his cell, Cell 330, on Galley 8. Smart threatened to hang all the hostages if Laureys didn't cooperate. Smart held his rifle in one hand, in the other, a rope.

Harold Laureys was a native of Superior, Montana. He first came to Montana State Prison in 1950, then again in 1952, while Jerry Myles was still at Alcatraz. His second sentence ended in March 1956. In the first month of his parole he stole a 1942 Pontiac sedan valued at $300 from a service station in Malta in northern Montana. Convicted of grand larceny, Laureys returned to his familiar haunts in Deer Lodge for five more years. He listed "farmer" and "auto mechanic" as his occupations, but every convict knew him as the joint's best lock picker, what they called a gopher man. It was the story around the joint that he had learned his skills from a man from India. With two paper clips and a fingernail file, Laureys could open any door.

288

The door Myles wanted him to crack opened from the west catwalk, near the northwest corner of Cell House 1. It was right across from Cell 250 on the northernmost end of Galley 6. This door led to the TB ward although its use for that purpose had been discontinued several years earlier. One of the upper three floors housed John Storey's school, which his students entered from the tower's outside door. In this modest cramped room, three rows of desks faced a battered blackboard.

Storey had tried hard to establish a respectable climate for learning. Only weeks earlier he had convinced Floyd Powell that he needed a better arrangement than this sorry cupboard of a room. The remaining two upper floors, occupying the north half of available space, housed clothing, beds and other assorted furnishings, and most of it in a jumbled mess as if the occupants had left in a hurry. Windows looked west and north from these concrete bungalows. The southern half of each floor was again divided into halves. Stark lavatories filled the west end; on the east, a treacherous steep stairway zigzagged its precarious path.

The door off the catwalk, had it not been welded shut years earlier, would open inward onto a small third-floor landing. Stairs led up and down to the left, the lavatory door was straight ahead, and the bigger room was entered through a door to the right. At the tower's ground level, one outside door opened into the tower on the west side from a breezeway between Cell House 1 and the hospital. This was the door through which Storey and his students entered. It was made of heavy oak and secured with an inset lock that couldn't be smashed off.

Myles and the other ringleaders wanted the catwalk door to the tower forced open. That way, they could come and go into the cell house tower undetected. Guards with binoculars on Towers 4 and 5 on the west wall watched convicts through the west windows of Cell House 1, but they couldn't see the catwalk door. Guards on Tower 6 on the northeast corner of the big wall could have seen the door through the north cell house windows if they had walked west on the wall at least forty feet, but they would be standing in plain sight of Lee Smart or any other convict with a rifle. Myles posted lookouts to watch every tower. He joked about shooting tower guards.

Myles told Laureys to crack the catwalk door, which was a solid sheet of steel. Opening the full door would be impossible because of the welds. On the top half, a half-moon of steel bars surrounded a smaller "wicket" door. It was barely large enough for a man's body to squeeze through. Prying with crowbars and swinging a sledgehammer, Laureys and Frodsham and other convicts battered the bars open wide enough to allow Laureys to disassemble the lock. He did so in less than a minute.

Laureys prided himself on speed. He later bragged that he sprung seven locks in a total of less than two minutes inside Montana State Prison that day. Laureys could have opened the wicket door, but he heard Smart tell Myles that they should take their hostages to the top of the tower. Fearing the hostages were as good as dead if that happened, Laureys pretended the lock wouldn't open. By the time Smart figured out Laurey's ploy, all the hostages were locked in cells on Galley 2. For the moment Smart abandoned his idea of killing them.

As night settled over the prison, Laureys finally opened the wicket door. He snaked behind Smart into the tower and walked down the stairs onto the ground level. Smart examined the thick concrete floor. "Where should we start digging?" he asked Laureys, who pointed to a corner farthest from the outside wall. Surprisingly, Smart agreed. Laureys hoped the digging would distract Smart and his fellow rioters from harming the hostages. Like most convicts who watched the growing pill-fueled desperation of Myles and the others, Laureys didn't want to see the guards die. For most prisoners, the party had ended when Smart shot Deputy Warden Rothe.

***

At Beck Funeral Home, Dr. Benjamin and Ralph Beck, the coroner, examined Ted Rothe's fatal wound. The bullet had entered his right chest, imposing a hole similar in size to a nickel, or no larger than a quarter. It tore through Rothe's right lung, his heart's right auricle, his aorta artery and then his left lung, finally lodging in his left chest. Dr. Benjamin concluded Rothe died instantly.

The .30.30-caliber 1894 Model lever-action Winchester loaded seven rounds in all: one in the chamber and six in the magazine. Loading a live round required ratcheting open the lever, and either inserting a shell manually straight into the barrel as the firing mechanism stands open, or closing the lever again, the action of which propels a shell from the magazine into the chamber. This lever action induces an unmistakable crack of metal against metal.

Circumstances would suggest that Lee Smart entered Rothe's office with a live round already in the chamber, and possibly with the hammer cocked. Driving the lever at that fatal moment should have distracted any of the three men fighting inside Rothe's office.

And then there was the matter of ballistics. The slug in such a rifle is about the size of the tip of a man's little finger and its departure from the barrel forces a powerful kick. Smart's point-blank firing at Rothe, at a distance of no more than five yards, knocked the larger man from his feet. Being near-sighted, Smart couldn't see particularly well. In his vanity he rarely wore his glasses, preferring instead contact lenses that gave him fits. Smart's cellmate, George Alton, had never before seen these little glass saucers that Smart attached to his eyes. Smart rarely revealed his secret; only Alton and a few other convicts knew Smart's vision wasn't good. Rothe presented a large target, weighing about two hundred thirty pounds and standing more than six feet tall. Smart would try to convince his fellow convicts that he intended only to wound the deputy warden.

For a hep teenager who supposedly never had fired a rifle, Smart shot Rothe with deadly precision, hitting him square. Smart either knew more about firearms than he admitted, or he fired a reckless shot that just as fatefully could have missed Rothe entirely. The ricocheting slug might have buzzed the room, striking Rothe, Myles, Cox, or even Smart.

In the mortuary, Benjamin and Beck inserted a stainless steel rod into Rothe's wound to determine the bullet's path. With the deputy warden lying face up, his big arms stretched beside him, the rod veered about forty-five degrees to the right, proving that just as Sergeant Cox had described, Rothe was turned somewhat to his left, at a right angle from where Smart fired, as he defended himself against Jerry Myles' slashing knife.

***

Just after nightfall, Floyd Powell stood on Main Street in front of a growing crowd of news reporters and shouted toward the prison: "Those who want to fight get in one corner. Those that don't get in the other." To some people it appeared the warning was intended for show because it produced no observable response.

Powell again went into the prison. Just inside the street entrance of Tower 7, a guard unlocked a metal trap door heavy enough to kill a man if it fell on his head. Powell descended into a cave-like stone tunnel. Through the clammy air, under naked light bulbs, he walked west under the prison yard until he reached a locked grill door. Once he passed through that door, Powell stood in a concrete tunnel extending north and south at a right angle to the first tunnel.

This long tunnel, impressive in its ghostly fortification, flanked the convict dining room. Gun portals appeared every twenty feet. Shallow in depth to allow a good aim down a rifle barrel and little else, they were equipped with hinged metal doors that latched on the tunnel side. Jagged metal like shark teeth implanted along the top of each portal discouraged escape from inside. Even a thin convict couldn't have fit through the compressed opening. At either end of the tunnel, narrow metal ladders inset into concrete disappeared upwards into pools of darkness. At the top, crude handrails helped the climber navigate into another stairwell that led to a black solid steel door opening into a gun cage in each cell house. In Cell House 1 to the north, this was the same gun cage where Alton and Smart had stolen the catwalk rifle; in Cell House 2 to the south, this gun cage was kitty-corner from the cage where Jimmy Hubbard subdued Officer Backman. Had rioters found keys to the locked steel doors, they could have climbed into the tunnel, surprising Powell.

When Powell entered the main tunnel, he turned right, walked a few steps to the north, and then, ducking through another short security door, climbed four steps into a gun cage that surveyed the dining hall. The gun cage had three features. The most open view came straight ahead. To the left, a steel plate covered all but the top ten inches of the bars. At the right corner of the gun cage, a crude metal tunnel just large enough for crawling led to the west side of the dining hall. Small windows made with a cutting torch opened into the bakery and kitchen. Guards who crawled through the tunnel were forewarned to protect their eyes because convicts sometimes sloshed the peepholes with hot grease and boiling water.

Powell looked west into the glare of the dining hall. Seeing nothing, he yelled for Myles, Alton and Smart. Convict runners, called canaries by their peers, scattered into the hallway to Cell House 1, to Powell's right. They returned with Myles, who pushed Walter Jones ahead of him. Handcuffed with a knife held to his throat, Jones walked carefully to the gun cage. Smart stayed hidden in the hallway between the kitchen and bakery, pointing his cocked rifle at Jones' back.

"What do you think you can accomplish with this?" Powell asked Myles, who replied that he wanted news reporters to write stories about conditions inside the prison. Powell demanded that the hostages be released. He warned Myles not to harm anyone else. An argument ensued. Angry and defiant, Myles told Powell: "Make one move to come over those walls and all of your hostages die." A runner hurried away to find Alton. Myles rained insults on Powell, ending his tirade with the admonition, "You can go to hell!"

Myles stalked off, leaving Alton to guard Jones and reason with Powell. Alton told Powell that Myles wanted at least thirty newsmen to come inside the prison to take photographs and talk with convicts about conditions. He said they wanted Benjamin Wright, who headed the state parole board, removed from his job. They saw Wright as a man who conspired to keep parolees inside the prison. Privately, Powell understood their frustration with Wright, but he told Alton he had no authority to fire Wright. "What we will do is get three reporters in here on the condition that they give their word that they won't print a word of what was said to them unless every hostage walks out. Then they're free to print whatever they want to," Powell told Alton, who warmed to the plan.

"Give me forty-five minutes," he told Powell. "I've got to convince the others." Powell left the tunnel and returned to his office where he met with news reporters, informing them he would use every means he could find to save the hostages.

Nobody pressed the warden to explain why he had gone inside the prison the first time. After the waves of prison riots in the 1950s, the American Correctional Association had specified in a new list of rules that guards should never run to the scene of trouble. Most certainly that would mean the warden. "The histories of many unfortunate riots show that officers who rush unguarded and unwarned into actual or staged group disorders have been taken as hostages, overpowered, or killed," the ACA wrote in its manual of standards.

Yet Powell had done just that. He reacted impulsively to John Simonson's phone call, dialed at the insistence of Jerry Myles. Powell charged into the prison with his other top administrator, Elmer Erickson, without knowing the circumstances. He didn't have a riot plan. He didn't alert tower guards to trouble inside. When he became a hostage the prison lost its leadership, and he came close to being killed. If not for the unlikely benevolence of Earl Jackson and the good will of several convicts who had occupied and distracted Jerry Myles, he would have been executed.

It was nearly midnight, eight hours after the riot had begun. Powell retired to his office to think. This was the worst crisis of his prison career. As the cell houses fell silent under a starlit Montana night, the nation awoke to America's latest prison riot.

- 18 -

Deer Lodge and the national news

In the county jail behind Deer Lodge's courthouse on Missouri Avenue, telephone inquiries overwhelmed Sheriff Everett Burt and his three deputies. Burt had gone to Bozeman that day, April 16, 1959, to attend the state's first Law Enforcement Academy. When Powell County's sheriff heard about the riot, he started the long drive back to Deer Lodge on Highway 10, arriving late that evening.

He found hundreds of people milled around the prison near the warden's house. A line of prison guards and law officers looped around the minimum-security fence on the south and continued to the north along both east and west sides of the main prison walls. Unsmiling, purposeful men holding rifles stood every hundred feet or so, their uniforms displaying a jumble of jurisdictions: prison guards, police and sheriff deputies from Butte and Anaconda, and Highway Patrol officers.

At the jail on Cottonwood Avenue, Burt and his deputies – Undersheriff Oliver Touchette, Deputy Harold "Chick" Fanning and Deputy Bill Arthur, jailer and dispatcher – managed the growing volume of calls the best they could. The single phone rang seconds after being hung up, bringing excited voices from as far away as England and Mexico.

Most calls came from news reporters wanting official information. Other people inquired about the welfare of their friends and relatives in Deer Lodge. Occasionally routine complaints about stray dogs, bar fights, speeding cars and other small-town minutiae filtered onto their log through the flurry of riot calls. If that wasn't enough, more and more people appeared at the jail demanding news of the riot and asking how the sheriff intended to keep their families safe from convicts.

Burt flicked a switch that illuminated a red light mounted on the downtown Masonic Temple building at Main Street and Milwaukee Avenue, three blocks distant, to catch the attention of a city police officer. Usually that light was used when an officer left his car to walk up and down the business district rattling doors; the patrol car didn't have a two-way radio. Tonight, Deer Lodge's tiny police force could be anywhere, most likely trying to manage the growing crowd outside Montana State Prison.

Burt was Powell County's new sheriff, having been elected the previous November. He and his deputies tried to hold back the flood of cars pouring into Deer Lodge from surrounding towns. Eventually, he was sure, the number of curiosity-seekers trying to gawk at the riot grew larger than the town's population, maybe as many as 5,000. Never had he imagined anything so big.

***

A block from hostage Ralph Knutson's home on College Avenue, National Guard troops began arriving at the grade school gymnasium, a tall creaking structure that was one of two buildings remaining from Montana's first-ever college campus. It had none of the amenities of home, except for ancient washrooms in the basement where dripping water echoed.

Late that evening, about 160 troops went to eat dinner at the coffee shop in Hotel Deer Lodge on Main Street, several blocks north of Montana State Prison. Walter Justice, the manager, watched them devour his inventory of roast beef, then his pork chops, then all of his chicken fried steaks. More of them returned for coffee, bacon and French toast at 3:15 Friday morning. In that single meal, the troops consumed hundreds of eggs and eighty gallons of milk.

Highway 10 doubled as Main Street through Deer Lodge and passed within spitting distance of Montana State Prison's east wall.

Almost from the start, law officers detoured traffic away from the prison. Northbound motorists entered Conley Avenue at the prison's south end, drove east a block to Fourth Street, then traveled north four blocks to College Avenue where they returned west to Main Street. The townsfolk couldn't remember seeing that much traffic. When the wind died down, choking dust from the back roads hung in the air. The riot had put Deer Lodge on the map.

Local volunteers, sworn as deputies, blocked off surrounding streets and all the alleys that connected them. They brought their own food, coffee and flashlights, and most came armed with hunting rifles and pistols. They stood two men to a post, more than willing to chase away anyone who challenged them. North of the prison, more deputies closed Second Street, where some of the guard hostages lived.

Despite the show of force, people slipped through yards and alleys onto the boulevards along Main Street from where they could look across the big wall into the windows of Cell House 1. It was rumored that the hostages were held there, and more and more the crowd turned its attention to the prison's north end.

Photographers set up their cameras on the sidewalk. Reporters stood shivering, their wind-chapped hands shoved into deep pockets in their overcoats, whispering to each other as they watched the dark hulking building across the street. In the twilight the tall barred windows resembled long black teeth.

Prison guards, law officers, and soldiers streamed in and out of Outside Administration, the building that housed Warden Powell's office. On Maryland Avenue, between Outside Administration and Powell's house, members of the Deer Lodge Fire Department waited with a pumper truck. A man shouted and swore at a National Guard officer trying to shoo him away, and volunteer firefighters, feeling obliged to help, forced him into retreat with a blast from their water hose.

Soon after the riot began, Officer Murry Giles climbed into Tower 7. He and other guards who had started working at Montana State Prison after the 1957 disturbance were a close cluster, an unofficial union of unadorned men in thankless jobs, and when things got tough they looked out for each other.

Guards pleaded with Powell to rush the prison. They knew what harm Myles and the others were capable of doing. Emotional outrage over Rothe's murder and Cox's wounds and the hostage taking permeated every fiber of their beings, giving them great determination. Had Powell given the command they would have charged inside to save their comrades.

From his vantage point, Giles watched a drama of historic proportions. Of all the wall towers, Tower 7 was the most pivotal. It linked the deceptive quiet inside the cell houses with the near-hysterical hustle outside; at twenty-two feet in the air, Giles could see every piece of the story except for what was hidden behind cell house walls. After darkness fell Thursday night, he steadied a ladder propped against the street side of the wall for Highway Patrol officers who would climb into the tower. Below him, flashbulbs popped. Later someone would hand him a front-page clipping from the *Seattle Post-Intelligencer* showing him kneeling outside Tower 7, his officer's cap cocked on his head, as carbine-toting patrol officers ascended the ladder.

Early Friday morning, about 3 o'clock on April 17, Giles saw a rifle at the bars of Cell House 1. He sent word to Outside Administration that rioters might try to shoot someone outside the walls. All of the guards knew about the captured .30.30's. Sheriff Burt and Police Chief John Wilson decided to clear onlookers from the yards along Main Street. With great difficulty they pushed everyone back to the alley that paralleled Main Street behind Powell's house.

At the 4B's Cafe kitty-corner from Tower 6 at the prison's northeast corner, customers ate breakfast within rifle shot of Jerry Myles, who watched them from the east catwalk just feet from where he had subdued Officer Gus Byars the previous afternoon. Burt tried to close the cafe, but it was filled with soldiers, law officers and newsmen. Business was good. The owner agreed, however, to shut off the lights and move customers away from the south and west windows, a decision more prudent than he realized.

Minutes earlier, Jerry Myles poked the barrel of a rifle through the window bars, aiming at the cafe about seventy-five yards away. "I think I'll shoot a few," he said, cocking the gun. Hostage Walter Jones, who sat handcuffed inside the gun cage a few feet away, spoke as calmly as he could.

"That wouldn't be very smart," he said.

Myles eyed Jones suspiciously. "Why not?" he asked.

Uneasy at what might happen next, Jones told him: "Well, you'll use all your ammunition and I thought you wanted to save your last shots for you and me."

Myles lowered the rifle.

***

Lyle Gillette had been a guard at Montana State Prison for only eight days. On Thursday, April 16, he worked the breakfast shift, starting at 6 o'clock and ending at 2 o'clock. Later that afternoon, after he had changed out of his uniform, his wife handed him a grocery list. In the car, he switched on the radio, and in the short drive downtown to the store he heard a special news bulletin about a disturbance at the prison. He hurried through the aisles, filling his wife's order, and when he arrived home with a sack of groceries she told him the prison had called and he was to come back to work, and fast.

Many years distant this man would become Deer Lodge's mayor after a long career as teacher and coach in its public schools. On this day he was new in town, a history major in search of a profession, having graduated in March from Eastern Washington University. He wasn't even supposed to be a guard. The guard work was only part of his "break-in," as they told him, before he joined the prison's one-man teaching staff. That man, John Storey, was now held hostage.

At the warden's office, someone handed Gillette a twelve-gauge shotgun and ten rounds of ammunition and sent him inside Tower 7, below Murry Giles and other guards in the tower. He began a shift of sixteen straight hours. Locked inside with another young guard, a kid he knew only as Johnson, he saw the drama from ground zero. Through the grill door to the street he could see the growing crowd, agitated but safe, and freedom was life. On the west side he looked through the bars to Inside Administration where Ted Rothe had lost his life. He was looking at death.

***

It was late Thursday evening in the radio room at the top of Cell House 1, in the southeast tower. Convict Robert Foster decided to quit playing records, which he had been doing since before 5 o'clock. Myles and Alton and their helpers had locked most convicts in their cells, leaving only those men sympathetic to their riot free to roam the cell houses. Foster tuned the radio to Butte's *KOPR*, broadcasting a stream of news reports into earphones up and down the galleys. For the first time, many convicts heard of Rothe's death. George Alton appeared in the radio room, angry with Foster. "I didn't authorize the radio. Turn it off!" he told him. Fifteen minutes later, he reappeared with a demand to tune back to *KOPR* and leave it there. Alton, Foster thought, was getting his orders from Jerry Myles.

Deer Lodge didn't have a radio station but *KOPR* and *KXLF* broadcast riot news continually. The first urgent bulletins broke the radio waves about dinnertime Thursday. By itself, Ted Rothe's cold-blooded murder would have been arresting news. The drama captivated Montana and the nation.

News reporters raced to neighborhood doors, pleading with residents to use their phones to relay their latest findings to their editors. Some newsmen paid residents to keep their phones on direct long-distance connections. So jammed were the phone lines in Deer Lodge that outside inquiries spilled into nearby cities. In Butte, an editor at *The Montana Standard* took a call from a correspondent for the *London Daily News*. "We have heard that you have another of those nasty riots in your state prison," the correspondent said. After securing all available information he hurriedly closed the conversation. "I'll have to get busy to keep London informed."

Dan Powell, by this time a high school junior in Waupun, was browsing in the library when he heard over the school's loudspeakers an announcement of a "prison riot in Deer Lodge, Montana," and instantly fell to wondering about the welfare of his older cousin Floyd, who had taken him squirrel hunting in the Wisconsin woods. Dan's older brother Fred, who was working in a department store in Massachusetts, saw the news on a street corner when he glanced at a new edition of the *Boston Globe*. There, above the fold on the front page, was a story and photograph about the riot.

Before the next dawn, more than 100 newsmen would arrive in Deer Lodge to cover the big story. And a big story it was.

"Pictures were taken and news gathered by men willing to forego the thought of sleep," wrote Clyde Reichelt of the *Great Falls Tribune*. "It was a time when sleeping was almost out of the question because at any moment the situation could break wide open and it was the man with a camera or the pencil ready to take notes that might get the scoop of the year."

***

Early on the evening of April 16, Mary Jo Burns crossed the alley to visit her neighbor, Jean Giles, who had just finished supper with her three young children. The Gileses had rented a house on Kohrs Street from Ada Holt, a social studies teacher at the junior high school. "Have you heard anything from Murry?" Mary Jo asked, trying not to alarm Jean, who had been preoccupied with the children. Mary Jo fidgeted, realizing Jean knew nothing of the riot. She told Jean what she had heard on the radio and then went home.

Murry was working second shift; he didn't usually arrive home until a few minutes after 10 o'clock. Not wanting to alarm the children, Jean put them to bed. She paced the living room until a knock came at the front door. It was nearly 11 o'clock. The town mortician, Ralph Filcher, stood under the porch light. Expecting to hear the worst, Jean swung the door open. Filcher spoke quickly, wanting to reassure her. "I saw Murry on the tower and he asked that I get a message to you that he's okay," Filcher said.

Jean Giles wouldn't see her husband for another full day. Virtually every guard, even off-duty guards like Alex Cuthill, came voluntarily to the prison. Cuthill, a retired Butte police officer, was in Butte when the riot broke out. He rode to Deer Lodge with Police Chief Emett Sullivan and eight other police officers.

***

Operators at the Deer Lodge exchange of Mountain States Telephone sat along the tall switchboard in high-backed chairs, furiously plugging calls. At the first news of the riot, operators occupied all seven positions at the switchboard. Two additional operators assisted with long distance routings. Normally, only five operators went on duty. Milton A. Johnson, the local exchange manager, described the scene: "Our seventeen lines for long distance calls were in constant use and all other facilities were taxed to the maximum during the prison emergency.... The local switchboards looked as though they were alive with calls."

The telephone company routed long distance calls through Missoula, Butte and Helena. One circuit was kept open for emergency outgoing calls from the prison. Mary "Irene" Evans, who had been chief operator for five years, worked continuously for thirty-six hours. Others worked twenty-one hours straight. At least ten operators who lived in Deer Lodge worked around the clock; others from the Butte district office came to assist.

The company set up a special line inside a Deer Lodge motel for *LIFE* magazine photographers. Nine of their pictures would be devoted to a cover story in this popular family magazine known for its outstanding photography. One of the pictures would show Ted Rothe lying in his casket at Beck Funeral Home. To the horror of mourners, a cameraman climbed through a window. He focused his Hasselblad at Rothe reclining in satiny state, his big hands carefully folded across a new suit.

In the electrical repair shop at the back of Thompson's Photo Studio, cameramen working for *Associated Press* sent fifty pictures to New York over a direct continuous circuit using the Baehr

Electric telephone connection a few doors down Main Street. In hours, newspapers across America would be delivering these pictures to an audience of millions. Howard Thompson, who owned the studio, watched with fascination. It was the third time, beginning with the pea riot, that *Associated Press* had used his shop.

Now, within seventeen minutes after film came into his shop, he watched pictures transmitted for world distribution. Ten of those minutes were devoted to developing and printing, seven to send the picture. A photoelectric tube in the transmitter developed light waves from the photograph. Those light waves, in turn, became sounds waves on the telephone lines. In New York, a mechanism converted the sound waves back to light waves and hence, created the actual photograph.

***

On Thursday evening, in a statement issued from his Helena residence, Governor Hugo Aronson expressed his sorrow to Ted Rothe's family: "The hearts of all Montanans go out to the wife and two children of deputy warden Ted Rothe who was killed in the line of duty at the Montana State Prison." Aronson said he sent a telegram to Mrs. Rothe "expressing the sorrow of myself and of all Montanans." On behalf of guards held hostage, he was "waiting prayerfully ... our deepest sympathy goes to their families in this tense hour," and he noted: "This is a tragic occurrence and one which we all regret. I speak sincerely and from my heart when I say that I am truly sorry. This is a black day and I want to pay tribute to this fine young man who served Montana to the end."

Warden Powell, meanwhile, issued a three-point ultimatum to rioting convicts. He demanded that all hostages be released, that the two principal ringleaders (whom he did not name) surrender to officers at Tower 7, and that convicts not taking part in the hostilities segregate themselves in the far corner of the prison yard. Powell told news reporters that troops and law officers would storm the prison with rifles, machine guns and tear gas unless his demands were met.

More significant, however, was what Powell didn't say. Having been held captive for three hours by the men who killed Ted Rothe, he had ample time to observe that Jerry Myles and Lee Smart would never give themselves up. His curt characterization of "two principal ringleaders" left to the imagination whether he meant Myles and Smart, or Myles and Alton, or Smart and Alton. Powell didn't immediately reveal Lee Smart as Rothe's killer. He also knew unsympathetic convicts couldn't gather in the prison yard. Ringleaders had locked them in their cells.

In brief comments to news reporters, Powell described the riot as "a spur-of-the-moment thing," although his guards and anyone else familiar with the situation would have considered his comments less than truthful. The guards had warned Powell and Rothe about rumors of a disturbance. The domino collapse of security and the hostage taking embarrassed him. Now a prison warden's worst nightmare was his.

Fortunately for him, the wall around the prison was a veil and life behind that veil was a secret kept from most everybody. Powell described the revolt as a cover-up for a failed escape attempt, and told reporters: "A few of the convicts got on top of the catwalk and took a few rifles. How they did it I don't know. It is not an organized thing. Most of the convicts want no part of it."

In stories appearing in Friday morning newspapers, Jack Zygmond of the Associated Press quoted "prison officials" who identified these supposed ringleaders: Myles, Smart, Alton, Wallace Bear Jr., and Thomas Ray Jr. Bear had walked out with Powell four hours after the riot began, and Ray was virtually unknown and a minor player, if involved at all. No mention was made of Donald Toms, who had searched and handcuffed the warden, or of Carl Frodsham, who had thrust a knife in Powell's stomach, or others Powell knew well, convicts he personally observed taking an active part in the riot.

Many people began to compare the riot with what had happened in 1957. The pea riot was more truly a riot in the conventional sense, involving most men from both cell houses. In his public comments, Powell didn't point out the obvious difference: Jerry

Myles. On this day in 1959, Myles and Smart had shown their inclination to kill. No convict or guard doubted their intent. They held an entire prison of more than 400 men hostage. Prison being the place it is, other men could start killing either from revenge or from desperation.

In prison, a place of mind-numbing routines, new developments induced new reactions, new leaders, and new dangers. Guards held prisoner in Cell House 1, guards in the towers, and all the convicts on the blocks knew that Myles and Smart, and to a degree, George Alton, were only the most recognizable threats. Death could come from anywhere. Hostages shuffled inside their cells as pilled-up convicts threatened them with beatings and worse.

In terms of criminal liability and the further potential for human suffering, this riot would live in infamy. Disheartened that his reform efforts had culminated like this, disbelieving that his friend and protégé Ted Rothe was dead, feeling badgered by news reporters clamoring for more insight into conditions inside the prison, Powell looked at the scene with dismay. Hadn't it been only a few hours since he had met with architects to talk about his vision of a new prison? Hadn't he been leading Montana State Prison into modern times? Now this.

In December 1958, about four months after taking his new job, Powell presented a report to Montana's prison commissioners that said: "Major problems facing this institution can be summed up very briefly. We are operating a physical plant in very poor condition and with a minimum of staff and a shortage of trained personnel. One of the most difficult things with which I was faced was the lack of experience in the staff charged with the responsibility of supervising the inmates." In the winter of 1959, the Montana Legislature approved Powell's request for more money for salaries, which drew gratitude from guards. It also approved another measure calling for a $5 million bond issue to expand the ninety-year-old prison. When the riot began, construction of a new minimum-security building on state-owned land west of Deer Lodge had not been completed. Before the riot, Powell and the Board of Prison Commissioners shared a fear that crowding men together without proper classification levels, known as grades, could lead to trouble.

Powel refused to appoint a spokesman to work with news reporters, preferring to dispense information as he saw fit. An acrimonious relationship began almost immediately. Nevertheless doing their jobs to feed a public hungry for news, reporters quickly found other sources, usually prison guards and police officers who had overheard conversations. Hence came the news from various unnamed sources of a planned assault on the prison scheduled for 4:30 Friday morning. Then came the word from an "informant" that troops would storm the prison at 6 that morning. Radio stations broadcast the news, alerting convicts in the radio room of Cell House 1. Morning newspapers informed their readers of an "imminent" attack that didn't come. Frustrated National Guard officers, especially Bus Ellsworth of Deer Lodge, began to question Powell's ability to quell the riot.

***

Few people understood that Jerry Myles was no ordinary convict. Only Powell and a few other top-level prison officials knew that he had led a mutiny at USP Atlanta. This lifer, his ego bloated with conquest, had captured Montana State Prison by using techniques he had observed in 1946 during the bloodiest escape attempt ever at Alcatraz Island. As more news of the riot broke, clichés began to describe him:

"small-time burglar"

"flamboyant homosexual"

"six-time loser"

In fact, none of these descriptions was accurate. "Small-time burglar" related to his most recent crime in Butte, albeit his general pattern of behavior, but failed to reflect his propensity to defy authority. He wasn't a stupid petty thief who blundered his way to jail. He was a man of superior intelligence, struck crazy by a trail of emotional and psychological spoilage. More than a professional criminal, Myles was a professional convict.

He was never a "flamboyant homosexual" in the sense of feminine behavior or appearance. At times he regretted his impulses, feeling he soiled men to whom he felt attracted. At other times he revealed the "wolf" that Walter Jones perceived him to be, driven by his urge to dominate other men. In the 1950s, people generally believed that homosexuality meant flamboyance, but guards knew better. In prison, sex between men was common and sometimes, hardly clandestine. Queen though he was, Jerry Myles wasn't alone.

Myles' reputation as a "six-time loser" stuck, although the chore of sorting out his multitudinous offenses baffled federal and state prison officials wherever he served. As Myles served time in one prison he was wanted for one or more unrelated crimes elsewhere. Since 1932 he had committed at least fifteen crimes in eight states. Crimes included burglary, grand larceny, conspiracy to commit robbery, transportation of stolen securities, escape, mutiny with weapons, carrying a concealed weapon and even loitering. He served time in three federal prisons and six state prisons, possibly the source of his "six-time loser" reputation. Three of those state prisons were in Illinois, one in Georgia, one in Indiana and then, finally, Montana. Myles served his largest block of time in Alcatraz, a sentence that consumed seven years. Among his shortest was a three-week jail sentence for burglary in Phoenix, Arizona, in 1932.

Little was known about Lee Smart except for published details of his murder conviction. Newsmen mistakenly reported that Smart had been hitchhiking before he killed Charles Denzil Ward; therefore, Smart became known as a notorious hitchhiker rather than a car thief. Alton, being even more of a mystery, received less press than the others. He was described only as a burglar with a previous escape on his record.

***

After 10 o'clock, Gert Knutson stood at the door watching for her husband Ralph to come home from his afternoon shift. When he didn't appear, she asked a girl living upstairs to stay with her children. She walked through the dark toward the prison until a guard stopped her one block from the warden's house, refusing to let her pass. "I have to find out if my husband is one of the hostages," she begged. He escorted her to Powell's house, where she learned Ralph was a hostage. Although four months' pregnant with a baby who would be named Ronda, she stayed awake all night, staring at the prison with other wives through a large picture window in the warden's living room.

Near the back of the prison wall, in a tiny house a mere one hundred feet or so from Tower 5 on the northwest corner, Betty Simonsen paced the floor, frantic with worry. Her husband John hadn't returned home from work and now, hours later, she looked through the window to the prison looming before her and cried.

Betty knew all about convicts. Both parents made their living at Montana State Prison. Her father, Ray Hoy, and her mother Edna, a matron in the women's prison, lived in a house just behind hers. Betty and John had moved to Deer Lodge a few months earlier after John quit a construction job. Hearing news of the riot, Betty's sister, Margaret Moughton, came from Butte to help console Betty and help with her year-old son.

"I know he's dead," Betty sobbed, picturing John suffered at the hands of mad criminals with knives and other weapons. It was a blessing that she didn't know her husband had come face to face with Ted Rothe's murderers. John, after all, had seen for himself what they had done to the deputy warden. Like Betty, each hostage wife had her private torment. Some stayed away from the prison. Others stared at it and a few walked incessantly back and forth in front of it, ignoring the chapping wind. Friday's newspapers would report this story:

"Two red-eyed wives of Montana Prison guards walked into the prison office at 4 a.m. Friday, seeking word of their hostage husbands.

"They were Mrs. Robert Wyant, 29, mother of two, and Mrs. Vernon Kelpin, the mother of three children.

"Both women, who obviously had been crying, said their husbands had worked together in the smelter at Anaconda until they became guards six weeks ago.

"The women said no one from prison headquarters had informed them of their husbands' danger. Mrs. Kelpin said, 'I was away at work all day and other officers came to me and told me he was a hostage.'

"Kelpin was assigned to Cellblock No. 1 and worked the 2-10 p.m. shift. Wyant was assigned to the infirmary.

"Asked about the attitude of her husband toward his new job, Mrs. Kelpin said, 'He enjoyed it. He liked it very much.'

"Officials finally invited the two from the cold doorstep into the warm prison office."

The hostages wives, like Floyd Powell and the others, feared the worst with good reason. As day turned to night, hostages wondered when they would die.

Lee Smart (center) drew attention from a newspaper in nearby Butte.

- 19 -

Walter, Jerry and the newsmen

Early Friday morning, sometime after midnight, Jerry Myles peeked through the bars at Walter Jones on Cooks' Row. "I think we'll use you," he told Jones. "But I am still going to kill you."

Jones tried to stay calm. "I know," he acknowledged quietly.

Myles led Jones up the stairs to Galley 6, two tiers higher, where he locked him in another cell. Jones couldn't sleep, tortured by the certainty that Myles would act on his promise to commit murder.

George Alton and other convicts prodded remaining hostages to the same galley. Alton stopped in front of Clyde Sollars. "They have spotted where you fellas are, so we gotta move you to protect you," he told Sollars. "Now, you either move willingly, or we will move you, and we are just the sons of bitches that can, so don't try to be a hero." Jimmy Hubbard came to Officer Chris Pletan's cell. "They're wise to where we put you, so we're moving you again," he said. Neither Alton nor Hubbard explained whether they meant protection from other convicts who might harm the hostages, or from the armed force outside the walls. In those early hours most everybody, hostages and convicts alike, feared an attack from outside that could set off a killing spree inside.

Frodsham, Toms and others kept their hostages at bay with knives, escorting them in pairs to cells along Galley 6. They directed the hostages to walk in a duck-like crouch; Myles and the others thought they couldn't be seen from the wall towers that way. Pletan entered Cell 240 with Officer Ray Quilici.

Alton stood at the grating door leading onto Galley 6, his gun aimed down the stairwell. As hostages passed him on their way upstairs, Myles warned them to keep their matches cupped with their hands. "If you try to signal the towers you'll get it a lot sooner," he promised.

Officer Victor Baldwin described the scene: "They took us. They would open up each cell separately, and Alton had the rifle, and he was very, very well loaded. I mean he was heavily built up. He acted like a crazy man sometimes, but apparently he held his head pretty good. As long as we didn't make any false moves, we were all right. He treated us well, and he stayed clear of us, but we were covered. No chance of getting away. No chance of trying anything." Any man who could slip his captors needed only to sprint across the exercise yard to one of the guard towers, but the cell house was a fortress. Relative geography meant nothing. Here, convicts ruled. Here, a view to the street was a tease. And what if one of them escaped? What would happen, then, to the others?

At the entrance to Cell 242, Toms searched Baldwin, pocketing his tie clasp with his name engraved on it, his fingernail clipper, and his time book that listed his work assignments for the week. Inside the cell, Baldwin and "Little" Jones heard Frodsham coming down the galley, asking for wristwatches. Jones hid his inside the cell. When Frodsham appeared, Jones thrust his bare arms through the bars. Baldwin hadn't time to react, and Frodsham took his watch.

Officer Vernon Kelpin, meanwhile, saw Hubbard approach his cell. "They have decided that if the National Guard comes in you fellows have had it," Hubbard told him. He said death would occur by any means convicts saw fit, and it was a sadistic list: shooting, stabbing, burning, hanging or beating.

***

Walter Jones couldn't be certain of the time, because Donald Toms had stolen his wristwatch, but he guessed at least three hours passed before Myles returned. It was dark, sometime before dawn. Like Jones, Myles hadn't slept. Fatigue showed on his thick face.

"We want you to do some talking," Myles said, opening the cell door. Myles told Jones to turn around, then snapped handcuffs on his wrists.

Myles prodded Jones with his rifle barrel down the galley to the north end where convicts had laid a twelve-inch wooden plank across to the guards' catwalk. Jones tried to keep his balance as he lifted his legs over the galley railing. One slip and he would plunge thirty feet.

"It would be something if you fell and splattered all over the floor down there," said Myles, taunting him. Concentrating on the plank, Jones silently thanked the Marines for high off-the-ground training at the recruiting depot in San Diego. He made it across, but as he lifted his leg over the railing on the other side, he slipped and nearly fell, and he felt his body go weak. Myles watched him, unconcerned. Once Jones got onto the catwalk, Myles pushed him past the steel door that led into the northwest tower, then through a gun cage diagonally positioned from the other gun cage where George Alton had seized the rifle on Thursday afternoon. Lee Smart had made this gun cage in the northwest corner his defensive headquarters. Here, within steps of the tower door, he could watch hostages and the guards on Tower 6 on the north wall at the same time.

As Myles paused to talk with Smart, a concussion that sounded like a gunshot invaded Cell House 1. Myles instantly swung the muzzle of his cocked rifle against his hostage's stomach. He listened, his eyes wide and his face flushed with anger.

The small army congregated outside on the street heard it too. A highway patrolman deflated the ensuing panic outside when he reported that a guardsman had accidentally discharged his rifle. Jones saw in the eyes of his captor a wild vacant stare of madness, born from the twin evils of psychopathy and fatigue, and for a few tense seconds he braced for the gut-ripping bullet. Defusing what might have become a bloodbath, a fellow convict yelled a warning to Myles that a car backfired on the street. Myles relaxed his angry face. He looked at Jones almost remorsefully. His words came clean and measured:

"I wonder where you and I would have been tonight if I'd had a family when I was a kid."

***

Jones made a mental count: twenty married hostages who had forty-one children among them. He wondered if Jerry Myles, who now considered himself an orphan, had made the same appraisal. Was it longing for family that stopped the impulsive Myles from pulling the trigger?

Jones followed the catwalk around the north end and then to the east side, where Myles and Lee Smart and George Alton had captured Officer Gus Byars the previous afternoon. Myles jerked his hostage to a halt. "You're going to talk through the windows to the people outside," he said. Earlier, on Thursday evening, Myles had instructed Robert Foster to build a public address system with a microphone from the theater. Now Myles guided Jones to a loudspeaker that faced Main Street.

"What do you want me to say?" Jones asked.

"Tell them not to storm us. They say on the cell headset radios that the troops are going to attack. Tell them if they storm I'll shoot you and kill the rest of the hostages."

Again Jones recognized the conflict in Jerry Myles. His desire to show who was boss would eclipse his fleeting feelings for family and friends. The hostages would die after all. Jones ignored the loudspeaker. At one of the broken windows, Jones leaned his face into the cool night. It was just ten degrees above zero. In the mountains the temperature drops sharply at night, and the chill felt like bee stings on his cheeks.

"This is Jones! J-O-N-E-S!" He didn't want a National Guard sharpshooter to mistake his identity. "Newspapermen, can you hear me? I want to talk to you." Quickly, reporters and their cameramen assembled in the middle of Highway 10 to hear the haunting hoarse voice. Reporters furiously scribbled his words by yellow light from pale streetlamps. "Do not, whatever you do, storm this place because they are ready to kill us. Hostages will die violent deaths by burning or hanging. These men mean business, so play it cool. I repeat, don't storm or we'll lose all!"

Twenty-four hostages remained inside, counting himself and the two men housed in the hospital: George Axtell, the typing teacher, and the injured Officer Backman. Then Myles stepped to the fourth window from the catwalk's south end, brazenly showing his body from the waist up in the glare of spotlights. His blue shirt hung unbuttoned over a white t-shirt. "I hate this man, but he's doing the right thing now," he yelled, referring to Jones.

"This is a dead man speaking," Myles said. Calling the prison a "dungeon," he stated his demands: "All we want is a chance to be heard. We want the public to know about the brutality inside, the living quarters, and the lack of medical attention." Then it became clear that he indeed had been compiling a family count of his own: "We are holding eighteen men in here who have families. We don't want to see anyone killed; all we want to do is reach the public. We are willing to die for that purpose. This is a prison of torture ... of brutality. If you send the National Guard in we'll kill them."

When he finished with his speech, Myles traded his rifle for a knife. Gripping Jones by the arm and pressing the knife against him, Myles paraded his hostage up and down the catwalk in full view of the people outside. He pressed Jones close to the windows, using him as a shield, while Smart covered Jones with a rifle from the corner. Despite his nervousness, Jones laughed. "What do you think I'm going to do, fly out?" A convict yelled to Myles that he might get shot if he didn't get away from the windows. "Naw, I got Jones with me, and if they get me, so what?" he replied.

"I couldn't care less," Jones told him.

Smart broke his customary silence. "You're a damn fool, too," he offered from the corner.

Confident that Jones' warning would forestall an invasion, Myles shuffled the taller man back onto Galley 6 and then to Cell 248 across from the steel door leading into the northwest tower. After Myles left a convict arrived with coffee and sandwiches. "I'm hungry, but I can't eat with my hands handcuffed behind my back," Jones told him. The convict opened the cell door. As Jones stood on the galley, the convict fed him an egg sandwich, bite by bite, and held a cup of coffee to his lips. Grateful, Jones drank it all. Back in the cell he stretched out on the cot and dozed, but awoke in pain. He had rolled onto his handcuffs, jamming them tight.

***

As dawn broke Friday, Alton came for Jones. "We're going to take you to the dining room to talk to the warden," he said. Jones had heard talk about the tunnel. He knew convicts were playing for time. From scraps of conversation he overheard, they would make a case for prison reform. Myles seemed taken with the idea. It gave him a forum, swelling his importance as the ringleader in charge.

In the dining hall, convicts stationed Jones in front of the gun cage before hiding in the hallway leading to Cell House 1. They heard shuffles inside the gun cage, indicating Warden Powell had not come alone. Indeed, Powell had brought Father Lynam and former warden Bill Benson. Myles and the others suspected a trick. They wouldn't talk unless Powell came alone. Later, in his cell, Jones heard worried hostages whispering to him. They hoped he could save them from gruesome deaths. "Stick with it, Jones," one of them said. "It's your baby."

A few hours later the cons marched Jones, dreadfully tired, to a second meeting with the warden. His arms ached. Smart leveled his rifle, while Alton pressed a knife to his throat. The knife seemed more for show than anything. Jones realized a remarkable change in Alton's demeanor. He seemed heavily doped up, but in a second of lucidity, he whispered: "Jones, this is turning out real bad." Jones, elated, thought his instincts had been right. If only he could turn Alton against Myles and Smart he might break the riot.

In the dining room, Jones relayed the convicts' grievances to the warden. Some were valid complaints, although Powell already had improved living conditions and the cons knew it. They wanted the bucket system eliminated in Cell House 2, the 1896 building. They also wanted lights installed in old cells, and brighter bulbs in newer ones. They complained about the lack of a full-time doctor and a full-time dentist; they weren't happy that a trained convict treated patients and gave inoculations.

The convicts demanded that Powell fire Benjamin Wright, the state parole board director. Jones knew that with only three parole officers to cover Montana, the parole system was hardly adequate. Just in its infancy, it was struggling to meet the needs of a prison where so little casework had been done. Jones understood the convicts' concern, but he had watched Wright and his tiny parole staff try to cope under difficult circumstances.

Powell tried to explain that as much as possible was being done, and that a new Legislature-approved prison budget would come available on July 1. Powell, Jones and other prison administrators hoped voters would approve the bond issue to build a new prison.

Myles and the others asked that three newsmen be allowed into the prison to hear the convicts describe their conditions. He surprised Jones with his stipulation that Jones would go outside the walls to escort the reporters inside. Powell agreed to this demand on the condition the hostages be freed. Not a word would be printed, he vowed, if the ringleaders didn't cooperate.

When Myles and Alton prepared to release Jones at mid-morning, they discovered they had lost the key for the handcuffs. Harold Laureys, disoriented from lack of sleep, couldn't find anything suitable to pick the lock. He used a hammer and chisel to break the chain. As this was being done, Myles warned Jones, "Tell that warden that if you don't come back I've got six hostages set up to hang, and I'll burn the rest of them."

He gave Jones eight minutes to return, and then he went to the hostage cells where he told the despondent guards to clean themselves up, and clean their cells, because company was coming.

***

George Alton and Jimmy Hubbard escorted Jones up the west steps into Inside Administration and into the lobby past Ted Rothe's office. He departed through the east grating door, a handcuff still clasped to each wrist, the broken chain dangling like a bracelet.

When Jones stepped through Tower 7 to freedom, Father Lynam shook his hand.

Jones found Warden Powell, who was briefing the selected reporters: Fred Zavaterro of United Press International, Keith Fuller of The Associated Press and Art McDonald of radio station KREM in Spokane. "You know, we're not going to resolve this thing peacefully," Jones told Powell. "Myles and Smart are not going to give up. They're going to take as many as they can with them." Jones quickly described the location of the hostages, and what he knew of the tunnel plan. "They're all set up to be killed, some will be hanged. I am going back in. I don't know for how long. The inmates are touchy. Any little thing will set it off." He spoke of the "specter of death" inside Cell House 1 and warned: "They're shook. The inmates there are in control and they're shook." Then he spent a moment with his father Walter and his older brother Gordon, a physical therapist at Community Hospital in Butte. They stood in the crowd of hostage families.

"I've got to go in again," Jones said.

His father, a sixty-nine-year-old retired mine boss from Butte, leaned close. "Will you be back, son?"

The younger man hesitated. "I don't know."

Anxious to return within eight minutes, Jones started for the Tower 7 entrance. Powell touched his shoulder. "You don't have to go back," he said quietly.

"Let's go for broke, warden," Jones replied, determined to disguise his fear. He stepped to the base of Tower 7 to reach for a key lowered by Lieutenant Pete Lynch. "Sure you want to go back inside, son?" asked the older kindly Lynch. Jones nodded, then stepped through the grating door into the gloom. Jones mounted the steps to Inside Administration where, met by armed convicts, he was returned to Cell House 1. While Powell and the newsmen entered the tunnel leading into the gun cage, Myles met Jones. "I didn't think you would do it, Jones, but it's a damn good thing you did or twenty-one men would have died."

Alton hardly could contain his glee. "Now I think we can accomplish something," he said, smiling. Jones hoped he was right.

***

Seven convicts came to the dining hall to relay Myles' demands to the newsmen. Much to their disappointment he didn't show his face. Myles pressed for more concessions. He now wanted newsmen to enter the prison to see conditions for themselves, and to take photographs. Powell again agreed to these demands, but only if Myles first released the hostages.

Zavaterro of UPI described his impressions from where he sat on a wooden box in the dining room gun cage: "Below us were the convicts. The fellows that did most of the talking were George Alton and Jimmy Hubbard, a dark-haired burglar with a gold tooth. There were other convicts who came in from time to time to spell out their troubles.

"With them was the prison sociologist, Walter Jones, 24, a husky six-footer. He had a pair of broken handcuffs on his wrists. He was there to help the men explain their grievances.

"George Alton, a wiry little convict in his mid-20s, passed his hand wearily over his forehead and through his curly brown hair. 'I can't think,' Alton said in a voice that was nearly a moan. 'I'm tired.'

" 'Take it easy,' Jones said. 'Be quiet.' "

Fuller, chief of bureau for Associated Press in Denver and a former prisoner of war in Germany, also wrote of Alton's behavior: "Alton acted strangely, appeared incoherent and uncoordinated. He complained that he had not had sleep since the riot began at 4:30 p.m. the previous day and blamed lack of rest for loss of the ability 'to think straight.' A guard told newsmen later, however, that Alton was 'hopped up,' perhaps from medication taken from the prison dispensary."

Hubbard led convict complaints with his evaluation of the parole system. "Lots of first timers get sprung too soon," he alleged. "Anybody knows that a second or third timer who's been a model prisoner is a better parole risk. And anybody who's in for life knows he doesn't ever have a chance of getting parole." Other complaints included condemnation of the bucket system in Cell House 2 and of the lack of segregation for young first-time offenders. One convict protested use of the Hole.

But it was the parole system that angered convicts most. One by one, Alton called them in front of the gun cage to speak their minds. Typical was the second convict interviewed, a man who went unidentified: "A 30-year-old man has no hope. It's easier to get a parole as a lifer. They parole the crime, not the man. A man's crime has nothing to do with it. A man in for murder might be a better parole risk than someone else. On the other hand a man in for a lesser crime might be a greater parole risk."

Said another prisoner: "It is the parole system that's wrong. It killed Rothe."

"How's the food?" one newsman asked.

A convict pointed with satisfaction to salt, pepper, ketchup and mustard containers on the fifty or so tables stretching across the dining hall. "You see these? We didn't have them before the new warden came."

After two hours the convicts fell silent, seemingly at a loss to find much more to criticize. "That's just about it," one of them finally said.

"We have concluded our part of the bargain," Warden Powell told the convicts. "Now I'm looking for the hostages to walk out as agreed."

Alton spoke up. "I'm really going to try to sell this, warden, but you know I don't have the say."

"I think you do," Powell rejoined, hoping he was right. Secretly, the warden had come to accept that Jerry Myles would never release the hostages. To complicate the situation, Alton appeared a pathetic sight, nothing at all the fiery little man by reputation.

Their interview ended. The three newsmen filed down six steel steps into the tunnel, convinced they had just seen a staged show. While the rank-and-file convict population might feel genuine concern toward conditions, their concern had nothing to do with the riot. Like they were saying out on the street, "It's Jerry's riot."

***

Back in Cell House 1, Jerry Myles refused to release the hostages as he had agreed earlier. Swaggering up to Jones, he outlined a new demand: "You go get the newsmen and photographers and tell the warden that when I see a story or a picture in a newspaper – any newspaper – the hostages go free."

Visibly dismayed, his authority eroding, Alton argued with Myles. "But we promised that the hostages would go free the minute the newsmen came in," Alton implored him.

"No! Get it in print first!" Myles shouted. Moments later he wanted his story printed in "thirty or forty newspapers" before he relented on the hostages.

Alton could see that Myles had no use for him anymore. A few hours earlier, when Alton had gone to the wicket door, Myles aimed a rifle at him through the opening.

"Don't shoot!" Alton called, worried that Myles might do just that.

Myles seemed to think that Alton had turned against him. "Why are you intervening in trying to keep the guards alive?" he demanded of Alton. "You shouldn't have no liking for them, because they are on the other side of the fence from you."

Now, hearing Myles' latest tirade, Alton gave up. Concluding little hope remained for escape, even as convicts hacked away at rock and packed earth beneath the northwest cell house tower, he walked away. Finally he accepted what had been obvious to him all along. Myles didn't want to escape. He thrived on power. The hostages gave Myles leverage for more publicity. Myles, the dethroned con boss, was king again.

Jones observed that Myles' betrayal jolted Alton's sense of right and wrong. It seemed that the doped-up Alton had neither the courage nor the will to resist the marauding Myles. Smart, for his part, had been practically mute, staring impassively across the yard at the west wall towers, coddling his rifle like a teddy bear. He spoke to ask a convict to find him clean underwear and socks, but he otherwise remained silent, seemingly accepting Myles' leadership. Smart behaved much like Jones had expected he would. The social science officer's research showed an anti-social, self-centered teenage boy devoid of conscience and guilt. He could easily beat a polygraph test. Jones never saw Smart get excited, but he knew he was dangerous. Smart's immaturity made him prone to senseless impulses, as his cold-blooded murders of Charles Denzil Ward and Ted Rothe showed.

Meanwhile, Powell explained to reporters in the street why he had allowed only three newsmen to go inside the prison to hear convict demands. He said it was agreed that convicts would release their hostages if the newsmen wrote their stories. "They didn't keep their word," he said of the convicts. "They reneged on the state offer, so the newsmen did not release any of the information gained from their talks with the convicts. It was no intent to bypass the Montana press. It was a prisoner request to get the story throughout the country."

The reporters filed stories for the next morning, detailing their encounter with Alton and the others in matter-of-fact prose.

***

Throughout Friday's daylight hours, Myles shouted demands from Cell House 1. A *LIFE* magazine photographer snapped a picture of Myles reposing in the sunshine on one side of a tall barred window, caught in conversation with another prisoner, Don Lee Smith, who stood on the other side. They looked like two men on a coffee break. *LIFE* would misidentify Smith as Lee Smart, who did not appear in the window but stayed sequestered in the northwest tower, his emotionless eyes scanning the broad exercise yard that separated Cell House 1 from the west wall.

Basking in his newfound fame, Myles spoke like a political candidate at a press conference, outlining his vision for the prison in broken verbal constructions and responding to questions that newsmen shouted from the street. His voice resounded clearly from the brick and rock fortress. To the guards outside who knew it well, it was a voice speaking from the darkness. They heard growling voices like that, voices full of discontent and anger, hundreds of times a day. This was a new thing, this broadcasting to the street, because it linked two polar worlds, the inside and the outside.

"I was one of the guys over there when Rothe was killed," Myles informed them. "It was an unfortunate accident for which I might be hanged for. If I get life, I want to be treated as a decent man with medical care and like a human being."

"Why was Rothe killed?" a newsman shouted.

"He attacked me after I told him this was a riot." He described Rothe as "the most hated man in this prison but he was a very foolish man."

"Are the hostages okay?"

"They are alive."

Myles railed against Warden Powell: "He is a Caesar. He tells us we have to release hostages first, then get news stories and photos. But I'm not turning my hole card loose."

At another time, Myles presumed a role as spokesman for all prisoners: "We're not fighting for today, but for the next guy who comes in here. The governor won't listen to us, he never will. They give us everything in the world on a string and then take everything away from us one at a time."

He asked that Chicago broadcast journalist Len O'Connor be allowed into the prison because "I believe he would see through any phoniness." O'Connor was known for his gritty reporting from the street and his biting commentary about public policy. Myles evidently liked his blunt manner. O'Connor was a fat man in a rumpled suit. He talked and looked like somebody who would know his way around a prison, but Myles didn't explain his interest in O'Connor or how he knew of him.

Myles also criticized Benjamin Wright, the parole supervisor. That morning word got around that Wright's presence might cause a hostage bloodbath, and by afternoon, he announced his departure, revealing that he had resigned on March 23 but hadn't intended to announce his resignation until June. He said he would quit his $7,000-a-year job immediately to prevent any delay in hostage negotiations. This news came much too late for some people who had viewed Wright as the fuse to a powder keg. Convicts had called for his dismissal during the pea riot twenty months earlier, and a legislative committee in early 1959 recommended his firing.

Wright had come to Montana from Walla Walla, Washington, where he was supervisor of classification and parole at Washington State Reformatory. A statement from the parole board, signed by chairman Clark E. Simon of Billings, vice chairman L.W. Fahrner of Helena and Ted James of Great Falls, read in part: "It is the unanimous opinion of the board members that Mr. Wright is an extremely capable and dedicated man. We feel the state of Montana has indeed been fortunate in having a man of (his) outstanding abilities pioneer the way in the pardon and parole system in Montana. His has not been an easy task. Insufficient funds, inexperienced and too few employees and unwarranted criticism have all combined to make his job intolerable."

At forty-two, Benjamin Wright pondered a career change. He planned to return to college to study for a doctorate degree in sociology.

***

Spent, George Alton walked away to sleep. Walter Jones watched his best hope for overthrowing Myles disappear down the galley. Alton's constant policing of both cell houses kept order. Without Alton's protection, Jones would have died for sure. Alton had stopped Smart from shooting Jones in the back. The reckless teen with wild eyes hungered for more blood and wanted to make an example of Jones. And Myles, still filled with a fury toward the Powell administration, had told Alton of his intention to beat and hang Jones. Alton talked him out of doing it.

Desperate, Jones offered Myles a compromise. "Let me go out with six hostages," he told Myles. "I'll come back and you keep the rest of us until something has been published."

Myles refused. "No, it's all the way or nothing."

"Okay, let me go out and tell the warden about this new setup," Jones replied. "I'll come back."

At 3:30 Friday afternoon, Jones left the prison again. He met Warden Powell in the middle of Main Street and told him of Myles' new demands. When Jones tried to walk back into the prison, the warden stopped him.

"No, Walt, there's no reason for you to go back in."

"I promised, Warden."

"Jones!" Powell ordered. "Stay here." They walked across the street to Powell's office, where Father Lynam joined them. "Your usefulness has ended," Powell told Jones. "The more concessions we grant, the more they'll ask. There will never be a guarantee they will turn the hostages free. If you went back, it would be just another life endangered."

Lynam argued that Jones should return inside to prevent a massacre of hostages. "Walter has been doing courageous work to prevent further tragedy," he reasoned in his lilting Carroll College professorial manner. The priest offered to go himself. The warden refused on both counts.

On Powell's orders, Jones left for home on College Avenue. He took one last look at the stark profile of Cell House 1, which appeared deceptively innocent in the bright afternoon sunshine. He feared for the other hostages, convinced Myles would act on his threats. Jones walked down the street to the Rothe apartment in the commissary building to pay his respects. He told Ted's family that he had admired Ted for his sensitivity and his puckish sense of humor. He felt that he couldn't find the right words to put sense to a senseless murder.

Only twenty-four hours had passed since the riot began, yet in the compression of time and tragedy it seemed like days. Back home in Butte, Jones' elated mother told newsmen: "My prayers have been answered." Said Gordon Jones: "We're proud of him. He's a great kid brother."

When Myles realized Jones wouldn't be returning, he flew into a towering rage. He stormed in front of the hostage cells on Galley 6, screaming, "I'll burn you all!" Officer George Schaffer, the cook, would lament: "We sure figured we'd had it. I've never seen a man so mad."

Late Friday night, Warden Powell received a tip that Myles and Smart planned one final attempt to drive their tunnel under the wall. They had sworn that if they weren't free by daybreak they would kill all the hostages and commit suicide. The weary man from Wisconsin wondered what it would take to stop Jerry Myles.

Walter Jones confers with Father Gerald Lynam outside the prison after Jerry Myles freed him to bargain for a hostage release.

Courtesy Old Montana Prison Archives

- 20 -

Threats of execution, and prayers

When the three newsmen started their Friday interviews from the dining hall gun cage, Floyd Powell stepped back into the tunnel and walked to the south end where a few convicts had congregated on the other side of a gun portal. Fearful of more killings, they pleaded for Powell's quick intervention. As the others turned to leave, one man flicked a piece of paper through the portal.

Powell read the handwritten note under the tunnel's bare light bulbs. The convict asked that he enter the prison through the back gate just after midnight on Saturday morning. They would meet behind the theater where the convict would disclose the ringleaders' escape plan. Powell later wrote down his thoughts: "Was it a means to retake me? Was it their intent to walk out with me and other hostages with a gun at our heads or a knife at our throats? I had no way of knowing. I finally decided to risk it as time was running out and something had to bring this thing to a head."

Hostages might not survive another day.

***

Officer Gus Byars fumed inside his cell. In previous weeks he and some of the other guards had overheard whispers of an impending riot. Byars had warned Warden Powell and Deputy Warden Rothe, but they said their own informants had told them a riot wasn't going to happen. They told Byars to return to work and mind his own business. At least that's the way he heard it. The same thing happened to Officer Larry Cozzens who tried to tell Rothe about the rumors. "I know everything that goes on inside this prison," Cozzens would remember him saying.

Byars came to work at Montana State Prison in 1958 after a tour of duty in Butte's underground mines. As the prison's new auto school instructor, he taught basic mechanics to a class of nearly twenty-five convicts in a room beneath the theater. Engine repair came easy for him. He was raised on a farm near Milton, North Dakota; he had learned to work on machinery when he was a boy. He attended auto mechanic school in Fargo, North Dakota, in the 1930s. In the U.S. Army he commanded a tractor battalion that pulled artillery. He came to Deer Lodge, made his home in the Guards' Quarters, and settled into twelve-hour shifts, six or seven days a week. When he wasn't teaching he relieved guards at various posts in the prison. It was like he had two jobs for one paycheck.

In the auto school, most of the convicts at first wanted to learn how to start a motor without a key. Some of them aspired to learn more. Two of Byars' best students were George Alton and Lee Smart, both men he regarded as quiet, diligent workers who followed class rules.

Byars had no confidence in Floyd Powell. Like many guards, he felt demoralized and unappreciated. He thought of the warden as abrupt and arrogant. Powell's daughter Judie, for one, thought of him differently: as a likable, concerned person willing to listen. In Byars' opinion, guards valued Rothe for his knowledge and his firm, man's man personality, but many of them considered him stubborn and unwilling to listen to their advice, even when they brought him information from the canaries. Byars was one of the guards who thought Powell felt superior to them. To a lesser extent, he believed, so did Rothe.

Since Powell's arrival, convicts tried once to escape through the roof of Cell House 1 by cutting a hole in a heating unit. They had climbed atop the block of cells into a space beneath the cell house roof barely high enough for a man to stand. Hiding their activity through careful timing and an elaborate arrangement of lookouts and distractions, they clipped away the sheet metal to expose an opening wide enough for a large man. Their plan was to shoot tower guards from the roof before rushing the walls. Canaries alerted guards, ending the escape before it began.

Byars knew how escape-minded convicts coveted firearms. He detested carrying an unloaded rifle when he worked the catwalk in Cell House 1. "Carrying an empty rifle is a way to get killed," he told his fellow guards. On the afternoon of Thursday, April 16, when Byars relieved Officer David Hinton on the catwalk, he locked the rifle in the gun cage, refusing to have anything to do with it.

Now, nursing his burning eyes, he felt sure Myles and Smart would have killed him had he been holding that rifle.

***

Separated as they were in cells along Galley 6, some hostages became aware of preparations for their executions. Those guards locked up near the south end saw nothing. Guards closest to the north end saw the weapons of death that appeared on the catwalk across from them Friday morning: loops of wire coiled like wary snakes, glass jugs filled with golden liquid that looked like gasoline. During the night, cons worked their way down the galley, placing open pans of lighter fluid beside some of the cells.

Walter Jones had seen the wire and fluid. Myles had pointed out the wire, trying to scare him. Early Friday morning, Officer Victor Baldwin watched three shapes appear in the sprinklings of daylight. Molotov cocktails stuffed with rag wicks stood in a row on the catwalk across from the galley.

In the early light, Officer Vernon Kelpin watched Jerry Myles construct firebombs on the catwalk. Myles removed the brass end of several light bulbs, filled them with lighter fluid, and then wrapped each bulb in toilet paper before reattaching the brass ends. All the time he was talking with various convicts about progress on the digging, but Kelpin and other guards who watched him doubted his riot would end with an escape. Myles held the deadly light bulbs with fascination, like a child coveting his favorite toys.

Hostages fell quiet in their cells. Some stared wishfully through the bars at a pristine cap of snow on Mount Powell's volcanic crown. So near, so far. Some dozed fitfully. Others wept. It seemed a time for that because death had come close enough to whisper.

***

The previous evening, after hostages settled on Galley 2, convict Clifford Amdahl helped them write notes to their wives. He supplied pencil and paper, then slipped their terse notes through the gun portals into the tunnel where waiting guards hurried them outside. Brief as they were, those notes gave comfort to women who waited tearfully on Main Street. Clyde Sollars wrote cryptically to his wife: "Helen, take the car home and stay home." Ralph Knutson declined to write a note, believing it was a trick. Gert Knutson, one of the few wives who didn't hear from her husband, hoped he was still alive.

***

Sitting in Cell 230 on Galley 6 with fellow hostage Bob Wyant, the hospital guard, Lieutenant Charlie Brown thought about the last will and testament he had written on a scrap of paper he hid in his pocket. A confirmed bachelor, he lived in a single room in the Guards' Quarters, furnished with a military-style bed, a footlocker and a sink. He had little to give in the event of his death, but hours earlier on Galley 2, he thought the time had come to dispense of his worldly possessions.

In some ways Brown was a cartoon character in his own right. He was a big man, bigger in stature than most of the men who worked for him. He stood well over six feet and weighed at least 250 pounds, and he dwarfed his rail-thin captain, Everett Felix.

Sometimes Brown was a joking man. Sometimes he showed a mean streak. Guards never knew where they stood with him. It was like he didn't know how to operate under the Powell-Rothe administration. He seemed to prefer turmoil, and he disliked schedules, and therefore he had a hard time living with the regulations that flooded from Powell's office.

Having worked at Montana State Prison since 1949, he had seen the worst of past wardens and their deputies. He was, after all, a man who knew the prison better than most everybody who worked there. Cons accustomed to knowing most guards as Mister this or Mister that, or addressing them as "key holder" or in times of anger, "screws" and "bulls," called him Charlie. He liked his name; everyone thought of the Peanuts comic strip. Some guards thought he wasn't a friendly man when they saw him around Deer Lodge. He was different in Butte or Anaconda, where he reacted to those same men with a blush of friendliness that surprised and embarrassed them. In Deer Lodge, he bore the responsibility of his position like a yoke, as if it were his and his alone.

Donald Toms, a young prisoner with little common sense, had a soft heart for the big lieutenant. When Toms searched him at the doorway to Cell 230, Brown admitted he had hidden his blackjack club and a second set of keys while he was kept in the Hole. Searching Brown's jacket, Toms found the will. He handed it to another convict who, after reading it, said to the lieutenant: "I know what you want. If anything happens to you, I'll take care of it." He started to walk away, then turned back. "You've got a heart anyway," he said.

Toms returned to ask for a pencil, which Brown provided, and then came again seeking Brown's wristwatch. "I got this for a Christmas present and I want it back," Brown told Toms, who replied: "You'll get it back. You know me, Charlie."

***

In a guard's life, control is everything. They hold the keys and enforce the rules. The power of the court stands behind them, and the state pays their salaries and sanctions them to hold convicts in captivity. Guards were wise to the truth that many prisoners weren't bad but stupid. They wrote checks on money they didn't possess, or drank themselves into illusion and forgotten the slap of the law, or fell into bad friendships or hard times.

The best ones matured as they did their time. Eventually a maturing man can come to despise his personal nonsense and put an end to it. That's the magic of wisdom, although prisons aren't known for it. The guards learned that what they heard at night, those sniffs and sobs and the caterwaul up and down the galleys, wasn't always grief over confinement but regret over the crimes that got them there. Those cons were the best ones, the ordinary Joes who had done something stupid and felt remorse for it. Jerry Myles and Lee Smart and men like them were different. They were psychopaths to the core. Prison wouldn't change them but make them stronger.

Guards held the keys, and that was their power. They were otherwise plain men. Now susceptible to attacks that could include mortal injury, they sat defenseless inside cells built for convicts, protected again by the concrete and bars and common sense of the better convicts and ultimately, they hoped, by God's will. They had little at stake but to survive. This wasn't their prison, except in the occupational sense, and some already had decided that if they lived to see the outside they wouldn't come back. They smelled death and it revolted them and shot the bile high in the throat. Death seemed a high price to pay in exchange for their meager salaries, and who would look after their families?

One of the hostages, Larry Cozzens, felt relieved when he found more than a dozen other guards held captive inside the Hole. As acting sergeant in Cell House 2 he had made enemies, and he thought that the convicts who took him hostage meant to kill him. He sat inside a cell, stripped of his keys and his dignity, and wondered who would be first to have a go at him. That night, after he had been moved to Galley 6, he found out. James Randall, drunk with the thrill of power and a bellyful of pruno, clattered a sparkling-sharp meat cleaver across the bars.

"Cozzens, I'm going to butcher you like a steer," he warned, loudly, shouting words that would appear in court documents. "I'll cut your head off."

Cozzens could see that he wasn't fooling. "Randall, what did I ever do to make you hate me so much?" he asked him, wondering why he even bothered. In prison nobody needed an excuse for irrational behavior.

Randall paused, as if he was trying to think. "You wouldn't give me my medication one day," he replied, visibly hallucinating on pills or pruno or both. He again slammed the cleaver against the bars, calling to nobody in particular to let him inside to teach Cozzens a thing or two.

Cozzens draped a mattress from the cell cot over his shoulders, thinking he could take one slash before trying to grab the other man's ankles to catapult him over the galley railing onto the concrete floor three tiers below. To Cozzens' great relief, George Alton appeared with a rifle to chase Randall away. Hostages counted that Randall returned at least four more times, although in subsequent court proceedings Randall denied threatening Cozzens. Other hostages who saw and heard the confrontations hoped Cozzens would hold his tongue. If Randall persuaded Myles to open the door, Cozzens might die. It was like that in prisons during riots, and it would be like that today.

Cozzens turned to Tom Stanford, his cellmate. "I wish I could just go home," he said, speaking aloud the thoughts of every hostage.

"I wish you could too," replied Stanford, a burly logger from Hamilton, Montana, who had come to work at Montana State Prison after timber prices slumped and his mill closed. Only a few days earlier, while Stanford worked relief on the catwalk, a convict had attempted to cross the monkey bars, just as George Alton had done to capture Gus Byars. Stanford warned the convict away with his rifle. "If you come across I'll blow a hole in you," he threatened. The memory of that incident loomed large. Stanford wondered if that man had been working for Jerry Myles.

Less than a year earlier, Stanford organized a union to improve conditions for guards. He contacted a business agent for the American Federation of Labor and he personally convinced several guards to join. He felt pride at seeing his name on the charter that hung in the union hall.

***

As acting afternoon sergeant in Cell House 1, Officer Chris Pletan had come to know by name most every man who lived there. Some of them, he knew, wouldn't hesitate to murder a guard. "My stomach was in my throat most of the time," he recalled in a later interview. His story is worth hearing verbatim:

"Then began our long wait to see what was going to happen next. They had already advised us, of course we knew that the deputy warden had been killed, and they wouldn't hesitate to kill anybody else if need be. Looking back on this I seem to remember times when I knew there was something wrong because Myles and Smart were always together. They'd be sitting in their cell together, or outside together, or wherever they could get. They'd be sitting by the hour, talking in low tones. I never could figure out what they were up to. I reported this a couple of times to the deputy warden and he just shrugged it off and says, 'Ah, keep them apart, separate them, do whatever you can.'

"Being in charge of the cell houses, I moved them. They used to have cells opposite each other. I put one up on the 7 galley (Smart) and the other down on 1 galley (Myles). This didn't help anything because they were still together, and I knew they were cooking up something but I just didn't know what. Of course, it would be impossible anyway to keep them apart unless you kept them locked up all the time.

"Myles was a very good inmate, that I could see. One thing about him, he liked authority. He liked anybody that had authority. He liked someone that could give authority and give it out right. He used to do anything I'd ask him to. He'd wash the walls, and clean the cell up, he'd do anything. Of course, prior to this, he was what they call the 'king boss.' We called him 'Little Hitler.' He had the rule of all the inmates. If any of the inmates wanted anything they had to go to Myles to get it, and that had been the condition there for a long time. And of course, when the new warden came in, he took this authority away from him and placed him in the ranks with the rest of the inmates. And this aggravated him very much, and I think that was the reason why he agitated this riot. He still wanted to show the inmates and the public at large and the guards that he was still the boss."

When moved from Galley 2 to Galley 6 in the wee hours of Friday morning, Pletan crawled on his hands and knees because he heard voices in the dark telling him he would die if he didn't. Myles told his fellow convicts to turn off their flashlights. To Pletan's surprise, nobody stopped him from lighting his smokes. Once inside their new cell, he and Officer Ray Quilici burned an entire book of matches trying to signal Tower 5, the northwest wall tower, a stone ghost against the night sky. Pletan held the flaming matches close to his face, hoping to illuminate the silver badge on his officer's cap.

Twice, two convicts came to Pletan's cell to threaten him. The first time, on Galley 2, they called him foul names. When they came again after Pletan had been moved to Galley 6, they wanted to get inside. By that time, late Friday morning, both men appeared heavily doped. One of them shouted for someone to open the door. "If we can get in there, we'll tear you apart," he promised Pletan, who had already discarded his necktie to avoid being choked with it.

Pletan describes the scene: "It wasn't long after this riot began that the inmates started brewing up some potent drinks. ... Two hours after that they were drinking whatever they could get ahold of. Of course they had been in the hospital and raided that and taken all the pills they could get their hands on. I remember one, he was an Indian if I remember right, or a Mexican, that came up to me when I was locked up and he says, 'Are you guys nervous?'

"We said, 'Yes, pretty much.' He said, 'Here, have some of these,' and he handed us a fistful of pills of every description. I said, 'Well, I'm not about to take that stuff.' He said, 'They won't hurt you,' and he swallowed them all down. It wasn't long before he was flat out on his back. Of course, as time went on things were getting worse. Lots of them were pretty well intoxicated, already staggering around and blabbering. Myles and Smart, the ringleaders, kept their heads pretty much."

Such irony it was: in those early hours, the psychopaths (and in addition, the petty burglar, George Alton) stopped intoxicated convicts from clubbing and slashing the hostages into gruesome deaths.

Wild drinking and drug taking led to an orgy of sexual violence on Cook's Row, where older convicts raped younger defenseless men at will. Lookouts watched for George Alton and others who would stop the raping, but Alton, now prancing on the clouds, would have been little help. Walter Jones and some of the other hostages were forced to observe these humiliating acts. A convict scraped a gleaming knife across Jones' throat, taunting him to fight.

***

Pletan was sick. Being a severe diabetic, he needed an insulin shot. He called for Myles, who in turn told an errand runner to find some soda for Pletan to drink. Myles warned other convicts to leave Pletan alone, then left. They continued to threaten Pletan until Jimmy Hubbard showed up. "Take it easy, you guys," he told them. "What the hell's the matter with you?"

Hubbard asked Pletan what was wrong. "I'm on the verge of a coma," he replied. Hubbard left to find some insulin. He returned with three convicts, one of whom was Carl Frodsham. "Follow us," Hubbard said.

Pletan thought they might be taking him to the hospital, or even to a place where they would beat him senseless. A lot of the men had their beef against a cell house officer. It's the way it was. But in anachronistic moments in prison, compassion sometimes shows its friendly face. And Pletan, unsure whether he would live or die in the next five minutes, found his captors escorting him to the grating door at Inside Administration. Hubbard yelled to guards on Tower 7 that Pletan could leave if a newsman replaced him. They waited a few minutes. Nobody came, but Hubbard released Pletan anyway.

"They mean business. They're not fooling," Pletan told the sea of intent faces that surrounded him as he emerged onto Main Street from Tower 7 a free man. Guards escorted him across the street into Warden Powell's house. Trembling for insulin, he nonetheless talked with the warden for about five minutes, telling Powell everything he had observed and heard inside. Then he was driven home where his wife and two children, thirteen-year-old Joy and fifteen-year-old Ray, greeted him at the door.

***

Jerry Myles stared through the bars of Cell 218 at John Simonsen and Clyde Sollars. "I want you to talk to the reporters who are coming in here," Myles told Simonsen, ignoring Sollars.

"I don't have anything to say to the reporters that would do you any good," Simonsen replied.

Like a bulldog itching to attack, Myles pressed his flushed face against the bars. "You know, white collar worker, I used to think that you were a pretty damn good guy and I respected you, and you did me a few good turns, but since this new outfit came in you have turned out to be quite a prick. Since you lost your authority in here and you had to listen to the other man," he said, referring to Warden Powell, "you are nothing but a damned runner."

Frightened, Simonsen tried to change the subject. "What are your complaints, anyway?"

Myles named poor living conditions, a bad hospital and insufficient medical treatment. He tried to convince Simonsen that he disliked teenage boys being mixed with the older, tough cons. "You know I don't go for these kids as I have been accused of," Myles reasoned in a psychopathic contradiction familiar to doctors who had examined him in other prisons. "I don't believe in taking on these kids and pumping 'em."

Simonsen reflected: "I don't know what made him decide to do what he did, but when he was telling me this, I just sat there on the bunk and looked at him and listened to him, and when he finished, he looked at me, and he cocked his head to one side and he said,

'I'm not getting through to you,' and he shook his head and walked off.''

Simonsen and Sollars hoped Myles would forget the conversation, and that more pressing matters would distract him from returning.

***

At Deer Lodge's Church of the Immaculate Conception, only two blocks from where National Guard troops began preparing for a possible assault, Father Lynam knelt in prayer before the Blessed Sacrament. He had spent part of Friday morning inside the dining room gun cage, trying to persuade convicts to surrender.

His prayers concluded, Lynam strolled into the garden behind the residence of Father Edward Moran, pastor of the Deer Lodge parish. "I pray God this crisis will be over soon," Lynam told news reporters. "There is little to say, in fact, almost nothing. There is terrific emotional impact behind those walls. Perhaps too many words, some of them unfounded, have already been spoken or written."

Somebody asked how he tried to persuade convicts to give up their hostages and end the riot.

"I endeavored to persuade them to realize that further loss of life, including perhaps their own, would be catastrophic for all concerned," he replied. "I endeavored to persuade them that their own interests would be better served by capitulation, and reliance on due course of law, and future mediation, rather than force."

Having spoken his scholarly mind, the priest walked into Father Moran's home for a quick supper before returning to Montana State Prison to keep vigil outside the walls.

***

At the start of the riot, worried ranchers armed themselves with rifles, shotguns and pistols. Vowing to protect their families at any cost, including shooting convicts on sight, the ranchers threw together a vigilante patrol that drove and walked around a prison ranch southwest of Deer Lodge through Friday and into the night. Bundling in hunting clothing and sheepskin jackets to fend off the biting night air, dozens of men fanned out in fields and forests with assistance from a couple of sheriff deputies and A.D. "Buck" Lightfoot, the ranch foreman. Said one rancher: "If one of those cons tries to walk out of there, we're going to have a real story."

Most of the men were members of the Deer Lodge Valley Protective Association, a citizen group organized in the wake of the pea riot and a series of subsequent prison escapes. They remembered the recent escape of Wilbur Brown, who abducted a Deer Lodge farmwife in plain sight of her husband and children. Said Wilbur McGee, the association's president: "The thing we're after now is security for our families and we have not been getting it."

Between shifts the men brandished their weapons for photographers over beer at the Gem Bar in nearby Racetrack, happy to oblige for any camera that came around. Some of them drank too much, ending any chance of a straight shot at an escaping convict.

***

It was late Friday, more than a full day after the riot had begun, and night had come to Deer Lodge. Floyd Powell walked around the prison perimeter, stopping to talk with tower guards. At Tower 2 on the southwest corner at the vehicle sally port entrance, he told two guards he would return at midnight to enter the prison. "Be alert in case the convicts try to rush me," he told them. He pledged them to secrecy.

Powell returned to the tower a few minutes after midnight, passing through three security doors in a long hallway that flanked the sally port. His informant waited behind the theater, and there, Powell heard his chilling story.

Myles and Smart had decided that if they failed to tunnel outside the north wall they would tie up a hostage, soak him with naphtha, the cleaning fluid, take him into the yard in view of the towers and set him afire. Everyone would hear his screams. Myles believed this would lead to an armed assault on the prison. Convicts could kill a few of the assailants, steal their weapons, and escape in the confusion.

"It was the plan of very desperate madmen," Powell wrote. "One has to realize there were about twelve or fifteen (prisoners) facing serious charges for murder, complicity to murder, kidnapping, attempted escape, assault, and a number of other charges. Some of them would no doubt hang, and others faced years of confinement. They knew they had little to lose no matter what they did from here on out."

Powell went to his big house, found an empty bedroom, and prayed. Only by the grace of God would these hostages live.

- 21 -

Hostages and hostage wives

On Friday afternoon, Jerry Myles decided to move his hostages again. Harold Laureys threw the levers to open the cell doors. Hostages emerged in pairs. Myles aimed his rifle down Galley 6 from the far north end. "If the troops come in we're going to burn you," he yelled to them.

Donald Toms, who had begun the riot as Myles' bodyguard, now was his chief enforcer. Toms herded nine men into 250, the last cell on that galley: Clinton Fowler, Ralph Knutson, Charlie Brown, John Simonsen, Erwin Seiler, Vernon Kelpin, David Hinton, George Schaffer and John Storey. Into the adjacent Cell 248 went eight more: Victor Baldwin, Everett Felix, Larry Cozzens, James Jones, Clyde Sollars, DeForrest Thompson, Tom Stanford and Bob Wyant. In Cell 246 went the remaining three: Gus Byars, Marvin Wallace and Ray Quilici.

Each cell had two metal bunks, one above the other; a toilet and small sink, and a crude metal cabinet affixed to the wall. Myles had run off the convicts who occupied those cells. They resented the intrusion, fearing a violation of their modest belongings as the hostages pressed inside, shuffling to find a place to stand or sit. Yet the residents of those cells didn't dare argue the point; Myles was a frightening man and Toms looked in the mood to kill. Myles hollered down the galley for Laureys to close the cell doors. He shut the doors simultaneously, locking them in place.

At the back of Cell 248, Wyant, the hospital guard, found an earphone dangling from the bunk. He held it to his ear. Over the next few hours he listened to radio broadcasts, sometimes music and sometimes news, transmitted through the radio room in Cell House 1.

That evening, and he didn't know when because he had lost track of time, he heard a startling report. Authorities had pushed spectators away from the prison to Fourth Street, a block east of Main Street. The announcer spoke ominously of reports that convicts intended to throw flammable fluid on their hostages, then set them afire. Wyant told his fellow hostages what he had heard. Most of the guards worked at one time or another in the prison dry cleaning plant and had seen the barrels of naphtha. They felt sure that Myles and the others heard the broadcast as well, and that they would be set afire because of it. Only the National Guard, they knew, could save them.

As if on cue, Myles appeared at Cell 248, glaring at the frightened but defiant men who stared back at him. "If you know any prayers, you better start saying them awful hard," he warned.

Crammed into cells barely large enough for two men, hostages wondered aloud what would come next. "I think the purpose of this eight-man deal is that they're in the last ditch," Simonsen whispered next door to Captain Felix, trying to offer an explanation to the highest-ranking officer among them. While walking down the galley past the windows, Simonsen glimpsed Highway Patrol officers perched outside Tower 4, across the exercise yard to the west. Now the cell house wall obstructed his line of vision.

Toms and the others told hostages to remove their shoes, then Toms threw them through the bars into Cell 244. They left Captain Felix's shoes lying on the galley outside his cell. Some of the hostages refused to obey. None of the convicts noticed.

Late Friday afternoon, the effects of pills and mood-altering concoctions such as the pruno brew began to show. Various men once enchanted with rioting had consumed their medical "fruit salads" with no concern for the result. Subdued by tranquilizers, propelled by uppers, they stumbled around Cell House 1, their eyes glassy, their pupils dilated. When they could get close they egged hostages on, trying to force them to react in a way that would convince Myles to open the cell doors.

Toward evening it was clear they had exhausted the supply of medications stolen from the hospital and other places, including the cabinet in Ted Rothe's office, because they now chewed the medication from asthma inhalers like gum to get high.

After dark, a matter-of-fact voice rattled down the galley. Hostages heard him tell somebody that convicts intended to throw Molotov cocktails into the cells at dawn. Hostages surmised that's why they had been robbed of their shoes. They couldn't stamp out flames without their shoes. They decided they had been grouped together to burn more completely.

Earlier, at dusk, Myles had shown Officer Seiler two bottles. "This is gas here, and if anything happens we will throw some on you and light a match on it," he told Seiler, and the guard knew he wasn't kidding. Hostages watched a convict handing a Molotov cocktail through the wicket door to Myles, who appeared to be assembling an arsenal of fire-catching liquids inside the tower. They watched Jimmy Hubbard give pills to Myles and other convicts. He brought Myles two shells for the rifle; from their near vantage point, hostages could see the shells in Hubbard's hand.

***

Hostages whispered back and forth between cells. Nervous but not hysterical, they debated what to do. Rothe's murder made one point clear. Lee Smart wouldn't hesitate to kill again. But where was Smart? Myles was putting on a show for the crowd outside. He yelled intermittently from the east-facing windows, making various demands. The hostages couldn't see him, because he was on the opposite side of the cell house, but his voice rang like a hammer strike on cold iron.

When he talked with the hostages, he played the friend and then the bully. He joked about setting up a movie to help them pass the time, and for a moment, acted like he might do it. Moments later his humor dissolved into dark descriptions of death. Jerry Myles became one man and then another, and it was here on these galleys and behind these bars that death stood a constant vigil, without mercy.

Guards knew Myles would act on his threats. Pills and fatigue hastened his deteriorating emotional state, yet he managed to remain in control of his riot and of himself. The way the guards put it, he was a con's con. This was "Little Hitler" at his best, forming the world as he saw it, taking charge of his home. Here was his family, an eclectic collection of thieves, robbers, rapists and murderers, and he counted among them the guards, for without them, his position of power wouldn't be complete.

Jerry Myles needed prison. He needed his domain. Now he had influence with his captive audience both inside and outside the walls. Had he been a madman, he might have killed all the hostages in those early hours, much as Joseph Cretzer tried to do in the Alcatraz outbreak attempt in 1946.

The Deer Lodge guards could see he was a more complex type of convict, a man full of contradictions unfamiliar to them. He seemed unusually bright but at times a coward; that's what fellow convict Bill Rose said about him. Had hostages known of his pattern of behavior in other prisons they would have had greater cause for worry. His bluster hid experience of the ages: six state prisons, three federal prisons including the legendary and notorious Alcatraz. This was a man prone to hostile outbursts when the world didn't agree with his thinking. Now he found himself in the biggest show of his long prison life, in a violent riot of his making, armed with more weapons than he had dreamed of possessing.

Now accepting death as inevitable, hostages wondered only whether their demise would come from Myles, from Smart, or from hopped-up convicts who they felt sure would murder them in cold blood for the pleasure of watching them die. Hubbard stopped at the cell doors to remind them, almost nonchalantly: "If they say you are going to die, you are going to die." Most hostages, individually and privately, resigned themselves to this fate. Some prayed silently. Some shook with fear; it was an involuntary reaction that swam over the brain like the tide. Some stood at the bars in defiance.

Others hung in the gloom against the back wall, trying to shut the specter of death from their thinking the way that eyelids block the light.

Their reactions fell into the natural order of things. Survival became the single engrossing thought. They couldn't see how they could be saved. Still, they wanted to put up a fight. When the cons came for them, it would be quick and vicious. Every man locked in those cells knew how ugly it could get. They knew the men who roamed free in the cell house and knew their crimes. Most of the guards were not educated men, but what they saw and endured in the prison every day made them wiser to the potential of human brutality than most people outside the walls. It would be bad, but they would fight.

Officer Cozzens suggested they throw cotton mattresses from the cell cots against the bars as a shield against a spray of gasoline. Waiting until they saw an empty catwalk, Cozzens and other hostages in Cell 248 pushed two mattresses against the bars to test their assumption. They fit perfectly.

After returning the mattresses to the cots, they rehearsed a drill. Each man would seize a corner of a mattress to press it quickly and accurately into place. When the fire came, their lives would be measured in seconds. None of the hostages disputed Myles in his determination to make them human torches if Warden Powell sent his guards to assault Cell House 1. Thin cotton mattresses made a feeble defense against firebombs. In minutes, probably seconds, flame would dissolve the barrier of thin cotton in a hot lick.

Myles and Smart would fire bullets through the mattresses anyway. The hostages would feel what Rothe felt. The hurt of it turned in their minds. Hostages thought death by shooting more desirable than burning alive.

***

Margie Cozzens, twenty-nine-year-old mother of six children and wife of Larry Cozzens, kept her children out of school Friday because other children "would probably ask a lot of questions." She related to news reporters: " 'Mother,' they kept asking me, 'will Daddy get out all right?' " She said Floyd and Dorothy Powell had treated her and other hostage wives well. "They turned their house over to us. I don't think Mrs. Powell slept all night. I hope they get them out soon. I don't think the warden can last much longer. He looks awfully tired."

A day earlier, on Thursday afternoon, Twyla Thompson had come to the prison from the family home at 200 Second Street to meet her husband DeForrest after work, as she often did. Being the prison bandmaster, he worked days, and he should have emerged from the big wall about 4:30. She couldn't get a straight answer about his whereabouts. Not until later Thursday night did she know mutinous convicts held her husband hostage. "I didn't sleep last night and I won't sleep tonight," she said Friday. "I won't sleep until he is out." She prayed that their 11-year-old daughter would see her father alive.

***

Sometime Friday night, Jimmy Hubbard entered Cell House 2 looking for Bo Sherman. Hubbard apparently was having second thoughts about the riot and now was trying to affect a role as peacemaker. He asked Sherman to try to persuade Myles to free officers Clinton Fowler and Clyde Sollars. This would be Sherman's second meeting with Myles. Earlier, Sherman had asked Myles to release Larry Cozzens, a man Sherman told Myles had never bothered anybody. Myles had replied: "I almost killed that son of a bitch today."

Before Sherman had gone to work in the minimum-security garage outside the big walls, he supervised Myles in the garment shop for a short while. They had become fast friends. Myles even confided to Sherman intimate details of his mutiny in federal prison in Atlanta. But after Myles went into Isolation in December 1958, he sent messages through other convicts asking Sherman to sneak tobacco to him. Tobacco wasn't allowed in Isolation. Sherman refused, feeling angry that Myles would expect that of him. Myles cooled to their friendship.

Sherman, outwardly opposed to the riot, met Jerry Myles on the west catwalk of Cell House 1 in a summit of sorts. Officer Baldwin watched Myles emerge from the tower to meet Sherman. A younger stout man with a shock of blond hair swept back in the style of rock swinger Jerry Lee Lewis, Sherman loomed over the shorter Myles. Speaking quietly to avoid being overheard on the galley, Sherman tried to negotiate a release. He faced the window, looking outside, his thick hands gripping the bars. Wary, Myles stood away. Smart pointed his rifle at Sherman and Frodsham held a knife on him from behind. Sherman didn't like Smart. "To me he was just one of those hepcat punks," he recalled later. "Walked around, and every time you seen him, you wanted to grab them britches and sack them up on him, because he wore them right down to the crack of his ass."

After a heated argument with Myles, Sherman left. "I tried talking to him, and I still couldn't do nothing with him. I couldn't do no good with him. He wouldn't listen to me no way."

Sherman went to the auto mechanics school below the theater. He tried to sleep but partying convicts burst into the room. "I left because they was running around in there drunk, and one guy hollering at another, one of them punks, 'Come here, bitch,' they was drunk, staggering all around, and then they come in and they made, oh, I don't know how many more gallons of that old pruno. I am doing twelve years, and I am trying to do it, and I am trying to get out, and I didn't want no life jolt for killing some drunk-some staggering drunk son of a bitch, and that's what it looked like it was going to lead to."

Sherman returned to Cell House 2, which by then had erupted into a drunken brawl. Intoxicated convicts lurched up and down the galleys. Nearly every convict who passed Sherman carried a shiv. Sherman and four of his friends walked around to Tower 1, in the southeast corner of the prison yard, where they asked the guard if they could leave the main prison. Before he fell asleep in a bunkhouse, Sherman told former warden Bill Benson everything he knew about the riot. Like many of the convicts that night at Montana State Prison, Sherman wanted Jerry Myles stopped.

***

Each of the hostages took careful note of their captors. Donald Toms and Carl Frodsham had conducted most of the hostage shakedowns. Jesse DeWeese and others had lookout duty on the catwalk. Some threatened hostages with foul and abusive language. "I get my nuts off seeing the faces of these silly son-of-a-bitching screws sitting in there like that," one bragged.

Don Lee Smith sometimes stood watch in front of Cell 248, where George Alton had posted him. He conversed congenially with hostages, trying to put across the impression he was cooperating against his will. Smith ignored their requests for help, saying that only Myles could help them. The guards thought of him as a Myles hero-worshipper.

Myles had posted lookouts, including a convict known to most hostages as "Muscles," all over Cell House 1. All these men, either loyal to Myles or fearful he would kill them if they didn't cooperate, watched the office across the street and the flag below, bringing regular reports on what they had seen. Others monitored newscasts in the radio room.

When Myles wasn't watching hostages, friendly convicts trickled along the galleys to Cells 246, 248 and 250 to offer encouragement. At great risk, Jack Evans brought hot coffee, tobacco and matches, as did Cliff Amsdahl. Harold Laureys, in charge of opening and closing cell doors, appeared again and again to ask if anyone needed medical attention. He also talked about how poorly the prison had been run and how the riot would change conditions for the better. Richard Walks on Top and Harold Powder Face brought a few sandwiches. So did Floyd William Ecker, who told hostages he understood their concern for their families because he had children himself, but that he had to "move carefully" or he would be killed.

Simonsen described the cell house mood: "Right from the beginning, we realized the seriousness of our situation. Although there was no joking, there was a lot of good clear thinking. We were trying to think up something to turn the situation. You could talk most of the time with your cell partners, although more or less of a roving patrol of prisoners was keeping an eye on us. Some of the inmates talked to us. It's hard to say why. Some said they didn't know exactly what was going on. I believe all of the inmates were scared."

Joe Rodish and Bob Griffin came to Cell 248 to give Clyde Sollars a partial pack of cigarettes, but more importantly, to tell him they were working on ending the riot. "Sit tight, Mr. Sollars, and we will get you out of there," Rodish said. They returned later, bringing a bar of candy to each of the eight men in the cell. They also offered cigars to Lieutenant Brown in Cell 250.

Before he left the prison, Bo Sherman returned to say he was working on their release. Sollars tells the story: " ... several of the fellows were trying to make (Myles and Smart) think that they were working with them, in hopes that they could get the two rifles together so that they could overpower them, but that they wouldn't try it with one rifle in one place and one rifle in another, because there was too few of them to do anything like that, but they were in hopes of catching the two rifles in one place...."

***

Jerry Myles pushed relentlessly with the tunnel. He sent rotating crews of convicts, including the bakery workers, through the wicket door on Galley 6 and down the stairs into the ground floor room of the northwest cell house tower to dig.

Officer Seiler watched convicts carry sledgehammers and chisels into the tower. On Thursday, he had assisted with a convict yard crew, supervised by Sergeant Gus Beierle, which used some of the same tools. Beierle had worked in place of Lieutenant Spalding, who had spent the day on another assignment outside the prison walls. Had Spalding been taken hostage Myles might have killed him at the start, and the others too. Spalding had fired Myles from his con boss job. Myles hated him for carrying out Rothe's orders and the hate was deep and ugly.

The tunnel began less than a dozen paces from the hospital's east wall, across the breezeway between the hospital and the cell house tower. Myles had barricaded the tower's thick oak door that led outside to the breezeway with diggings from the tunnel. Now reachable only by the stairs that led upstairs to the wicket door into the cell house, the tunnel site had become a veritable fortress. In a gloomy space webbed with heating pipes and barely large enough to swing a pickaxe, reluctant bakers chipped half-heartedly at rock and concrete. Brown clay soiled their white uniforms. Hands accustomed to pots and pans became calloused and dirty and sweat odor filled the clammy dungeon of a room.

Lee Smart, who had been outwardly passionless in his slaying of Ted Rothe, grew edgy. He prowled like a cat from one high window to another, his cold eyes straining to identify uniformed figures behind the broad tower windows across the yard. George Alton, his cellmate and friend, had quit. Smart knew Alton was finished. Without Alton's leadership, other convicts who at first supported the riot would quit. Alton's bravado faded; he knew time was running out. He had seen the National Guard soldiers in the street, watched the flash of gun barrels on wall towers.

Convicts in the kitchen reported a dwindling food supply; normally it came daily from the prison warehouse. Men locked on the blocks grumbled about their hunger. A few convicts instructed to distribute sandwiches had barely managed to assemble a single meal. Some convicts awoke from their naps to find single slices of bologna between pieces of dry bread lying on the concrete floors of their cells, tossed through the bars. The remains of Thursday's dinner, piping hot when the riot began, sat spoiling and neglected.

Baldwin and the other hostages in Cell 248 ate one hot meal. It was a mixture of spinach, green beans and boiled eggs cooked in the kitchen in a metal pan. Somebody handed them spoons and saucers, and they ate with a fury.

Smart sensed danger in Cell House 1. More and more he felt alone because his fellow convicts looked glum and watched him, never took their eyes off him as a hawk watches its prey. He didn't trust anybody, not even his friends on the band gang. The cell house had grown teeth. He and Myles decided to keep their rifles apart. If convicts attacked one of them, the other could shoot. Lee jacked a live shell into the chamber of his stolen rifle.

He didn't feel troubled about murdering Ted Rothe. His mind didn't permit him such regrets. Spending his life in prison distressed him more. His violent life made him appear older than he was. He was still a teenager, even after more than two years' confinement in Montana State Prison and two murders. Life in prison had aged him more than his years. He had come to recognize the gravity of his imprisonment, at least enough to know what it meant to do hard time. He wanted out. He dreamed of being on the road again, free of screws and clanging jail doors and buzz cuts by sadistic prison barbers. He wanted to play rock and roll records, to get himself a car, to find old friends, to raise some hell. Didn't people know he was a rebel? His killing of the traveling salesman was a dusty recollection in his young mind. Lee Smart yearned for his freedom.

The rifle looked too rugged for his girlish teenage hands. As he caressed it, he turned to Walker, one of his most reliable lookouts and a worker on the tunnel crew. "If this thing turns out bad," Smart said, "I'm ain't doing any more time."

***

As Friday night wore on, Jerry Myles kept vigil at the wicket window inside the tower, pointing his rifle through the opening at the hostage cells. Officer David Hinton, who couldn't smell the flammables because of his head cold, nevertheless stayed awake in his dark cell haunted by Myles' warning that if hostages tried to signal the towers, he would douse them with lighter fluid.

From his vantage point on the back corner of the top bunk in Cell 248, Everett "Guff" Felix could see little more than the wooden plank leading from Galley 6 to the catwalk near the door where Myles stood guard. Various convicts, some of them heavily induced with narcotics, tried to walk the plank.

331

By nightfall Friday, Donald Toms was in terrible condition. Several times he staggered across the plank, covering his eyes with his hands. The few convicts still involved in the riot gripped his belt to hold him steady. Toms looked rather clownish bungling along the board in his blue denim convict uniform. Pills invited courage and foolishness, magnifying his child-like terror of heights. Hostages hoped he would fall to his death before he killed one of them.

Guards in Cell 250 watched Myles struggle through the wicket door at various times, aided by a few of his friends who stuffed his thick body through the opening. When not conversing on the catwalk or patrolling through Cell House 1, Myles stayed inside the wicket door, eyes locked on his hostages. "By that time Myles had taken the gun away from Alton and Toms, he was head man, and he was looking right down our necks from the hole," Officer George Schaffer, the cook, was to describe. Schaffer felt "distress" at the show of force: "There was a hundred knives around here."

Schaffer heard one convict boasting that he would cut hostages' throats. No hostage doubted his intent. When Myles wasn't threatening to burn hostages alive, he was promising to hang them. When forced down the galley to Cell 250, Schaffer had seen a rope draped from Galley 6.

***

Some of the wives remembered that shortly after midnight on Saturday morning, Floyd Powell's assistants told them to go home with this icy advice: Nothing would happen until morning unless the hostages were already dead.

When Margery Cozzens arrived at her West Side home on Oregon Street next door to the Baldwin house, her six-year-old daughter Dawn, her face wet with tears, ran to the door. "Mama, the man on TV said they're going to burn up Daddy!"

Margery had heard convicts shouting to the street, threatening to burn their hostages alive. Someone said they had forced hostages to stand on boxes and then looped wire around their necks. One rumor described hostages forced to stand on the railing along the galley, ropes straining at their throats. Throughout Thursday night and Friday, Margery and other wives had waited at the prison, their eyes scanning the tall barred windows for any signs of hope. They seemed oblivious to everything but what they couldn't see. They tried to stare right into their husbands' minds. It was a syndrome as close to extrasensory perception as anybody had seen, common to wives who gathered outside prisons and mine gates and anywhere else where tragedy put their men in danger.

Some of them, like Gert Knutson, sat mute in chairs pushed against the big living room picture window at the warden's house. They wore curlers in their hair and scarves knotted under their chins and pedal pushers. Some sat wrapped in heavy coats, unaware and uncaring of the heat from the house's big furnace, their minds trying to comprehend a place behind those bricks and bars that they had never seen. Margery Cozzens, at home, prepared for the worst. A devout Mormon, she knelt in prayer with her children.

***

Betty Wyant was one of three hostage wives that a *LIFE* magazine photographer captured on film as they stared through the warden's window toward the prison. The riot was Betty's second tragedy of 1959. Two months earlier, a truck hit and killed Betty and Bob's five-year-old son Mark in Anaconda. She had driven to Deer Lodge from Anaconda at the start of the riot and had not slept Thursday night. Most of the time she walked back and forth on the sidewalk across Main Street from the prison, ignoring the chill of the spring winds sweeping off the mountains.

Mingling in the crowd of onlookers, Betty watched Myles shout from the cell house window from where he stood on the east catwalk. She feared for her husband, but when she thought of Bob she thought of Mark. One sadness became another. When prison guards told her late Friday to go home, she let her protective instinct guide her away from the lights of Deer Lodge into the night to Anaconda, toward the safety of her surviving sons, Greg and Kurt.

***

In Floyd Powell's kitchen, Marlene and Babe Lightfoot made sandwiches and coffee until their fingers ached. They fed hostage wives, prison guards, National Guard soldiers, news reporters and others who swirled around the warden's house on Main Street. Marlene mourned for her friend Phyllis across the lawn in her family's new apartment. Her father, shot dead. Hadn't they just been talking about spring activities at the high school and graduation and all their dreams? The gritty horror held tight and no matter how hard Marlene worked it wouldn't let go. It was terrible and real and stuck to her mind like glue.

After midnight, long after she had lost any rational perspective of time and circumstance, young Marlene Lightfoot climbed onto a bed in the warden's house. At least on stage the drama was make-believe. Good or bad, it stayed behind at the end. She fell into a deep sleep that wouldn't last long, because with every sleep comes an awakening.

- 22 -

Jerry's escape fantasy

After dark, as Jerry Myles and Lee Smart huddled in the northwest tower, other convicts passed notes describing the tunnel to prison guards through the dining room gun portals. It had come to that. This riot had been furious at first, full of an intoxicating glee of power and madness. Now several prisoners worked to end it. Some thought it was the right thing to do. Others wanted to save their necks.

The notes revealed the extent of Myles' fantasy. He would burrow into a storm sewer. He and others would emerge outside the walls wearing guard uniforms stripped from their hostages. To desperate convicts disinclined to details, the plan might have appeared feasible, even brilliant. But the storm drain didn't exist, and dozens of armed men fortified the street and neighborhood fronting the north wall. The truth was that even Myles knew the escape wouldn't work, and he didn't care.

As he had learned at USP Atlanta, a tunnel plan sustained a mutiny. Energy of this kind would keep doubters at bay, and followers like Donald Toms would continue to believe Myles knew what he was doing. George Alton, a smarter man, had seen the folly in it.

Most everybody sensed the beginning of the end. Convicts whispered urgent warnings through the portals that when Myles quit working on the tunnel, he would kill his hostages. Their notes described gruesome deaths by burning, hanging or shooting. Some of the informants thought that they might suffer the same fate if help didn't come soon.

A few ticks after midnight on Saturday, April 18, about the time that Floyd Powell was meeting with his mystery informant inside the prison walls behind the theater, Myles admitted to himself that the tunnel had run its course. At the end of it, which extended at the most ten feet from the opening in the tower floor, a shield of stone and sheet metal blocked more digging.

Conley and McTague had built the 1912 cell house to last, and to discourage escapes. Even if Myles had succeeded in breaking through that forbidding foundation, only a team of Butte miners might accomplish the next feat: nearly forty feet of hard digging to reach the outer prison wall, which stood atop rock at least six feet deep and four feet thick. National Guard snipers, hiding behind a hedge across the street at the north end of the prison, watched Cell House 1 with binoculars and scopes. In their thinking, Myles might surrender or die, but he wouldn't escape.

Inside the cell houses, passion that prevailed during the takeover had evaporated. Myles had lost much of his influence, which now was limited to the tower, the hostages and those areas of Cell House 1 that he could view from his defensive position from inside the wicket door. Pills, pruno and fatigue had subdued most of his runners and spies. Myles had lost his influence over the convicts in Cell House 2, as well as the dining hall that linked both cell houses, and the Inside Administration offices above it where Rothe was shot. Powell and the guard commanders knew this. If not for the hostages they could have charged into the prison from several directions with no resistance from hungry and scared prisoners.

Psychiatrists at other prisons had concluded again and again that although Jerry Myles was prone to psychopathic behavior he understood the consequences of his actions. For Myles the tunnel had been a diversion, allowing him to prolong the end. In the past thirty-some hours he had attracted more publicity and attention than in his entire forty-four years of life. He showed he was really the king boss. His memory skipped through the years to the elation he had felt wearing the red robe at USP Atlanta. How good it had felt against his skin. How powerful he had felt wearing it. If his riot in Deer Lodge failed, isolation and disgrace would follow. He knew that from his long lonely life in Alcatraz. He didn't intend to be captured alive.

Myles reached into his pocket for Floyd Powell's watch. The warden and the others would be coming for him soon. Riots don't continue forever. Myles learned that hard lesson in Atlanta. He saw it at Alcatraz, where waves of screws came for blood. Bernie Coy, who led the bloodthirsty escape attempt in 1946, had tasted a sensation of power and influence that most convicts after a few years behind bars didn't bother to even dream about anymore. For Coy and Marvin Hubbard and their four accomplices, it was destined not to last, and it wouldn't last for Myles, either.

It was easier to start a riot than to end it. Myles didn't fret over the ending. Earlier, after he hid his hostages out of sight of the towers, he switched on the lights of Cell House 1. Friday evening he shut them off again, and now he sent his tunnel crew back to their cells in the dark. Just he and Smart and a few others remained. Myles met Smart in the third-floor tower room adjacent to the wicket door. They argued about their hostages. Smart wanted to shoot them. Myles countered that to fire on the hostages would invite an immediate counterattack from the National Guard. It was too soon for that, he told Smart. The hostages, Myles said, would save them. Killing the hostages would be easy when the time came. They would fire pointblank at the men inside cells across from the wicket door on Galley 6. Or they could burn them. Killing the screws would require no effort at all.

Over the next couple of hours Myles and Smart roamed the shadowy tower, sometimes together, sometimes alone. Followers like Herman Cardinal and Carl Frodsham watched them but stayed out of their way. Myles and Smart had nothing left to do but die. In ordinary life they were simply a lonely career criminal and his demented teenage boyfriend, but they held the rifles and so the power.

From windows on the second, third and fourth floors they watched four wall towers, the sprawling exercise yard, the hospital, the theater, and the long sidewalk that ran north and south along the west side of both cell houses. They watched little lamps burning in the towers and occasional bouncing beams from flashlights. They knew that men who wanted to kill them stared back from behind those tower windows. Neither side could see the other in the dark of the mountain night. The wind still worked its way from the west, spitting little noises. Myles and Smart heard a few words now and then, indistinguishable but spoken by the men who hated them. A wooden door slammed, as if blown shut by the wind. They heard metal hitting metal, sometimes like the clink of a coffee pot, sometimes harder, like the clunk of a rifle on a metal railing.

The TB ward was full of ghosts. Men had died there. Myles and Smart thought they could hear the ghosts walking. It felt cold and spooky. Myles and Smart were almost ghosts themselves, and they began greeting death as an old friend. Their faces look ashen in the weak light from moon and stars. Cardinal saw their faces, and he crept away into other rooms and hid.

Their rifles in hand, their countenance being as soldier sentries watching for enemy attack, Myles and Smart vowed they wouldn't be taken alive. Soon the National Guard would come for them. They agreed that before daylight, they would shoot and burn the hostages. Then they would shoot each other.

***

Miracles being what they are, Captain Everett Felix and his men remained alive through the most desperate and unstable of circumstances. Felix ran a mental checklist: a riot led by a psychopath wanting to show who was boss, a loaded rifle in the hands of a cold-blooded killer, fatigue and drugs inviting hallucinations and desperation, weapons of execution appearing in front of their cells, negotiations that had produced nothing, and although Felix had lost track of time, an afternoon and a night and a full day evaporated with no sign of rescue. The hostages already figured that only luck had saved them. Death was only a trigger pull away. Hope already faded among most of them.

338

The more religious men prayed to God. They saw no comfort in the human realm. As they sat helpless in their cells, only the mercy of Jerry Myles spared them, and that wasn't much to savor.

Of course, Felix and the others didn't know the full story, and it was worse. Floyd Powell and the National Guard were at odds. National Guard commanders had intended to storm the cell houses early Friday before dawn, but a radio broadcast destroyed their element of surprise. Hostage Robert Wyant heard the news on his radio earpiece in Cell 248. National Guard troops had moved close to the walls. Whispers communicated this revelation to hostages in the other two cells.

In all three cells hostages soaked sheets and blankets from the cots in the toilets to smother flames. Myles heard splashes. His voice roared down the galley: "One false move and I'll give it to you right now!"

Wyant and the other men in his cell sat quietly, three men on each bunk and two on the floor, trying not to make a sound. Soon came another radio broadcast. Troops had pulled back. Captain Felix and his fellow hostages didn't understand why the National Guard had retreated. In response to the radio broadcast, Myles got word out that the rioters had tied up five of the hostages hand and foot, and placed wires around their necks. As his story went, they planned to push the scared men off the galley if an assault was made. And that was another miracle. Despite his threats, he didn't do it, and the men of the second shift remained unharmed.

***

Furious that he hadn't been included in this invasion plan, Floyd Powell concluded that the National Guard was trying to usurp his authority by hurrying an assault at the cost of hostage lives. Conversely, Guard commanders thought Powell had waited too long already. They had heard threats of burning and hanging shouted from Cell House 1. They reasoned that Myles and Smart might kill their hostages at any moment. The riot had gone on much too long.

Another delay might result in a crazed killing spree of defenseless men.

On Friday evening, Powell told news reporters that the riot was stuck in a "sort of sweating out stage" and admitted he had no definite plan for regaining the prison. He either didn't know or didn't acknowledge that National Guard commanders planned an assault for early Saturday morning. He said it was still his intention to find a way to free hostages unharmed.

The warden also told newsmen he was easing restrictions in their coverage of the riot. He told them that he had appointed J.L. Hoffman, deputy registrar of motor vehicles, to represent the prison administration in news matters. Hoffman lived in Deer Lodge and worked in the state office across the street from the prison.

Even if he had been inclined, Powell could not personally handle demands for interviews. Governor Aronson's office in Helena already had fielded calls from news agencies in London, Winnipeg, New York City, Seattle, San Francisco and Nashville, among other major cities. Every newspaper editor and broadcast news director in Montana and most surrounding states made repeated inquiries. The presence in Deer Lodge of big city newspapers and national magazines confirmed the tremendous public interest in the riot. Among the journalists working at the prison was a team of *LIFE* magazine photographers and writers, and a reporter-photographer team from the *Denver Post*.

***

Two of the National Guard commanders, Bus Ellsworth and Richard Kendall, lived in Deer Lodge. Many people, distressed at the violence on Main Street, would remember concers that the new warden was forcing a big prison mentality on a small prison town. To Powell's credit, he had done much in his eight-month tenure as warden to advance the prison into modern times. He knew from his experience at Wisconsin State Prison how a good prison should run, but changes of such a magnitude took time. However beneficial that reform had been, he hadn't worked at the Deer Lodge prison long enough for his progressive ideas to be accepted. Then came terrible developments: a slain deputy warden, prison guards held hostage by desperate convicts, and no resolution in sight. Powell felt terrible about the death of Rothe, his friend and partner in reform. Yet some people would allege years later that Powell had let the riot happen to drive home the need for a new prison. Distrust ran deep.

When word of the riot reached Helena late Thursday afternoon, Adjutant General Mitchell immediately ordered six more National Guard units to active duty at Montana State Prison. One came from Helena, four from Missoula and one from Anaconda. Several members of the Deer Lodge unit, Battery A, 443 Armed Field Artillery Battalion, already were in uniform. By evening, at least 150 combat-geared guardsmen arrived at the high school football field near the old Trask gym, just two blocks from the prison.

After Powell's escape from his captors Thursday night, Governor Hugo Aronson had placed the warden in full charge of operations, which by Powell's definition meant he could give orders to Maj. Gen. S. H. Mitchell of Helena, state adjutant general and commander of the Montana National Guard, and Supervisor Alex Stephenson, commander of the Montana Highway Patrol. Counting various city police officers and sheriff deputies and his own prison guards, Powell on the riot's second day commanded nearly three hundred armed men, all of them eager to avenge Rothe's murder.

But how? Before Friday had ended, National Guard commanders claimed they began mapping a second plan for taking back the prison, openly defying the warden. Powell hadn't slept since Wednesday night. Exhausted and besieged, he tried to manage the swirl of activity the best he could. He discarded his tie and brown sport jacket; now, with a hunting cap cocked on his strawberry mane, he found himself surrounded by newsmen wanting information and by prison guards seeking guidance. Meanwhile, four of Montana's highest-ranking National Guard commanders convened in the state criminal identification bureau behind Powell's office.

That midnight meeting marked the beginning of the end of Powell's career at Montana State Prison. This sudden reversal in

[]

leadership, this apparent absconding of his authority by Montana's National Guard, would trouble Powell for his remaining days at the prison, in ways he couldn't imagine.

Publicly and in his later memoirs, Powell took full and exclusive credit for planning a tactical assault that blended all forces at hand. He did thank Guard commanders and the Highway Patrol for helping, but said that the idea belonged to him. He later wrote: "I found Denny Spalding (a prison lieutenant loyal to him), who had been constantly available, lending me his support, and told him my plan. I'll never forget his remark to me. He said, 'Warden, with the Lord's help we can do it.' To work, it had to be accomplished with absolute secrecy."

Bus Ellsworth, a man who would become Powell's nemesis, tells an opposite story. "Floyd Powell did not plan the assault," Ellsworth stated flatly years later. "General Mitchell called for a meeting of the Montana National Guard commanders and other key personnel in the warden's office across from the main gate of the prison." Attending various strategy sessions were Ellsworth, assistant state commander Lieutenant Colonel Richard Kendall, group commander Colonel Meyhew Y. Foster of Missoula, Guard colonel and former acting warden Bill Benson, and occasionally Robert Zaharko, a Deer Lodge highway patrolman.

Mitchell, who shuttled back and forth from Helena, put Foster in charge of National Guard operations in Deer Lodge. Foster, like Benson, was a seasoned combat veteran. As a soldier in the Fifth Army's 36th Division he had been an artillery spotter from the air over southern France in World War II. He had participated in the liberation of Rome two days before D-Day and had fought the Germans through Italy into Austria. Foster also fought in the North Africa campaign. Artillery was his specialty.

Foster and Ellsworth described the preparation this way: Into Saturday's wee hours, the planners reasoned through one assault strategy and then another. They didn't know if they could catch the riot ringleaders in the northwest tower of Cell House 1, and they didn't know how many weapons they had, but they knew how to attack. The takeover of Montana State Prison would become a military invasion, planned with all the deliberation of a frontal assault.

Foster wanted National Guard officers to lead seven teams of rifleman, firefighters and medics in a charge on the prison before dawn. Each team would include one prison guard and at least four enlisted guardsmen.

No maps existed of the prison's interior. Foster and the other commanders decided that prison guards would guide them to their destinations. Some of the soldiers, in fact, had worked as prison guards. In total, fifty National Guard troops and eight prison guards would participate in the assault.

Years later, Foster said he and the other Guard commanders didn't include Warden Powell in their plans. Foster said he knew little of Powell, had never talked with him and wasn't sure what he looked like. Powell's absence from the planning sessions didn't worry Foster at all. "I just wasn't really concerned about it. I had this mission to go in and rescue those hostages," he would recall.

The plan went like this: Ellsworth would lead the overall assault but also a team of his own. Kendall would lead a team and Major Hugh McElwain of Missoula another; Captain Reuben Dwight of Helena and Captain Dale Dahlgren of Missoula would lead a team together; and Lieutenant Burton K. Walsh of Missoula, Lieutenant Francis R. Pulliam of Missoula, and Captain Horace Gregory Jr. of Missoula each would lead their own teams.

Benson, armed with a pistol, would accompany the first team into the prison. Foster would enter with the third team, then go straight to Cell House 1 to help find the hostages. After nearly three years of World War II artillery combat, this would be Foster's first infantry fight. Dr. Benjamin of Deer Lodge and Father Lynam, the Catholic priest, would follow the combat teams.

Zaharko, the Deer Lodge highway patrolman, attended the final briefing. He remembers that Floyd Powell wasn't present, that Guard commanders and law officers had concluded Powell was "in way over his head," and that the final meeting amounted to a strategy session to invade the prison without the warden. During that session a Butte photographer snapped a picture through the room's only window, a small pane of glass that was high and barred, as Foster sat at the table, his men standing around him.

Zaharko knew the prison's interior as well as anyone who met that night, with the exception, possibly, of Benson. Having been a patrolman for four years, Zaharko had gone inside the prison walls dozens of times, often to return escapees he had apprehended on Montana's highways. He had served four years in the Army Air Force during and after World War II including time at the first atomic bomb site at Yucca Flats, Nevada.

His military training included the firing of various weapons, including machine guns. As the meeting progressed Zaharko's role became clear. When the National Guard invasion began, he would fire rounds from a machine gun through the north windows of Cell House 1 toward the wicket door used by the ringleaders. The plan assumed his incessant firing would drive Myles and Smart to cover, preventing them from killing the hostages. Powell later would say that he devised the machine gun plan and that he personally had instructed Zaharko on how he wanted it executed. Zaharko said Powell had nothing to do with the plan and had not talked with him about it.

The plan was decided by two o'clock in the morning. Foster and the other men looked at each other, and finally all eyes stopped on Ellsworth and Kendall. Deer Lodge was their town. The hostages were their neighbors. They should decide. They nodded their affirmation.

***

In the stillness of that cold deep night, while the valley slept, Deer Lodge guardsman Emery "Buzz" Weston drove to the armory at the City Pavilion across the train tracks to retrieve a rocket launcher. As the Deer Lodge Guard's administrative supply technician, he was in charge of such matters.

Soon after that, Captain Dwight of the Helena National Guard headquarters unit came to the elementary school gymnasium on College Hill looking for Master Sergeant William Rose of the

Missoula Guard and Sergeant First Class Floyd Hoff of the Deer Lodge Guard. He drove them three blocks to Outside Administration, where Kendall outlined their role in an attack plan. Rose, a bazooka expert, and Hoff, his loader, would begin the attack on Montana State Prison. Dwight then drove them around the prison to Tower 5 at the northwest corner. At the back of the car he opened the trunk. There lay the rocket launcher, powerful enough to stop the Third Reich's best tanks.

- 23 -

The National Guard and the bazooka

An armed invasion at night can be rude to a sleepy man. About three hours after midnight, long before the curious eyes of the Saturday sun would pry from the east, National Guard commanders summoned their troops to a briefing inside the historic college gymnasium on the hill.

The men who didn't live in Deer Lodge had been sleeping on cots on the gym floor. Most of the Deer Lodge men had gone home to their own beds but few slept. It was clear to all of them that an attack on the prison was imminent.

Ron Scharf was one of them. He had barely slept at his home on Fourth Street when the phone rang and he knew why. All the troops sensed urgency. They heard the stories of hostages on their death row, their murders possibly imminent. So too, then, would be the National Guard invasion. Late Friday night, the Deer Lodge soldiers were sent home until further notice. National Guard commanders wanted to create a diversion. They hoped convicts watching from Cell House 1 would misinterpret the departure as a disassembling of the Guard. With great fanfare, guardsmen left the old gym.

A curt voice on the phone told Scharf to hurry back to the gymnasium. "Don't attract attention," he heard before the click.

"Are you going into the prison now?" his wife asked.

"Not now," he said, not wanting to alarm her and knowing he had done a poor job of it.

She looked at him, already knowing the truth.

***

The gymnasium where National Guard troops camped stood tall and stark in plain view of the upper east-facing windows of Cell House 1. History connected the two buildings, just three blocks apart: the gym had opened in December 1913, a year after completion of the cell house. From any of the high galleys, Jerry Myles and Lee Smart and their lookouts watched military comings and goings at the gym and its adjacent football field. This show of force, while intended to intimidate the convicts, also afforded a measure of convenience. Guardsmen parked their military trucks in a line on the field. The gymnasium, with its locker rooms and showers, made a suitable barracks for the troops.

When the call to action came the young men huddled around their commanders in the gym, straining through bleary eyes as they examined prison mug shots. Look close, they were told. These were the ringleaders of the riot. These were the men who murdered Ted Rothe. These men, they were told, must be stopped.

So this was Jerry Myles. He looked like a man who knew his business. He didn't look at all scared, like some of them do when they pose for a mug shot on their first day inside the prison. The guardsmen saw the sass in him. He had come to Deer Lodge on a long trail of tears. It showed there, in the battered road map of a face. His eyes looked electric, full of sparks, and he defied authority with a cocky tilt of his head.

And this was Lee Smart, the boy who had murdered a traveling salesman up north. An emotionless punk kid, to be sure, but they saw Rothe's reflection in his cold eyes and felt anger. And then came George Alton, the man least familiar to them. He was an enigma, really, but his handsome face looked hard and tough. The papers hadn't written much about him. They said he was a burglar and habitual criminal. Some of the guardsmen had read Associated Press accounts of his interview at the gun cage in the dining hall.

Myles, Smart and Alton. To these guardsmen they were just faces, frozen at the snap of a camera, faces without voices, without bodies that gave proportion to their criminal looks. From their throats had come threats, from their minds some contorted view of the world. The guardsmen didn't know that Myles was more dangerous than Smart, and Smart worse than Alton. They saw faces locked in time by a camera lens. A picture of a face didn't reveal how a man carried himself, but the guardsmen could see disturbed thought behind the eyes that stared back at them. These were the men they would hunt.

The Scharf brothers, Ron and Jack, didn't hear specific orders to shoot the ringleaders, but the implication was clear. "Memorize those faces," they were told. The soldiers would save the hostages – at any cost.

While most of Deer Lodge slept, fifty National Guardsmen and their commanders huddled for a briefing. Acting on orders from the midnight strategy session led by Colonel Foster, officers divided the troops into teams. Then they described each team's mission in the assault on Montana State Prison.

Among them was the 443rd Field Artillery, staffed with men from Deer Lodge. Lieutenant James Girard, the commander, had met Ted Rothe only the previous Sunday. Girard was driving to Rock Creek Lake, a popular destination for families in a crease of the Flint Range high above the valley west of Deer Lodge, when he saw a stalled car. A big man stood beside it on the dusty rutted road, and when Girard got closer, he recognized the new deputy warden. After they shook hands Rothe introduced Girard to his wife and mother, who waited in the car. A tire had gone flat on their big sedan. He couldn't get the jack free from the trunk. Girard helped him change the tire; the road was rugged and full of sharp rocks that played hell with two-ply tires. Rothe said he was turning back to Deer Lodge. "Let's get together real soon," he suggested, and Girard drove toward the lake, anxious to talk again with his new friend.

***

Girard slept at his home on the West Side when the phone rang deep in the bottom of the night. "Hurry!" said the husky voice, and he did. He knew his duty, and at the age of thirty-one, he was old enough to have earned his way through the ranks of the National Guard. His training included parachute jump school at Fort Benning, Georgia. Girard had been a guardsman long enough to understand that inevitably he would carry live rounds into a tense situation. He was a Deer Lodge man, through and through. He had grown up in this little town where but a whisper was heard after the sun went down. He made a good living as a machinist working on trains at the Milwaukee Road car shops. He had a personal stake in the riot, too. Hostages Victor Baldwin and Larry Cozzens were his neighbors. They lived just a few houses away on Oregon Street.

***

Buzz Weston heard his commanders say that anyone caught running should be shot. The hostages, once liberated, would be evacuated in an orderly manner to avoid mistaken identity. That was the plan. Weston knew better. In the dark, confusion would prevail.

Each man armed himself as if going to war. Like his fellow guardsmen, Jack Scharf carried an M-1 carbine. Its clip held eight shells. He drew a drab olive denim bag over his shoulder. Inside it he placed at least six pouches of ammunition, two clips to a pouch. That made ninety-six rounds. His leaders had said that although the ringleaders had rifles they had little ammunition to fire back. Nobody knew for sure.

***

Walter Jones would have killed Myles and Smart. He would have shot them, or beaten them in hand-to-hand combat. He never got the chance. Throughout his twenty-six hours inside Montana State Prison he thought of one scenario and then another. He was a Marine, taught to fulfill his duty without question. His duty here was clear. The ringleaders had intended to kill him. Jones would have taken their lives without regret.

He left the prison on Friday evening wishing he could have stopped the riot. He tried to sleep in his basement apartment on College Avenue, but reporters from *LIFE* and other news magazines tried to force their way inside. Jones roomed below a family residence with Mark Joroleman, whom he had hired a few months earlier to be his social services assistant. Reporters yelled bids for his story: "Five hundred dollars! We'll give you five hundred!" The roommates pushed them back and slammed the door.

The reporters missed a good story. Even to the *Saturday Evening Post*, the magazine to which Jones finally gave his big interview, he never mentioned his plot to kill Jerry Myles.

On Thursday night as he stood handcuffed on the galley, facing the shorter man, Jones considered knocking him to the floor with a "major ankle sweep," a judo technique that involved using his instep to whip one ankle against the other. If the timing was right and the execution of it flawless, both of Myles' feet would fly sideways and he would fall hard. Falling to the mat during a judo match drove the wind from the lungs. Jones knew that from practicing judo in college. His club often did public exhibitions. On the galley, Myles would crash to a steel walkway. Better yet, he might slip through the railing, falling to the concrete below him.

If Jones missed, Myles would fight. Jones was sure of that. By comparison with the sallow Smart, Jones thought of the older psychopath as a scrapper, strong and willing. Jones had confidence in his judo skills. He waited for the right moment to attack, watching the short rhythm of Myles' little girl feet. He never had the chance. Smart always stood close to Myles, his rifle pointed at Jones. He knew Smart would shoot him if he attacked Myles. It had occurred to Jones again and again that the riot wouldn't have lasted, or even begun, without the rifles. It was always about the rifles.

On Friday, when Jones left the prison for eight minutes, Floyd Powell reached into his coat for a snub-nosed .38 revolver, small enough to conceal in his hand. The warden asked Jones if he wanted to take the gun back inside. Jones wanted to kill Myles and Smart and end the riot, but he knew they would frisk him and find the gun. He and the other hostages might die. It was tempting. Two quick shots. That's all it would take. George Alton wouldn't interfere. Two quick shots, and the riot would end.

Later, in his apartment, fatigue swam over his brain like the tide. He puzzled over what he might have done differently, but he was safe and the hostages were still alive. But so was Jerry Myles. After all the magazine reporters went away, he fell asleep. The mocking face of Jerry Myles filled his nightmares. When exhaustion took over he didn't hear the attack on the prison.

***

Prepared for battle, the troops filed outside while Deer Lodge slept. Some of them had emerged from the gym just like this in their high school football uniforms, running into the embrace of the cheers and lights on the playing field across the dirt road.

Their hot nervous breath trailed behind them in the cold mountain air as they marched in columns south on Fifth Street three blocks to Conley Avenue, avoiding pools of yellow light beneath the street lamps that would betray their activity. Just north of the old prison brick plant they turned west toward the prison. They slipped past silent dark houses. Wind blowing eastward from Mount Powell raked through the naked trees. At the Guards' Quarters on the corner of Main Street and Conley Avenue, kitty corner from the southeast corner of the prison's minimum-security compound, they stopped for a prayer. A National Guard chaplain asked God to walk beside them, and that He protect innocent hostages from harm.

Then these soldiers of the night double-timed across Main Street, circling the compound to Tower 2, the southwest tower. From there they crept around the west side of the big wall to a reinforced door below Tower 4. This was the tower in the middle of the west wall and the one that overlooked both the main prison yard and the women's prison compound behind it.

***

Floyd Powell and his family disputed the National Guard's version of the assault. In his memoirs, Powell said he asked his trusted friend, Lieutenant Spalding, to find duplicate keys for Cell House 1. As Spalding pawed through the key drawer, prison guard Harold Phillips appeared. At the riot's beginning Phillips had stood watch in Tower 1 above the gate through which the guards of the second shift had entered and left the main prison. Now, seeing Spalding busily pocketing keys, he asked if an assault was coming. Fearful that Phillips might reveal the secret, Spalding invited him to join the attack force waiting inside the women's compound.

Ralph Filcher parked his Powell County ambulance at the tower. Deer Lodge guardsmen filing toward the door under the tower glanced nervously at the car, knowing it doubled as a hearse. Filcher chatted quietly with his friend, Officer Murry Giles, who lowered the key to Filcher outside Tower 4. Like other guards, Giles had moved from tower to tower during the night.

Lieutenant Colonel Kendall, a Deer Lodge man, told Filcher he should bring the ambulance "to view the dawn of a new day," leaving Filcher the impression that nobody doubted the ambulance would be needed. Dr. Benjamin, normally examining patients at a clinic downtown or in the hospital on the hill, appeared at the tower carrying a doctor's bag in one hand and a rifle in the other. Prison guards opened two fortified doors beneath the tower. Guardsmen filed into the exercise yard of the women's prison, where they made a line against the big wall that separated the women from the men.

They stood along the sidewalk, their rifles raised and ready for the attack. Just feet away, women begged them from behind barred windows in their cottage not to hurt or kill anyone. "I know it's cold out there, honey," Ralph Filcher heard one of the women call to somebody. "If we could turn the lights on in here, I'd make you a cup of coffee." Some of the "naive young guardsmen," as Filcher called them, inched closer to the woman's voice.

A prison guard barked at them. "Get away from her," he instructed them. "She's in here for stomping a man to death in Miles City."

***

Wearily, Floyd Powell looked around him. Two days earlier he had been designing plans for his new prison. Now, in a dramatic shift of extremes, his deputy warden lay dead, convicts governed his prison, and combat-readied National Guardsmen waited for their commanders' orders. Shadows and metal helmets hid unsmiling and mostly young faces. This riot had made national news. Twenty-two of Powell's custody guards and staff waited to die. Thank heavens Jones and Officer Pletan were safe, he thought. Bus Ellsworth and other National Guard commanders had stolen the show. The soldiers lined up now outside the prison wall, nervous at their impending charge into the prison but determined to save the hostages.

As their fellow guardsmen assembled in the women's prison, Master Sergeant Rose and his loader, Sergeant First Class Floyd Hoff, entered an outside door at the base of Tower 5 on the northwest corner of the long prison wall. The other soldiers waited with their rifles about 100 feet away. Rose carried a bazooka. John Wilson, the police chief, accompanied them. Behind them, across the street where hostage John Simonsen lived, his distraught wife paced the living room floor.

They climbed a tight stairway into the guard roost. Through the windows of Tower 5, Rose and Hoff saw the riot scene up close for the first time, but it was quiet. Before them lay the sprawling prison yard, empty and dark, and the gothic cell houses. They looked abandoned, like haunted old buildings inhabited by spirits. To their left inside the tower, a wooden door opened onto the north wall. To their right, a second wooden door opened onto the west wall. Outside this door their view of the northwest tower of Cell House 1, almost due east over the hospital roof, was unobstructed.

In the twilight they could see little of the prison. Cozy circles of yellow light surrounded a few yard lamps atop tall thin metal poles. Both cell houses looked mostly dark. Only a few shadowy figures moved inside. City streetlights silhouetted the giant structures. It shocked the senses to think the cell houses hid hundreds of men, all of them waiting, many of them no doubt awake, sensing and fearing a rush of fury.

Rose couldn't see detail on Cell House 1, but light from a yard lamp shone on the tall windows of the building's corner tower. It would be enough to make a clean shot.

Earlier, Rose had offered to fire phosphorous shells through the windows to create an inferno that would fry Myles and Smart. Ellsworth and Kendall and the other commanders declined, unsure whether the ringleaders might be holding hostages in the tower. Instead they wanted a concussion effect. They wanted an earsplitting violent explosion that would convince the ringleaders that they meant business. When the order came Rose would fire a round into the brick casing around those windows, eastward from his position on the big wall, and about 100 yards away.

Rose was born in Sultan, Washington, in 1926. His family moved to the Montana resort town of Seeley Lake when he was a toddler. He lived there until he enlisted in the U.S. Marine Corps in 1943. He served as an automatic rifleman in the Third and Fifth Marine divisions in the South Pacific during World War II.

A year after his discharge in July 1946 he enlisted in the U.S. Army, then served four years in Austria. In 1954 he joined the Missoula Police Department as a patrolman after working for a lumber company. The same year he joined the Montana National Guard. By 1959 he had earned the rank of master sergeant, and now, as he stood in Tower 5 in the chilling hush that comes before dawn in the mountains, waiting to initiate an unprecedented attack on a prison, Rose felt comfort in his experience with the bazooka he held in his hands. In the summer of 1958 he taught a National Guard class. His students fired 800 practice rounds from this very weapon.

Hoff, his loader, knew the Deer Lodge men well. He had been raised in town and attended high school with many of the guardsmen who waited to attack. Hoff found the scene surreal. On lazy Deer Lodge summer evenings, the kind every child of the prison town would remember into adulthood, he and other high school boys had gone to the field outside the minimum-security compound on the prison's south end to watch convicts play softball.

Also known as a bazooka, this launcher measured three and a half inches at the mouth; hence, it was known as a "three point five" in military jargon. When assembled, it measured sixty-one inches long. It was a light weapon, weighing only fifteen pounds. Developed at the end of World War II to counter Germany's best tanks, the launcher fired an ice cream cone-shaped shell capable of penetrating nearly a foot of armored steel. It had a range of 960 yards but was most accurate when fired within 150 yards of its target.

National Guard commanders selected the weapon for its maneuverability. They chose Bill Rose to fire it because of his marksmanship. He belonged to the Montana National Guard's acclaimed rifle team that had brought home trophies from precision matches at Camp Perry, Ohio. In effect he was a sniper. A day earlier, he watched Jerry Myles and Lee Smart from the warden's office across Main Street. It seemed Myles in particular begged a shot to the head or chest as he stood at a window on the east catwalk, bellowing his demands to news reporters down on Main Street. Rose told his commanding officers that he could take Myles and Smart in two shots. One and two, just like that. Although tempted, they told him to hold his fire, believing such action would constitute murder.

In the darkened tower, Hoff swung the bazooka around, crashing it into a metal pot. Hot coffee splashed over the weapon. He cursed his nervousness. A bazooka was a touchy weapon. A missed shot would send a rocket streaking into Deer Lodge's neighborhoods to the east. The National Guard's convoy of trucks parked on Powell County High School's football field lay nearly straight in its path.

Within minutes Bill Rose would be ordered to fire the bazooka that would launch the assault on Cell House 1. He never thought himself a hero. To him, all the heroes had died in the South Pacific during the great war.

***

The riot went much the way Jerry Myles expected. He had mimicked similar outbreaks in USP Atlanta and Alcatraz Island to perfection. The Atlanta "mutiny," as it became known, included an attempted tunnel escape that was actually more of a ploy to buy time than a meaningful intention. In Atlanta and Deer Lodge prisons, Myles won an audience that stood outside helpless but spellbound as he held forth from a barred window. He enjoyed the control. It was familiar to him, and he felt full of himself at seeing the passive compliance in the streets. There they stood, his audience of hundreds down on Main Street listening to every word he spoke, making him famous in the papers and on the radios and television sets all over who knew where. He owned the prison now. This was more exciting than what had happened in Atlanta. He was young then and didn't know how to make the most of what he had done.

In Deer Lodge, he made a name for himself. No matter how it ended, they would remember Jerry Myles.

As well, comparisons can be drawn between Myles' doings in Deer Lodge and the 1946 riot at Alcatraz. Although Myles didn't participate in that one, he knew the full story. He knew of ringleader Bernie Coy's ingenious timing. Coy's principal partner, Marvin Franklin Hubbard, was a more violent convict with a history of gun-related offenses. He was second-in-command to Coy as Lee Smart was to Myles.

In both cases, inmates climbed onto the catwalk, subduing the guard and stealing his rifle. Both riots started on the premise of escape attempts, although neither attempt was plausible. Both Coy and Myles were longtime federal prisoners, neither known as a killer. Both had been cell house orderlies. Both chose riot partners who killed prison officials. In both cases the riot started during lunch relief. Both riots commenced after months of planning, involving contraband taken from prison industries. Lengths of takeover were similar: the Alcatraz riot had lasted forty-one hours, the Deer Lodge riot from its beginning until the moment the National Guard invaded would last thirty-six hours.

And one other lethal parallel, had Warden Powell and others known the full depth of Myles' riot experience, would have rocked them. In Alcatraz, one of Coy's psychopath partners opened fire on their defenseless guard hostages, locked in three cells with no chance to protect themselves. Three cells, just like Deer Lodge.

- 24 -

Sergeant Rose and the surprise attack

Bill Rose crept out of Tower 5 on the big wall. He would fire through the railings that flanked the walkway. To his right and below him toward Tower 4, his fellow guardsmen waited inside the women's compound, shivering as much from anticipation as from sixteen-degree temperatures. The wind still blew from the west, off the bib of snow on Mount Powell, and its cold breath fell over the wall into the tiny compound where the guardsmen waited. Somewhere in the train yards across the river where silver rails threaded through the roundhouse and car shops, boxcars banged as one coupling met another.

Few of the men had seen combat. Many graduated from high school during or after the Korean War and were "nothing but fresh-faced kids," as the folks said around town. These men were young but they were soldiers, and they came to save the hostages and quell a riot. This was a time of duty. They gripped their rifles with authority. This wasn't training at the armory but the real stuff. The guardsmen who were police officers knew how it felt to charge into an unknown situation where lives could be lost. Most of the others didn't. They waited nervously for the signal.

A woman's voice, from the cottage, drifted tenderly in the night. "Give 'em hell, boys," she implored them.

Once the troops entered the prison, men of high position would follow. Among them would be Colonel Foster, Highway Patrol commander Alex Stephenson, Bill Benson, Father Lynam, and Dr. Benjamin, who waited with his carbine and a first aid bag. The presence of a priest and a doctor brought no comfort.

The time had come. The young soldiers watched Lieutenant Spalding unlock the security gates to the main prison yard.

***

Less than an hour earlier, when he got word of the National Guard's intentions, Floyd Powell asked Police Chief John Wilson to call all newsmen into a private house at 920 Fourth Street, a block east from the prison behind the warden's office. After they assembled, expecting to hear an announcement, Wilson told them he was holding them in the house until further notice and that he had officers standing outside to make sure nobody left. He ignored their protests that this constituted an illegal police action and interfered with their constitutional rights to a free press. Powell had made it clear to Wilson that he didn't want convicts inside Cell House 1 hearing news of the invasion.

They wondered what had led to this. Just hours earlier, Powell had apologized to the newsmen for backing them away from the prison on Friday afternoon. "I realize you have been pretty shabbily treated," he told them. "I'm sorry you have been shoved around. It was for security reasons."

One reporter, Jack Bacon, working for United Press International, stood in a telephone booth at the 4B's Restaurant, talking with a radio station in San Francisco just minutes before the Guard invaded the prison. He had seen unusual preparations outside the prison, and he knew something big was going to happen. "I could tell the police were mad when I saw them coming," he said. Police told him all phones were "out of bounds" and that they were taking him to the makeshift pressroom near the warden's office where the reporters had been writing their stories. "I tried to explain this over the phone when all of a sudden I found a rifle about a foot from my head. I hung up in a hurry," he said in a later interview.

At the warden's office he found other newsmen who hadn't been lured to the house. "When we nervous newsmen had been herded into the central room police lambasted us because one radio station had told of unusual activity near the prison. The prisoners had radios too, the officer explained, and should not have been tipped off. We stood there wondering what next when suddenly all hell broke loose. The National Guard had opened up on the prison and we realized what the activities outside the prison had been leading up to. Nobody tried to stop us from getting to a phone after that."

***

Calling to the telephone on Tower 5, Kendall commanded Rose to load. It was fifteen minutes to five o'clock, April 18, 1959. Rose would aim to the right side of the highest window. The order to shoot came minutes later. The assault on Montana State Prison would begin thirty-six hours after the riot had become apparent to the outside world.

Rose squeezed the trigger. Nothing. He cursed. Inside the women's compound, Sergeant First Class Ron Scharf watched the top of the wall, his heart racing. Somebody was saying the bazooka wouldn't fire. The line rippled with impatient voices. Bus Ellsworth, waiting with the troops, got word that a radio station had just broadcast news of the pending assault. "We've got to go! Now!" he shouted toward Tower 5. Kendall buzzed Rose on the walky-talky.

"Hey! Rose! Fire!" he ordered.

In the emotion of the moment, Hoff had pushed the sixteen-inch rocket too far into the launcher. The magneto wasn't making contact. Hoff was no stranger to bazookas. A year earlier, as a member of the Deer Lodge unit, he had taken bazooka training at Fort Lewis in Washington State. Hoff and Rose carried the bazooka into Tower 5, reloaded it under a dim light, and walked back onto the wall. Rose tells the story:

"We had to be real careful after that because a loaded bazooka is touchy and a radio signal might set it off. After I got the order to fire I lined up on a light (it was nearly pitch dark) and let go. The shot was about 100 yards from the tower where we believed convicts Smart and Myles were hidden. When the bazooka rocket hit, the prison rocked with the blast and bricks and glass flew out. The first rocket hit next to a window (I had been ordered not to let a shot go into the cellblock) and the troops began to move.

"The bazooka blast also was the signal for the combat teams to assault the south door of the cellblock under cover of fire from highway patrolmen on the walls and in the towers on the west wall. They must have fired two thousand rounds. Lights flared up and bullets flew. It sounded like a battle going on."

Rose's bazooka shot made good fireworks. Prison guards, Anaconda police officers and highway patrolmen watched the rocket's milk-like splash against the cell house tower. Bits of brick rained through the smoke. John Wilson stood on the northwest wall with Rose and Hoff. When Rose fired, the concussion knocked Wilson backwards with such force that he nearly fell off the wall.

Rose's first shot woke Deer Lodge. Its thunder and echo rolled like a fast train through the prison cow camps on the western benches near Mount Powell, to the Racetrack bar a few miles south on Highway 12 where armed vigilantes met and drank for two nights, and across the wide valley checkered with farms and ranches.

Every wife of a prison guard heard the roar. Some launched out of their beds to the windows where they pressed their faces against the cool window glass, watching for evidence of what they had heard. Others raced into their yards. Amy Lee Felix, four months' pregnant and fidgeting in her apartment at the old Larabie mansion across the street from the high school, tore into the gravel alley in a dead run toward the prison, eight blocks away.

"We heard a terrific noise," Helen Sollars recalled. "My brother-in-law jumped out of bed, hurriedly dressed and drove to the prison office. He returned shortly and said the National Guard had fired a bazooka."

Being her senior year in high school, with the school's spring activities unfolding before her, Janet Brown hated being in the hospital for appendicitis. The doctor had removed her appendix, and the first day of the riot as she lay sleeping in her room at St. Joseph Hospital, a disturbance down the hall awoke her. A nurse came to calm her, explaining that a wounded prison guard had arrived. It was presumably Sergeant Cox. The next day, a Friday, several of her classmates brought her a radio to listen to news of the riot. By then it was widely known that a ringleader had murdered Ted Rothe, father of their classmate. That night, as Janet slept, Bill Rose fired the bazooka. "I almost split myself in two getting out of bed to look out the window and of course couldn't see anything," she recalled.

Across Main Street from the prison, a prison guard stepped into the pressroom where police held newsmen hostage. "You can go now!" he told them. They and the others held in the private residence rushed into the street in time to hear a second deafening blast. A halo of light and dust surrounded Cell House 1, near the northwest tower. It made an arresting picture against the dark sky as stars winked back.

***

As chief of bureau for the Associated Press in Denver, Keith Fuller oversaw news operations in Colorado, Montana, New Mexico, Wyoming and part of Nebraska. He came to Montana on Thursday, the day the riot began, for a casual get-acquainted meeting with AP editors and reporters. He spent the afternoon in Butte, then drove north to Helena. By the time he arrived there, news of the riot broke. Fuller rushed out of Helena for Deer Lodge, traveling those sixty-some miles with Tom Maddox, chief of the Helena bureau, and Jack Zygmond, bureau reporter. In a few hours Fuller had crossed the Continental Divide twice.

Less than two months earlier on March 2, 1959, Fuller had been promoted to the Denver bureau from Little Rock, Arkansas, where he had covered the segregation disturbances. He later would say that nothing about the legendary Little Rock episode compared with the sensational drama that unfolded in Deer Lodge. Personally, Fuller knew all about drama. During World War II he was an Eighth Air Force Command navigator. When his plane went down the Nazis imprisoned him for fourteen months in a camp at Moosburgh, Germany, near Munich.

He hadn't slept since Wednesday night, and now, at the sound of the first explosion, he raced out of the makeshift pressroom.

"The action in the assault on the prison recalled my last day in the German prison camp, the day we were rescued from the Nazis following an attack by our ground forces. Saturday morning ... I heard a bazooka boom. It was followed by lighter arms fire. I involuntarily hit the dirt. The action was so reminiscent of fighting at the battle to free us from the German prison camp that for a moment I thought I was back in the brig myself."

***

Donald Toms slept on a cot beneath the barred west-facing window on the third of four levels. The explosion catapulted the cot across the room, slamming him onto the concrete floor in a shower of brick and concrete. He crawled toward the door, stunned. The concussion, violent and exact, put his brain on hold. Toms didn't know what had happened, nor could he appreciate that he had survived. Men had died all over Europe from rocket blasts like that in World War II. Toms felt a hot salty trickle from his nose and mouth.

Jerry Myles had left the room moments earlier. He stood with Lee Smart at the mouth of their modest tunnel, wondering what to do next, when the round hit three floors above them. The explosion shook the castle-like cell house tower with uncommon strength.

Off and on during the preceding three hours Myles had watched the hostages through the wicket door. Sometimes he had pointed his rifle at them and felt within an impulse of shooting one, or maybe all of them. He knew they feared Smart more because of what Smart had done to Ted Rothe, but Smart seemed oddly distant now. He paid little attention to the hostages. He stared through the windows, his eyes expressionless but fixed on some distant point, over the walls and toward those wild rugged mountains. Myles wanted to save the hostages for last. Other cons had heard him talking about how he could use them to bargain when the National Guard came for him. Shooting them would be easy.

The explosion caught his sleepy mind by surprise. He didn't know where it happened, or what caused it, but it spoke with such authority that he felt afraid. He and Lee hurried up the concrete steps. Each carried a rifle. They needed to get to their hostages but bullets pounded on the wicket door like mad demons. The racket terrified them.

***

Inside Tower 6 on the northeast corner of the big wall, east from where Rose launched a rocket, Highway Patrolman Bob Zaharko waited. When the first bazooka round exploded, he bolted onto the wall, clenching a forty-five-caliber machine gun. If he did his job, and the gun didn't jam, the hostages might live.

Zaharko had watched the riot from the start. On Friday, he could have shot Smart and Myles. Through a four-power scope on a hunting rifle he brought from home, he watched them walk along the catwalk in Cell House 1. He marveled at how the scope brought into focus their facial expressions, as if he were reading their thoughts. Myles spoke as if his lips would never stop. Smart smirked like a brat who hadn't learned his lesson. If not for the safety of the hostages Zaharko would have shot them both. He was sure of that.

Standing on the wall past the short railing leading from the tower door, Zaharko struggled to keep his footing, twenty-two feet above the ground. He and the National Guard commanders had hoped that the bazooka rounds would stun Myles and Smart and anyone else hiding with them in the northwest tower, but they knew that if the ringleaders escaped into the cell house, they would kill all of the hostages.

Seconds after the first bazooka hit, even before the echo died away, Zaharko rained bullets through the north windows of Cell House 1 toward the wicket door on the catwalk, eight feet from the hostages. From the street below, newsmen heard glass smashing. Zaharko fired a shoulder-held weapon known as a "grease gun" that had a tendency to buck and shoot in upward lines unless fired intermittently. It was a World War II combat weapon built for French soldiers that Bill Rose had brought from Missoula. Zaharko fired drum after drum into the cell house. Some of the bullets hit the building's brick facing around the windows, but most sprayed into the cell house toward the wicket door, their soft tips pulverizing on the metal and concrete.

It was now or never. Zaharko had figured that at the angle he was firing, he wouldn't hit the hostages. He worried less about ricochets striking them than about Myles and Smart shooting them, and before he was done firing, he had poured nearly one hundred fifty rounds into Cell House 1. Sergeant Rose, from his perch at the other end of the north wall, watched Zaharko's brave stand from his vantage point near Tower 5. Rose would later commend Zaharko as "a one-man army" who "stood up unprotected" to save the hostages.

Inside, convicts crawled under their bunks, shielding themselves against flying bullets with their mattresses. One of them described them as angry bees buzzing in the cell house. It was some miracle that nobody was hit. The spray of bullets came with such fury that it was impossible to know how to get out of the way.

In the last three cells of Galley 6, closest to where Zaharko was firing, prison guards slammed mattresses into place against the bars. Thirty-six hours had passed since Gus Byars had been taken captive on the other side of the cell house. They hoped the National Guard could save them before Myles and Smart tried to kill them. The mattresses might stop the Molotov cocktails from exploding in the cells, but flames would devour the thin cotton in minutes. At least when Myles and Smart started shooting, they would fire blindly. Standing now in total darkness, unable to see outside their cells, hostages waited to feel the bite of the ringleaders' bullets.

Hostage Ray Quilici knew bazookas. He had fired them in combat in Korea. The explosion told him help was coming and that the National Guard meant business. He hoped they came in time. Pressing against the mattress, he listened to the machine gun barking and the glass smashing. He and his fellow hostages didn't realize how close they stood to the line of fire. They heard a war in progress.

Quilici decided that if he survived the riot, he would quit the prison. Less than a month earlier he had left his U.S. Forest Service job in Dillon, from where he had gone high into the timber-quiet mountains with pack mules to build roads and trails, to work at Montana State Prison's ranch at Tin Cup Lake on the bench lands below Mount Powell.

Three days after starting on that job, however, he was assigned to work inside the prison. Fitted for a customary guard's blue custodial uniform tailored by convicts, he then worked two shifts in towers followed by a few days in the yard and other places, including the theater, where he watched convicts sweep and dust. The riot started on his second day in the kitchen, a job that involved accounting for knives and chasing away unauthorized convicts. He had met barely a few of his fellow guards on second shift, and practically all the prisoners were strangers to him. He resented this turn of events because he was a man of the woods. He had neither the training nor the desire to stand among convicts working with knives and meat cleavers.

At Bob Zaharko's west side home, across the Clark Fork River and the swath of train yards that dissected Deer Lodge, the bazooka shot startled his wife Pat, who ran outside onto the lawn. The machine gun's rat-tat-tat echoed through the dark neighborhood. Being a "good law officer's wife," as she described herself, she didn't go to the prison. But she also didn't know it was Bob who was firing those rounds.

Sheriff Everett Burt, an exhausted man, dozed in a chair at the county jail. His family lived upstairs. Home seemed miles away; he dared not stray from the county telephone on the battered desk in front of him. He wasn't alone. His deputy, Bill Arthur, sat nearby, and the telephone was silent. A sleeping man would dream of it as a menacing black bug, waiting to chase him when he closed his eyes. That receiver, smug in its cradle, had moved from ear and back, maybe hundreds of times.

When the bazooka cracked he leaped from his chair. The roar of it stuck like syrup to the cool air. The sheriff ran outside to his patrol car. A machine gun chattered several blocks distant, followed by a second explosion. Burt hadn't been privy to the invasion plans. Like most everybody else in Deer Lodge, he knew only that time was running out. He had watched the desperation on drawn faces. Within two minutes he arrived at the prison, where he found throngs of people already milling in the street. Some wore pajamas, or street clothes over their pajamas, and they wore looks of fright and thrill and chaos at all once.

***

Seconds after Bill Rose fired his bazooka, Ellsworth and Kendall and the other National Guard commanders told their men to charge.

"Go! Go! Go!" Ellsworth yelled to them. Seven teams of men poured through the doorway separating the women's compound from the main prison yard. The riflemen came first, followed by medics and firefighters carrying extinguishers lest Myles succeed in setting his hostages afire. They stormed toward their destinations. They hadn't been warned about Zaharko's fusillade from the wall, which they misunderstood as convicts shooting at them.

The yard proved to be an obstacle course in the feeble light. Buzz Weston saw ditches and tried to elude them. Ron Scharf tripped on a metal stake in the horseshoe pit and fell. His helmet flew off. Jack Scharf, running behind him, thought his brother had been shot. He stopped to help, and in the darkness and confusion, neither of them understood what had happened.

From his cover near the west wall, ambulance driver and mortician Ralph Filcher watched bursts from Zaharko's Thompson as he stroked the walls inside Cell House 1. Filcher watched at least four orange pops of light, which he took to be shots from Myles and Smart, from a tower window. Outside Tower 6, Sergeant Rose lay prone to make himself less of a target. Two bullets, which he later decided were ricochets from Zaharko's attack, slammed into the wall less than a foot from his head. Shards whipped across his nose, drawing blood.

Gus Beierle, a prison guard, charged toward Cell House 2 in the torrent of gunfire. He carried seven keys in his hand; the guardsmen around him carried rifles and wore helmets. The gun noise cracked deep in his ears, and the beating of his heart, he was sure, could be heard all over Deer Lodge.

He'd had plenty of time to think about this riot. All day Thursday, just hours before it began, he stood in the sunshine in this very prison yard, watching convicts shovel and chop to replace a wooden sewer line with a metal one. Later that afternoon they said they needed more lumber to brace the pipe. When Beierle walked toward the woodpile, several of them followed. One of them, he noticed, held a knife.

Like most guards at Montana State Prison that day, Beierle found himself walking alone with convicts almost from the start. He came to the prison only two months earlier after leaving his job as an ironworker. At least he had experience around dangerous people. He had worked in the high-security unit at the state mental hospital at Warm Springs, thirteen miles south of Deer Lodge, for three years.

That afternoon, Beierle sensed something was wrong. He stayed close to the watchtowers, to the guards with rifles. The man with the knife melted into the stream of men headed to the cell houses. Anxious to get out of the prison, the young guard told his crew to surrender their tools. They complied quickly, as a rule, because the end of work meant recreation and then dinner. Shovels and pickaxes went into a basket, suspended on a rope from Tower 4. Hammers and other smaller tools went into a canvas sack. Up they went, pulled into safe storage in the tower.

Beierle went home at four o'clock. He worried about the knife. He'd barely changed out of his uniform when the phone rang. An agitated voice from the prison office told him to hurry back. Somebody had shot Ted Rothe.

At the prison, a sergeant gave him a Thompson machine gun and a revolver and sent him into the tunnel that fronted the dining hall. There, from the gloom of the gun cage, he watched convicts rush back and forth between the cell houses until night settled them. At first some of them came to the gun cage to whisper that if anybody made trouble for the hostages they would take care of it. Their bravado faded with the evening light. By midnight, at least a dozen of them lay sleeping on the tile floor.

Now came the sprint in the dark. Unprotected as he was, Beierle had only one advantage, and that was in knowing how to avoid the ditch and other obstructions. A bullet pinged off the historic theater at the south end of the exercise yard. A guardsman fell in the same instant and Beierle, thinking the shot had come from the cell house tower where Myles and Smart hid, figured he had been shot.

Years later, Beierle wouldn't remember the guardsman's name. Commotion can erase significant details like names and faces and it was a metaphor for the riot anyway: too many men who didn't know each other, especially the prison guards. Here they were, one man's life depending on another, but strangers to each other. The guardsman skidded on the asphalt in front of the theater, falling hands first into the gravel beyond it. Beierle pulled him across his hip and shuffled into Cell House 2. Torn skin hung from both palms on the guardsman's hands.

The soldiers on Kendall's team – among them Leo "Dude" Kemp, Darrell Jensen, Buzz Weston and Allen Denton, all Deer Lodge men – yelled fierce orders up and down the galleys, telling convicts to get into a cell, any cell. Beierle tried to lock them in, but none of the seven keys worked. He and the guardsmen implored the convicts to give up the right keys.

Barely thirty-six hours earlier this had been a place of terror for guards. Now cons who at first felt inclined to resist saw good reason to be afraid. Most of them had never seen troops prepared for combat. They looked like they might shoot. The men in Cell House 2 gave up the party. They hadn't seen Jerry Myles for a long time. His riot was over.

One inmate, known to Beierle as "Brooklyn," reached into a can of red paint. He pulled out the cell house keys, dripping wet, which two days earlier had been taken from Officer Cozzens.

As Kendall's team entered Cell House 2 from the front, more Deer Lodge guardsmen, led by Ellsworth, tried to enter from the back door from which Officer Fred Dawson had escaped on Thursday afternoon. Captain Earl Hansen, the Scharf brothers, Don

Jensen and Darrell Jones all pushed and swore, but they couldn't jar the door. Convicts had barricaded it with sacks of potatoes. Ellsworth's team missed most of the action inside.

Other teams raced to the dining hall, various industries, the hospital and other buildings, but they found little or no resistance. The danger remained in Cell House 1.

Smoke curled out of the northwest tower of Cell House 1. The air fell heavy with dust and a whiff of sulfur and crushed brick. It was impossible to know if the bazooka shot had stopped the ringleaders from killing their hostages, and the hostages, in their weary minds, couldn't make complete sense of the pandemonium.

Before the attack, hostage George Axtell, the typing teacher, dozed on convict Bill Ingle's bunk in the infirmary, near a barred window within twelve feet of the tower. The first bazooka explosion showered glass all over him. He watched soldiers run past the windows. He thought it looked and sounded like a war outside. For the first time since he had been taken hostage he felt truly afraid.

Soon Bill Benson and several other guardsmen appeared at the hospital door. Axtell and his fellow hostage, Officer Lawrence Backman, fared better than the others locked in cells on Galley 6. They didn't want the convict orderlies who had protected them with genuine concern to be harmed.

Axtell recalled: "We could hear shouts of the guardsmen. They entered the hospital. Then they escorted us along the walls of the building [west] to the women's quarters and out a back gate. We had a run of about 100 yards to make this gate. I heard three distinct shots."

***

What everybody in Deer Lodge would remember most was a drama bigger than themselves, than their prison, than their little dot of a town, but their memory of the details would come later. The assault was sensational beyond their wildest imaginations. It came in snapshots, much like cuts of a movie: Volleys of shots from unknown places. Soldiers running with guns. Choking smoke. A quest for survival.

Few of the men on either side of the bars understood the big picture. Ask the men who hit the beaches of France at D-Day, hostage Everett Felix being one of them, and what they remembered most came from their will to somehow avoid imminent dying. This invasion of Montana State Prison, evidently scripted by National Guard commanders whose clear immediate objective was to save the hostages, could go horribly wrong. Felix knew that. Ellsworth and Kendall and the other commanders knew it too, and so did Warden Powell.

Sergeant William Rose of the Montana National Guard with the bazooka he fired three times at Cell House 1.

Courtesy William Rose

- 25 -

Jerry, Lee and their last stand

The rifle team led by Reuben Dwight and Dale Dahlgren, and including group commander Meyhew Foster, raced to the main door of Cell House 1. Their mission: save the hostages.

They found the locks jammed with thread, wood chips and other debris. Dwight shot the locks out of the thick oak door with five M1 rounds. Blocked from the inside, the door still wouldn't open. Dwight and Dahlgren lifted a nearby wooden bench, took a long run, and slammed it against the door. They tried again and again until the door budged open.

Inside the stone vestibule, at the very location where convicts had seized several prison guards on Thursday afternoon, they found the inside door barricaded in the same manner. Again, they bashed the door with the wooden bench until it opened. By that time three teams of riflemen and two teams of firefighters had assembled behind them, and they all ran inside. When Sergeant Tom Vukosovich of Anaconda, a longtime cell house officer on the breakfast shift, hit the light switches, Bob Zaharko quit firing as they had planned and retreated to Tower 6.

The soldiers found nobody loose except a few kitchen workers, but they hadn't expected problems from the hundreds of other men in the cell house. Dwight and Dahlgren had their orders. They would rescue the hostages on Galley 6 before Jerry Myles killed them. They hoped the hostages weren't dead already. Dwight, a former Marine and a Naval prison deputy warden who someday would figure into Montana prison affairs more than anyone could have imagined, climbed the stairs to Galley 6, pistol in hand, watching the wicket door.

Survival of the hostages now would be measured in seconds.

***

After hearing what Officer Victor Baldwin later described as "a great big boom" that shook Cell House 1, Captain Felix yelled, "This is it!"

Baldwin and Felix and their fellow hostages stood fast against the mattresses they had thrown against the bars, fighting the temptation to fall to the floor to avoid the bullets that plinked like raindrops against the wicket door. They heard a cry that came from somewhere in the cavernous cell house. "They're coming in!" the voice observed, either from fright or from relief, or maybe both. Hostages shouted instructions to each other in the darkness. The mattresses sealed the openings, isolating each cell from the other. Each group of men wondered what was happening to the others. As they pressed against the mattresses, they worried that Myles and Smart would kill them before their rescuers arrived. How long had they waited for this moment?

Would they live? Would they die?

***

Carl Frodsham, who huddled inside the cell house tower with Jerry Myles and Lee Smart, had heard on the grapevine months earlier that they were planning a riot. "It was awful quiet, everybody suspected that something was coming off sooner or later but they didn't know when because of the quietness," he said. He remembered bitterly how Smart belittled him when he asked how the riot got started. Frodsham was a strong man. Smart would have been no match for him in a fight, but Frodsham knew his place in the prison pecking order: "He never told me nothing. I tried to inquire and he told me to shut my mouth and do what I'm told if I want to keep on living."

Earlier that morning, Frodsham wandered around inside the tower until Donald Toms, who by that time was acting as a straw boss for Myles and Smart, told him to rest. Frodsham found someone sleeping in his bed down on Skid Row. He returned to the tower through the wicket door. He saw Myles and Smart awake in the same room where Toms and Walker were bedding down for the night. Myles and Smart had taken turns napping on Friday, and to Frodsham they looked awake, alert and defiant.

Frodsham already had logged seven years of his young life at Montana State Prison. He knew where he stood. Seeing it his place to take orders from the ringleaders, Frodsham asked permission to sleep. Myles nodded and motioned him away. Frodsham climbed the stairs to the fifth and top floor. He undressed, removed his artificial leg, and fell asleep on a mattress.

The first bazooka round hit with a fury, knocking Frodsham onto the floor. As he scrambled to reattach his leg and pull on his blue convict clothes, he tried to understand what had happened. The explosion, he decided, had happened on the west-facing window on the floor below him.

Frodsham hobbled down the pitch-dark stairwell as fast as his wooden leg would allow him, trying frantically in the yellowing beam of a guard's flashlight to find his way to the others. Partway down the stairs on a landing, he came face to face with Smart, who looked stunned and reckless. Instantly the teenage convict jerked his rifle into firing position.

Myles shouted a warning. "Don't shoot! It's Frodsham!"

Smart hesitated before lowering the rifle. Frodsham shook. Given a second more, Smart would have killed him.

"I meant no harm," Smart offered. Pale light from a small window made a ghost of him. He thought Frodsham was a National Guardsman who had crept into the tower through the roof. "No one is going to leave this tower alive," Smart vowed. His voice echoed in the stairwell, and it was the voice of a dead man and sounded shrill and unsettling. Frodsham wished he had stayed in Cell House 1.

Kevin S. Giles

***

The guards fought their own demons in the dark. Only a couple of dozen feet away from Myles and Smart, behind the mattresses pressed tight against the bars, they heard the shooting stop. They didn't realize that the cell house lights had come on, or that men who came to rescue them stood on the galley. "We weren't even through barricading when we heard, 'Who's in that cell?' " Baldwin remembered.

"Officers!" Felix yelled.

"Let me see!" came the reply. Felix peeled a corner of the mattress away to see a soldier holding a rifle. Their rescue seemed quick after the hours they spent waiting for death. Actually, Felix and the other hostages had waited several minutes after the first bazooka round hit until the moment that Dwight and the others appeared at their cells.

Dwight found twenty hostages huddling behind mattresses in cells 246, 248 and 250. He called by radio for Vukosovich to open the last three cell doors on Galley 6. Guardsmen lined the galley, their rifles trained on the door leading into the cell house tower.

When the doors opened the hostages burst in ones and twos onto the galley. To a man they stole a look at the wicket door shielding them from Myles and Smart before running down the galley to the zigzagging stairs at the block's end. Only Baldwin, of all the hostages, stopped to retrieve his shoes. Bill Benson, their former warden, waited on the "flag," the cell house lobby, to slap them on the back as they ran past him. Hostages grabbed at Benson and Foster to show their appreciation. "Go on out!" Benson yelled. "We've got them now!"

"We went just as fast as we could safely do it," Benson wrote in a widely published newspaper column. "I told the inmates to stay in their cells. There weren't any of them running around at all. A few stuck their heads out, but they pulled them back quickly. We passed about thirty prisoners. The hostages were in three locked cells. They started downstairs on their own. None was injured. Some had to

378

stop and pick up their shoes. ... Prisoners told us the leaders had gone into the cell tower through a steel door."

Led by National Guard troops and prison Lieutenant Pete Lynch, hostages tumbled out of Cell House 1 into the chill of the morning: Officer Victor Baldwin, Lieutenant Charles Brown, Officer Gus Byars, Officer Lawrence Cozzens, Captain Everett Felix, Officer Clinton Fowler, Officer David Hinton, Officer James "Little" Jones, Officer Vernon Kelpin, Officer Ralph Knutson, Officer Ray Quilici, assistant steward George Schaffer, Officer Erwin Sieler, administrative assistant John Simonsen, Officer Clyde Sollars, Officer Tom Stanford, teacher John Storey, Officer DeForrest Thompson, Officer Marvin Wallace, and Officer Robert Wyant.

Other Guardsmen followed them down the galley, throwing mattresses over the railing to provide partial protection should the ringleaders shoot from the wicket door. They kept the remaining convicts locked in their cells, subduing complainers into silence at bayonet point. Within seven minutes after the first bazooka shot, hostages ran for freedom.

"They appeared running out of the darkened yard so fast, it caught all of us by surprise," Ralph Filcher said. Years later, Guardsman Buzz Weston marveled that none of the hostages were mistaken for convicts and shot. They left the prison through the same doors through which the National Guard had entered. Female convicts pressed to the windows of their cottage, cheering.

Escorted by a phalanx of fellow prison guards, police officers and others, the hostages trotted around the prison's southwest tower and through the minimum-security compound. They passed the guards' dining room where many of them had eaten two days earlier, unknowing of the riot. They emerged outside the west wall of the prison, then turned north toward Warden Powell's house. Filled with the exuberance of freedom, the former hostages of career convict Jerry Myles hardly noticed the cold gravel beneath their stocking feet.

***

Three floors below the ringleaders, National Guard troops congregated around the outside door to the northwest tower of Cell House 1. Dwight and most of the others who rescued the hostages had appeared, leaving Major Hugh McElwain of Missoula and a few soldiers in charge of securing Cell House 1.

The team led by Francis "Russ" Pulliam, a mustached National Guard lieutenant and Missoula assistant police chief, had gone first to the hospital. Now he and others bashed open the outside tower door with a wooden bench, just as Dwight and Dahlgren had been done at the other end of the cell house.

By this time Ellsworth's teams had secured Cell House 2. Ellsworth now stood at Cell House 1 with Pulliam, asking for volunteers to go inside with him. Pulliam stepped forward. So did prison guard Harold Phillips, Highway Patrol Supervisor Alex B. Stephenson, Lt. James Girard of Deer Lodge and Master Sergeant William Weston of Missoula. Weston was a brother of Emery "Buzz" Weston of the Deer Lodge unit.

Myles and Smart and the others had piled earth from the tunnel against the door as a barricade. Ellsworth and a few guardsmen dug and pushed to free the door. When it opened, they stepped into a dark room. It was cold like a tomb. Watching the stairs above them, the men stole a look at the mound of dirt that constituted Myles' supposed escape attempt. Their flashlights revealed an empty tunnel that was pathetically short for all the labor it must have taken to dig. Ellsworth dropped into the tunnel on his hands and knees for a better look. Nobody was there.

The men climbed the narrow concrete steps. Phillips led, shining a light into the gloom. Ellsworth and Pulliam, each carrying M-1 carbines loaded with eight rounds apiece, followed the light's wandering gaze. As they stepped onto the third floor landing, at the wicket door, an odor of paint thinner or naphtha blew over them and they tensed, fearing for an instant they would be doused. Pulliam realized it had been poured all over the landing and that he was walking on it.

To their left they saw a bathroom door, to their right the steel door leading into the cell house. Straight ahead stood a closed wooden door. Phillips lunged forward, lifting his leg to kick it in. At the instant his foot connected, a flash came from the landing above. A shot roared through the concrete rooms, numbing their ears. Ellsworth, who stood behind Phillips and Pulliam, couldn't tell whether it had come from the doorway where Phillips stood, or from above them. Then he heard Pulliam cry out.

"Oh God, I'm hit!" he shouted, and he fell backward against Ellsworth.

Pulliam had earned battle stars for his fighting at Iwo Jima and Okinawa. He was one of the first sixty Marines who occupied Nagasaki after the atomic bomb's searing destruction. After his discharge in 1945 he had worked his way through the ranks of the Missoula Police Department. He was the son of a U.S. Army first lieutenant. In Missoula, he joined the artillery wing of the 443rd Regiment as a pilot, flying L-19s as an artillery spotter. He felt comfortable in combat.

An hour before the invasion began, Pulliam crouched inside the tunnel that flanked the convict dining room, watching for activity through the gun portals. When he got word of the pending assault he hurried through Tower 7 into the street, and down to the prison's south end where he met other excited guardsmen. Clouds of nervous breath drifted around their helmets.

Now, in a dark stairwell in a surreal conflict with men he didn't know and couldn't see, the first sensation of a bullet wasn't pain but the absence of feeling. He had been trained to know what that meant. He felt his left arm and his left leg go limp. His fingers flopped to and fro like untied rope.

Above them, Carl Frodsham watched Jerry Myles shoot at the men below. The rifle's bark filled the stairwell. Myles stood on the half-landing between the third and four floors. At a distance of only about eight feet, he had fired practically point blank. Hitting Pulliam had been mostly fateful; Myles had no skill with firearms, nor in the darkness could he have discerned individual men. Still, Frodsham knew Myles was now capable of killing. Frodsham reflected: "Jerry Myles was, ah, so hopped up that if one guard would look cross-eyed at him, he'd of been dead."

Phillips raced down the stairs to safety. Ellsworth carried the bleeding Pulliam to the bottom floor. Stephenson saw blood on Ellsworth and thought he had been hit and grabbed him instead. Pulliam fell to the floor.

When they got Pulliam outside, Dr. Benjamin and National Guard medics started first aid. The bullet had ripped Pulliam's right forearm, severing tendons. It passed through the wooden rifle stock, deflecting off the metal butt plate into his hip and back. Prison guards rolled the gurney from Ralph Filcher's ambulance into the prison yard. It was too wide for the door through the prison wall. On the way back out they had to turn it sideways. Pulliam clung to the edge to avoid falling off.

Two prison guards helped Filcher take Pulliam to St. Joseph Hospital in Deer Lodge where Benjamin cut away his fatigue jacket. Pulliam saw that his arm was little more than an inch thick in places. With his good arm he reached behind his back to free the 45-caliber pistol from its holster. He asked a medic to empty the ammunition from it. Instead of pulling the clip the medic jacked each shell through the chamber. Pulliam watched a nurse in her nun's habit dance in fright as ejected bullets bounced off the tiled floor. Once Benjamin was sure Pulliam could stand the trip, Filcher drove the injured soldier to Fort Harrison in Helena, where doctors took him into surgery.

After Pulliam left the prison in the ambulance, Ellsworth and Benson shouted for the ringleaders to surrender. They got no response. Ellsworth ordered a third bazooka shot to the tower. The second bazooka shot, which pierced the eighteen-inch brick wall and blew fragments and dust into the fourth-floor tower room, hit in the same place as the first.

Sergeant Rose knelt on the wall outside Tower 5. He bumped the bazooka on the metal railing, accidentally jarring the sights. He didn't know it, but the bazooka was set for a range of 900 yards. His shot went high, tearing a clean hole through the parapet's west side. Mercifully the round exploded on the tower roof instead of blazing into the neighborhoods beyond. Ellsworth and Benson told guardsmen congregated around them to fire at will into the tower windows. Angry that Pulliam had been shot, they poured hundreds of rounds through every window, but mostly the big west windows where the bazooka rounds had hit. Chunks of brick rained on them.

***

Minutes after Myles shot Pulliam, Frodsham and the others heard the whistle of a third approaching bazooka round, which exploded above them. They hid in the top floor from which Frodsham had just come. This room was unlike the others. Just below the parapet surrounding the tower's roof, this room had no big windows looking west and north. Except for a south-facing attic-like window barely wider than a human face, the room resembled a gun bunker in its concrete simplicity. The other rooms opened level with the landings that led to them; this room had its own staircase leading downward to the landing near where Myles had shot Pulliam.

Myles and Smart milled anxiously around the room, each of them clutching a rifle they had seized from catwalk guards more than thirty-six hours earlier. Bleeding and confused, Toms staggered against the north wall near the top of the stairs. Frodsham crawled into a corner where the metal railing surrounded the stairwell. He sat on the floor, his back to the wall. Walker was last onto the stairs, closing behind him the door that opened onto the landing. He crawled through the gloom, stopping at the wall between Frodsham and the window.

About ten minutes after Myles shot Pulliam, Ellsworth ordered tear gas canisters shot toward the small window at the tower's fifth floor. That was the only room left in the tower that hadn't been hit by the barrage of bazooka and rifle fire. "We had an awful time getting the tear gas through the bars into the tower room," Benson would recall.

To the convicts hiding there, the aim was good and the room became a hellish muddle. Frodsham pressed a handkerchief to his mouth and nose. "It stung. I mean it *stung*," he would recall. Vapor filled the room. After the guardsmen stopped firing from the ground outside, Ellsworth and Benson yelled to Myles and Smart to surrender if they wanted out alive. Benson stood in the yard in plain sight of the tower. He cupped his hands around his mouth.

"Jerry! Jerrrrrryyy! Are you in there?" Still nothing. Benson waited, hoping Myles would show himself in the window. Then the Korean War combat veteran's burly voice echoed against the brick facade. "Jerrrrrryyy? I'm going to kill you!"

Still nothing.

Minutes later, the Guard shot more tear gas into the room. As soon as it began to clear, Frodsham heard Myles or Smart say, "It's time." The words came low and full of resignation and it was unclear to him, in the dark, who spoke them.

Hours earlier, Frodsham had heard Myles and Smart talk about a suicide pact that included Toms and George Alton. Now it appeared that Smart wanted Walker, Toms and Frodsham to die as well. Frodsham hadn't seen Alton since Friday. They had met in their early teenage years in the state reform school in Miles City. Frodsham was eight years old when he was sent there. His parents had separated in 1934.

Frodsham figured Alton had "chickened out" of the suicide pact. Frodsham hadn't been asked to join in it. He was considered a "helper" and therefore had no claim to the status that Myles and Smart thought they enjoyed. Nor did he have reason to think they would intentionally kill him, at least not before he entered the tower that night. He "had no dealings" with either Myles or Smart, which in prison vernacular meant he had no reason to fear either of them. Originally Myles and Smart agreed to commit suicide. Now, under siege after a murderous riot, Smart's movement and language became deadly deliberate, like he wanted to take on the world. Frodsham suspected that Myles didn't trust Smart to kill himself.

Frodsham thought Myles was different from Smart. He sensed Myles as the more dangerous of the two, but he didn't know why. Myles, of course, had a long history of violent outbursts followed by attempted suicides and his proclivity toward maiming himself to attract sympathy, even to punish his wrongs. This time was different. Myles held a loaded rifle powerful enough to kill a man with the first shot. Rothe's quick demise was proof of that. From radio reports Myles knew his riot captured the nation's attention. He was the star of the show. He wouldn't risk an ending that showed him the weak, pathetic, unloved man he was.

Myles bragged to Frodsham and others that he had killed six convicts in Atlanta. Guards, too, suspected Myles had a darker side than even his record showed, and they speculated that he had killed other men. Nobody could distinguish his bragging from the facts. Guard talk over coffee figured Myles the dominant male in his love affair with Smart, but they also thought Smart to be outwardly the more dangerous of the two men.

Smart murdered without hesitation, as he had demonstrated with Charles Denzil Ward and Ted Rothe. Myles found Smart's unrehearsed killing instincts attractive. In the past Myles had punished himself after falling in love with other men. He couldn't help himself with Lee Smart, who he thought to be pretty. Smart acted decisively; Myles acted impulsively. Smart's brooding girlish face disguised his rage. Myles wore his angry tormented emotions like a Halloween mask, hiding little. With no hesitation Smart could summon that animal within him to slay men. His dark interior came not from a youth's wrong-minded compulsion, but from some devilish workings that showed in his eyes.

Myles liked to manipulate. Smart liked to execute. The psychopathic Myles saw the world not as it was but as he wanted it to be. His great elaborations to draw attention to himself had started early in his childhood with his first adoption. Smart didn't care how other people perceived him. He was a rebel gone bad. At times he appeared quiet and soft and unassuming; at other times, as a man possessed. Captain Everett Felix had shivered at seeing Smart's haunting stare. Felix felt that he could look right through Smart's cold eyes to some unknown but terrifying secret inside of him. Those eyes looked back with raping arrest, like a pipeline from one soul to another, transporting a vulgar, passionless violation that was much like the images he painted.

Lee Smart considered himself something of a martyr. He fought the world. He and his friend Dave Neal considered themselves "lions" who would bend a knee to no man. This poem, written by

Lee's friend, found its way into Smart's permanent file at the prison:

DAVE AND LEE

Some men were born Rebels
Just like you and I,
Just to Love, Laugh, and Live
Not afraid to die

Our moral code's our Creed
We have no God you see,
We make our rules to follow
To no man bend a knee

When our lives come to an end
You can bet one thing for sure,
We've lived our lives as Lions
We die with conscience pure...

By David Neal

***

Through the vapor cloud in the tower room, Frodsham glimpsed Lee Smart approaching. He carried the rifle like he planned to use it. Lee would kill others before he ever killed himself. Frodsham knew that. Every con knew that. Lee wouldn't be taken alive. Frodsham crouched against the wall, suddenly comprehending the boy's intentions. Smart aimed the rifle at Frodsham's head. A deafening shot filled the room. Blood and brain tissue showered Frodsham's face and glasses. Smart's thin body crumpled in Frodsham's lap.

In the echo came the unmistakably frightened voice of Jerry Myles. "Lee! Lee?" Stunned, Frodsham replied matter of factly, "Lee is dead."

Seconds later came another shot, but more muffled. Frodsham strained to see through the mist. Feeble light from the window revealed only that the back of Smart's head had been blown away; it came to Frodsham in a flash that Myles had seen Smart's head silhouetted against the feeble light from the window, just a few feet away, before Myles fired.

Frodsham called to Toms and Walker, asking what happened. Toms crawled across the room to the bed, where he found Myles' burly body sprawled on a mattress lying on the floor beside the bed.

The man who said "prison is my home" had left prison the only way he knew how. Born without a family to call his own, he left the world without a single real friend. Later a card, stained red with his blood, would be found on the floor. Its typed message read:

"Nary a word said o'er my grave
"Not a soul to rant and rave;
"No marker of errant past
"An individualist to the last..."

Jerry Myles was dead, a victim of his own hand.

***

On the ground below, National Guard heard a distinct rifle shot, followed a few seconds later by another.

After the shootings, Toms fumbled with the rifle that Smart had pointed at Frodsham's head. It was cocked and as Toms fiddled, it went off with a thunder. Outside, the guardsmen heard the third shot and didn't know if anyone was left.

Benson yelled to the tower that he had a message from Warden Powell. Toms told him to take it back, then abruptly handed Frodsham the rifle and told him to stand by the window. Toms went downstairs to surrender, leaving only Frodsham and Walker. Frodsham leaned the rifle against the wall. Then Walker handed Frodsham the second rifle when he too decided to go downstairs to surrender. "I took both rifles and set them on the table and that was the last time I touched those rifles and the third time I touched those rifles," Frodsham would later tell County Attorney Malcolm

"Scotty" MacCalman. "I just put the guns down. I didn't do no shooting whatsoever."

Jerry Walker didn't think much of Myles, but he liked Smart: "I never knew Lee real good, but I did like him, what I knew of him."

Walker told MacCalman that he didn't remember the first bazooka shell hitting. He insisted he was passed out in the tower from pills, about eight of them. He awoke when he heard a rifle shot. "When I come to, I don't know, there was that tear gas, or something, and Myles was laying across the top of me, but I didn't know who it was at that time, and I shoved him and he was dead, and so I looked around, and everybody else was laying around, so I got up and walked downstairs, and when I got down to the bottom of the stairs, that's when they grabbed me." He said he thought Myles had killed himself. Frodsham offers a conflicting recollection. Walker, he said, never moved from where he sat next to Frodsham until after the fatal shots, and he was awake.

Walker to MacCalman: "I wouldn't even hit a guard, and I didn't hit one of them, but there are a lot of them that I dislike, but nevertheless I didn't have it in my mind to hurt any of them, or to have anything like this come off and have anybody killed, or shot up, or anything like that."

Frodsham told MacCalman: "After Walker was out of the tower, I hollered down to – not to shoot, that I was coming down with my hands in the air and awful scared. They finally seen me through that one window there and this one National Guardsman says hold it and I told him not to shoot, I told them to come and get me and they called up and told me to come down and I came down fast but with my hands in the air."

Bill Benson and Bus Ellsworth met Frodsham as he emerged from the tower. Seeing the blood and tissue matting Frodsham's hair and shirt, Benson asked Frodsham if he was hurt. Frodsham said Myles had killed Smart and then himself. "Okay, if they are dead, is there anyone else up there?" Ellsworth asked.

"No," Frodsham replied.

"Then go on up and get those rifles for me."

Frodsham cussed, adding: "No sir, not me." Guardsmen led Frodsham at gunpoint into the prison yard and told him to strip naked. Captain Dwight told them to shoot Frodsham if he moved, and he told Frodsham to remove his artificial leg. Hopping on his one foot, Frodsham took a wild swing at a guardsman and missed.

Ellsworth and Benson entered the tower again. They found Smart dead by the small window, the back of his head torn away. Across the room, Myles sprawled partially on a mattress that lay on the floor, his face gone. A stench of warm blood filled the room. Seeing the bodies, Ellsworth concluded that Myles had shot Smart and then shoved the rifle muzzle into his mouth to kill himself. He found an empty shell casing on the floor beside Myles' body, and another spent casing in the chamber of the rifle.

The rifles that prison guards had wanted for security, that Floyd Powell and Ted Rothe had feared would fall into convict hands, that were stolen from the guards by knowing convicts, that had killed Rothe and kept the prison under siege for thirty-six hours, now had finished the drama.

***

Ellsworth and Benson dragged the bodies to the edge of the steep stairwell, where they kicked them into a plummet. Myles' head slammed on the concrete steps as he bounced to the bottom, knocking the remains of his brain free in a garish finale. The bodies tumbled onto the landing below. Ellsworth and Benson left them lying in the company of a sniffing black prison cat.

Outside, a National Guard lieutenant summoned Ellsworth to Cell House 2. There, lying on a bunk inside a cell belonging to someone other than him, a blond but balding young convict calmly read a magazine. "Here is that fellow that we have been looking for," the guardsman told Ellsworth. Remembering the handsome face from prison mug shots, Ellsworth bent close. "The game is up, George."

- 26 -

A finale, 36 hours later

Like other people milling around him on Maryland Avenue, Powell County Sheriff Everett Burt waited for news of the hostages. Fire trucks lined Main Street flanking the prison. People arrived from every direction to watch this unquestionable climax of the longest prison siege in Montana history.

Hostage families came running onto the pavement between Floyd Powell's house and his office, watching the prison for their loved ones. It seemed like only minutes had passed since the second bazooka shot. The crash of it, a sound few would ever forget, filled their ears. Already daylight rimmed the eastern mountains, casting just the slightest distinction of pink dawn on the improbable scene in front of the prison: hostage wives wrapped in a bewildering assortment of clothing (one of the hostage wives, awakened from her sleep, said, "Boy, I look like an old witch."); prison guards and law officers outfitted in shades of blue and brown; volunteer firemen equipped for calamity; newsmen in long coats with collars turned up; photographers poised with flashbulb cameras; solemn combat-clad soldiers armed with carbines. Anybody who had missed the riot's unraveling might think they had walked onto the wardrobe department of a movie set.

The first shouts of recognition alerted the crowd. Down the street to the south, from the gate below Tower 1, a line of dusky blue uniforms emerged. A procession of exhausted disheveled men, mostly hatless, approached the warden's house in the dim light.

They came as ghosts, men feared dead. They came as refugees from the night and from something worse, something unexplained, from a place that was as deep and dark and unfamiliar as a grave, and to see them that way, running scared and looking faint and hungry and tired and happy at all once, the crowd for a moment recoiled in disbelief. But they came to the outside real and whole men, and it took but a second to comprehend they were alive and free. In a jubilant scene that nobody who witnessed it would forget, the men fell into the arms of the emotional crowd.

***

Gert Knutson hadn't heard the bazooka explosions. She had set her alarm clock to ring at daybreak, when she planned to hurry back to the prison and hope against hope. Gert decided Ralph wasn't coming home. She hadn't received a smuggled note from him as the other hostage wives had from their husbands.

During her vigil at the prison she had heard talk of burning and hanging. She had watched those drawn worried faces. Ralph, she decided, might be dead. On Friday her head had ached with such intensity that she telephoned the clinic downtown. "I'm sending up some medication," the doctor told her. Someone came to her house with sleeping pills. Dizzy with fatigue and anxiety, Gert swallowed one and lay down on the bed. She tried to shut from her mind images of her husband being murdered in cold blood. "I was so sure that they were going to do away with him," she recalled. Before she left the house in the morning, Ralph appeared at the door.

Hostage Clinton Fowler went home to his wife and his adopted one-year-old sons, where news photographers snapped pictures of the reunited family. The convicts were "definitely doped up," the thirty-three-year-old guard told reporters. "There were as many as nine of us in a cell at one time, but they kept changing us around. I don't think we were scared, but we were all nervous." Fowler vowed to return to work at the prison. "We've got to pick up again," he said.

Some of the hostages talked with newsmen in the warden's office. George Axtell, stiff with an injured back, offered his matter-of-fact appraisal of recent prison conditions: "This was the third prison riot for me. Two years ago I was captured here but they released me. A year ago we had a sit-down strike.''

The hostages of Galley 6 told of their ordeal:

"The one to thank for our rescue is the Lord," said a weepy-eyed hostage Erwin Seiler, father of six. "That was a bad time in there. Butcher knives and cleavers and guns went by us in our cell all the time."

Hostage Marvin Wallace told newsmen: "We were just plain lucky to get away. It is a wonder that we weren't actually set afire. They meant business. The takeover was excellently planned and moved like clockwork. The cons did not make a single mistake.

"I was feeling pretty desperate, but I finally fell asleep for a few minutes. As luck would have it, that was the moment our boys opened up on the cellblock. A few minutes later, we heard footsteps down the hall and were literally jerked to freedom. I can tell you I feel mighty happy about the whole thing."

Hostage George Schaffer: "From 3:30 p.m. Thursday we were dead. They were always looking right down our throats with their rifles and threatening us with cocktails. ... We wanted the rescuers to come in yesterday. (Friday) We had no inkling they were coming when the guardsmen finally came."

Helen Sollars would recall: "Clyde was more than ready to come home. Coffee, sandwiches and cake were being served at the warden's house but he did not want to stop, even that long. Clyde was a wrack of nerves. He couldn't eat, sleep or sit still. All he could do was pace the floor in utter frustration."

Hostage Victor Baldwin: "We received a royal but tearful greeting and reunion with our wives." His wife replied: "I was dead afraid for the National Guard to try to rescue them. I didn't want them to go in, but thank God they did."

Few of the hostages lingered. Within ten minutes most of them had gone home in the burst of an April morning, leaving the prison and the corpse of Jerry Myles behind them like a bad dream.

***

During the riot's last hours, Marlene Lightfoot and her mother Gladys, exhausted from their hours of kitchen work, slept in their clothes in one of the many bedrooms at the warden's house. An explosion shocked them awake. When they ran outside to the chatter of machine gun fire, another boom followed. Minutes later, less than ten perhaps, they watched hugging and weeping as hostage wives rush to meet their husbands.

Some of the hostages who didn't have wives or girlfriends waiting came into the house. Officer Lawrence Backman, his shirt stained with blood, sat at the kitchen table trying desperately to drink soup. A newsman pestered him for comment, but Backman only could look into the bowl, searching for answers that he couldn't muster. Emboldened by the emotion of the past few days, Marlene pushed the reporter toward the door until he left. Backman looked at her. "You're a treasure," he told her.

Inside the prison, guards escorted accused convicts into the Hole beneath Cell House 1, isolating them in what Warden Powell called "strip" cells. Among them were George Alton, Donald Toms, Carl Frodsham, Jerry Walker and Jimmy Hubbard. As the remaining convicts stayed locked in their cells, handed coffee and sandwiches through the bars, teams of prison guards and National Guardsmen searched the prison's interior.

Earl Howard Jackson, who conceivably saved Warden Powell's life two days earlier, was returned to his cell in Cell House 2. He had been held in the bunkhouse outside the main prison wall since his escape with Powell. The warden didn't know whether to punish him or applaud him.

At about daylight, Bill Clawson, a part-time Deer Lodge city police officer, walked south from the northwest tower of Cell House 1 toward Inside Administration when he heard a voice calling for help. Startled, he whirled and drew his pistol. About halfway up the tower, he saw a man's bloodied face peering from a barred window. "Don't shoot!" the man pleaded.

Inside the tower, Clawson and a prison guard found convict plumber Herman Cardinal. He was in a bad way: retching and blinded from tear gas, and bleeding from his nose and ears from the bazooka shots. They led him to Inside Administration, where he lay mumbling and confused on a wooden bench until medical help arrived. Eventually the story came out: the first bazooka blast knocked Cardinal into a concrete wall. Terrified, he had stumbled down the tower stairs into a room full of guards' uniforms, where he hid behind racks of clothes. None of the men who rushed the tower had seen him there.

Cardinal, who like some of the hostages was a former Smelter worker in Anaconda, had a history of robbery, escape and assault. He found trouble even when it didn't concern him.

***

Their mission completed, the men of Deer Lodge's field artillery marched back to the grade school gymnasium. Ron Scharf would remember the women who stood watching on their porches, waving white handkerchiefs as a sign of thanks. Deer Lodge had its prison again.

After the drama in the dark, Saturday's sun shone almost curiously on the riot scene. Sheriff Burt and Undersheriff H. "Chick" Fanning entered the prison at Tower 7, the main gate. They walked into the yard to the outside door of the fateful tower of Cell House 1, where they stood talking with Police Chief Wilson and a prison guard about what had taken place.

Tear gas wafted out of the tower, wetting their eyes. Wilson advised them that Ralph Beck, the county coroner, would arrive soon. Burt and Fanning decided they had the authority to retrieve the bodies of Myles and Smart. Captain Dwight, whom they would come to know as "Lou," handed them two National Guard gas masks.

"We went up in the cellblock tower, and there were two crumpled bodies lying there that were practically headless," Burt would recall, seeing the bodies lying on the landing where Ellsworth and Benson left them. "Smart's body was lying over, or covering, some of Myles' body. Only some of the lower jaw to the back of the neck and to the back part of their heads was still intact with the rest of the body. Their faces and the top and side parts of their heads were gone, and there were pieces of skull, flesh, blood and brains scattered all over the floor and walls and ceiling of the small room where they killed themselves."

The room was a mess. Apparently it had been abandoned as a guards' quarters years earlier, because bed frames and mismatched furniture filled the room at crazy angles. Curtains still hung from a rod above a small window. Beneath the window was an old suitcase that looked packed and ready to go. Great sheens of blood showed where Smart, and then Myles, had died. Other patches, some showing the striped design of their prison shirts, showed where their bodies had been rolled around.

Burt and Fanning dragged the bodies by the trouser legs down the concrete stairs into the daylight, leaving a red smear. The human body in a fatal shooting coughs up a revolting volume of blood, as anybody who saw that scene that day would attest.

Outside the tower Ralph Beck met them. "Dwight says drag them out into the yard for the cons to see them," the sheriff recalled Beck telling them. Burt and Fanning complied. Dozens of convicts stood in the yard at rifle point, many of them stripped naked. They stared at the remains. Prison guards paraded George Alton past the bodies of his fellow ringleaders, displayed deliberately, he thought, for his benefit. After a few minutes Burt decided people had seen enough. He found blankets and covered the remains of Jerry Myles and Lee Smart.

Carrying a camera from the sheriff's office, Burt and Fanning returned to the tower, where they took several rolls of pictures. Years later, after Burt had left office, their photographs disappeared from a locked drawer. Burt alleged that Floyd Powell had taken them, promising their return. Burt never saw them again.

Within half an hour Burt and Fanning helped Beck zip the bodies into black bags. The coroner hauled them to the funeral home on Missouri Avenue where Ted Rothe lay in state, awaiting a Sunday funeral. When Beck and mortician Ralph Filcher opened the bags, tear gas overwhelmed them.

Having seen the bodies, and the room where the shooting occurred, Burt would disagree with Beck's conclusion that Smart killed Myles and then himself. And because the National Guard had moved the bodies and removed the rifles before he entered the tower, Burt had no chance to examine the scene as a law enforcement officer might. People who didn't know any different accepted the story that Smart killed Myles. Numerous people had visited the scene, moving the bodies and rifles and other evidence, and tracking through the puddles of blood. This led to conflicting interpretations of what had happened there in that dark tomb three stories above Deer Lodge. It was easy to conclude that a teenage killer had taken one more life, but it wasn't true.

***

After daybreak, Warden Powell walked to the 4B's Cafe, kitty corner from Tower 6 on Main Street, where he perched on a stool to eat a breakfast of ham and eggs. "I guess you could say all is well that ends well, and this one ended in great shape," he told newsmen. Of Rothe: "He was a good friend and a good man."

Later he gave a news conference, in which he thanked the National Guard and the Highway Patrol. "We were able to work together with split second timing and with full cooperation," he said. "Only in this way was it possible to save the lives of the hostages and not lose a single man in last night's successful operation." Powell said the uprising "was not a riot. It was definitely an escape attempt. When the tunneling-out operation failed and came to an end, the ringleaders decided to kill all hostages last night. Upon learning this I saw only one course of action, which was taken successfully." He promised a complete investigation and said he would report the results to Governor Aronson and the Board of Prison Commissioners.

In regards to newsmen, Powell said: "If any incidents have occurred this is unfortunate and I am sorry. However, I must strongly point out that security had to come first. One slip could have cost the lives of several men. While I believe the public should know what is going on in an emergency situation like this, the lives of the hostages had to come first. I am certain everyone realizes this and understands now that we only did what was essential while still giving the press what information we could." And finally, at prospects of another riot:

"I only hope no one is foolish enough to try it. The bodies of Smart and Myles should be ample evidence as to the rewards for such actions."

However, Powell denied newsmen's requests to go inside the prison. "That would be a concession. I made no concessions to anyone."

Meanwhile, authorities conducted no forensic tests, nor did they take fingerprints from the rifles. No independent investigation would be accomplished. Powell's description of the riot as an "escape attempt" distracted attention from his inability to end it. Few questions were asked about the fateful presence of Jerry Myles, diminishing the magnitude of a murderous riot that could have been even worse.

***

Governor Aronson described Floyd Powell as a "very tired man" but said the warden was "working hard at the job of restoring the prison back to normal and preparing a complete report on the unsuccessful escape attempt." The governor's statement read:

"A complete and thorough shakedown is now going on at the prison. Prison officers, assisted by Montana National Guard troops, are in the midst of this. The troublemakers, like (George) Alton, are being put in isolation in so-called "strip" cells with a change of prison clothes, a bucket and a mattress.

"Discipline is firm and tight, but fair. As soon as the shakedown is completed, the warden said he will interview every prison employee and every prisoner who was in the prison at the time of the escape attempt Thursday afternoon." And Aronson said of the prison staff: "These people helped perform a miracle and deserve the fullest credit for it."

Attorney General Forrest H. Anderson, after touring the prison Saturday, called the riot "an insane outbreak by a few bad boys," and he renewed his campaign for a new prison, saying Montana was "trying to keep 20th century hoodlums in a 19th century jail." In characteristic prose, he offered a cynical assessment: "This is like trying to run a zoo with the elephants in monkey cages and the monkeys in the elephant cages, in which case you can't control either the monkeys or the elephants."

Anderson said Rothe had been "one of the finest and most promising young correctional officers in the United States." And he praised Warden Powell, whom he described as a "mature and astute prison manager."

Clinton Fowler was one of the first hostages to come back to work. Being the library guard, he'd had nothing to do with the security breakdown in the cell houses. Floyd Powell sent him to the tower where Myles and Smart died to scrub clean their remains. Fowler sensed Powell's irritation and thought he was being punished for being taken hostage. Fowler recalled that it was the first time Powell had spoken to him and that it would be the last.

Fowler went into the tower with rags and buckets, half-heartedly swiping at the dried blood and tissue until workers came with a fire hose to flush away the blood of a psychopath and his teenage lover. In the deputy warden's office, they washed Ted Rothe's blood from the walls with rags. There it went, the most graphic reminders of the riot's beginning and of the riot's end. In its final simplicity, the Montana State Prison riot of 1959 had been reduced to the color red.

***

After he ate his breakfast in the corner restaurant, Floyd Powell walked back inside the prison. He was gratified to see that his prison guards now stood vigil at grating doors leading from Tower 7 into the main prison yard, although armed National Guard troops occupied the cell houses. Powell glanced into Ted Rothe's office, now empty and silent. Powell hated the scene before him: combat troops and law officers swarming through his prison, probing every crevice and corner without asking for his permission or seeking his direction.

Inside riot-weary Cell House 1, where the raspy voice of Jerry Myles echoed in the ears of every man who had known him, Bill Benson inspected the higher galleys. Benson thought he knew the prison well, as well or better than Powell. Benson held Powell in low regard, thinking him an unfit warden. Many years later, Benson's son Ted would relate that his father was incredulous that Powell had allowed himself to be captured when the riot began Thursday afternoon. To Benson, a hard military man who had spent thirty-nine months fighting the Japanese in the Pacific during World War II, Powell's capture showed his inattention to dangerous details. But Benson kept his tongue; he knew many secrets. His account of Powell's escape after being taken hostage differed completely from the warden's. Benson told others he had seen Powell emerge from his ordeal not a hero but a shaken man.

Benson told his son that when he met Powell in August 1958, when Benson's temporary job as warden came to an end, Powell had spoken extravagantly of a new prison. Only after the riot would Benson, furious with Powell, relate what most angered him: that Powell had told him in a private conversation that he had taken the Montana job only to build a new prison, and if he didn't get his way, he would quit. To Benson, Powell seemed nonchalant toward the people who would work for him.

Now, on the morning the riot ended, as Floyd Powell walked onto the "flag," or the ground floor, of Cell House 1, he spotted Benson walking above him. Benson still wore his Montana Highway Patrol uniform. He had been patrolling near Bozeman when he heard of the riot's outbreak. He had driven straight to Deer Lodge. For the riot's duration, Benson had been a mainstay, putting into action his hybrid experience as combat soldier, former warden and law officer. Saturday's early morning assault, said an admiring National Guard colonel, showed "Benson's touch," and while

Benson had accrued little actual experience in running a prison, people said he knew plenty about leading men.

According to Benson, Powell shouted to him in a formal voice. "Mr. Benson, what is your official capacity here?"

Surprised at Powell's tone, and clearly understanding his inferences, Benson shot back: "Well, Mr. Powell, I'm here to help the warden quell a riot."

Benson fumed. Without the National Guard's intervention, he thought, Myles and Smart would have killed all the hostages. Convinced that instant that he would help Powell no more, Benson climbed off the galley, left the prison, and drove straight to Bozeman in his patrol car. After a drive that took more than two hours he arrived at home in time for lunch. As he devoured sandwiches at the kitchen table he spouted his anger over Powell, telling stories to his spellbound wife and four children in a rare show of candor. Benson, a picture of military discipline, wasn't a man to share his frustrations with his family. This afternoon he told all. And never again did he speak with Floyd Powell, whom he described to his son as "that damn peacock."

***

On Saturday afternoon, after their relatives had gone home, Clyde and Helen Sollars visited the Rothe family apartment to pay their respects. At the sight of the grieving Mrs. Rothe and her two teenage children, Clyde broke down and sobbed. When they left some of his pent-up emotion had passed. Clyde said to his wife, "Mom, if I'm going to keep working at the prison I have to go back inside those walls soon, or I'm not sure I can go back at all." He returned to work the next day, determined to overcome his fear. That weekend Clyde and Helen finally found an open phone line to call their daughter Joan at her military base in San Antonio, Texas, to tell her Clyde was safe. She came home on furlough the following August to attend the wedding of her sister. Clyde got his billfold and shoes back, and forty-eight-dollars cash. He never did find his watch, an anniversary present from his wife.

After his release Saturday morning, Larry Cozzens slept soundly for nearly seven hours at his home on Oregon Street. At noon he awoke and began to dress for work. "What do you think you're doing?" demanded his wife, Margery. "Nobody expects you to go to work. I don't ever want you to go there again." She stood in the doorway, blocking it. Like some of his fellow hostages, Cozzens was driven by curiosity and the lure of returning to the prison as a victor. "I picked her up, kissed her, and went to work," he recalled. "I was made sergeant then."

Victor Baldwin slept all day and through the night. On Sunday afternoon, he told his worried wife Bonnie, who wanted him to stay home, that he was returning to the prison for his regular two o'clock shift. That very day, he wrote a poem for her:

> Heart, oh heart,
> My beloved heart,
> How I'd hate
> For us to part.
>
> But raise them well
> Oh darling mine,
> Keep them well
> And strong and fine.
>
> And think you not
> Of me too long,
> For me grieve not
> And you be strong.
>
> Your love they'll need
> Our children five,
> Pay me no heed
> Keep them alive.
>
> Let memory wan
> of me my dove,
> and try to fan

the spark of love.

That in your heart
Lies dormant dear,
Should I depart
While I am here.

[written April 19, 1959]

***

Inside the walls, the scene resembled a military camp. More than one hundred guards and other prison employees were actively engaged in the aftermath. They at first confined 438 inside convicts, excluding kitchen and hospital crews, to their cells. Meanwhile, the National Guard took control of the cell houses. Galley by galley, soldiers led convicts at gunpoint into the yard and told them to strip. Disheartened prisoners stood in rows, nude in the sunshine, listening to the crashing in the cell houses.

Guardsmen ransacked their cells, stripping each one of personal belongings including family photographs and letters from home, tossing it all from the galleys. They carried the debris outside and threw it onto a mountain of rubbish that contained everything from chairs to curtains to books and toiletries, even leather making tools, toothpick sculptures and other hobbies. They swept metal detectors over hundreds of mattresses and pillows strewn across the yard; of everything removed from both cell houses, only the bedding would be saved. Troops recorded each convict's name and cell number. They examined the convicts' mouths, their hair and even their rectums. After inspections the prisoners marched nude into the dining hall, where they sat silently with guns trained on them.

Even after his ordeal, Baldwin felt regret and sadness at seeing the spectacle. He thought it strange, feeling that way. He might have died. His survival seemed nothing short of heavenly intervention. None of the men who had helped Jerry Myles and Lee Smart take over the prison stood among these convicts. Those men – George

Alton, Donald Toms, Jimmy Hubbard and others – remained locked in dungeons.

The Guard planned to stay at the prison for a week to help guards conduct a complete shakedown. "We're going over it with a fine-tooth comb," Warden Powell said. "We're searching every nook and cranny, every crevice."

Most of the convicts had not participated in the riot. Baldwin saw standing among the nude convicts those men who had tried to help and protect the hostages. "I cannot say this was completely fair to some since most of them didn't want trouble any more than we did," Baldwin would recall. "They were kept locked up too and I don't know if they got fed the whole time." One convict told him later: "They yank you out of your cell, march you out into the yard, search you, take all your clothes, tell you to turn around, bend over and spread your 'jaws,' then march you down into the dining hall bare naked to sit and look into the bore of a rifle till you damned near can't stand it. Then when you're finally marched back to your cell you ain't got nothin' left, not even your dignity."

Reuben Dwight recalled: "The cells were filled with radios, hot plates, coffee pots, record players, innerspring mattresses, four poster beds, dressers, mirrors, shelves, pickled pigs feet; you name it and it was in those cells."

It was the legacy of years of permissiveness and neglect. Evidence would suggest that Floyd Powell's campaign to reform the prison hadn't purged the cell houses of contraband, despite his early efforts to remove draperies. George Alton and Lee Smart hid gasoline in their cell without fear of being caught. Like many other convicts, they knew shakedowns were mostly predictable, infrequent, and incomplete. Workers hauled loads of contraband in a two-and-a-half ton truck to the city dump along the old Emery Mine road. When they set the heap afire everyone could see the smoke.

Using metal detectors, soldiers uncovered 382 knives of one kind or another. Many had been sharpened on grinders in the inside toy shop from spoons and other contraband metals. Prisoners remained locked in their cells until their Sunday meal in the dining hall. The next morning they went back to work in the shops and industries, and for most of them, the routine of prison life began anew. Twenty-five soldiers helped prison guards herd them around. Floyd Powell said the only post-riot instance involved Officer Lester Barton. A convict threw a mirror at him, but missed.

***

Victor Baldwin saw another change right away. Reuben Dwight was taking control, and doing so aggressively. A convict being escorted to an Isolation cell smarted off to Dwight, who ordered pushups as punishment. The convict refused. Baldwin watched Dwight draw his forty-five-caliber automatic pistol from its holster. "You sure have nice teeth," he told the man, brandishing the gun in front of him. The convict dropped to the ground and started doing pushups as Dwight counted to fifty. Many of the guards liked Dwight. They didn't trust Powell, and with Rothe gone, they wanted a deputy warden who would stand on their side.

Looking back, Powell realized the foreboding signs of the riot, or what he called a disturbance or escape attempt: fewer requests for office interviews, unusual quiet in the dining room during meals, a lack of ostentatious behavior among convicts in the yards and shops.

Powell estimated the riot's cost at $205,000, including $100,000 to call out the National Guard and $5,000 for repairs to cells and doors. In the months afterward he made various structural changes to the prison to improve security. Most of them were minor but prudent renovations. In his continued attempt to prune away at the old prison's infrastructure, Powell vowed the Cell House 1 tower where the ringleaders died would be demolished. It never was, and decades later it remains a visible reminder of Jerry Myles and Lee Smart and their last stand.

- 27 -

Three funerals

Ted Rothe had struggled to be fair. At times in his frenzied short tenure at Montana State Prison he worried that he might be too severe with the men he was hired to guard, and even those he was hired to lead. He had pushed them hard. He demanded of them much like they demanded of him. He dreaded the opposite as well. Being a man of spiritual and professional conscience, he fell into the inevitable contradictions of being a leader. He knew that being too rigid with the men could lead to trouble. Being permissive could too.

It was a dilemma for a man who felt a God-bent commitment to his work. Soon after Rothe came to Deer Lodge he began a quest for higher moral ground. Floyd Powell was writing regulations of all sorts that governed the behavior of men on both sides of the bars. The warden described a manner of custody, common in all prisons, intended to restrict human behavior. What his regulations couldn't include was a plan for human salvation. Ted Rothe, an attentive Christian and a good and decent man, saw a mission for himself, and while not a crusader, he wanted to do what was right.

Walter Jones and guards who worked for Rothe would conclude that his sense of fair play killed him. This was not an indictment but a sad resolution that psychopaths like Jerry Myles and Lee Smart, whose contorted minds would not permit remorse, appreciated neither God's wisdom nor Ted Rothe's principles. They all died together in a way, their lives extinguished in a powerful struggle over good versus evil. Those three men were the polar extremes, the best and worst of Montana State Prison.

At a little church on Missouri Avenue, across the street from the county courthouse and not far from the high blue mountains that the local folks called God's Country, the Reverend Kenneth Schwengel had built a congregation of sixty-some members in what he called an "over-churched" town. He had come to St. John Lutheran Church in 1952 soon after he left the seminary. By the time the Rothes arrived in Deer Lodge in the autumn of 1958, Schwengel knew the prison well. In his work as a part-time chaplain he watched toil and toll, despair and desperation. Each time he entered the prison he marveled at how tower guards raised and lowered big brass keys on a long rope, but more meaningfully, that he was never trusted with keys to open doors himself.

To him this was a metaphor for redemption; in Matthew 16:19, the Lord would hand over the keys to the kingdom of heaven. So struck was Schwengel by this that more and more of his sermons captured a prison theme. He had seen the prison's rough edges. Schwengel knew how the prison life weighed on Ted and his guards. Three guards and their families belonged to his church. The Rothe family, soon after their arrival in Deer Lodge, became members as well. Schwengel remembers that they attended services nearly every Sunday.

Before long Rothe asked for private conversations with his pastor about how his Christian faith could guide him in his work. He came to the sanctity of his pastor's study, his big eyes brooding with concern. At the prison so many challenges presented themselves at once that the deputy warden reasoned that without his faith he would lose his way. He shared specifics with his pastor, too. He lamented that the prison didn't have a classification system that would isolate harder convicts. If Rothe mentioned Jerry Myles, the pastor didn't remember it.

***

It was Sunday, April 19, 1959. In a twenty-minute ceremony at St. John Lutheran, Reverend Schwengel commemorated the riot's first victim as one of "all the other saints and martyrs of God." Ted Rothe was only the second employee since 1908 to die at a convict's hands at Montana State Prison.

As the deputy warden lie in his casket at the front of the church, Schwengel eulogized him as "compassionate and diligent." He called his friend "a leader in one of the world's most difficult professions," and said that Ted Rothe had "returned to the shepherd and bishop of our souls." He did not ask the Rothe family to forgive Lee Smart for murdering their loved one but told them instead, "We are by nature sinful and unclean." A female soloist sang two church hymns. The pastor quoted the Twenty-Third Psalm.

After the service, Floyd Powell walked weeping through the crowd outside the church, grieving for the friend he had known for eight years and six months. Lieutenant Charlie Brown sobbed bitterly against a tree. The emotion of being a hostage drained from him as he shook in his bright blue Sunday suit. Other guards milled around on the winter-brown lawn in their uniforms, some cradling their hats in their hands. Hostage Walter Jones, interviewed outside the church by several newsmen, said of Rothe: "We differed. We agreed. His experience prevailed." He said Rothe had made him see that "you can't change (a prison administration) from black to white overnight if you don't have the money. It's the money that's the important part." Jones did not intend to quit the prison unless "I have irrevocably lost the confidence of the inmates." He said of the nightmare just past: "The wonder of it is how you can grow accustomed to the idea you are going to die. We all really thought we would."

Last to leave the church was Ted's wife Elsie, who through tears told reporters: "If the prison reforms he worked for are carried out, his tragic death will not have been in vain. He died like a man, doing what he believed in." Elsie helped her mother-in-law, Katie Rothe, out of the church. Ted's mother had been visiting at their home when the riot began. The day before her son died protecting himself, Katie Rothe had joined Floyd and Dorothy Powell on a trip to Montana State College in Bozeman, where the warden had delivered a speech. Ted's brother, Paul, and a sister, Edna Galbraith, had come from Milwaukee for the funeral. That afternoon the family prepared to leave for Wisconsin, where Ted would be buried at Theresa, fifty-three miles from Milwaukee. Elsie Rothe and her children would return to Deer Lodge to finish the school year. Phyllis would graduate that spring with Powell County High School's Class of 1959.

***

Carol Havemann Page, a fellow graduate, had gone to Butte for the district music festival the week that Ted Rothe died. She and other members of the Assembly of God Church in Deer Lodge spent many Sundays inside the prison for church services. The prisoners liked to sing "Amazing Grace" and "the Old Rugged Cross" from their dated hymnals. Then Carol sang solos like "His Hands" and "It Took a Miracle" before the sermon.

Guards had been careful to protect Carol and the others, seating them on stage in the Clark Theater before any prisoners entered. "The only time I felt any fear was when they brought the woman prisoners to the church," she recalled years later. "The men were polite to our group but the women seemed much tougher. They would glare at the girls in the group. I was this young seventeen-year-old girl and was glad that we were protected and could go 'out' of the gates."

Carol knew Phyllis Rothe as a quiet girl. They had several classes together. "She was out of school for a short time after her father was killed and when she came back, most of her classmates didn't know what to say," Carol remembered. "We were so young and didn't have much experience with death."

For many graduates of Powell County High School that spring, the pain they felt for the Rothes became a defining memory of their graduation. Barely six weeks after the riot, Janet Brown, another 1959 graduate, sat at the same table with Phyllis at their senior banquet, a tradition at the high school. Janet remembers thinking "how brave it was of her to come," and how blue she felt when a classmate sang the Doris Day tune "Whatever Will Be, Will Be," written for the 1956 remake of the Alfred Hitchcock film "The Man Who Knew Too Much":

When I was just a little girl
I asked my mother what will I be
Will I be pretty, will I be rich?
Here's what she said to me
Que sera, sera
Whatever will be, will be
The future's not ours to see
Que sera, sera
Whatever will be, will be

"All of us at the table including Phyllis just looked down in our laps," Janet remembered. "It was so sad and especially for her, it was hard not to cry."

On the day of Ted Rothe's funeral, a coroner inquest into his death was announced. After a short deliberation the jury reached the same conclusion as Dr. Benjamin had done the afternoon of the shooting. Rothe, a young man of much promise, died instantly from a bullet that Lee Smart fired from close range.

***

As the Rothe family buried their husband, father and son, Floyd Powell was learning he had trouble of a different sort. The National Guard didn't want to go home. Powell wanted to get the prison back to normal, but he needed a deputy warden. Powell was a harried, tired, grieving man. His fatigue showed in his face, adding more mileage to a life of hard prison work. Aside from Ellsworth and other critics in Deer Lodge, he did get plenty of thanks from service clubs and politicians for his efforts during the riot. Yet he buckled to the National Guard and in doing set his fateful course.

Publicly, it was an innocent appointment, even a lauded one. Powell appointed Reuben Dwight of Helena, thirty-seven-year-old operations and facilities manager for the National Guard, as his acting deputy warden. "Captain Dwight was one of the heroes of the successful attack and is a former deputy warden of the 12th Naval District at Treasure Island off San Francisco," Powell told the newspapers. Powell later admitted that this decision resulted after "considerable pressure from the National Guard intermediate leadership." Key among them was Bus Ellsworth, who wanted Powell gone.

The warden said he wanted to gather his staff to thank them for their loyalty, but already several officers had "resigned or disappeared," including some hostages and other guards who had decided that the job was too dangerous. They would blame Powell for failing to run a safe prison. The warden, however, saw the situation differently. "It gave me an opportunity to point out by this example how important it was to follow policies and procedures, especially where security was concerned," Powell said.

***

On the day of Ted Rothe's funeral, a former district parole supervisor said in the newspapers that he no longer felt obligated to keep quiet for his true reasons for leaving state employment. William J. Orsello of Helena, once a police officer, called the Montana State Prison riot "a sorry situation that the life of a good sincere person was taken because of the negligence of the proper persons."

Orsello, then thirty-five, was one of the first parole officers hired after the Board of Pardons was created in April 1955. He had resigned suddenly in December 1958, saying only that he disagreed with board director Benjamin Wright on certain matters. But on the day after the riot ended, he told a newsman: "This last tragic incident could have been avoided entirely if authorized persons, such as the Board of Pardons, had taken the proper actions. Instead they have placed self-political interests before ethics. The board has known this unsettled situation since the 1957 riot. That was the reason for my resignation.

"Because I could not convince the board of the uncomfortable situation that existed both within the prison and within the organization itself, my conclusion in December was that the board and its directors were insincere in the parole program and considered their duties as a secondary matter. I have personally observed that the way they operated this system has been nothing but a joke, both to the state and to the inmates. I have worked with inmates long enough to know that they know their place and all they ask is fairness."

And also on Sunday, the chairman of a state House of Representatives committee that had investigated the Montana Pardons and Parole Board said Wright was the cause of much discontent at the prison.

"We knew he was despised by the prisoners and was not capably administering the work of the board," said Representative P.J. Gilfeather, a Democrat from Cascade. The investigation had been conducted during the 1959 legislative session. Wright's resignation was one of three recommendations made to the full House by the investigating committee. Gilfeather said his committee was unanimous in its recommendation for Wright's resignation, and he described Wright as "not an organizational man. He was a self-seeker." Despite Wright's help in arranging the mechanical operation of the parole program, "we find that Wright has a great deal of professional and personal difficulty with people working for and in connection with him, in fact to such an extent that it is a detriment to the program and has and is affecting the morale and quality of the work being performed, not only by himself but the staff as well."

On Saturday, the Board of Pardons accepted Wright's resignation, but said criticism of him was unwarranted.

It was true, although not commonly understood, that Wright's role in the riot was much to do about nothing. Jerry Myles didn't care about parole. "Prison is my home," he had said. What would parole mean to a man who valued an influential prison life above freedom in the streets? Shouting a few criticisms about Montana's parole program from the cell house windows during the riot didn't

413

make Myles a champion for reform. It meant he had heard talk around the prison that came to mind as he delivered his disjointed speeches. He ranted about poor medical conditions, and he raged about Rothe, and about the despised parole system. From his platform on the catwalk of Cell House 1, Myles held forth to an audience of hundreds who stood in the street. And so Wright fell victim to the riot, deserved or not.

***

At the mortuary a block east from the church where Ted Rothe's family and friends said goodbye, the body of Jerry Myles lay unclaimed in a simple casket. Myles belonged to the netherworld now. No longer did the gray cloak of a prison wall comfort and inspire him.

In his turbulent life he had come to embrace the bars and cells and isolation as his lot in life. He belonged to prison and prison belonged to him. At Montana State Prison and all the prisons that had held him, he had been somebody, at least in his own mind. That might have been all that mattered to him, or least what mattered most. In his intelligent but skewed mind he saw his world as he wanted it to be. In the end, in that final moment when he pressed the cold tip of a rifle barrel against his head, he saw himself dying in glory. That could be the only plausible explanation for the mayhem he had inflicted in the past thirty-six hours in Floyd Powell's prison. That self-seeking glory spent itself when the trigger released the firing pin. Even in taking his life, Jerry Myles felt power over others.

News reporters, pressing Walter Jones for a better explanation of the man whose riot had killed Ted Rothe, surrounded Jones outside the church. Jones replied that Myles "might as well have come from nowhere," and he expressed hurt that what Myles had said about Rothe being the most-hated man in the prison (again shouted from the cell house) had been widely circulated. That was what Myles might have felt, but it was far from the truth. The news organizations covering the riot and the funeral did little to advance the story beyond verbatim comments from the central figures.

Jones knew that most everybody had misunderstood Jerry Myles. Outside the church, Jones told news reporters that when Myles "lost his leadership" he lost everything, and that Myles was "dedicated to die" from the time Rothe broke him as con boss. Myles was determined "to die in glory as he interpreted it," Jones informed them. He was offering insight into the real cause of the riot, although what he said didn't get much play in the press.

A block away in the mortuary, Ralph Filcher prepared Myles and Lee Smart for burial. Filcher would attest that they had suffered no wounds other than their revolting head injuries, although the convict population rippled with rumors that National Guardsmen fired additional rounds into their dead bodies.

Filcher embalmed them the normal way, and then dressed them in prison-made dress suits usually given to paroled convicts. The clothes resembled 1940s zoot suits. They were brown with double lapels and made of heavy wool with a houndstooth pattern. Parolees hated them, customarily discarding them in alley garbage cans after leaving the prison. The prison tailor shop had quit making the suits; the last of the inventory was used for burials. Filcher fitted ties around the necks of Myles and Smart the best he could; it's doubtful either man had worn a tie in his life. Because Lee's face was reasonably intact, Filcher prepared him for his mother and brother, who asked to see him. When they arrived at the funeral home, Filcher led them to their loved one. He was struck by the similarity in appearance between Lee and John, and recalled that Mary Smart was "quite calm" when she saw her son, seemingly resigned to this morbid conclusion.

"He was a stinker, but he paid for it," she had told news reporters Sunday in Seattle as she boarded a bus for Deer Lodge. "He couldn't pay anymore. He blew his head off," she said, believing his death was a suicide. She recalled his plea to be hanged after his conviction for killing Charles Ward, the novelty salesman. "He said, 'I can't live in prison.' " Mary Smart didn't spare herself. "It's partly my fault. I don't think any kid goes bad if his mother and father do their job." She said of her dead son and his funeral hundreds of miles away: "They call it the product of a broken home."

On Monday, the day before her son's burial, Mary Smart penned a letter to Floyd Powell in her room at Hotel Deer Lodge, five blocks north of the prison on Main Street. "I neglected to request that if there is any cash remaining in Lee's account, of sufficient amount to warrant a check, I would appreciate receiving it," she wrote. "If his balance is small and it can be credited to George (Lil George) Alton for cigarettes." Three days later, Powell mailed her a check for $25.92.

In his coroner's register at the funeral home, Ralph Beck noted that Smart had died of a "gunshot wound to the head" and ruled his death a suicide. At the bottom of the page he wrote a reference to the county when Smart had killed the traveling salesman: "Choteau County should be proud of the justice they gave to this animal." Beck logged the brief Myles entry on page 140 of the register. "Murdered by Lee Smart," he wrote, adding: "Any remarks I would make would not be proper for official records."

Thus that became, for the ages, the most official ruling of who killed whom in the murder-suicide. This scenario became the standard explanation, ventured even by Warden Powell who said he found one rifle with a spent bullet lying beside Smart's body, and one rifle with a live bullet in the chamber lying partly beneath Jerry Myles.

Powell and Beck held to this theory; Ellsworth and Sheriff Everett Burt had concluded the opposite. Ellsworth, being one of the first men to enter the tower room where the shooting occurred, found Myles and Smart and the rifles lying differently than Powell later described. Carl Frodsham's account of being handed the rifles after the shootings was different yet. Burt said so many Guard soldiers and prison guards entered the room to view the bodies that they ruined it as a crime scene. Although Powell described the shooting scene with certainty, testimonies from Ellsworth and Burt and others contest that he went into the tower before the bodies were removed.

Myles fired one shot at Francis Pulliam, the Guard lieutenant, in the stairwell of the tower. Witnesses to the aftermath said they found shell casings near the south-facing windows, indicating shots had been fired at the National Guard troops as they rushed the cell houses. Prison guard Gus Beierle, bazooka marksman Bill Rose, Captain Dwight and others involved in that charge thought someone had fired at them from the tower. Those bullets could have been ricochets from Bob Zaharko's stream of fire from the north wall, but men thought it probable that Myles and Smart, knowing the end was coming, fired some of their ammunition.

No fingerprints were lifted from the rifles. Nobody took into account that the surviving convicts in the tower had moved the rifles; Carl Frodsham, in his deposition, said he laid them both on a table after others, including Jerry Walker, handled them. No autopsies were done to confirm where the bullets had entered the bodies and from what distance, and because the bodies and rifles were moved around, it was impossible for Sheriff Burt to reconstruct the scene. There's no evidence that anyone in authority considered whether one of the surviving convicts in the tower shot Myles and Smart to end the riot.

Regardless, most everybody seemed pleased with the outcome. It was a crime of convenience. Powell and Beck and Ellsworth and Burt and many others who disagreed on the sequence of events in the tower at least agreed on this: Ringleaders Myles and Smart got what they deserved.

***

Three days after the riot ended, Jerry Myles was laid to rest at eleven o'clock in the morning in the prison burial section of Hillcrest Cemetery, known as Potter's Field. His casket, purchased from Montana Casket Co. in Butte, was a style commonly used for indigent burials. It was steel with a flat top, furnished with a white satin lining and pillow. The body that had belonged to a veteran of many prisons, and of much loneliness, looked strangely out of place in there, his wrinkling remains reposing in such unseeming opulence.

Never in his long prison life had Myles known luxury. He had slept on crude metal bunks and cheap mattresses. He had entered Montana State Prison with practically no possessions. Even his violin disappeared. Had his lonely stringed melodies in dark cells long ago been his final appreciation for culture? Despite his notoriety he died a stranger. Prison officials didn't know if he had survivors. He told them he was an orphan, and essentially he was. Nobody wrote him a letter for the final many years of his life. He knew not a soul on the outside, save lost acquaintances from past prisons, and who were they to care?

A hostile wind from the high mountains to the west raced through the brown grass, matted from winter snow. In the barren plot of Potter's Field, where other convicts rotted anonymously into the ages under tiny blank concrete markers, the earth awaited Jerry Myles. True to his wishes and to community sentiment (in Deer Lodge one would hear, "the bastards are getting more than they deserved") no one attended his burial other than funeral home attendants and Protestant chaplain A. H. Rogen, a Lutheran pastor from Anaconda assigned to state institutions in the Deer Lodge Valley.

Cemetery workers quickly lowered the casket. With a last nod to the day's light it sank into the clammy subsoil. No flowers, no regrets. People were fond of saying that Myles would be going deeper still, and that it was a damned good thing for anyone who ever knew him.

Three hours later, Rogen read prayers for Lee Smart in the Perpetual No. 1 section of the adjacent city cemetery, at the second grave from the north corner on the west side. He was buried in a plot purchased by his mother, just across a little lane from the Odd Fellows and Masonic sections. Graves of longtime Deer Lodge families surrounded his plot. Burying the young killer among them got tongues wagging in town, for his violent exploits both in and out of prison were by then well known. The presence of his mangled body, his head blown to bits, violated the sanctity of a calm place.

To the people who knew and respected Ted Rothe, this teenager deserved worse. But young Lee was his mother's son. Mary Smart mustered more dignity than anyone would have expected. Beneath a pine tree that would shield Lee's grave from winter's breath and summer's stare, she parted with the rebel son she loved but barely knew.

There they stood, saying goodbye, and for some, good riddance: Lee's brother John, just seventeen, who would declare years later that he had quit knowing his brother even before the murder of Charles Denzil Ward; three of Mary Smart's friends, and among a few others, Police Chief Wilson, who served as a pallbearer at Mary Smart's request. Wilson came only because he thought it was the proper thing to do. Mary Smart, despising his uniform as a symbol of the police, prison guards and National Guard troops she believed had killed her son, told him she hated him and everyone else in uniform for what they had done to Lee.

Earlier she had told Floyd Powell that "I'll hate you as long as I live," and that she wished guards had killed Lee instead of him dying in a murder-suicide. Powell took that statement to mean that she still thought of her son as an innocent victim. To Wilson she said abruptly, "People like you I don't like but I have to have pallbearers." Young Lee's father did not attend. He had been largely absent in Lee's life anyway. A bouquet of flowers appeared, compliments of relatives in Washington.

***

Janet Brown's mother worked with a friend from Butte who sometimes ate lunch at their house in Deer Lodge. A woman stopped the friend on the street downtown, asking if she was the mother of the boy who shot Ted Rothe. Indignant, the friend made it clear she was not. "How hard it must have been for the real mother to come to a town that must have hated to bury her son," Brown recalled. "I also remember thinking about the prisoner that was with him and that he was also killed and he was just buried in a prisoner grave with no one to care about him. I wondered also if he had been given a choice if he would have turned himself in or chosen to die."

The teenager's death had come twelve days short of three years since his murder of Charles Ward in cold blood. Lee's attorney in 1956 had argued that the boy could be rehabilitated into living a lawful life. Now he was gone, shot dead. His mother bought a handsome marble grave marker to remember, as mothers do, the man she had hoped he would become. For Deer Lodge people who visited the cemetery in a hush and respect that one feels in such places, the headstone annoyed them. Lee's date of death, "April 18, 1959," was an icon for the worst of Montana State Prison. Years later the headstone is gone. Cemetery workers don't know when it disappeared or why. Only a depression on the ground indicates the presence of Smart's remains.

On the same day as the ringleaders went below the soil, prison workers sealed the tunnel that Jerry Myles had forced his fellow convicts to dig. Floyd Powell wanted to put the riot behind him. Shovels and rock and leaden earth don't bury one's past, however, as the warden would find out.

- 28 -

Floyd Powell's legacy

Mary Smart wrote Floyd Powell a month after the riot, asking for her son's personal belongings, "including clothing, wrist watch, pictures, papers, letters, or anything at all that was his at your very earliest convenience." Powell responded by letter that prosecuting attorneys had seized Lee's possessions as evidence until they completed their investigation. "I do not know whether or not any of it will be used in the prosecution of those who participated in this tragic incident with Lee," the warden wrote. Powell didn't tell Mary Smart that chances were good that most of Lee's possessions had been burned at the city dump after the National Guard's wholesale cleaning of the cell houses.

Over the next year she bombarded Powell with letters. In March 1960, she wrote: "Attached is 44 cents in stamps to reimburse your office for postage charges in the very small package. If you are not allowed to accept them, please credit George Alton or someone else with them.

"I am very surprised to learn that this is all that is left of Lee. It is very difficult to believe that two wallets, one homemade address booklet and a pair of glasses are all that were salvaged.

"Knowing Lee as I do, I feel certain he would not have carried an empty wallet. It would seem he would have had pictures in the wallet. That his clothing should be taken by other prisoners is understandable and I hope whoever got them has enjoyed them."

And then she wrote in an insightful understatement: "Mr. Powell, there are many phases of this whole situation that are very perplexing." She implored Powell to resurrect anything that might constitute a memory of her boy. "I'm again asking you to send me the rest of Lee's property with the exception of his magazines," she wrote the warden. "These are probably giving someone pleasure. Lee was my son. What he did never altered the deep love I had for him. Mostly because I know he was mishandled and put thru much more at the hands of various city and state officials of Montana than most men could have endured. He was no more responsible for what he did, nor could he help himself. Harboring hatred and animosity toward him can hurt him no more, but it can hurt his brother and me. Denying us the pleasure and comfort we can get from his pictures, sketching and other effects that were dear to him cannot hurt Lee, but it can hurt us deeply and it does just that."

In Powell's final letter to Mary Smart, he wrote: "I do not believe anyone here harbors any hatred or animosity toward Lee or toward you or Lee's brother. I and others of the staff have searched everywhere we could for items of Lee's, but I am sorry to say we found nothing except what was sent to you."

His admission that nobody hated Lee Smart was a remarkable act of kindness toward a grieving mother. It was also a disguise of the truth. As a final gesture, Powell returned her postage stamps.

***

Two months after the riot, Floyd Powell wrote a letter of explanation to the Board of Prison Commissioners. The warden renewed his campaign for a new prison, referring to the riot as a "disturbance" and blaming the violence on "a grossly inadequate physical plant, and with a lack of trained staff."

He wrote: "In bringing about the change ... to a condition where the employees and administration were running the Institution rather than the inmates, created a great amount of tensions from time to time. Between the Deputy Warden and myself we met these crises many, many times, and, if I may say so, the progress which we had made in the seven and a half months was very, very noticeable."

Powell said the average length of service of prison guards when the riot occurred was eleven months. "To bring about the tremendous change needed to make the Montana correctional system a workable, valuable, efficient, adequate activity, is an almost insurmountable job," he wrote.

Powell eulogized Ted Rothe: "He devoted long, hard days to the extremely difficult task of trying to convert the Montana State Prison into a decent correctional facility. It is doubtful that we can ever again obtain a man as capable, experienced, and with exceptional ability as Mr. Rothe possessed."

Most of Powell's five-page letter reviewed details of the riot as he saw them, and his general tone showed a confidence that he had done everything right but that circumstances had let him down. "I planned the attack to the last detail myself and led the assault," he wrote the commissioners. The National Guard, of course, strongly disputed that statement. Powell offered only a hint of vulnerability: "We, Mr. Rothe and myself, expected ever since coming here that sooner or later we would be given a test."

***

Jerry Myles' riot began Floyd Powell's demise at Montana State Prison, although the end would be nearly two years in coming.

The warden's grand vision of a new prison suggested him to be a man before his time. His drawn plans revealed ingenious progressive thinking, and in the broad picture of things, it remained clear that he had taken the Montana job with hopes of pinning his name to potentially one of the most dramatic prison reforms in America.

Powell spoke authoritatively about modern corrections philosophy, yet many of his employees thought daily operations suffered for lack of leadership. A blizzard of memorandums sent from his office more often overwhelmed his employees than taught them about professional prison procedures. Powell couldn't overcome a weakness that he wore like a scarlet letter: that people felt he distrusted them. Yet Powell, in turn, thought that the National Guard deliberately undermined his work to make his look incompetent.

When prospects for a new prison faded in the wake of the riot, Powell grew increasingly bitter, blaming his staff. Through 1960 and 1961, he often worked seven days a week, convinced he must show his department managers how to do their jobs. He drove them without mercy until even Dennis Spalding, whom he had promoted to captain to replace the departed hostage Everett "Guff" Felix, complained to Powell during a tense meeting of prison managers: "Some men you inspire and the ones you can't you drive and we're just about at this point. We're worn out, we're tired and everything else."

Powell decided he should teach ranch manager Lou Harris how to ranch. Some weeks he spent twelve to fourteen hours a day trying to show Harris what he thought should be done. He tried to become *de facto* business manager and later proclaimed he had taught Elmer Erickson everything he knew. He tried to scare Erickson by spreading a story that he might lose his job to a National Guard officer, and when Erickson challenged the truthfulness of this statement, Powell then accused Erickson of spreading the rumor. In a meeting in Powell's office that was recorded and transcribed, Erickson protested Powell's behavior. "You have a funny little way of twisting things around," Erickson told the warden.

Dwight, who increasingly found himself at odds with the warden, accused Powell of trying to make decisions for plumbers, electricians and every other worker at the prison. The growing internal struggle threatened the prospect of a new prison, as rank-and-file guards progressively split into two distinct factions. The larger group supported Dwight, whom Powell personally had proposed as the new permanent deputy warden. With Rothe gone, Powell thought it was time to settle the prison and move forward. But he later wrote that Dwight was disloyal to him and a pawn for the Guard.

All three of Montana's three prison commissioners approved Dwight. As the warden's first assistant he would be paid $5,000 annually in addition to free housing and commissary. The smaller group backed Spalding, who was known by some as "a Powell man." Perhaps unfairly, guards loyal to Dwight accused Spalding of spying for Powell, branding Spalding as "Powell's informer." Spalding denied their accusations. Powell criticized Dwight for failing to "develop" sergeants and lieutenants; Dwight shot back that Powell had told him that Spalding was responsible for doing that. Powell remained indecisive on whether Spalding or Dwight should lead the custody force. To illustrate a situation he thought could contribute to another riot, the deputy warden alleged that each of the four custodial lieutenants worked independently of each other, lacking clear communications, similar to the practice before the 1959 riot.

Contrary to Powell's glowing public statements and his frequent missives to the governor's office, some troublesome conditions remained that had existed before the riot. The laundry still had a con boss. In many instances guards lacked proper training, and they still came and went with alarming frequency for most of the reasons that prevailed before the riot. Divided loyalties and misunderstandings over policies and procedures led to internal confusion, resentment and jealousy.

And then there was the riot itself. Incredibly, no formal investigation followed the most violent prison disturbance in Montana history. Powell continued dismissed the riot as an "escape attempt" and a disturbance, despite Ted Rothe's wasteful death. The true story was known among guards and convicts who had watched the prison fall like a house of cards. Only in the dozens of depositions taken by County Attorney Malcolm "Scotty" MacCalman after the riot did a picture of the afternoon of April 16 emerge. Taken as a whole, it was a disturbing progression of events. The conniving Jerry Myles had spotted every weakness. For thirty-six hours, the prison became his. Newspapers did little to uncover the full story. Myles' long prison history, including his incarceration in Alcatraz, remained largely untold.

An investigation would have uncovered multiple shortcomings the day the riot began: too many guards leaving the prison at one time to eat dinner, catwalk guards vulnerable to attack, telephone lines inadequate and their repair and installation behind schedule, rules governing convict movement unenforced, doors left unlocked, shovels and pickaxes stored in the cell houses, early warning signs like an empty exercise yard and absenteeism in typing class neither recognized nor reported, and the deputy warden left unprotected.

Powell raced into the riot without first taking stock of it, and without alerting tower guards. This was in contradiction to the standards of the American Corrections Association, which warned that a prison warden should never risk being taken hostage, therefore depriving the prison of its leadership. Having fallen into this trap, Powell could not assume command in those first critical hours. The people outside didn't know what to do because the prison had no plan for countering a riot, nor did a map of its interior exist.

The timing of the rifles couldn't have been worse. All winter, much of which Jerry Myles spent in Isolation, Powell and Ted Rothe had negotiated with guards and their union about removing the rifles. On the eve of Powell's decision to take them away, Myles returned to his cell, at a time when George Alton and Lee Smart had stored enough gasoline to fling it on a catwalk guard. Most of this information remained undisclosed until it became testimony in the lengthy criminal trials and appeals that followed. Never, however, did Powell admit that the prison had been less secure than he had led the public to believe. His friend Ted Rothe was as much a victim of security breakdowns as he was of Jerry Myles and Lee Smart and a prison rifle.

Powell's detractors, some of whom continued to believe that he had let the riot happen to demonstrate the need for a new prison, watched for more evidence to support their theory. On August 18, 1959, an earthquake struck at Hebgen Lake near Yellowstone National Park, killing twenty-eight people, most of them campers in the Madison River Canyon. Its tremors carried 150 miles northwest to Deer Lodge, where dishes tumbled out of cupboards and some people reported being shaken from their beds. At the prison, Cell House 2 rocked, wedging some cell doors shut and nearly tossing the catwalk guard onto the floor below. Some of the rock slabs surrounding the roof of the 1896 building fell to the ground outside.

Victor Baldwin and other guards thought damage was minor. At the time they thought the old cell house sound enough to be rebuilt, and in retrospect would think of it as a historic building. Powell summoned a state building inspector who, after seeing daylight peeking through cracks between the roof and the walls, concluded the building was unstable and should be torn down.

Governor Aronson and Secretary of State Frank Murray told Powell to proceed. Almost immediately, Powell assigned convict crews to dismantle the fortress-like building. He called the earthquake "the most critical time in the history of the state prison." He sent seventy-eight Cell House 2 convicts to double bunking in Cell House 1, creating worse overcrowding than before the riot. He now had nearly 400 men sharing 200 cells. Nobody disagreed that Cell House 2 lacked modern amenities that made it outdated. It was the warden's motive that came into question, at least among some of the guards, and as the gothic circular towers disappeared in nibbles and bites, Powell complained to bureaucrats in Helena about overcrowding.

Dolores Munden, who as director of the state criminal identification bureau reported to Warden Powell, was among the employees who thought he was more talk than action. She wrote a poem about Powell, calling him "Rehab Red," and the poem read in part:

> On a hot day in August, the year '58
> A redheaded fellow appeared at the gate
> "From Wisconsin I come to make my name great,
> I'll save this institution from a terrible fate."
>
> I'll build up the place and spend lots of money,
> And those who don't agree will find it not funny.
> I'll live high and mighty and fatten my tummy,
> I'll throw my weight around just like Gene Tunney.
>
> He changed all the rules and made lots of regulations,
> Most of them were laughs but some were sensations.

He referred to the place as his own private nation.
And put all of us in a very low station.

About his home state, he always did boast,
How great and advanced, it just was the most.
Most of us rebelled in our own private way,
We hoped and prayed Rehab Red wouldn't stay.

Powell's problems carried onto Main Street, where some business owners openly questioned his leadership. Owen Gehrett continued to deride Powell in sharp-tongued editorials on the front page of his newspaper. But the National Guard remained Powell's primary enemy.

Seven days after National Guard troops ended the riot, Governor Aronson praised them in an address to the Montana National Guard Association at Hotel Florence in Missoula:

"The Montana National Guard set a high standard for split-second timing and excellent planning on that day. This was a complex plan that depended upon every man for its success. Every guardsman came through with flying colors and no lives were lost. Only one man was wounded and he is recovering satisfactorily. ... I have always supported the Montana National Guard to the maximum. Sometimes this has been in the face of opposition, but I have not wavered. This support included an appearance in Washington, D.C., to fight against the proposed slash in the National Guard in Montana and elsewhere in the nation. This was averted, something for which we can all be thankful."

The governor's list of special commendations excluded rank-and-file troops, just as prison guards, many of whom had worked thirty-six or more hours straight to save the hostages, got little attention. Meanwhile, Francis Pulliam remained in the hospital, awaiting surgical grafting to repair deep wounds in his left forearm and left hip. His disability would be permanent. To add insult to injury, Floyd Powell would disparage Pulliam for going into the tower against his orders but the Guard said that wasn't true. Pulliam said his orders had come from his National Guard commanders, not from the warden.

Deputy Warden Dwight still had National Guard connections in Helena. Powell soon complained that Dwight was his "weakest link," although he earlier had described him as having "good potential" and personally told Dwight that he had already become a better deputy warden than Ted Rothe. Confronted with this contradiction by his department managers, Powell admitted that that conversation had taken place, but said he had told Dwight only that he might be better than Rothe *someday*.

One man, more than others, kept the pressure on Powell. He was Bus Ellsworth, who in his civilian life was a Deer Lodge insurance broker and formerly manager of Deer Lodge Interstate Lumber. He represented what Powell denounced as "those people downtown." Georgia Briggeman, who had become Powell's personal secretary four months after the riot, worked alongside the warden in his office in Outside Administration. She detected no problems until the business manager, Elmer Erickson, told her that "something is brewing in Helena," and she became aware that Ellsworth and his close friend, Deer Lodge attorney Joe McElwain, were trying privately to get Powell fired. Ellsworth's intervention with the governor meant Powell's tenure as Montana's prison warden, a tenure Powell himself had admitted was plagued by "one crisis right after another," would end.

***

On November 22, 1961, Ellsworth and three other Deer Lodge civic leaders went to Helena to persuade Governor Donald Nutter to replace Floyd Powell as warden. With Powell present, they alleged that another riot was imminent if Powell remained in place, and they warned Nutter that three of Powell's top administrators – Lou Harris, Elmer Erickson and Reuben Dwight – would resign rather than continue working for him.

Ralph Beck, the mortician, Dr. Gordon Anderson, a Deer Lodge physician, and McElwain accompanied Ellsworth. Powell's accusers told him in the governor's presence: "We are not interested in getting your job, but in the welfare of the prison." They warned Nutter that Powell's policies would force another riot within thirty days. Powell said that was ridiculous.

Three days later, Powell fired back a letter to Nutter condemning what he saw as political motivations: "I stand ready to risk my reputation as a prison warden on my record as administrator of the Montana State Prison. I believe the time has come to determine whether the Warden is to be the Warden, as I am sure would be in accord with your wishes, or whether prison policy is to be constantly shifted and turned to meet the whims and wishes of every pressure group with a personal axe to grind.

"My administration of the prison has been honest, forthright and progressive, in line with my best judgment based on my experience and training. I am sure you will agree that if pressure groups with personal or selfish motives, be they political or otherwise, are allowed to exert undue influence upon the Board of Prison Commissioners or its members as was the case in the past, that a very dangerous situation may well be created within the prison again."

Powell wrote that during his three years as warden, "we have, under my direct supervision and management, raised this prison from a filthy, racket riddled, dope infested, poorly operated institution (as evidenced by the reports from many surveys and inspections by committees and individuals, on file in your office)...."

Powell had worked hard to convince his supervisors in Helena that he was moving the prison forward. For instance, in his final quarter report to the Montana Board of Prison Commissioners in 1959, he listed physical changes made since the riot, including the construction of four new classrooms in a tower of Cell House 1. At Tower 7, the main gate that led into the prison, a ground-level addition had been completed. This addition, which would house a new turnkey and receiving office, was built below the tower, which before the construction had jutted from the top of the big wall. Cyclone fencing and security gates were added on either side of the addition, extending to the walls of Inside Administration. This created a courtyard of sorts that sheltered people coming and going from the rest of the prison yard. Powell also replaced the grill door at the Tower 7 street entrance with a solid metal door.

After the razing of Cell House 2, Powell built a dormitory in a portion of the dining hall, but only thirty-five prisoners could sleep there. The bulging Cell House 1 brought worry of new unrest. In October, he began using Rothe Hall, west of Deer Lodge, as a minimum-security dormitory. Built of cinder block and painted pale green, it was named in honor of the slain deputy warden. It stood alone in the foothills below Mount Powell, looking a forlorn and weak stepsister to the behemoth cell houses and the surrounding gray wall in downtown Deer Lodge. Rothe Hall wasn't much at first. It didn't even look like a prison, but it was a glimmer of Powell's dream. He moved the first prisoners there before the snow fell.

Much like before the riot, guards came and went with alarming frequency. In Custody, twenty-nine guards were fired in the final quarter of 1959. Twenty-one of them failed to make probation, three guards were "showing effects of alcohol on duty," two had been in poor health and unable to carry out duties, and three didn't report for work. That's what Powell wrote in his report, anyway.

***

Convinced Dwight was trying to undermine his authority through National Guard affiliations, particularly Ellsworth, Warden Powell demoted Dwight from deputy warden to guard officer on January 22, 1962. He told Dwight to report to Inside Administration the following Monday for assignment. Dwight would be paid the maximum guard's salary of $335 a month in addition to $30 a month commissary allowance. Within thirty days, the Dwight family must vacate the deputy warden's apartment, the same quarters where the Rothes had lived. Powell named Spalding his new deputy warden.

Protest came from all directions. Many guards had preferred Dwight's vigorous leadership style. Townspeople who remembered the National Guard as the savior in the 1959 riot interpreted the demotion as one more example of why Powell should be removed. Owen Gehrett wrote that as a Marine who fought at Guam, Bougainville, Saipan, Guadacanal and other Pacific island landings, Dwight wouldn't back down from a fight. Gehrett quoted Powell on the demotion: "There might be a possibility I will be fired over this action, but I couldn't care less...." And the National Guard, of course, came to Dwight's defense.

Privately, Ellsworth convinced Governor Nutter to fire Powell. On the morning of January 25, 1962, Nutter met with Ellsworth. The governor told him he must agree to become temporary warden until a permanent replacement could be found. That very afternoon, Donald G. Nutter, Montana's fourteenth governor, died in a plane crash thirty-five miles north of Helena near the canyon hamlet of Wolf Creek. Nutter's Air National Guard C47 plane had just left Helena to fly to Cut Bank, where he had planned to address a meeting of the Montana Barley Growers. Nutter, a conservative Republican much attuned to Gehrett's editorializing in Deer Lodge, had left Helena convinced that he needed a warden of his choosing at the prison. Now, minutes out of Helena, his plane sputtered in a rainstorm. He had survived sixty-two combat missions as a B24 pilot in World War II. At the age of forty-six, he died with his companions: State Agriculture Commissioner Ed Wren, aide Dennis Gordon and three crew members.

***

That same day, nearly three years after Jerry Myles had planned his riot, Warden Floyd Powell admitted defeat. Just hours before the governor crashed and died, he submitted his resignation, effective March 31.

In a letter to the Board of Prison Commissioners, Powell recounted what he found on his arrival at the prison in August 1958: " ... the prison atmosphere was dangerously tense, and the prison was generally overcrowded, disorganized and a dangerous mess – a powder keg set to explode at the slightest spark of provocation. ... Inmates were openly exercising a shocking degree of control over the management of the prison inside the walls. The hardened professional criminal element, the homosexuals, the prison racketeers, the thugs within the prison population were freely plying their nefarious trades and providing the bulk of the 'rehabilitation' treatment received by the younger, unsophisticated first offenders and the weaker inmates. The medium of exchange within the prison was dope and pills of one kind or another. Numerous weapons were hidden within the institution and contraband articles were being smuggled in and out of the prison. Accountability for state materials and supplies was practically non-existent; inmates destroyed, bartered, lost and in other improper ways, disposed of state property."

***

On Monday, January 29, 1962, Reuben Dwight spoke publicly against Powell. "Warden Floyd E. Powell, who invariably refers to himself as a trained and experienced penologist, is in no way qualified to allot himself fancy titles," he said in a statement released to the news media. "Although he has taken some correspondence work in custody, he is not educationally qualified to be called a penologist." Dwight now took full swing at Powell, doing all he could to discredit him.

News of Powell's resignation wasn't known publicly until February 8, when Governor Tim Babcock appointed Ellsworth as acting warden.

Dennis Spalding quit his job when he heard of Powell's resignation. Ellsworth, in turn, reappointed Dwight as deputy warden. Ellsworth, then forty-eight, had been Powell County's sheriff from 1947 to 1954. He was still a National Guard lieutenant colonel, commander of 1st Battalion, 190th Field Artillery. During World War II he had served in Europe with the 87th Infantry Division. He was a political appointee, but Deer Lodge residents seemed relieved. "It's the best thing that's happened to us in fifteen years," said retired railroad employee Noel Boyer. Said Mrs. Leon Nelson, a Deer Lodge City Council member and a licensed practical nurse: "Bus Ellsworth is a good man in anybody's terms." And Charles MacGregor, a local barber, had heard an outpouring of anti-Powell sentiments in his shop since the riot. "I thought it was kind of odd that they had to go out of state to find a man to run a state institution," he said.

Ellsworth insisted he hadn't wanted the job. "It wasn't in my plans at all. All I wanted to do was clean up an unhealthy program. It came as a complete surprise ... today was the first I knew about it."

***

Floyd Powell didn't survive the riot, and whatever public confidence he had engendered in his first months in Deer Lodge fell as a casualty as well.

He had worked relentlessly to draw plans for a new prison that would include ten major buildings. The centerpiece would be a maximum-security unit that would house more than 200 prisoners. The existing Rothe Hall would be expanded into a medium security unit.

Powell's plan first needed approval of Montana voters, then subsequent legislative validation of the bonds. In anticipation that his dream would come true, he had barnstormed around Montana, gaining support from organized groups of church women, career law officers, the Montana Sheriff's and Peace Officer's Association, from clergy and business owners. Lacking no confidence, he skillfully explained all the technical details of the new prison, including the need for a tunnel to a guard station inside the dining hall and other security precautions. On November 8, 1960, voters rejected a statewide referendum for the bond issue, 120,749 to 78,291. In Powell County, where Deer Lodge was the county seat, voters turned down the bond issue by nearly four to one, the largest opposition of any county in Montana.

The warden continued to preach his vision that only a new prison would propel Montana into an era of reform. He hoped that the 1961 Legislature would "provide a new facility so badly needed" to improve security and separate first-time offenders from hardened criminals and to keep sexual predators from molesting younger prisoners.

His dream remained just that. Governor Nutter had asked for a moratorium on all new construction of state buildings, proposed cuts at the prison, and wanted to reduce state subsidies of the prison ranch. The Legislature cut the prison's budget by more than $500,000 for the 1961 biennium, inflicting the cuts on education and training and even Powell's personal staff.

It could be argued that Montana wasn't ready for Floyd Powell, or Powell for Montana. Montanans believed that the man, not the money, needed to run the prison. This was a fickle view; Powell, despite his perceived shortcomings as a leader, had at least brought prison reform to public debate. He set higher standards for the prison than Montanans had known through the woeful Burrell years. His inability to turn others to his vision hurt him, but the riot of 1959 hurt him more. He couldn't shake the twin images of personal arrogance and public tragedy.

A modern prison was long in coming. Accommodations at Rothe Hall relieved some of the overcrowding at the historic prison on Main Street, but nearly twenty years would pass before the state closed it. Coincidentally, the new prison had many of the progressive features that Powell had envisioned, such as classified segregation, more sophisticated security, and a budget that reasonably paid for rehabilitation programs. In part because of the 1959 riot, more attention was paid to the power and influence of individual men on either side of the bars.

***

A week after Jerry Myles fell in his last stand, *LIFE* magazine described Montana's 1959 prison riot as "one of the most desperate jail outbreaks in U.S. history." Such an iconic description made good copy for a national magazine, but it missed the point. Myles considered Montana State Prison his home, just as he had found comfort at Alcatraz Island and a series of other state and federal prisons. He wasn't trying to escape the prison. His escape was from the anonymity of a lonely loveless life. For thirty-six hours in 1959 he was somebody, the king boss, a big man who ruled the news. People would remember him that way, however tragic, however pitiful. That's how a reformist warden would be remembered, too. Neither name would be spoken in Deer Lodge without a mention of "riot" in the same sentence.

Forty years and more later, people talk about two men who blew into this small prison town in western Montana the way stiff summer winds hurl tumbleweeds off the foothills. Jerry Myles turned to dust in Deer Lodge. Floyd Powell's vision of reform, however needed, surely died there too.

THE END

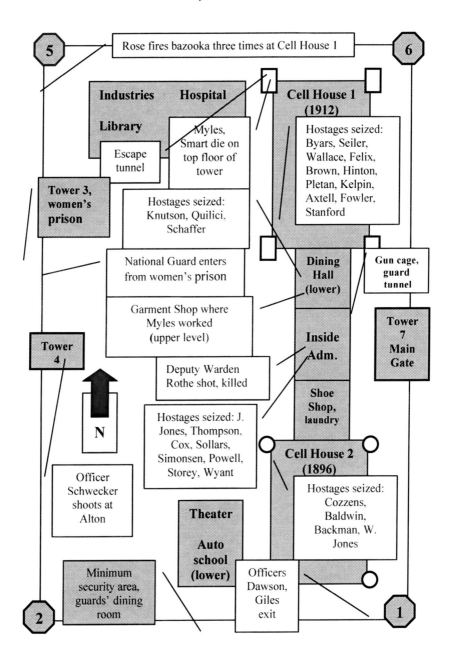

Author's Notes

As in any book that reconstructs an event, "Jerry's Riot" required hundreds of interviews with people familiar with those pieces of the riot that most personally affected them. First, thanks to the good folks of Deer Lodge, my hometown, who unselfishly gave of their time. I appreciate their patience and hospitality.

The staff at the Old Prison Museum in Deer Lodge contributed magnificently. Curator Jim Haas, who later died of cancer, was a champion of this book and a good friend. He and former museum director Andy Towe, as well as former office manager Elaine Way, allowed me to inspect every record available, much of which was stored in cardboard boxes in various rooms of the old prison. A major source of information came from dozens of legal depositions taken from guards and hostages by County Attorney Malcolm "Scotty" MacCalman in the week after the riot. Once I assembled their statements and corresponding court records into a timeline, I began to see how the riot unfolded. In addition, the prison's "big book," a journal-type history of each inmate's criminal track record, helped me understand the people behind the riot.

To ensure accuracy, I've made this book as organic as possible, drawing from primary sources and trying to corroborate elements of the riot with two or more sources.

Several dozen times I inspected the inside of the prison. With the help of retired longtime guard Bob McNally I entered the tower room, on the corner of Cell House 1, where Jerry Myles and Lee Smart died. I explored the tunnel (later opened to the public) where hostage negotiations took place. I've been inside the cells where hostages were held. Much of my orientation of the prison came from recollections of conversations with my father, Murry, who during his employment as a guard often described various occurrences inside the walls. Only a few of his specific recollections of the riot appear in this book because he died a few years before I began my serious research. I regret not pressing him harder for an oral history.

As new guards were required to do in the 1950s, I "walked the wall." A stiff wind blew that day, probably much like the day the riot began. I fought to keep my balance on a wall without rails. It was a frightening exercise but nothing as dangerous as duck-walking on ice, as guards often had to do.

Former guards Don DeYott, Noel Davidson, Lyle Gillette, Gus Beierle and Harold "Chick" Fanning contributed their memories and historical knowledge. So did Carl Parish, a maintenance worker caught in the riot, and Kurt Weiel, a civilian who worked in the prison's machine shop, as did many others in and out of uniform.

Archivists at the U.S. Bureau of Prisons uncovered a substantial body of information on Jerry Myles. His entire file exceeded seven hundred pages, which contributed to my chapters about his early prison life. I found a respectable collection of prison records and court documents at the Montana Historical Society and at the Montana Supreme Court library, both on the state campus in Helena. Numerous leads yielded other documents from private sources, including former inmates who described routines and conditions inside the prison. Floyd Powell's memoirs, on file in Deer Lodge and at the Montana Historical Society, helped me understand his thinking and motivation. Two of his cousins, Alden and Dan, told me about the family's younger years.

After a bit of detective work I found George Alton, the surviving ringleader, who invited me to his home. He too had buried his memories. As we talked at his kitchen table on a warm Labor Day afternoon, he swallowed one cold beer after another, pouring forth with welcome candor. At one point he waved me to stop and pressed his hands over his eyes. "You're really shaking me up here with these questions," he said. Later he wanted to continue, emphasizing the importance of "making things right." He expressed remorse, saying the riot was never intended to happen the way it did.

After the riot Alton spent two years in a dark cell inside the former women's prison building in the compound where National Guard troops had assembled for their pre-dawn assault on Cell House 1. That building had been renovated into maximum security for the special purpose of punishing Alton and the others who had assisted Jerry Myles in his riot.

A jury convicted Alton of second-degree murder in Rothe's death. His appeal to the Montana Supreme Court failed. The state paroled him in 1966 and released him from parole in 1981. In that time Alton had married. He and his wife raised a son and a daughter. When I met him he lived in a mobile home from where he could see miles in every direction. One can't help but appreciate the metaphor: a man held captive for most of his youth by walls, fences and locked doors living in a wide-open place, insistent he'd never once broken the law since his release.

I interviewed Carl Frodsham, another primary participant in the riot, at Montana State Prison. Veteran prisoner Bill Rose gave me valuable perspective, as did former prisoner Edward Wayne Edwards.

Former hostage Victor Baldwin supplied extensive information in several conversations and letters. He toured the old prison with me on a numbing gray day, recalling with surprising clarity the details of his capture forty years earlier. When I interviewed former hostage Everett Felix, the guard captain, in his home in Corvallis, he remembered the riot as if it were yesterday. Former hostages Gus Byars, Larry Cozzens, Clinton Fowler, Ray Quilici and Tom Stanford all consented to interviews. Walter Jones Jr., the hostage and sociologist, patiently explained to me relationships among the men involved. Today, fewer than half of the twenty-six hostages remain. Their memories remain vivid and their pain is evident.

Helen Sollars and Gert Knutson, widows of hostages Clyde Sollars and Ralph Knutson, recalled their feelings and helped me understand the sequence of events. Similar help came from hostage wives Margery Cozzens, Amy Lee Felix and Betty Wyant. Margaret Moughton of Butte recalled scenes in the Deer Lodge home of her sister Betty, who was married to hostage John Simonsen. Phoebe Parish, sister of hostage DeForrest "Frosty" Thompson, shared her memories of his ordeal and confided that she thought his memories of the riot eventually killed him.

National Guard sources helped me reconstruct the invasion of the prison to save the hostages. Former Guard commander Ed "Bus" Ellsworth, who later became the prison's warden, toured the old prison with me, and in person and in correspondence was a technical adviser. Deer Lodge restaurant owner Ron Scharf and his brother Jack Scharf, among the first National Guard riflemen to enter the prison that morning of April 18, 1959, did the same. I was fortunate to get first-person accounts from other key players in the Guard attack: commander Meyhew Foster; William Rose, who shot the bazooka, and Floyd Hoff, who loaded it for him; highway patrolman Robert Zaharko, who stood on the wall firing a submachine gun into Cell House 1; Emery "Buzz" Weston, another Deer Lodge rifleman, and Francis "Russ" Pulliam, who was shot in the assault. Ted Benson of Bozeman, son of the late Bill Benson who was interim warden before Floyd Powell's arrival, recalled for me many conversations with his father about the riot.

Several current and former Deer Lodge residents offered their perspective. Among them: Elmer Erickson, the prison's former business manager; Dolores Munden, former records supervisor; Jim Blodgett, former deputy warden; Ben Goldie, once married to Phyllis Rothe; Marlene Lightfoot Olmstead, Janet Brown, Carol Havemann, Sue Lintz, Bert Gangl and several other members of the Powell County High School class of 1959; Georgia Briggeman, Floyd Powell's personal secretary; Ada Holt, my junior high school social studies teacher who had compiled a written interview of hostage Chris Pletan; Dave Collings, a retired sheriff, and Bill Wood, whose uncle was hostage "Frosty" Thompson. Everett Burt, who was Powell County's sheriff at the time of the riot, and his under sheriff, Harold "Chick" Fanning, put their thoughts on paper. Former Deer Lodge mortician Ralph Filcher, whose family socialized with ours when I was a boy, helped a great deal.

Among the many people helping me with records research were Sharon Applegate at the Powell County Clerk of Court office, Dana Jennings Eldridge and Linda Moodry at Montana State Prison and

Terry Thomas at the state Registrar of Motor Vehicle office in Deer Lodge. Librarians at the Montana Historical Society and the Montana Supreme Court in Helena assisted me with volumes of court documents produced after the riot.

Much gratitude goes to my mother, Jean Skinner Giles, who became my partner in my early research, helping me examine documents and reason through evidence. She interviewed several fellow residents in Deer Lodge, including Betty Hoffman, Dolores Munden and Gert Knutson. Heather Giles Peacock, my eldest daughter, spent considerable time reading the manuscript and suggesting changes, as did her husband Jim. My brother Jeff advised me on earlier chapters. David Conley, my longtime friend and journalism colleague, kept me going with his encouragement and counsel as I chased this book for ten years. Thanks to my wife Becky for tolerating my obsession with the old prison for so long.

Some sources declined interviews. Among them were Ted Rothe's children, Phyllis and Jim, who declined interviews out of respect for their mother's wishes. However, Phyllis told me that she visits the old prison every chance she gets to remember her father. Ted Rothe was by all accounts a fine man. Even today, people in Deer Lodge who remember the riot feel pain for the Rothe family, victims of senseless violence.

John Smart said he knew little about his older brother Lee except that he had killed somebody in Montana and then died in a prison riot. He didn't want to say more. Lee left a wide paper trail in Montana and, as his mother's anguished letters show, a trail of broken hearts.

Floyd Powell's memoirs, which he intended to publish finished his career in Washington State. When he left Montana in 1962 he became supervisor of classification and parole at Washington State Penitentiary at Walla Walla. In 1963 he became associate superintendent of custody at Washington Corrections Center in Shelton, and for a year beginning in 1969 he was acting superintendent. He later became Washington's Jail Commission director. When he retired he had spent thirty years working in prisons in three states. He died of heart failure at age 76 in 1988.

Floyd's daughter, Judie Powell Heimbigner, offered considerable perspective on his work at Montana State Prison that differed from other accounts. She describes her father's accomplishments in Deer Lodge with pride and remembers him as determined, dedicated and caring.

Walter Jones, whom Alton took captive on April 16, 1959, retired from his prison career in Alaska. Jones quit Montana State Prison in the fall of 1959, barely a year after he had begun working there, to become a state parole officer, covering eleven southwest Montana counties. Soon he took his career to California, and eventually to Alaska. He is retired and living in Arizona.

Jones and Alton have not talked since the riot, but they share a mutual appreciation for one another's efforts. Jones remembers Alton as the sensible ringleader who he thinks stopped Jerry Myles and Lee Smart from killing hostages. Alton praises Jones for his courage, and in turn believes it was Jones who saved hostages.

Many of the hostages are gone. Hostage Everett Felix, the guard captain, died after I interviewed him for this book, as did hostage Victor Baldwin, National Guard commander and former warden Ed "Bus" Ellsworth, and business manager Elmer Erickson. Some of the hostages, like Felix, Tom Stanford and Ray Quilici, never entered the prison again after their liberation the morning of April 18, 1959.

One who did, Ralph Knutson, returned to the prison for two months, then went back to the Smelter in Anaconda. But the union went on strike in August 1959, and in the spring of 1960, he returned to the prison. "Oh, was he nervous," his widow, Gert, remembered. "He talked most of the night. He was always looking for something. And looking for keys. He was always looking for keys. He was always feeling around.... He was on one of the towers for awhile after he came back. And one night he thought he was on the tower and he was walking around the bed and making the rounds. He caught on the covers and he fell and came down on my hip with his knees and I was pregnant. Ronda was born in September of that year. Man, that was terrible."

Donald Toms, paroled in 1970, committed suicide on Christmas

Eve of 1990 in Washington State. Jesse DeWeese, who played a minor role in the takeover, left prison on parole in 1977. He died in 1995. Herman Cardinal came and went from Montana State Prison on various convictions. He was paroled in 1987 and died in 1991. Earl Jackson left the prison on parole in 1979; the state Parole Board had no further record of him. Carl Frodsham's brief parole in 1973 ended after a sexual assault of a newspaper carrier. At this writing he remains at Montana State Prison. Jerry Walker, also known by various aliases, left MSP in 1998.

MacCalman, the county attorney, tried fourteen men altogether. He had charged most of them with first-degree murder on the grounds that they were principals even though most of them weren't present when Lee Smart shot Ted Rothe. All but two were tried in Deer Lodge before District Judge Sid Stuart. Security was heavy in the Powell County Courthouse. Sheriff Everett Burt supplied two deputies and the prison sent two guards and sometimes three. "It was a touch-and-go situation out there in the courtroom, lots of days," Burt remembered. Only one of the men was found innocent. The two accused men who said they couldn't get a fair trial in Deer Lodge went to court in Great Falls and Bozeman, and they got the stiffest sentences of all. "This has been a prison town since territorial days," MacCalman said in reflection. "It showed that the citizens of Deer Lodge treat the prisoners just the same. Better than most places. Most of them served their sentences in no time."

This leads us to the architect of the 1959 riot. I searched the prison cemetery, a vague brown patch of prairie grass, for his grave. Jerry Myles is buried under one of the dozens of coffin-like depressions scattered over the uneven ground, but which one? He's a ghost, anonymous and lost to the ages as he had hoped.

Few people close to the riot could talk about it without emotion. The pendulum swing of such an event hastens to remind us of a thin line between life and death and how humiliation intrudes on dignity.

In some interviews, tears told the story when words failed.

Kevin S. Giles

CPSIA information can be obtained at www.ICGtesting.com
Printed in the USA
BVOW071714240313

316309BV00001B/4/A

9 781591 137184